FLOWERING SHRUBS & SMALL TREES

FLOWERING SHRUBS
& SMALL TREES

ISABEL ZUCKER

Revised and Expanded by Derek Fell  Photographs by Derek Fell

Grove Weidenfeld

Derek Fell wishes to acknowledge the help of Wendy Fields and Cathy Nelson in preparing portions of the revised manuscript.

A FRIEDMAN GROUP BOOK

Copyright © 1990 by Michael Friedman Publishing Group, Inc.

Published in the United States by
Grove Weidenfeld, New York
A Division of Wheatland Corporation
841 Broadway
New York, New York 10003-4793

FLOWERING SHRUBS AND SMALL TREES was first published in the United States in 1966 under the title *FLOWERING SHRUBS*, copyright © 1966 by Isabel Zucker.

Library of Congress Cataloging-in-Publication Data

Zucker, Isabel.
  Flowering shrubs and small trees.

  Rev. ed. of: Flowering shrubs, 1966.
  1. Flowering shrubs.   2. Flowering woody plants.
I. Fell, Derek.   II. Zucker, Isabel.   Flowering shrubs.
III. Title.
SB435.Z8 1990   635.9′76   89–25963
ISBN 0-8021-1242-0 (alk. paper)

FLOWERING SHRUBS AND SMALL TREES
was prepared and produced by
Michael Friedman Publishing Group, Inc.
15 West 26th Street
New York, New York 10010

Editor: Melissa Schwarz
Art Director: Robert W. Kosturko
Designer: Marcena J. Mulford
Layout: Margaret Lem
Photography Editor: Christopher Bain
Production: Karen L. Greenberg

Typeset by BPE Graphics
Color separations by Universal Colour Scanning, Ltd.
Printed and bound in Hong Kong by Leefung-Asco Printers Ltd.

First Revised Edition 1990

10 9 8 7 6 5 4 3 2 1

A Personal Appreciation of Flowering Shrubs

*I first met Isabel Zucker and her devoted husband, Myron, when I was catalog manager for Burpee Seeds.
She came breezing into my office at Burpee's Fordhook Farms, near Doylestown, Pennsylvania, one hot summer's day to choose pictures for an article she wanted to write. Dressed in a full-length mink coat, she was a feisty, outspoken perfectionist and a real dynamo. She was already well-known in the garden industry for her sharp tongue, but respected for her writing ability, her encyclopedic knowledge of garden plants, and her progressive ideas for promoting the benefits of gardening. As a founder and the president of the Garden Writers Association of America, she conducted meetings at the annual symposiums in a dogmatic, no-nonsense manner. She was the type of person who could accomplish a great many things without wasting time.*

Isabel was extremely proud of her book Flowering Shrubs, *which was originally published in 1966. She once told me that she had not permitted her publisher to change a single word, not even a punctuation mark, in the original manuscript. In deference to Isabel's wonderful writing style and the accuracy of that original manuscript, I have retained as much of it as possible in this updated edition. I have added a few additional pruning tips to the plant listings and have updated the variety recommendations. The section on rejuvenating shrubs is new since many people today purchase properties where existing plantings have grown out of bounds and need to be pruned to a desirable shape. I have deleted a lengthy chapter on the importation of shrubs as well as all references to the Nickerson Color Fan, a system of identifying precise colors that is no longer in use. The list of sources has been substantially simplified and revised. Listings of azaleas, rhododendrons, crabapples, magnolias and a few other major plant categories have been expanded, and a chapter on vines added since many vines can be grown as shrubs, and indeed are considered to be shrubs. The number of plant descriptions has been increased from 696 in the original book to 730. Last, the title of the book has undergone a slight change, to* Flowering Shrubs *and Small Trees.*

Perhaps my biggest contribution to bringing Isabel's opus back to life are my full-color photographs, which replace the photographs in the original book. Though the original edition contained a small color section, the majority of the photographs were black-and-white, taken by Myron Zucker in his basement studio at home, where he arranged flowering stems and other plant parts for meticulous close-up shooting.

For many years, Isabel served as director of the National Garden Bureau, an information office sponsored by the American Garden Seed Industry. Her principal responsibility was to write four timely syndicated news sheets a year and distribute them to daily and weekly newspapers throughout the United States. When Isabel retired, I was appointed in her place. I visited with her and Myron at their gracious home and six-acre garden in the wealthy Bloomfield Hills section of Detroit, and left with a station wagon full of files and office equipment to take back to my home on the outskirts of Philadelphia, where I made my office and carried on Isabel's work.

In later years, Isabel suffered ill health, and in 1986, she passed away. Myron, who had a business of his own making automotive parts, lived another two years. Flowering Shrubs *had long been out of print when Isabel died, so as a memorial to her, Myron approached the Garden Writers Association of America for help in getting the book reprinted. I remember how delighted he was when I called him with news of its acceptance. Weeks later he called me again to say he had not been well and wondered if there was anything he could do to help expedite the work. He even offered to do some typing. I assured him the project was in good hands, and he died in his sleep the next day, September 28, 1988.*

Isabel and Myron were a remarkable couple who traveled to most of the world's great botanical areas, Isabel taking notes and Myron taking pictures. They left a valuable legacy in their book Flowering Shrubs, *and I am very pleased to play a part in bringing it back in this updated, full-color edition.*

Derek Fell
Cedaridge Farm
Bucks County, Pennsylvania

TABLE OF CONTENTS

A PERSONAL APPRECIATION OF
FLOWERING SHRUBS AND SMALL TREES
BY DEREK FELL
page 5

ABOUT THE BOOK
page 8

About the Book

Somehow, despite early acquaintance with the strawberry bush, snowball, weigela, and lilacs in the garden of my childhood, courses in woody plants in college, and planning the plantings of countless shrubs in gardens I have designed, I never really appreciated shrubs until the spring our daughter was nearly three and our son was born.

In addition to caring for husband, household, and children, I was in the midst of redesigning and replanting the grounds around six school buildings. That season all our perennial borders went untended, the annuals never were planted and only the shrubs carried on, giving their usual bloom without any attention whatsoever.

Appreciation of shrubs grew as they helped me over various hurdles. For instance, there was the time when the PTA called for 25 corsages to be ready within three hours. Clearly visible from the telephone, through a window across the room, were two large Father Hugo's roses and two Chinese lilacs, all in full bloom. Even as I said I would make the corsages, I knew where the flowers for them would come from.

When the neighborhood in which we lived gradually became commercial, and we were looking elsewhere for a home, I wanted more land. My husband protested that I didn't have time to take care of the half-acre garden I already possessed. But, I told him, the next garden would depend largely on shrubs and flowering trees, which wouldn't require the same care as perennials. Nor would I have to give that care—others could do it since shrubs are larger than perennials and more readily seen. Furthermore, I was going to buy and grow all the shrubs that could be grown in our area and put together a picture book of shrubs.

Now, almost fourteen years since this six-acre garden was started, the shorter and fewer perennial borders still go unweeded some years, but the garden is not dependent on them for design, color or bloom. Shrubs provide all these things.

In pursuit of knowledge about shrubs I have walked the rows of hundreds of nurseries in the United States, Canada and abroad, visited almost all of the major botanical gardens in the world, and grown hundreds of the shrubs in the garden.

Purpose

There are two reasons for writing this book. The first is to give the interested gardener a profusely illustrated book of shrubs available for purchase that will cut upkeep while beautifying the garden and providing flowers galore for use in the house.

The second is to furnish nurserymen, landscape architects and garden center operators with the book they have told me they need and want—one that pictures hundreds of shrubs so that they can show their customers and clients what the flowers and fruits look like, that provides up-to-date information on numerous aspects of gardening with shrubs and that uses currently correct botanical names.

If I have accomplished both of these objectives, to interest the home gardener and assist the professional, then the work of assembling the book will have been worthwhile.

Scope

Since it is obvious that all of the shrubs hardy in the United States and Canada cannot be grown in a single garden, so that they can be photographed as they flower and fruit, I decided to include in this book only shrubs and small trees hardy in Zones 6 through 1 of the Hardiness Zone Map.

The shrubs and small trees included in this book are those readily available for purchase since they are listed in catalogs or lists of nurserymen in either the United States or Canada, most of them located in the plant hardiness zones given above. The nurserymen's associations in both countries have cooperated by furnishing me lists of their members. I circularized them, and from the catalogs of those

who replied, compiled the lists of shrubs, small trees and flowering vines included in this book. Sufficient description is given of each plant in Chapters 12, 13 and 14 so that you can choose those that fulfill your requirements.

Nomenclature

Quite early in the work of assembling this book I realized that, as far as nomenclature was concerned, the nursery catalogs and lists left much to be desired. If I used the names as given in them, I would often have to list the same plant under several variations of the same botanical name (many retail and most wholesale nursery catalogs list plants under their botanical names). So I had to decide whether to use what I knew to be sometimes botanically invalid and other times incorrect names or straighten out the nursery catalogs, giving their incorrect names as synonyms for the currently correct botanical names. Though the latter course meant checking and re-checking botanical names in one reference after another, this is the course I chose to follow.

Because there is no one up-to-date botanical authority, numerous authorities have been checked. In reviewing all the botanical refer-

ences we have found that occasionally botanists disagree regarding the correct name of a particular shrub. In these cases Mr. Swink, a noted taxonomist, has given me the score of botanists for and against and I have decided which botanist or botanists to follow.

Following the advice of Dr. George H. M. Lawrence, director of the Hunt Botanical Library, Carnegie Institute of Technology, Pittsburgh, and Dr. Harold W. Rickett, from the New York Botanical Garden in The Bronx, I have dropped capitalization of species names but retained the spellings of names that end in ii.

Descriptions of Shrubs

Despite my insistence on the correct botanical names for the trees and shrubs in this book, the descriptions are not given in botanical terminology, but in the simplest possible English. Thus, an "inflorescence" becomes either a cluster or a spike, depending on its form, and a leaf is not "pubescent," it is hairy. This book, obviously, is not written for botanists. I happen to be a horticulturist and I write for gardeners.

The other aspects of the book are explained in the chapters to which they apply.

Part One

Using Shrubs

1

SHRUBS ARE FOR EVERY GARDEN

Plant for plant, dollar for dollar, and backache for backache, you'll get more satisfaction from flowering shrubs than you will from any other class of plants you can grow in your garden.

That's a broad statement, but it's true.

A shrub is planted but once, unless you're the sort of person who is perpetually moving plants. It will last a lifetime or more in that one place, if carefully planted then given reasonable care. There are two shrubs in the garden at Mount Vernon that verbal tradition says were given to George Washington by Lafayette during his 1784 visit. One is a calycanthus or strawberry shrub, the other an oak-leaved hydrangea. Think how many human lifetimes these two shrubs have survived!

Shrubs are easy to grow. Most of them require no constant care—just good planting—to thrive and produce a wealth of bloom. Most shrubs need no fertilization, very little pruning, little or no spraying for pest control. Thus your upkeep of a garden of shrubs is little compared with a garden composed of any other type of plants.

Shrubs really produce what you want most, if you're the average gardener—they produce flowers by the armful. Even the shrubs that can be accommodated in a small backyard garden will give the household more blooms than it can use. Cutting sprays of bloom is an easy way of pruning shrubs, while at the same time allowing use of the prunings for indoor decorations of many kinds.

In addition shrubs have another advantage: they are available in a wide, wide variety of heights, shapes, foliage colors, foliage textures and forms, flower colors, flower forms, fruit shapes and colors. There is at least one shrub in bloom practically every month of the year; during the five months of heavy shrub bloom there are so many in flower that one garden cannot possibly accommodate them all.

Thus, regardless of where you live, the garden color scheme you decide upon, the height or shape or anything else you de-sire, you'll find that there's a shrub available that will precisely fill your needs. In fact, there probably will be several shrubs to fill the bill, so that you'll have a choice.

Shrubs have something else to give a garden. They give it a lightness that no evergreen, not even a graceful hemlock, can give it. If you ever have first walked through a garden solely of evergreens and then into one that features shrubs, you know precisely what I mean. They give a garden variety in form, height and foliage texture, such as no other type of plants gives. If you plan well, shrubs also will give your garden a constantly renewed, constantly changing focus of attention, which shifts from place to place according to the season of the year—thus adding a kind of interest much harder to obtain from other categories of plants.

Shrubs are indeed for every garden—and every garden needs at least a few of them.

This is a spectacular specimen of Azalea mollis *hybrid planted at the edge of a woodland.*

2
GETTING
ACQUAINTED
WITH SHRUBS

What are these woody plants that we call shrubs? And how can one distinguish them from the other woody plants we call trees? There are several definitions and comparisons that will help.

The first is a comparison of the form in which trees and shrubs grow. A tree is a plant that grows with one stem (trunk) from the ground. A shrub, on the other hand, usually grows with several to many stems emerging from the earth.

These definitions, however, are not always accurate because a tree that has been cut back or injured often grows again with several stems whereas a weak shrub or one especially trained may have only one stem. Furthermore, there are times when a normal tree will sprout more than one stem or trunk and a normal shrub will grow sparsely with but a single stem. Thus, these definitions and this comparison are applicable only in a broad sense.

A second way of distinguishing a shrub from a tree is by its new growth. This is usually at the tips of existing branches if the plant is a tree, while a shrub also may grow by sending up new shoots or stems from the ground.

Even if both of these definitions of a shrub are kept in mind when viewing a woody plant, it still is not always easy to say "this is a shrub" or "this is a tree," which is why botanical descriptions often read "shrub or small tree."

For the purposes of this book, plants growing usually with several stems will be considered shrubs and those normally achieving only one main stem or trunk will be considered trees.

GETTING TO KNOW THEM

The shrub most people know best is the lilac. It is such a long-lived shrub that many still exist next to old foundations where houses once stood. While the houses are long since gone, the lilacs still thrive.

To get acquainted with lilacs (if you aren't already) and with other shrubs, take a walk around any residential neighborhood near you that has older houses and gardens. You wil probably see a variety of species.

April, May, and June are the months of "big bloom" for shrubs, so take your walk, if possible, during these months. You'll see some of the owners of the gardens out working in them. Ask them the names of the shrubs you see in their gardens. Chances are very good that they'll know.

Never think that you are bothering these people or taking up their time unduly. Good gardeners delight in sharing knowledge of plants and gardening.

Thus, in your own neighborhood or one nearby, you can learn about the shrubs that grow well there. However, this walk around a few blocks serves merely to whet your appetite for shrubs and their flowers. You will find that, regardless of the state in which you live, there are other neighborhoods and more distant places where many more shrubs will show off for your edification. Colleges in most states have beautifully planted campuses, where shrubs are used in great quantity and usually in great variety. There may be a botanical garden or arboretum or two for you to visit. Or perhaps finely landscaped gardens are open to you when garden tours or pilgrimages take place in your town.

Chinese lilac (Syringa chinensis) *makes a spectacular summer-flowering lawn highlight.*

In addition, commercial nurseries have rows of shrubs. There are nurseries in every state—in every province.

Visiting the neighbors, the university campus, the botanic garden, the arboretum, may be done during weekends, as part of your family's recreation program. Visiting local flower and garden shows adds to the places and things you can include in this program. Garden pilgrimages or planned visits usually include weekends, since more people can attend then.

You will find many outstanding examples of flowering shrubs in public gardens, such as this forsythia in Fairmount Park in Philadelphia.

NURSERY VISITS

If you know exactly what you want to buy and are going to the nursery in order to buy it, consider yourself welcome at any time. If, however, you are visiting a nursery in order to learn about shrubs, in order to ask questions, then confine your visiting days to Monday and Tuesday, the slowest days of the week for the nurseryman.

SHRUB LISTINGS

In getting acquainted with shrubs, sooner or later, in this case sooner, you are going to meet botanical names. In this book, the shrubs are listed alphabetically according to their botanical names because these are their only valid names. Botanical names as well as common names are in the index. If you know only a common name, look it up in the index and it will lead you to the botanical name, the description of the shrub and, usually, a picture or two.

Some people will not like the listing of shrubs in this way because the botanical name is either Latin or Latinized. They will feel that the botanical names are too hard to pronounce or to remember, that it is too much bother to use them, or that people who use them are all snobs. Actually, the person using

Rhododendrons adorn the woodland setting at the New York Botanical Garden.

a botanical name is not snobbish but sensible, for this is the only name known all over the world for that particular plant and the only one by which it surely can be bought. It doesn't make much difference whether or not you pronounce botanical names correctly, just so you can spell the one belonging to the plant you want. The nurseryman will recognize it, and perhaps he doesn't know the correct pronunciation either.

As to its being a bother to learn botanical names or too hard to do so, let me ask you a question. Do you have a hobby? If so, didn't you have to learn a new terminology or "language" in order to talk to others about that hobby? For instance, in stamp collecting the word "mint" means "unused." To the general public it doesn't mean that at all.

Another example of specialized language: the first time we exhibited an Irish setter at a dog show, I discovered, much to my astonishment, that "bitch" was a respectable word in dog show circles!

And so it is with every new hobby. There's a new language to learn. So why balk at learning a little Latin, since this happens to be the language of shrubs and shrub identification?

Certainly some of the words are long and are tongue twisters. But what did you do when you were in about the 4th grade and one of your classmates told you, with great glee, that the longest word in the English language is antidisestablishmentarianism? Did you avoid this word? Of course not. You learned it immediately, so you could show it off to a less informed classmate.

This doesn't mean that everyone who learns the Latin names of plants is doing so to show them off to people not in the know (though some of them, being only human, certainly learn a few names for this very reason). Most people learn a Latin name so they can buy the precise plant they have in mind and not have another plant foisted upon them.

Here are two true stories of what can happen when you want to buy a specific shrub but don't know (or won't learn) the botanical name.

The first concerns a reader who wrote me to ask the name of a small shrub that had beautiful purple berries in early autumn. It seemed to her that it would fit exactly a certain corner in her small yard. This shrub, I told her, is callicarpa, or beauty berry, and there are several species of this genus available, all of them effective at that time of year. I warned her to take the correct Latin name of the shrub with her to the nursery when she went to buy it, since callicarpas are not found in every sales lot.

She must have failed to do this. Result: next autumn I got another letter from her complaining that the shrub she had purchased, which had borne beautiful pink flowers in great masses in May, didn't bear a single berry that fall!

This doesn't seem like much of a story, does it? But to me

The decorative berries of Callicarpa japonica *persist even after leaves have fallen.*

it meant that she had been sold beauty bush rather than beauty berry and, instead of a small shrub with insignificant flowers but handsome purple berries in fall, she'd bought a shrub that will grow 12 feet high and stretch 12 feet across, which has abundant and lovely pink flowers in May, bears no berries at all, but has attractive greyish seed heads after the flowers fade. In her small garden, the ultimate size of that beauty bush, lovely as it is, will be a problem!

The other story concerns my aunt. She told me, when her garden was quite new, that she wanted to buy an old-fashioned fragrant mock orange. I wrote down its Latin name for her—*Philadelphus coronarius*. She scoffed at the thought of a Latin name.

So, a couple of years later, she told me about her mock orange, which had intensely fragrant blooms, but double, not single like the ones she wanted. She had, quite evidently, been sold *Philadelphus virginalis*, instead of *Philadelphus coronarius*. To make a long story short, she finally owned eight mock oranges, some with fragrant blooms, some not, and not one of them was the old-fashioned species she wanted! While she steadily refused to "bother with the Latin name," she kept bemoaning the lack of that old-fashioned mock orange every time we met!

So, as you see, it pays to know botanical names, not only on the nursery sales lot, but also if and when you travel. Here's one short story to illustrate.

My husband and I were at the Taj Mahal, not in the beautiful park around the building, which every tourist sees, but in the working garden where the plants for the park are grown. Many were in pots set on the concrete paths that border the garden. Some I knew on sight. Others I wasn't certain I knew. About one of these I said to my husband (who certainly wouldn't know the answer, but was the only person around to address, since the guide obviously was bored to tears with me), "I wonder if that's——?" giving the botanical name I thought might belong to the plant in question.

You could have knocked me down with half a feather when, from behind me, came the botanical name. The person who uttered it was certainly a most ragged looking man. He was one of the gardeners, knew the botanical name of every plant in the garden, and we spent a happy half hour "Latin naming" each other to my edification. I didn't speak his language, nor he mine, but in the universal language of botany we were both at home.

BOTANICAL NAMES

After all those stories, perhaps a short explanation of botanical names is in order. The first thing to keep in mind about them is that they are given to plants, shrubs included, by taxonomic botanists who are seeking to *classify* plants, not by horticulturists who want only to *describe* plants so that it is possible to tell one from the other.

The second fact you need to know about botanical names is that they are not necessarily static. Botanists disagree about some of them, particularly about varieties and cultivars, and

occasionally change one or more names. This usually is because, in searching botanical records, they find that a plant has been given another name previously (and, according to the International Code of Botanical Nomenclature, a plant must bear the first name assigned to it) but sometimes for another reason. In making these changes in botanical names, botanists quite generally ignore the effects on the nursery business or on gardeners.

Despite the fact that botanists give the names to provide a means of reference, a botanical name, in many cases, does describe a plant, at least to some extent. And, whether you like botanical names or not, they just happen to be the only ones that really identify a plant to a horticulturist as well as to a botanist.

Most plants have botanical names consisting of two words. The first is the genus or generic name; the second the species or specific name. Both the genus and the species are groups of plants; the genus usually the larger of the two.

Although two taxonomic botanists discussing in my presence the definition of a species agreed that "a species is what a good botanist thinks a species is," I am going to step in where angels fear to tread and define a species. It is a unit or group of individual plants that bear a close resemblance to one another —so much so that this particular group will not be mistaken for another group combined with it in the same genus. The individuals in this group called a species will vary only slightly from one another, perhaps in such relatively minor details as precise shape of leaf, flower color or something similar.

Above is a breathtaking view of a woodland garden planted with a rich assortment of shrubs and small trees.

Cercis canadensis *grows into a small tree.*

Cersis chinensis *becomes a shrub with multiple stems.*

When several species resemble each other so that some physical feature, such as a leaf or flower form, is the same as that in other species, and these species may be considered to have some common ancestry, they are grouped into a genus. Thus, as previously stated, the genus is a group of plants and the species also is a group of plants, but the plants in a species more closely resemble one another than those in a genus.

The minor details indicated two paragraphs above, where they exist, are cared for by a third name—the varietal name. This makes clear the further way in which a particular plant differs from others in the same species. When a variety has been developed in cultivation, rather than found in the wild, it is called a "cultivar," a coined word. Cultivars are not natural hybrids such as occur in the wild but most are hybrids often deliberately perpetuated. The specific names of the parents must be omitted in designating hybrid cultivars because the cultivar name cannot favor either parent. Cultivars that are seedlings or bud sports may have both generic and specific names before the cultivar name to indicate their parentage.

Cultivar names usually are in English rather than Latin, and are set off by single quotation marks. The cultivar names that are in Latin usually are names that have been in existence longer, often names of species or varieties now found by botanists to be cultivars instead.

This may sound complicated, so let's try one botanical name to see how the nomenclature system works. *Cercis* (pronounced Ser-siss in English, though in Latin it would be Ker-kiss), is the botanical name for redbud, a small tree or large shrub that blooms in early spring. One species is called *canadensis* because it was found growing in an area that was at that time part of Canada; another is *chinensis*, found growing in China. The two species differ in habit of growth, in their ability to stand winter cold, and slightly in flower color—reasons why they are separate species.

Cercis canadensis has red-violet flowers. To distinguish the wild, white-flowered form from this species, a varietal name has been added and the white-flowered form is called *Cercis canadensis alba*, *alba* being the Latin word for white.

There also are several cultivars or horticultural varieties of *Cercis canadensis*, one of which is named 'Wither's Pink Charm', Withers being the name of the man who found it. It also has flowers in the red-violet range, like the species *canadensis*, but a different shade, much more pinkish-violet than red-violet. The proper name of this plant is *Cercis canadensis* 'Wither's Pink Charm'. The cultivar name, in this case, indicates the difference in flower color, just as does the varietal name *alba*.

In the example above, the cultivar 'Wither's Pink Charm' was not a hybrid and had only one parent, the species *Cercis canadensis*. When a cultivated variety (cultivar) is a hybrid and thus has two parents, the rules of nomenclature require that neither parent be favored. This means that the specific name of neither can precede the cultivar designation. Thus, for these hybrid cultivars there is a different designation. The generic or genus name is given first, followed by the cultivar name. *Philadelphus* 'Enchantment' is an example of such a listing. However, if the cultivar name is a Latin name then the genus name is followed by an × , meaning hybrid cross, as with the name *Abelia* × *grandiflora*, the result of a cross between *A. chinensis* and *A. uniflora*.

WHAT LATIN NAMES CAN TELL YOU

The following exposition of botanical (Latin) names is intended to bring a little interest, meaning and fun to this usually dull subject. These names, chosen for each plant, usually at the discretion of the discoverer, can be either useful in describing or identifying the plant or merely interesting.

The "interesting" names are those that indicate the place of origin of the shrub (e.g., americana, amurensis, koreana, orientalis, persica, virginicus) or that are the name of a person (baileyi, fortunei, kolkwitzia, schlippenbachii, wilsonii).

Both baffling and helpful are the names that describe something about the plant, distinguishing it from others in the same group. Many of these descriptive terms are used over and over again in different plant genera, so once you know what they mean your knowledge carries over. To understand these terms, it helps to know what features they are describing. A few examples are given here.

Some names apply to the general shape of the plant: arborescens—tree-like; compactus—compact-growing; nanus—dwarf.

Others tell about the plant's habitat: alpinus—growing in the mountains; maritimus—a seashore plant; and some about the season of bloom: praecox—very early; autumnale—autumnal.

When "flora" or some modification of this word is a part of the botanical name, you can expect some information about the flowers. This may be about quantity or size of bloom: floribunda—free-blooming; grandiflora—large-flowered; or form of flower cluster: paniculata—a "panicle" type of cluster, or racemosa—flowers formed in a "raceme," simplex—single, plenoflora or floreplena—double. Or it may tell about the flower color: alba—white, aurum—golden, lutea—yellow, rosea—pink, rubra—red, purpureus—purple; or perhaps about the odor: fragrans—pleasant smell, foetida—fetid.

Another important category of descriptive words is that including some form of the words "folia" or "phyllum," meaning leaf. For instance, when each leaf grows from the branch at a different level from another leaf, this is "alternifolia." A shrub with small leaves may be called "microphyllum," which is the word meaning small-leaved.

The shape of the leaf may be indicated by names such as "acerifolia"—like a maple (the genus *Acer*) or "trifoliata"—with three leaflets. Sometimes the leaf characteristic is indicated by such descriptive words as "incisa"—deeply-cut or "laciniata"—slashed. Or leaf shape may be the important characteristic and be indicated by such names as "rotundifolia"—round-leaved, "angustifolia"—narrow-leaved, or "prunifolia"—leaf shaped like that of a member of the genus *Prunus*

Here is a beautiful assortment of Clematis vines, 'Ernest Markham' (top), 'Nelly Moser' (center), and 'Ramona' (bottom).

(which includes plums, cherries, peaches, apricots and nectarines, as well as almonds).

At other times the botanical name describes the leaf tip, with such terms as "apiculata"—tipped with a point, or "mucronata"—tipped with a very short point. Or, perhaps the edge or margin of the leaf is important in identification as with "dentata"—having big teeth or "serrata"—having small teeth. Even the leaf texture may be denoted by such terms as "crispa"—curled or "rugosa"—wrinkled. A roughly fuzzed leaf surface may give the name "incana" to a shrub and finally, leaf color may be included in the plant's name as "variegata"— mottled or patterned, "marginata"—an edge or rim color different from that of the remainder of the leaf, usually lighter; or "polifolia"—white leaved.

So, the botanical or Latin names, once understood, may be helpful to you in many ways because they indicate the characteristics that the person naming the shrub considered most important to distinguish it from the others that are similar.

The reader who knows any Latin and who scans the botanical names in these chapters will note immediately that the genders of modifying adjectives quite often do not agree with the nouns that they modify. Apparently, even though there have been attempts to bring proper relationships between nouns and adjectives (e.g., *Rosa multiflora*), there have been so many shifts and modifications of names over the years that often the words in a given botanical name have differing endings. For instance, *Euonymus alata*. So, as long as the meaning is understood without precise Latin, pay no attention to the fact that the word endings often are not correct.

COMMON NAMES

After the Latin or botanical name of each shrub, which is the one currently correct for that shrub, you'll find in this book the so-called "common" or "vulgar" or "folk" name or names of the shrub. If you wonder how a shrub can have two or more common names, while it has only one correct Latin name, you have hit on the weakness of common names. They vary too, too much. It's as simple as that.

Different people in different parts of the world gave shrubs and other plants their common names. Thus common names vary from country to country, from state to state and even from community to community! For example, down in Kentucky a certain shrub is known as "hearts abustin' with love." More widely over the United States it is called strawberry bush, though it has other local names. Its botanical name is *Euonymus americana*—all over the world. Thus the gardener who knows the Latin names of plants can converse easily with nurserymen, botanists and plantsmen the world over, even if he speaks only English.

A close up of the flowers of **Rosa** rugosa.

CHANGING SHRUB NAMES

As previously stated, botanists give plants their botanical names and occasionally find reasons for changing a few of them. Also, as already explained, one reason for their so doing is that a previously published name is found and the International Code of Botanical Nomenclature decrees a change to it.

It seems to me that in addition to this Code botanists need a statute of limitations, so that a botanical name that has been valid for, let's say 50 years, cannot be changed. It certainly seems ridiculous that *Paeonia albiflora*, named in 1788, should now be changed to *Paeonia lactiflora* merely because a botanist found that *lactiflora* was assigned to the species about 12 years before *albiflora*. After all, the two names were given the plant by the same man and how, 200 years later, can any botanist know that the man didn't simply change his mind?

All would be well for the gardener despite these changes in botanical names if only every nurseryman would change the listings in his catalog accordingly. But nurserymen are busy growing plants and selling them. A few try to keep up with botanical changes and succeed. Most do not try.

So, while I am expressing my thoughts about changes in botanical nomenclature, I feel that just as botanists need a statute of limitations, nurserymen need some central agency to keep their catalogs correct botanically. After all, they no longer are using methods in vogue half a century ago, so why should they continue to refer to *Cornus racemosa* as *Cornus paniculata*, when this change in nomenclature was made about 50 years ago?

In general, the generic or genus name is correct in the catalogs, except for a few cases when a plant was known for many, many years by one name, later changed by the botanists for

Flowering quince (Chaenomeles speciosa) *blooms in early spring.*

valid scientific reasons that may be obscure to the gardener, and the nurseryman didn't see fit to change. Thus, in numerous catalogs you'll find the Japanese flowering quince listed as *Cydonia japonica*, which was its correct name for years and years. Botanists then shifted it to the genus *Chaenomeles*. Thus, the old name, *Cydonia japonica* is synonymous with *Chaenomeles lagenaria* or the newer *Chaenomeles speciosa* and the same plant is meant by all three names.

When it comes to species, variety, and cultivar names, there is much confusion in the catalogs. There is a too-common practice, by nurserymen and others, of using a varietal name as a substitute for a specific name. Thus, *Caragana arborescens* 'Lorbergii', the beautiful fine-leaved form of Siberian pea tree, often is listed merely as *Caragana lorbergi* without the capital letter that, according to the Code, is mandatory at the beginning of an English word used as a cultivar name. As you see, in the last case, the species name is left out entirely.

All of these discrepancies between catalog names and correct botanical names have been resolved, to the best of my ability, in the five years of work on this manuscript. It would have been much simpler and infinitely easier to use the botanical names found in most catalogs, but then one plant would have been listed by several to many botanical names, and the book would have been of little use to nurserymen, who really need to correct their listings. Furthermore, my German ancestors would never have permitted me to allow the incorrect names to stand.

Since there obviously must be some authority for plant names, and most of the authorities are out-of-date, having been published many years ago, it has been necessary for me to work from the oldest to the newest of the various publications listing botanical names. In some cases it has been necessary to choose which name I would use because authorities disagreed. In this case I have tried to choose the name given by the most recent authority.

I hope all this checking of botanical names will make it possible for you to avoid buying the selfsame plant under three different botanical names from three different nurseries. Also, for this same reason, all synonyms found in the catalogs, as well as those in botanical literature, are given in parentheses after the presently correct botanical name of the shrub.

If you are wondering why I place so much emphasis on the nursery listings, consider this: Who grows the plants offered for sale? Nurserymen. Who ought to know which plants will grow in a given area? The nurseryman who grows them year in and year out. Then what better place to find a listing of plants that grow from plant hardiness Zone 6 northward in the United States and Canada (the area included in this book) than the catalogs and lists of nurserymen in these zones in the two countries?

A nursery sales lot operator may buy plants from any zone at all—and the same applies to the garden center operator unless he is the nurseryman. I have seen many plants that would winter perfectly in Virginia and similar climates sold on lots here in Michigan where they are certain to die, long before the winter cold becomes severe. Many nursery sales lot operators neither know nor care about the ability of a plant to grow in a given climate. Nurserymen ought to care—if they expect to stay in business.

In addition to providing a listing of shrubs grown in Zones 6, 5, 4, 3, and 2, the nursery catalogs provide sources for those plants. What good would it do for you to know about a shrub, drool over the description, and want to buy it—if it isn't available? Many a description has been given in an article or book of a plant in a botanical garden, an arboretum, or some similar place, for which there is no commercial source. I learned the hard way, during my many years as garden editor of a large metropolitan newspaper, never to mention a plant for which I did not know at least one source, for, just as surely as I did, some reader wanted to buy it.

3
USING SHRUBS
IN THE
GARDEN

You notice that the title of this chapter is not Landscaping With Shrubs: I am not going to talk about any of the land-scaping principles, as these are available in plenty of good books. Instead, I'm going to try to show you how to use shrubs to fill the various needs of your garden.

GARDEN PROBLEMS

Every garden has problems, even if they're as simple to solve as finding a very low-growing, low-staying plant to use under a large picture window where the foundation looks bare. If

you'll look at the lists found in the appendix of this book, you'll see that there's a wide choice of low shrubs available to solve this particular problem, even though the lists cover only the shrubs in this book and therefore are not complete.

What are the problems in your garden? It would be an excellent plan for you to make a list of them. Nothing fancy, just jot down the places you're not sure what to plant and why you aren't sure. Add a dimension or two—height available, if it's restricted (as by an overhanging roof); width available, also only if it's restricted; depth available, ditto. From then on the lists and descriptions are your chief guides.

A beautiful shrub border featuring azaleas in the Connecticut garden of Mrs. Ruth Levitan.

HOW TO SOLVE YOUR GARDEN PROBLEMS

I often have wished that it was possible to pass on one's knowledge of a subject with the same ease that an outgoing chairman passes on a gavel to the incoming chairman. But, since that is not possible, the next best thing here certainly must be to point out the places in the garden where shrubs are most likely to be used and indicate how to plan these areas.

Most people who buy a new home or start renovating the planting of an older one start with the planting around the house—a logical place to begin. If you drive down almost any suburban street you will notice that these house plantings are almost entirely of narrow-leaved (needled) evergreens, and also that most of these plantings are deadly dull. Livelier and far more interesting plantings are achieved by using needled, broad-leaved and deciduous plants together. Look for yourself and you'll find that this is so.

You will notice that, in the paragraph above, I used the words "house planting." The term is interchangeable with "foundation planting."

House Planting

The most important point to remember in planning the planting around your house is that you are endeavoring to enhance the house, not smother it. The house is the important object, not the planting. On the house walls the openings are the most important features. And, of doors and windows, the doors are more important. So, look first at the doors, front, side, back, in that order. Are they so beautiful or so unique in appearance that no plants will help accent or enhance them? If so, leave well enough alone and use only a ground cover near the doorways. If not, what do the doorways need? If they are too narrow, adding a fairly wide shrub, preferably one with horizontal branches, on either side will make for a wider appearance. A too-wide doorway, however, will not be made to appear narrower by using a tall, narrow shrub on either side. It is better to balance the too-wide doorway with a wide shrub somewhere else, perhaps at a house corner.

Since a few shrubs around the house are sufficient to enhance its architecture, plant the doorways first and then look to see what other plants are needed.

The other openings—windows—may also need to be enhanced or accented. Full length windows, of course, are treated the same as doors except when on the same wall as a door, in which case the door planting still should be considered first and more important. Picture windows usually are enhanced by low plantings under them. Sometimes a ground cover is sufficient planting, at other times shrubs that

Flowering peach (Prunus persica) *and white bridalwreath* (Spiraea prunifolia) *bloom in early spring.*

when mature will reach to the bottom of the window will look better.

High windows may or may not need plantings under them—much depends on the house architecture and on your personal opinion. One thing, however, is certain: windows never were placed in a house wall to be obscured by planting of any kind, so select plants for your windows with due consideration of the footage between ground and sill.

It is possible that a house corner needs accenting. A high, narrow shrub will do this. Or it may need softening, in which case a tall-growing, fairly small-leaved and many-branched shrub may be the solution.

There are times when whoever planned the house did not do a perfect job, so that it seems unbalanced. For instance, a wing at one end may look far too heavy for the rest of the building. Try planting a large, visually heavy shrub or small tree at the other end of the building and watch the visual weight of the wing diminish.

Sometimes a huge chimney dominates the house. A shrub such as a pyracantha, espaliered against the chimney, its branches trained to any pattern that pleases you, will break up the mass of the chimney into smaller masses that are not so dominant.

So much for solving problems of house plantings. But bear in mind three things when you select the shrubs for this important location: (1) choose those that thrive in the exposure in which they are to be planted—in other words don't choose a shade-loving shrub for the south side of the house—you might just as well throw your money out of the window; (2) choose only shrubs that are absolutely hardy in your climate (if you want to try some that may or may not be hardy, plant them elsewhere than around the house), so that you don't have to build a burlap screen around a choice boxwood and look at burlap all winter through your picture window; and (3) think of the appearance of the shrubs you choose at all times of year and before you buy, eliminating any from your plan that do not look well at every season. This does not mean that only broad-leaved evergreen shrubs should be planted. Cork-barked euonymus (*Euonymus alata*), for example, is just as interesting and attractive in winter, with its odd corky wings and definite branching habit, as it is at any other time of the year.

Screening, Delineating

After their use in the house planting, shrubs are most frequently used for screening or delineating and both may be accomplished with the same shrubs in the same planting. Screening may be of the outdoor living area, of an unsightly view or of the neighboring property. In any one of these cases, the same shrub planting also may delineate the property line. While a single line of shrubs may be and often is planted as a screen, several lines or rows of shrubs are more frequently found in border plantings.

If you wish to plant only a single line of shrubs, why not consider a hedge of one kind of shrub or, if height is a factor, one kind of small tree? It is not necessary that this hedge be kept clipped since there are many shrubs that present an attractive appearance without this additional care. But, especially if only a short screen planting is required, it will look far more homogeneous and therefore attractive if only one kind of plant is used. The columnar form of buckthorn (*Rhamnus*), for instance, makes a handsome sheared or unsheared hedge. If, however, a shrub with showier flowers is desired, beauty bush (*Kolkwitzia*) will grow to a comparable height. This is best left unclipped and is only for a tall, wide screen, whereas the buckthorn, while it will grow tall, also will stay narrow. If you will look at the list of hedge shrubs in Part I of the appendix you

American bittersweet (Celastris scandens) (top) *can be espaliered against a brick wall. Hybrid pink rhododendron* (bottom) *positioned at the edge of a deck carries color high into the sky.*

will find that there is a wide choice of heights, widths, and kinds available. As a matter of fact, any shrub may be used for a hedge, but some are more satisfactory than others.

A long screen planting permits a wider variety of shrubs. If your property requires such a planting, look first to see what the neighboring property possesses that can be turned to your advantage. Evergreen or deciduous trees on the other side of the property line may lend the necessary height to your border without your waiting for small plants set on your side of the line to grow tall. Bright yellow-flowering forsythias on the other side of the line might be "faced down" with lavender-flowering azaleas (*Rhododendron mucronulatum*) on your side, thus furnishing you with a beautiful, early-spring combination of flowers without the necessity of buying the forsythias.

If there is no neighboring planting, then of course you have to do all of it. But remember that shrubs grow wider as well as taller. Buy only as many as will fill the entire space eventually or as will fill half the space immediately. Then later, as they grow, you can move half the plants to fill the other half of the space. If there is a reason why you need an immediate effect in one part of a shrub border, this "doubling up" of the number of plants and moving half of them later is a satisfactory solution, even though it entails extra work.

Planning Shrub Borders

How to design a shrub border? The easiest way is to take a sheet of cross section paper (available at any stationery store) and select a scale for your design—perhaps you wish to have one square on the paper equal one foot on the ground, but it is easier, considering the size of cross section sheets, to select a figure like 5 or 6 feet for the equivalent of each square. After measuring or pacing off the length the border will be, count squares according to the scale you have selected and mark the length of the border on the paper. Mark also the ultimate width you wish the border to be. If it has to be narrow yet tall, and you do not wish a hedge planting, select only sufficient kinds of shrubs of the desired ultimate height so that there will be two or three of each kind next to one another in the line. One successful way to design such a single-line border is select for bloom each month of the flowering season one shrub that grows to the chosen height and width, so that there always will be one group of shrubs coming into bloom as

flowers on another group are fading.

After choosing the shrubs, read their descriptions in Chapter 12 or, of small trees, in Chapter 13. When you are certain of your choice, make a circle in the appropriate square on the cross section paper to indicate where the center of the first shrub will be when you dig the hole in which to plant it. The distance between these centers should be equal to half the sum of the ultimate width of adjacent shrubs. Label each circle with a number, then make a list of shrubs indicating on it the name of the shrub that number represents. Thus number 1 might mean a plant of *Spiraea vanhouttei* and there might be three of these in a row, each circle numbered 1. Number 2 will indicate another plant. This list becomes your buying list when you go to a nursery: your diagram with its circled numbers will show how many of each kind of shrub you need to buy.

If more depth is available for your border, it may have two rows of shrubs. The easiest way to place these is in zigzag fashion with one lower-growing shrub in the front row (the row toward your property) in between each of the taller-growing shrubs in the back row. While this is the easiest way, it does not, by any means, give the best appearance as the plants grow. It is more satisfactory, for instance, to line up three shrubs of one kind in the back row, then a single shrub with particularly beautiful foliage, form or bloom, and in front of that single shrub group five or six very low-growing shrubs, with perhaps only one medium-high shrub in front of the group of three.

Always remember that even lower-growing shrubs will extend both up and sideways and allow sufficient space for them to do so.

These English boxwood (Buxus sempervirens) *were sheared with hedge trimmers to create evergreen mounds along the edge of a water garden.*

Azalea, Kurume hybrid creates a sensational flowering hedge.

The three-shrub-deep border allows for zigzag planting of back and middle rows if desired, and group planting of the front row. It also allows for a far greater variety of shrubs. But one shrub of each kind in such a planting makes it a collection of shrubs rather than a border, while groups of several shrubs of each kind in each row results in a more attractive and more harmonious planting. The shrub border is the place to try that doubtfully hardy shrub for if it fails to live its loss will not be too noticeable and it can be replaced with a hardier shrub the following planting season.

The choice of shrubs for a border depends on how frequently you will look at those shrubs. If the border is close to the house, perhaps around the outdoor living area or as a background for some garden feature to be seen from a window, do as you did for the house planting: select only shrubs that will look good all year (most certainly those in the row nearest the house). Try to select one group of shrubs to bloom in early spring and another to color or fruit in autumn, but choose them in relation to the border as a whole. In the same way, consider the border as a whole when you decide on the flower colors of the shrubs.

This does not mean that all the shrubs must have flowers of the same color or colors, but it does mean that you should not be spacing forsythias evenly throughout the border every 10 feet so that when they bloom you will have dots of yellow here and there. It is far better to design one group of shrubs with, for example, forsythias in the background and Korean abelia leaf (*Abeliophyllum distichum*) in the foreground, to bloom at forsythia time and concentrate your forsythias in that area or in two areas, perhaps at opposite ends of the border and with another kind of shrub in the foreground of the second grouping. Not only does color grouping give a more pleasing effect than color dotting, but clashing colors can be avoided by planning groups that bloom at one time, of colors that contrast or blend. It is to help you do this that the Bloom Time Chart is included in the appendices.

In a long shrub border it is the mark of an expert designer to use, just once or twice in the length of the border, a single outstanding shrub or small tree, which, even though it may grow high and wide, is set either near the front of the border or in the foreground—against the border but out from it.

It is not easy in a shrub border to mix shrubs that require acid soil with those that do not. It is far better for the shrubs and easier for the gardener to plant acid-lovers together in one area. Keep in mind that there also are shrubs that may be killed by acidifiers added to soil nearby. Shade-loving shrubs should, of course, be reserved for shaded areas and sun lovers set in sunny places. The same applies to shrubs that delight in moist soil and those that abhor it.

In a long border it is important that there be some blending and also some contrasting foliage textures. A bold-textured, large-leaved shrub may well be placed in the foreground of several fine-foliaged shrubs. Select each shrub to harmonize with its neighbors on either side but also keep constantly in mind the appearance of the border as a whole, so that there are not too many bold contrasts nor too long stretches of small-leaved shrubs.

Consider also the winter appearance of the border against the sky. There should be some variation in height if it is to be interesting, even if it means greater border width for a taller, wider plant in some places or cutting down on the number of rows of plants in those areas to accommodate the taller, wider plant.

Shrubs with distorted shapes do not belong in the border: Save them for use as specimens.

Red and white azaleas planted in a checkerboard pattern offer an unusual spring-flowering display.

This is a beautiful informal hedge of Hydrangea macrophylla *placed in the shade of a magnolia tree.*

Specimens

Planting a shrub for a specimen does not mean digging a hole in the middle of a lawn and planting it there. That is the poorest possible use of a shrub as a specimen. Usually it distorts the entire landscape.

A specimen shrub, one planted to show off its perfect or unusual form, foliage, coloring or bloom, may be used, as indicated in the discussion of shrub borders above, in the foreground of a border; or it also might be used to draw the eye to a certain spot in the garden (in landscape parlance this is called using the shrub as a "focal point"). Other possible uses are by a gate or other entrance to the garden or next to the place where one part of the garden (perhaps the outdoor living area) opens onto another part (perhaps a lawn area). Still another possible place for a specimen shrub is any place where you want to draw the eye of the beholder—for instance to the point where a path leads off a lawn into a wooded area.

Only a very large property will need more than one or two shrubs placed as specimens. Beware: too many competing beauties produce a feeling of restlessness.

Windbreaks

There are times when it is desirable to plant a windbreak of shrubs. In such cases shrubs should be selected first for their absolute hardiness in your area and second for their twigginess, for only plants with many branches and twigs really break the force of the wind. A windbreak planting of shrubs must be not only tall, but also thick so the wind's force is spent by the time it goes through the shrubs. Plenty of width must be allowed for such a planting, which should be at least three rows deep and better four.

Barriers or Obstructions

When you wish to keep people and/or animals in or out of specific areas or from cutting across them, shrubs and small trees can furnish useful barriers or obstructions. For this use, the most satisfactory choice usually is a tree or shrub with thorns.

Among the very best for this purpose are hawthorns, small trees that may be allowed to grow unclipped to full height or

A hedge of dwarf barberry (Berberis thunbergii atropurpurea 'Crimson Pygmy') borders a bridle path.

kept clipped to medium height and formal shape. They make a more formidable barrier when clipped, for then they grow so dense and their thorns are so sharp that a planting is virtually impenetrable.

There are, however, other trees and shrubs that can serve this same purpose. You will find a list of them in Part I of the appendix. Use them with discretion and you'll avoid lawsuits.

Other Uses

Shrubs are useful for ground cover plantings where it is desired to use something other than grass or deciduous or evergreen perennials. Shrubs are used also for planting on banks to hold soil in place (and to cover the ground). Indicated in the shrub descriptions in Chapter 12 are shrubs that may be planted in rock gardens and on tops of walls. Shrubs are a wonderful group of plants, available in sufficient variety and versatile enough to solve many a garden problem.

USING SHRUBS IN YOUR GARDEN

The procedure of planning the shrubs for use in your garden is, as you now know, the same in all cases. Select the area you wish to plant. Take sufficient measurements so you can make sensible decisions on the basis of ultimate height or spread of the plants. Look long and carefully at the area until you have an idea of the shapes of the plants you want to use. Also try to recognize any problems that exist in the area or if, within the space limits, you are free to choose any shrub you wish.

If there is a problem, state it either to yourself or your spouse or a neighbor, as much to clarify it to yourself as for the purpose of talking it over (the old saw about two heads being better than one still holds). Then use the descriptions of plants in Chapters 12 and 13 to help you decide which shrub or tree you want to use.

Remember, in choosing, that good-looking foliage all season is more important than beautiful flowers for two weeks and that, where the plant is prominent in winter, an interesting silhouette becomes of prime importance. Also, the smaller the garden, the more important each individual plant becomes.

If you need to use several different kinds of shrubs in one group, as in a border, look in the Bloom Time Chart to see which shrubs bloom together, before you read their descriptions and, once again, make your choice according to which kinds appeal to you.

No one else can choose for you. The best landscape architect will only suggest and recommend plants. It is of course far better if you see the actual shrubs before choosing which to plant, and this you may be able to do in one of the places suggested in Chapter 2.

Above all, have fun, for shrubs are plants that can delight the owner without a great deal of upkeep.

A beautiful vista is created with borders of flowering shrubs and small trees, especially azaleas and flowering dogwood.

Part Two

Growing Shrubs

4

HOW
TO PLANT
SHRUBS

The first requisite in planting is forethought, so that it will
not be necessary to plant twice. So, before you plant, think. Is
this the right shrub for the place you intend to plant it? If it
isn't, you are either going to have to move the plant or else be
sorry for years to come.

By the "right" shrub I mean the shrub that (1) will grow
well in the particular location; (2) will thrive and bloom with
the amount of light available; (3) will not outgrow its allotted
space, and (4) will enhance the place in every way.

SELECTION

The lists in Part I of the appendix will tell you which shrubs will tolerate damp soil, which will grow well in semi-shade, and so on. In Chapter 12, in the more detailed description of the shrubs, you will find the approximate ultimate height and/or spread. Consult these lists and figures before you buy and doublecheck them before you plant. It will pay you to do so for you will thus avoid making mistakes. It will pay you also to use common sense in interpreting the height-width figures. If the soil in which you are planting is high in organic matter, the plant may grow a little taller or wider than others of the same species or variety set in poor soil. If space is limited, therefore, select a shrub that will grow a bit narrower or a bit lower than the available space rather than one that will grow certainly to its limits and may exceed them when planted in excellent soil or given plenty of fertilizer and water.

HANDLING BEFORE PLANTING

Assuming your selection is made and you have bought the right shrub for the situation, the handling of the shrub from time of acquisition to time of planting becomes the important matter. Shrubs are living things and transplanting is a major operation in their lives. Recognize this in your treatment of them. Under no circumstances allow shrub roots to dry or shrub tops to be exposed to full sun while the shrub is out of the ground. The best thing to do, of course, is to plant within a few hours after the shrub is acquired. But sometimes this is not possible.

If you must wait to plant, set the shrub in a shady place. If the plant has an earth ball around its roots, check to make sure the ball is damp. Water it if necessary. If the shrub came to you with bare roots, open the package to allow air to reach the tops, but either keep it closed around the roots or open it, moisten the packing material around the roots if necessary, and repack around this area. Then put the shrub in a cool, shaded, airy place.

Should it be absolutely necessary for a bare root shrub to be held longer than one or two days before planting it, "heel it in" by inserting its roots into a V-shaped trench, the shrub lying supported against one side of the V. Cover roots with soil; shade tops with burlap. Water the roots and plant the shrub as soon as you can.

Balled and burlapped shrubs, watered when necessary, can wait a week or so before planting. If they cannot be planted by that time, heap peat, wood chips or a similar material around and between the earth balls to help prevent drying out until you can plant.

A young rhododendron has been balled and burlapped to keep the root ball intact for safe transportation.

DIGGING

When you are ready to plant, remember that under normal circumstances, you are going to plant this shrub only once, so you may as well do a good job while you are about it. This means first digging a good, big hole, large enough to hold the roots of the plant when they are spread out in their natural positions—and then a bit larger, especially in poor soil. This extra-large hole permits an additional amount of loosened soil around the roots of the shrub.

As you dig, lay the top soil carefully on burlap or a tarpaulin at one side of the hole, subsoil on burlap or tarp at the other side. If you have brought the shrub along with you, be sure to keep it well protected from the drying effects of sun and wind, with damp burlap or sphagnum moss over both roots and tops. Keep it covered at all times.

PLANTING A BARE ROOT SHRUB

Actual planting varies only slightly depending on whether the shrub is "B & B" (balled and burlapped) or bare root. Unwrap the bare root shrub, cut off any broken roots and branches and hold it in the hole so that the stems are about an inch below the level at which they grew before. You can see the former soil line on the stems if you look closely. Check the width and depth of the hole to make sure roots can spread out as they normally would.

If not, lay the shrub aside, covering it once more while digging the hole larger or wider or, if required, filling in a little with some of the topsoil from the pile. When the size is just right, hold the shrub in place once more so that it is vertical and in the center of the hole (unless all of its roots grow to one side, in which case you place the stems nearer the other side of the hole).

At this stage it is necessary to look over the shrub for its "front" or best side. There usually is one part that is far more shapely, more fully clothed with branches to the base, than any other. This is the side to set facing in the direction from which you most often will see the shrub.

Holding the shrub in this position, pull topsoil into the hole with your other hand, placing it under and around each root, as the root lies in normal position, and firming the soil to the roots by pressing with finger tips.

Once you have filled around the roots with topsoil, it makes little difference if you use subsoil to fill the rest of the hole. The roots will not be growing in it. If you are short of topsoil, use compost (if you have a compost pile), buy additional topsoil, or mix granulated peat moss with what topsoil

To plant a rhododendron that is balled and burlapped, dig a hole large enough to accommodate the root ball (top). Loosen the burlap and string before sliding the root ball into the hole (center). Mulch around the base with straw, pine needles, or shredded leaves to help the shrub suffocate weeds and retain moisture (bottom).

A rhododendron hybrid (variety 'Vulcan') comfortably planted in its new location.

you have, up to half peat and half soil. This peat should not be the extremely acid kind unless the shrub you are planting requires acid soil. (See the section of this chapter headed "Acid–Soil–Loving Plants"). Instead it should be either neutral or slightly acid. The reason for using peat to eke out your supply of topsoil is that peat improves soil texture as well as furnishing additional planting material. If your soil is sandy, and therefore drains too readily, peat mixed with it will help it hold water. If your soil is clay and therefore too retentive of water, peat mixed with it will help to lighten its texture so that it drains better.

When the planting hole is filled level with the tops of the roots, water thoroughly or soak with a solution of a wilt-reducing, root growth-promoting plant hormone. This comes in powder form and is not too easy to mix with water. If you will put the required amount of powder in a small container like a cup, add a little water and mix to a paste, then add more water until the paste is pourable, pour it into a pail or other container into which you first have put the correct amount of water, you will find it mixes readily. One 2½-gallon scrub- or household-pail full of this solution is sufficient to moisten roots of all but very large shrubs and small ones need only half a pailful.

The use of this solution is incomparably better than using water alone. Water certainly will settle the soil and help prevent wilting if the shrub has leaves. But the hormone solution does both of these, does a far better job in preventing wilting, and in addition stimulates root growth.

We plant dozens, sometimes hundreds of shrubs in a season, often in just a few days—and we have found that the transplanting solution pays its way, especially in late spring when shrubs are starting to leaf out or in early fall when we frequently move them with leaves still on. Shrubs in full leaf, like broad-leaved evergreens or deciduous shrubs that, for some reason or other, you need to move with the leaves on, are greatly benefitted by this treatment.

We are so sold on the use of the hormone treatment that, even when bare root shrubs arrive in early spring with leaves

still unfolded, we put a metal bushel basket on a wheel barrow, fill it with the hormone solution, and set the shrubs with their roots in the solution. We move them to wherever we intend to plant them in this container, so that the roots have been treated with the hormone before planting. Then we use plain water to settle the soil and firm the plants in place. This saves carrying pails of the solution to places not readily accessible to water, even though we still may have to carry the water alone.

We have been known to follow the same system with B & B shrubs, especially when they arrived in wilted condition. In this case we set the balls in the bushel basket of solution and leave them there for two to three hours to soak it up.

After you have soaked the soil around the shrub's roots with either the hormone solution or water, fill in almost all of the rest of the hole with topsoil or subsoil, firming it as you near the top by tramping on it with your feet. This tramping definitely will not hurt the shrub unless you step on the tops, which will only happen if you forget to gather and hold the branches in your hands.

Leave the soil cupped at the top of the hole for ease in future watering. Lay the hose in this depression and let water dribble into the hole until you are satisfied that the soil in the hole is thoroughly soaked.

If, because of the contour of the land, it is not possible to leave a cup near the top of the hole, then build a dike of soil on the downhill side of the hole, well above the surrounding soil surface, so water will be held. Leave cup or dike in place during the first growing season after the shrub is planted for if you plant in spring, you will have to soak the shrub's roots with water from the hose once every single week, unless there is a soaking rain. If you plant in fall, you need water artificially only until fall rains begin.

It is a good idea to check, a week after planting, to see if the shrub still is in a vertical position. Sometimes beginning gardeners leave soil around the shrub too loose and the shrub settles so that it stands at an angle. Sometimes it stands straight, but has settled so it is too deep in the hole. If this has happened, loosen the soil around the outside of the hole with a shovel and, grasping all the shrub's tops in both hands, pull gently but steadily. Usually you can pull the shrub upwards the necessary inch or two so that it sits at the correct level. If the shrub is no longer vertical, loosen soil on the opposite side from the one it is slanting toward and pull it gently back. It may be necessary to drive a stake on that side of the shrub, from two to six feet away from it, distance depending on the height of the shrub, and "guy" the plant by tying a soft cord around the main branch or branches and tying the other end to the stake, which has been hammered into the ground at an angle, so the top is further from the shrub than the bottom.

Rhododendron hybrid (variety 'Vulcan') before planting, balled and burlapped.

PLANTING B & B SHRUBS

To plant shrubs that come with balls of earth and burlap around their roots, follow the same general procedure as that described for bare root shrubs. A generous hole is dug. The ball of the shrub is held in the hole to make certain that the hole is sufficiently deep and wide, and topsoil is thrown into the hole so that the top of the ball will set level with the top of the soil. This soil is firmed. The ball is set on top of it and the plant inspected from several angles for verticality of tops and evenness of ball with soil surface, as well as for best side in the right direction. Necessary corrections are made.

Then comes the question that bothers most beginners—what to do with the burlap? The easiest way to handle this problem is to leave the burlap in place. As you water the shrub the burlap gradually will rot and disintegrate so it doesn't really make much difference whether or not it is removed. However, some gardeners become worried about leaving burlap in place. These people can make themselves feel better (and perhaps allow the shrub to grow new roots a tiny bit more rapidly) by loosening the burlap at the top, laying it back and doubling it outward so that the burlap is left only under the ball and a short distance up the sides. Only if you are certain

that the earth ball will not break, will not even crack, should you remove all of the burlap. Occasionally, when the shrub has been growing in very heavy clay, the ball will be so solid that there is no chance of its breaking or cracking. Then, if you insist, the burlap may be taken off and the uncovered ball lowered onto the soil you have placed in the bottom of the hole such cases are rare, however.

As with a bare root shrub, topsoil is thrown in, this time to cover three quarters of the depth of the ball, and firmed as it is placed. Then sufficient hormone solution (or water) is poured in to soak the earth in the ball and around it. Subsoil may be used to fill over the topsoil, but the hole should not be entirely filled. The usual cup-shaped depression should be left to hold water and the earth fill should be tramped. Once again, all the soil in the hole and the ball should be settled by a slow trickle of water from the hose.

Since the tops of broad-leaved evergreen shrubs, those usually purchased B & B, are in full leaf, it is only sensible to reduce water loss through the leaves while the plants are reestablishing their roots. To do this, spray the tops with any of the plastic coatings sold for the purpose. Be sure to spray both upper and lower surfaces of the leaves, for most of the stomata, the openings in the leaves through which water is lost, are in the lower surfaces.

The same spray materials may be used on bareroot shrubs should they have leaves on them.

Simply follow the directions on the package for dilution with water, then spray lightly but thoroughly. In due course of time the weather will cause the coating to disintegrate. Meanwhile it is practically invisible if you don't overspray.

Rhododendron hybrid (variety 'Vulcan') two weeks after planting, in full flower.

ACID-SOIL-LOVING PLANTS

Should the plant that is B & B be one of those that thrive only in acid soil (an azalea, a rhododendron, a mountain laurel or a similar plant) then you obviously must see to it that the soil in which it is planted is acid. This poses no problem for people who live where most soils are naturally acid; but for the people in areas with neutral or alkaline soils it may mean replacement of soil.

If you are in doubt as to whether or not your soil is acid, you can test it yourself by buying a soil testing kit (available at garden supply stores or by mail) and following directions that come with it to determine soil reaction. Or you can send a soil sample to your county agricultural agent or some other agency that tests soil. A phone call to your agricultural agent (listed under your county name) will get you the address of the nearest agency and the fee (if any) for such a test. To take a sample, dig a hole a foot deep and large enough for you to square off two sides with a spade. Put a piece of waxed paper in the bottom of the hole. Using the spade, cut down one of the squared sides, just as you would slice a cake, from top to bottom. Let the slice of soil fall on the paper, pick it up, mix it well and put a cupful of it in any glass container. Cover the container. Label it with your name and address, the name of the plant or plants you wish to grow in this soil and add a request for a test of the acidity of the soil. For accurate results take several such samples from various parts of the area where you wish to grow acid-soil plants. Such tests are well worthwhile because, should your soil already be sufficiently acidic, you will avoid both the work and the expense of modifying it.

You may be disconcerted when you receive an answer from the soil testing agency for it may be given in terms with which you are unfamiliar. Chances are it will tell you what the pH of your soil is—and a figure will follow. This figure is easy to interpret and you needn't know any more about pH than how to interpret it. The figure 7, following the pH sign, means that your soil is neither acid nor alkaline ("sour" or "sweet"): it is neutral. Any figure above 7 means that your soil is alkaline; any figure below 7 means that it is acid. The only other necessary fact you need is that the pH scale is logarithmic, so that pH 4 is ten times as acid as pH 5 and so on, on either side of the neutral point. (Most plants grow best when the soil reaction is between pH 6 and pH 6.5, slightly acid. No plants succeed in a very acid soil nor in an alkaline soil.)

The plants that need acid soil grow best in a pH of 4.5 to 5.5 so that is the figure at which you aim in treating or replacing your present soil, if it is alkaline or neutral.

The easiest, though not necessarily the best, way to acidify your soil is to mix an acidifying chemical with it. Aluminum

These are the components of a typical soil-test kit.

sulphate has been recommended for this purpose but it should not be used as, sooner or later, free aluminum will be left in the soil and this is far from good for the plants growing in it. Better acidifiers, with no deleterious effects, are ferrous sulphate or sulphur. The amounts of these to mix with your soil will vary according to pH as shown by soil tests.

The difficulty is that only a small amount of either of these chemicals can be added at one time, so that the acidity can be increased only slowly. Time between applications should be at least a month. For instance a pound of sulphur may be applied at one time over 100 square feet of soil. Since ¾ of a pound will lower the pH one point if the soil is sandy, this may be plenty if you have sandy soil. But if it is a medium-heavy loam, two or three times that much sulphur is needed and in heavy clay, far more than that, so much more that replacement of soil is far more feasible.

REPLACING SOIL

In this case dig out the existing soil to a depth of 18 inches. Make certain that drainage below this depth is good. Then mix acid peat with either existing soil or topsoil you have purchased, in proportions that may range from 50-50 to 75-25, the higher percentage being the acid peat. German and Swedish peats are acid and some Canadian and American peats are also. Their pH may range from 4 to 5.5 and the percentage of peat to use to soil will depend on this figure, usually stated on the bag or bale.

Any of the acidifying chemicals will work better and keep the soil properly acid for a longer time if the physical condition of the soil is good, as in the mixture suggested above where plenty of organic matter has been added in form of peat. Should you not need to replace your soil, because it is sufficiently acid, you should work in compost, acid peat, rotted leaves or even sawdust (plus 1 pound of ammonium sulphate to each bushel of sawdust) to improve its physical condition, if this is necessary. Of course if you have the ideal acid, woods soil, nothing need be added to it.

Many people make special beds for acid-soil plants, raising the beds above the existing ground level, especially if in a region of non-acid soil, so that the soil reaction can be completely controlled. Drainage must be provided if the natural soil is clay. The soil mixture previously suggested for a replacement for existing soil may be used, plus an acidifying chemical if necessary. However, it is not absolutely necessary to make special beds for acid-soil plants. If plants are set where drainage is good, it is sufficient to replace the soil around the earth ball to twice the width of the ball and to 18 inches in depth, including the depth of the earth ball.

This close-up of loam soil shows its crumbly texture (top). *A close-up of sandy soil reveals the large, loose, granules that let water drain too quickly* (bottom).

This is an example of clay soil, showing how it breaks apart in hard lumps.

It is most important, especially in regions where soil is not naturally acid, to buy acid-soil plants with earth balls around their roots. This is because some of the fungi present in the soil where these plants grow well live in and on the roots of the plants. These fungi are called mycorrhiza and they are thought to perform the same role that root hairs do for other plants: that is, absorb nutrients in solution in the soil water. And apparently, acid-soil plants must have mycorrhiza to survive. Some are undoubtedly present in the soil of the earth ball around the roots. Planting the shrubs in a mixture with plenty of organic matter will help keep these fungi growing and keeping the plants mulched will gradually increase the organic matter in the soil. (See Mulching in Chapter 5.)

Once soil is in good physical condition, with plenty of organic matter worked in, and is also acid in reaction, it should be tested once in six months or a year to make certain it stays acid in reaction. The water you give the plants from the hose, which comes from a well or a city water supply, may be sufficiently alkaline to gradually change the acidity of the soil. There are other possible factors that may do the same thing. So test at regular intervals to make certain of the soil reaction.

The foregoing paragraphs assume that your soil is alkaline or neutral and that you want to change it to have an acid reaction. But some soils are too acid to grow acid-loving plants and these need to be changed to have a less acid reaction. In this case add hydrated lime. Since you should not add any large amount at one time, start with 1 pound per 100 square feet, then test your soil in a month and, depending on the results of the test, add more. It is possible to add 5 pounds of lime per 100 square feet at one time, but never more, and even this will be deleterious to the plants growing in the soil.

Sandy soil always needs less lime than medium-heavy loam. Heavy soil needs most of any, which is the chief reason for replacing rather than attempting to change its reaction.

Is it worthwhile to try to grow acid-soil plants in a region where the soil is neutral or only slightly acid? I think it is. Rhododendrons are only a few of the acid-soil plants I grow. Azaleas number over 40, mountain laurels about a dozen, pieris about half a dozen, blueberries about a dozen, and so on through the roster of these plants.

We have a system for handling these plants that works well for us and might work for you under similar conditions. Since we live on a hilltop and gravel underlies the soil, drainage is no problem. Our topsoil is a clay loam, but not too heavy, testing pH 6.5. For all acid-soil plants but the heathers, we mix the existing soil and acid peat, in equal parts, add a handful of sulphur for each bushel of soil, and plant in this mixture. Heathers bloom best when soil is poor, so we mix acid peat and sand in equal proportions for these, adding the usual sulphur.

Once plants are settled they get special care just twice a year. In spring I make the circuit with a bag of fertilizer especially mixed for acid-soil plants and give each plant a bit, the amount depending on the size of the plant. Precise amounts are given on the bag. In autumn I duplicate the run, spreading a handful or two of cottonseed meal over the soil around each plant. This is a slow-acting organic fertilizer that has an acid effect on the soil.

Here is a close-up of a good loam soil, with its dark color and crumbly texture that allows plant roots to penetrate freely.

PRUNING TOPS

In all this discussion of planting shrubs you may have noticed that there has been no mention of pruning the shrub tops. This is because, given the dual treatment of hormone solution on the roots plus plastic spray on the tops, such pruning is unnecessary.

The reason for pruning the tops of newly set shrubs is supposedly to reduce the size of the tops in proportion to the inevitable root loss because of transplanting, so that the remaining roots are sufficient to nourish the tops left after pruning. Thus there would be a minimum of wilting because of insufficient water getting to the tops.

When tops are sprayed to reduce transpiration (that is, water loss) to a great degree, roots are stimulated to grow rapidly and make up for any loss in moving. If plants are thoroughly watered once a week, pruning tops becomes merely a bad habit left over from the dark ages. The only top pruning necessary is the removal of any broken branches or twigs, which obviously no longer are doing the shrub any good.

SPRING VS. FALL PLANTING

In spring the soil usually is very wet, digging is hard, and the weather uncertain. In fall the soil is mellow, easily worked, the weather likely to be clear and cool. So, plant in fall if you possibly can, unless you are planting shrubs purchased from considerably further south than where you live, shrubs of doubtful hardiness in your area or shrubs that prefer to be moved in spring (see list in Part I of appendix). Fall-planted shrubs almost certainly will bloom the following season; spring-planted shrubs may or may not flower the first season—usually they do not. This may be because they haven't strength to form flower buds or because these form but die.

SUMMER PLANTING

Shrubs that are purchased growing in containers can be planted all summer long and will thrive if planted carefully and watered regularly and thoroughly.

If you are moving and wish to take a shrub with you, you can do so even if it is in full leaf if you follow the directions given for use of hormone solution and plastic spray. Soak with the hormone solution the night before you expect to move the plant. Spray it with the plastic the day before moving. Dig with as large an earth ball as possible and burlap it carefully. Repeat the hormone solution soaking after replanting, and then water regularly and well.

5
SHRUB MAINTENANCE

In writing this chapter, the assumptions have been made that you have (1) selected your shrubs with due regard to your climate; (2) planted them carefully in a place suitable to their hardiness and their ultimate size, at the right depth and with plenty of good soil around their roots; and (3) not crowded your shrubs so they have room to grow naturally and normally.

If you have considered and acted on all these factors, maintenance should be relatively simple, especially when compared with what is necessary for many plants other than shrubs.

WATERING NEWLY PLANTED SHRUBS

Perhaps most important in maintaining newly planted (or transplanted) shrubs is watering them, because they simply cannot survive without water. Hang up a big calendar, one that hits you in the eye so you can't forget it, and mark on it the dates it has rained heavily. Any week in which there is a day-long or night-long soaking rain (which does not follow several weeks of no rain) is a week in which you can skip artificial watering.

Any week during which there is no such rain is a week in which you must water. Mark the dates you soaked the roots of your newly set shrubs on the calendar too, so you don't have to trust to memory as to when you need water next.

Sprinkling water over the soil surface around shrubs does them more harm than good so don't let the word "sprinkle" enter your vocabulary. The only word permitted is "soak."

If, like us, you often set out several hundred shrubs in a single season, weekly watering can become a terrific chore. I know because I'm the person who does it in our garden. In this situation, it is easiest to divide the garden into sections and soak the shrubs in one section each day in the week. This gets all shrubs soaked once a week without devoting too much time to watering each day and without too many backaches.

I find that perforated hoses, arranged around and between shrubs that are close together, do a good soaking job when water is allowed to run through them for half a day. When you water a single shrub setting by itself, take off the hose nozzle, turn the faucet on only a little so the water dribbles into the

Watering a newly planted rhododendron, either naturally in a day-long or night-long soaking rain or with a hose if it has not rained heavily for a week, is essential to the shrub's survival.

depression you left around the base of the shrub. Let the water do this for several hours.

When shrubs are set out in fall, after their leaves have fallen, they need be watered only until late fall rains set in, in the parts of the country where these occur. Winter snows (which melt and therefore moisten soil), where these occur, and rains will take care of watering for the next few months and by spring the shrubs' roots will be sufficiently established so water will be needed only when there is a drought. Planting at this time of year saves so much watering that fall planting is my recommendation for hardiness Zones 5 and 6 wherever there are rains at that season and snow or rain in winter. In zones north of these, spring planting is more satisfactory.

Shrubs set out in spring need weekly watering until late fall rains start. If you must plant shrubs in spring, water regularly and deeply. Even in Zones 5 and 6, spring planting is best for a shrub bought from one or two hardiness zones south because it has the whole growing season in which to become acclimated. Such doubtfully hardy shrubs should be moved only in spring and should be given protection the first winter.

After shrubs have been in your garden a season, they should need little or no watering unless your soil is practically pure sand (in which case water weekly, unless there is a soaking rain, and improve the texture of your soil so it holds water) or there is a drought.

DROUGHT

Shrubs past their first year in your garden can go without water for about ten days to two weeks before they are in trouble, because their roots grow deep enough so they can use water from lower soil layers even when the top few inches are dry. This does not apply to shallow-rooted shrubs like rhododendrons and this is the precise reason why such shrubs should be kept always under a mulch because, among other advantages, the mulch conserves moisture in the soil.

When the soil actually does dry out deeper than the top few inches, the first signs you'll see on your shrubs will be wilting leaves. Hydrangeas need a lot of water; leaves wilt and revive easily. Therefore the hydrangea is a good indicator of soil conditions. When hydrangea leaves droop, water hydrangeas, all rare shrubs and all others that wilt easily, like lespedezas. When viburnum leaves wilt, water all the shrubs in the garden.

MULCHING

Mulching, that is covering over the soil surface with some porous material that admits water, not only helps keep the soil moist under the mulch but also cuts down on weeding (since the mulch smothers all but stubborn weeds) and improves the soil.

When a mulch is applied, the soil bacteria start to work on the lower layer of it, decomposing the leaves, straw, sawdust or whatever you have used for mulch. This decomposed organic material contains nutrients that plants need for good growth. So, as this becomes incorporated in the soil, you will notice a marked difference in the growth of the shrubs that are mulched over those that are not.

Mulch materials are many. For shrubs (though not necessarily for all the other plants you are growing), leaves, straw, hay, sawdust, wood chips, grass clippings and weeds (before

Decorative, fragrant cedar chips make a good mulch to suffocate weeds and repel slugs.

seeds form on them) are all good. There are other mulch materials, good ones too, but why spend money on mulches for shrubs when you ought to be able to get those listed above either free or for the price of hauling them?

Leaves are available from your own trees or from those of your neighbors. Don't let anyone in the neighborhood burn leaves in the fall—haul them home and use them either as a mulch or on the compost pile. If they tend to blow away in high winds, hold them down with evergreen branches or chicken wire laid flat over the mulched area. They're much too valuable to be allowed to go up in smoke.

If you live in the right community, the city will be glad to dump loads of leaves collected from streets and parks right in your yard free of charge. Just let city hall (usually the department of public works) know you want leaves.

Straw sometimes is available for the hauling from new building sites where it is used to cushion bricks and protect newly laid concrete. People who live near the coast often can cut and haul salt marsh hay, which is exceptionally good because the seeds in it are those of aquatic plants, which will not grow in the dryer soil of a garden.

Sawdust is usually available free for hauling from a sawmill. If there is one near you, investigate it as a source. When sawdust is used for a mulch, add 2 pounds of ammonium sulphate (a nitrogenous fertilizer) to each bushel of sawdust, to nourish the soil bacteria that will start to decompose it. If plenty of nitrogen is not available, these bacteria may use what is in the soil in which the shrubs are growing, to the detriment of the shrubs.

Let your local power company, phone company or city forestry department know that you want wood chips and when

Shredded bark is a popular, inexpensive mulch to keep shrub borders neat and weed-free.

they are removing and chipping the overhanging tree branches in your neighborhood, they'll be pleased to use your yard for dumping their loads. Add ½ pound of ammonium sulphate to each bushel of wood chips as a nitrogen supplement.

Grass clippings are free as long as you have a lawn to cut. Catch them in a catcher attached to the mower or use a lawn sweeper after cutting the grass and dump the clippings over the soil around the shrubs.

I have not mentioned using manure for a mulch (though it is a good one despite the weed seeds in it) because most people cannot get it at all or must pay a high price for it. Should it be available near you at a reasonable price, use it, though not on shrubs that like acid soil. Perhaps even better than manure, because it has been sterilized so it contains no live weed seeds, is spent mushroom soil. If you live near a mushroom growing section, you often can have this soil free to haul home when they are changing soil in the mushroom houses, which they do once a year.

I also have not mentioned peat moss, so often recommended as a mulch. This is because I do not consider peat moss a satisfactory mulch, whether it comes from a bale or is granulated. While it is excellent when added to soil to improve texture and water-holding capacity, this ability to hold a great deal of water makes it a poor topping over soil. Rain or artificial water first must penetrate the peat before it reaches the soil and benefits the shrub roots. It cannot do this until the peat is saturated, which takes a very heavy rain or hours of watering.

Always soak the soil thoroughly before applying any type of mulch. It will take a bit of time to apply, but the mulch will save you sufficient time in the future to more than make up for that spent in application.

FERTILIZING

When you add ammonium sulphate to a mulch as you apply it, or scatter it over a mulch after you have applied it (which should be done once a year, for the reason explained previously) you are fertilizing the shrubs in the area as well as nourishing soil bacteria, because ammonium sulphate contains nitrogen, one of the chemical elements needed for plant growth.

There are a number of these; nitrogen, phosphorus and potash being the most important ones. Nobody knows exactly how one element reacts with the others for plant growth, but the three named, plus others in smaller quantities, are all necessary for good growth of plants.

Any complete commercial fertilizer contains the three elements already named. You will find the percentages of these in a given fertilizer on the package as a series of numbers as, for instance, 5-10-5. These figures mean 5 percent nitrogen, 10 percent phosphoric acid and 5 percent potash. The three figures always are given in the same order—nitrogen first, phosphate next and potash last. The rest of the fertilizer package contains material that makes it possible to spread these chemicals evenly and easily.

Thus, when you use a complete fertilizer on your shrubs, you are adding the three elements they most need to the soil around them.

The trace elements, needed only in small quantities by plants, are present in most soils in sufficient amounts for shrubs. Some of them are contained in chemical fertilizers as impurities. Therefore, in most cases, you need not worry about them.

If your soil is even reasonably good, most shrubs will grow in it, even thrive in it, without really needing fertilizer (just as long as they are not mulched). Of course there are some shrubs that do best in poor, sandy soil (see Part I of appendix) and these should never be given fertilizer.

Common grass clippings can be used as a weed-suffocating mulch around the base of shrubs and trees.

Since all shrubs have an ultimate height and spread beyond which they will not grow, even if fertilized, about all that fertilizer does is make them reach these limits sooner than they would without it. If you are in a rush for shrubs as large as they ever will grow, fertilize. If not, use the fertilizer for plants that need it a great deal more than do shrubs.

There are, however, four situations in which shrubs do need fertilizer.

1. A shrub has not leafed out, though it has been planted for several months. It is obviously alive because a twig bends without breaking and when you scratch at the bark you see green tissue underneath. In this case use a liquid fertilizer, mixing it with water according to directions on the package given under the heading "foliar feeding." Even if the shrub has no leaves, it can absorb nutrients through its bark. The solution for foliar feeding is weaker than that for fertilizing through the roots.

If the shrub is small enough, mix up a pailful of the solution and simply dump it right over the shrub. This is quick and easy and works well. If the shrub is large, so large you cannot dump several pails of solution over various sections of it, then spray the liquid fertilizer on the shrub.

Fertilizing through bark or leaves is an effective way to give a plant a boost since the plant can use the nutrients in the solution very quickly, sometimes in a matter of hours from the time they are applied. Foliar feeding is more expensive than the ordinary way of fertilizing a plant through the roots and the effects are nowhere near as long-lasting. Therefore, fertilizing through bark or leaves is no substitute for fertilizing through the roots.

It is possible to fertilize through bark or leaves daily if you wish to do so, with no harm to the plant. Even weekly application will help the plant while not exhausting the gardener.

2. A shrub shows obvious signs of lacking some chemical so it is time to try to determine the chemical needed (this is easier

Licorice root, a decorative mulch, helps to maintain soil moisture and suffocate weeds.

said than done) and supply it. Because of studies made on other types of plants, it is known that signs of lack of iron, manganese, calcium, and boron appear first on young leaves. Lack of sufficient nitrogen, phosphorus, potassium, and magnesium usually shows first on the lower leaves.

However, results of attacks by red spider mites, which are too tiny to be seen with the naked eye, often resemble nutrient deficiencies, so it is wise not to jump to conclusions too fast. To find out if red spider mites are causing the difficulty, hold a sheet of shiny white paper under a branch in the area that seems affected. With the other hand, hit the branch sharply, meanwhile watching the paper. If minute dark dots appear on the paper and, when carefully watched, they move, these are the mites. Spray with a miticide to control them.

How can you tell which chemical is lacking in a shrub's nutrition? Very little work has been done on this subject except with azaleas and there is no reason to believe that all shrubs would similarly show their lacks. Best thing to do, when a shrub's growth is not as vigorous as it was or when yellowing or mottling of leaves indicate possible lack of nutrients, is to use a complete fertilizer of a 10-6-4 formula at the rate of 1 pound to 100 square feet of area. If you are using a high-grade fertilizer, the chances are good that the manufacturer has added sufficient trace elements so the shrub will get these along with nitrogen, phosphorus, and potash.

Apply this fertilizer to dry soil only, scattering it as evenly as possible around under the shrub and as far out from the center as the spread of the branches. Soak the soil with water immediately after fertilizing.

Shrubs should not, under ordinary circumstances, be fertilized after July 1, because soft, new growth thus encouraged may be killed by winter cold. The best time to fertilize is in very early spring, but if a shrub later shows signs of deficiency of some chemical, try using a liquid fertilizer that contains the trace elements.

If the shrub does not lose the signs of malnutrition that caused you to use the complete fertilizer or the liquid fertilizer, try fritted trace elements sold as FTE, or a special fertilizer that contains all trace elements. This might be applied in late fall or in early spring.

Acid-Soil Plants

Acid-soil plants, the class to which rhododendrons and azaleas belong, sometimes show by the yellowing of their leaf blades, while veins remain green, that iron is lacking in their diet. The iron may be present in the soil, but in soils insufficiently acidic it often is in a chemical form that is insoluble and therefore the plant cannot use it. As you know, plant root hairs take up chemicals dissolved in the soil water.

Lime must be spread over an acid soil to make it suitable for planting a wide variety of shrubs.

Iron may be supplied to the plant quickly by applying a packaged iron amendment to the soil.

Remember that signs of iron deficiency also call for acidifying the soil further for, if it were sufficiently acid for the acid-soil plants, the iron in it would be in soluble form that the plants could use. So, at the same time as you apply an iron amendment to relieve the deficiency, add a soil acidifier like sulphur to make the soil more acid.

Occasionally it may be necessary to apply lime to soil in which azaleas or other acid-soil plants are growing. This happens only when the soil becomes too acid, below pH 4.5. This subject is more fully discussed in Chapter 4.

3. A shrub has been in your garden for several years and has not yet flowered; so it is time to try to help it to bloom. An application in spring and again in fall of rock phosphate, which contains phosphorus, the chemical most closely associated with flowering of plants, often helps the plant to produce blooms.

4. You may wish certain small shrubs or rare shrubs to grow a bit better. If so, use a 10-6-4 fertilizer at the rate of ½ pound per shrub in early spring and again before warm weather starts. Scatter it around under the shrub, over the soil. If the shrub is mulched, remove the mulch before you apply the fertilizer, replacing the mulch afterwards.

Special Fertilizers

There are numerous special formula fertilizers available, some of them highly touted for various types of plants, including shrubs and especially roses. Shrubs, however, will react just as well to a standard 10-6-4 fertilizer as to any of the special ones, with the exception of acid-soil shrubs. For these you can either mix a fertilizer that will have an acid reaction or you can buy one ready-mixed. Unless you expect to use large quantities, it is simpler and cheaper to buy it ready-mixed.

PRUNING

There ought to be a law against allowing anyone to touch pruning shears unless familiar with the natural form of the plant to be pruned. More crimes are committed against plants in the name of pruning than in any other way.

For pruning is not to be confused with hacking. Pruning is done for a purpose and, lacking the purpose, there should be no pruning. Furthermore, regardless of the purpose, the form of the shrub should be carefully retained. The butch cut seen on too many shrubs is a confession of ignorance. The person who cuts the top of a shrub off straight across obviously knows nothing about how a shrub renews itself, cares less, and in addition, has very poor taste.

Ignorance, too, is the reason for constant pruning of a plant. If it is necessary to prune a shrub that is not part of a hedge two or three times a season, then that shrub is in the wrong place. Move it to another place where it can grow as high and as wide as it should and replace it with a shrub that naturally grows in a shape that will fit the first place. The descriptions of the shrubs in Chapter 12 tell you their ultimate heights or widths.

The rhododendron is an example of an acid-loving plant that prefers a lime-free soil.

The beautiful arching branches of this forsythia are the result of little or no pruning.

Routine Pruning

Routine pruning, which should be done every two or three years, consists of removing: (1) dead parts of the shrub; (2) pieces that stick out too far and thus spoil the natural shape of the shrub; (3) parts that are injured or diseased or attacked by scale insects so that their removal will aid shrub health; (4) branches that are rubbing against one another so that, in time, one will rub the bark off the other, creating a place where disease may enter the plant; (5) suckers from the base of a grafted or budded plant which are not, of course, parts of the variety you wish to grow. In any of these purposes for pruning, the part to be pruned is better off the shrub than on.

Routine pruning also includes rejuvenation. Most shrubs that send up numerous stems from the ground will profit by having a few of the older, thicker ones cut off at ground level each year, thus allowing more room for the younger stems to develop. Shrubs that will profit from such pruning annually include weigelas, mock oranges, deutzias and spireas.

How to Do Routine Pruning

First of all the tools you use for pruning, shears and saws of various types and sizes, should be kept clean and sharp. If a badly diseased part of a shrub must be removed, the tool used should be disinfected after use by dipping it in a household disinfectant, then wiping it dry.

The first use of these tools should be to remove dead wood. This should be cut back to live growth. Scrape away a tiny bit of outer bark, if necessary, to find the green layer just underneath that shows that part of the shrub is alive. Make the cut just above the highest bud in the live wood.

Next, scrutinize the shrub with a view to its form and remove, only as far back as necessary, any branches that spoil it. Then remove any injured branches, cutting each one back far enough to remove the injury (or diseased areas, or scale-infested areas). In both of these cases make the cut just above the topmost bud that is pointing in the direction you wish a new branch or branchlet to grow. A bud that is heading towards the center of a bushy shrub is obviously not the one above which to prune. An outward pointing bud, even if lower on the branch, is preferable. The same sort of bud choice must be made when one of two rubbing branches is removed from a shrub.

Always keep in mind when pruning that when live wood is removed from a plant, some of the growth energy and substance is removed at the same time. If only a small branch is removed, this makes little difference, but if pruning is drastic, it will affect the plant's root system and some of the roots will die. The plant soon adjusts to the new state of affairs, and new growth will start from the top bud that is left on the pruned branch, or, if the branch has been removed entirely, then new growth will start in the buds closest to the cut. The more wood that is pruned off a plant, the greater the tendency of the plant to make new growth where the plant was pruned. Growth always will be on the side where the plant has been pruned—never on the opposite side.

Any shoots growing from the base of a plant known to have been budded or grafted, or any shoots growing from the base of a plant that have leaves on them differing from those of the rest of the plant should be removed as soon as you notice them. Trace the shoots back to the point of origin, which may be below the soil line, and cut the shoots off the plant at that point.

Other Types of Pruning

Pruning When Planting or Transplanting: Though broken roots or branches always should be removed at planting time, for obvious reasons, it is common practice to reduce the tops of newly set deciduous shrubs in about the same proportion as you guess their roots have been reduced in the transplanting process. I do not agree with this practice. If I buy and pay for a 3- to 4-foot shrub, why should I reduce it to a 2- to 3-foot shrub to make up for probable root loss? I might, then, just as well have saved money by buying the smaller size shrub to begin with.

If you will read, in Chapter 4, the thoughts about using root growth–inducing, wilt-decreasing hormone powder in solution on shrub roots and plastic coating on shrub tops, you will understand why I consider pruning tops unnecessary. If plenty of water is given to a shrub regularly after it is transplanted and it has been treated as outlined above, the existing roots can support the existing tops with no difficulty.

On rare occasions, if an enormous, ancient shrub is to be moved from one place to another, it is advisable to prune the

Heavily pruning this lilac will force new bushy growth and improve flowering.

tops, but then they should be cut to within 6 inches of the ground. If the remaining root system is well cared for, new tops will grow in due course of time.

Pruning for Renewal: This same type of drastic pruning, to within a few inches of the ground, is necessary when an old shrub or hedge of shrubs looks so unsightly that no ordinary pruning will do any good. Old or untidy shrubs like lilacs, or hedges of California privet that have winterkilled in a cold climate, all respond to such renewal pruning.

Ordinarily pruning for renewal is not so drastic. When a shrub becomes "leggy" and bears leaves only at the tops of long branches, first make sure it is getting sufficient light. If it is, then it may be rejuvenated by removing one or two of the older branches at ground level. One third of the branches should be removed each year for three years. Thus the plant's growth will not be upset by drastic pruning, but new shoots will have a chance to grow. I have found a keyhole saw ideal for the removal of these old branches because it is small enough to use between old and new branches without scraping bark off the new shoots when removing the old growth.

Pruning for Color: The newest wood is always the brightest on such red- and yellow-branched shrubs as certain dogwoods. If you depend on these shrubs for winter color in your garden, be sure to prune a little each year to keep the new wood growing. Some gardeners cut these shrubs to the ground every third year so that bright, new shoots will grow to make the winter garden gay.

Pruning to Increase Density: People plant hedges for privacy or to form divisions between various areas in the garden. Therefore, a good hedge is a dense one. The theory behind the frequent pruning of hedges to make them dense is that more than one shoot will grow in the place from which one shoot is pruned, therefore the more frequent the pruning, the more shoots that will grow and the denser the hedge.

Always prune any type of hedge so that it is broader at the base and tapers towards the top. This way air and light can reach the lower branches. If you prune the opposite way, wide at the top and narrow at the bottom, the lower branches soon die and the hedge no longer serves its purpose. As previously explained, a poorly shaped, old hedge of deciduous shrubs can be cut to the ground to rejuvenate it. Do this in late winter or early spring, fertilize the plants then, and watch the new hedge grow.

Pruning to Increase Bloom: Some shrubs tend to form flower buds after their normal blooming time is past if they are pruned directly after their flowers fade. Stems that flowered should be cut back for this type of pruning, and strong new shoots should be shortened. Shrubs that profit from this pruning include Anthony Waterer spirea, *Spiraea japonica* and its varieties, weigelas and buddleias.

Pruning to Train: When gardeners wish to grow lilacs or roses-of-sharon or some other shrub in "standard" or "tree" form (that is, with only one trunk) special pruning is required. One straight branch is selected to be the trunk. This is tied to a stake to keep it growing straight. All side branches are cut from it and all remaining branches are removed from the shrub and not allowed to grow. When the trunk is sufficiently high to suit the trainer, the buds near the top of it are allowed to grow and these will form branches that may be permitted to grow naturally with little or no pruning or may be clipped to any desired shape.

Weigela florida, *unpruned, creates a fountain-like effect.*

When a shrub of formal shape is desired, shrubs that lend themselves to formal pruning, like boxwoods, barberries, or privets, should be chosen. These may be trained to globe shape or other shapes by careful pruning, even though no trunk is desired.

Pruning Dead Flowers: Pruning also includes removal of dead flowers before the seeds form, so that food manufactured by the plant is not used in seed production when the seed will not be used. There are conflicting ideas as to whether or not such flower removal does any real good other than to make the shrub look neater. I have proved to my own satisfaction, by careful, controlled tests on my own plants, that removal of dead flowers results in more bloom the following year. So I feel that it pays to prune off faded flowers on pieris, lilac, rhododendron, azalea, kalmia, magnolia and hibiscus.

When to Prune

Routine pruning actually can be done at any time of year. But for the sake of appearances, try not to prune shrubs in winter, for the white scars left by pruning show and make the shrub look mangy. Any branches that have to be cut back stick out like sore thumbs until the leaves appear to hide the wounds. If you can stand such unsightliness, go right ahead and prune.

Any pruning other than that for sanitation should, if possible, be done at times most propitious for the particular plants being pruned.

Deciduous Shrubs

In general all of those that flower on the wood of the previous year's growth should be pruned when they finish flowering, for many start forming next year's flower buds a month or two after blooming. When you prune an early spring–flowering shrub like forsythia in late fall or in spring before it flowers, you prune off the flower buds.

Exceptions to pruning after flowering are the shrubs that are going to bear decorative fruits in fall. These may be pruned lightly in late fall, lightly in very early spring, or, if necessary, a little bit at both of these times of year.

Shrubs that flower on wood of the current season's growth all may be pruned in very early spring. These shrubs include: *Abelia grandiflora, Berberis, Callicarpa, Clethra, Hibiscus syriacus, Hydrangea arborescens* and *H. paniculata* and varieties of both of these, *Hypericum, Kerria, Ligustrum, Lonicera* (but not *L. fragrantissima*), *Philadelphus, Rhus, Rosa, Spiraea, Staphylea, Stephanandra* and *Tamarix* (but not *T. parviflora*).

The "die-back" shrubs, those that have roots that are winter-hardy, but tops that are not, should be pruned as early in spring as possible. If the winter has been mild, they may

Azalea mollis hybrids are beautiful planted along a house foundation.

need comparatively little dead wood removed, but if it has been severe, they will have died back and should be cut to the ground. These shrubs include: *Abelia grandiflora, Buddleia* (except *B. alternifolia*, which freezes back only occasionally), *Callicarpa, Caryopteris, Ceanothus, Tamarix* (sometimes freezes back) and *Vitex.*

A few deciduous shrubs that are not ordinarily die-back shrubs will have many more flowers if severely pruned right after flowering. The following may have about half of their branches cut back to two or three buds from the ground, cutting just above a bud: *Buddleia alternifolia, Deutzia, Forsythia, Hydrangea arborescens* and *H. paniculata, Philadelphus,* early-blooming spireas, *Spiraea bumalda* 'Anthony Waterer' and *S. bumalda* 'Froebelii', *Tamarix* (but not *T. parviflora*) and *Weigela.*

Broad-Leaved Evergreen Shrubs

These need very little pruning. Cut back the occasional dead branch and the occasional branch that spoils the shape; and prune off dead flowers. Removal of branches may be done at any time, but is best attempted in early spring so that new growth will hide pruning scars.

Shrubs that Require Little or No Pruning

After reading about all the shrubs that should be pruned, either every spring or occasionally, it comes as a relief to know that some shrubs should be pruned as seldom as possible, except to remove dead wood. These include *Amelanchier, Aronia, Azalea, Calycanthus, Cercis, Chionanthus, Cotoneaster, Cytisus* (in cold climates), *Halesia, Kalmia, Laburnum, Magnolia, Mahonia, Pieris, Prunus glandulosa, Rhododendron, Ribes* and spring-flowering *Viburnums.* If you select from these shrubs, pruning in your garden will be kept to a minimum.

WINTER PROTECTION

The only protection most deciduous shrubs need, if they have been carefully chosen for hardiness, is protection from animals that eat off twigs, buds, and bark. Against rabbits, ring shrubs with either chicken wire or hardware cloth high enough so that deep snow does not allow rabbits to eat over the tops of the wires, or spray with rabbit repellents. You will find rabbit repellents available in your garden supply store; chicken wire and hardware cloth at the hardware store.

There are several deer repellents on the market but, since we have no trouble from deer, I do not personally know how effective they may be.

Field mice may be kept from gnawing shrubs by sinking guard wires 2 inches into the soil or by setting out one of the various poison baits available.

Shrubs planted in very late fall sometimes heave out of the soil during the freezing and thawing in late winter. A mulch of any convenient material will prevent this.

Winter burn, or browning of leaves, is quite common on broad-leaved evergreens when the plants are placed so that they are exposed to the wind or where late winter sun touches them. This may be prevented by spraying the leaves of the

A forsythia bush looks exquisite when its bare branches catch and hold a bit of snow.

plants in late fall, before freezing temperatures arrive, with one of the anti-dessicant sprays.

These substances reduce water loss from the leaves, thus reducing the ratio between the amount of water the plant loses through leaves (or, in the case of deciduous shrubs, through branches) and the amount the roots are able to take up from the soil. This will be little or none when the soil is frozen. Both wind and sun increase the amount of water lost, but, as long as the soil is frozen, there can be no increase in water intake.

Rhododendrons survive winter better when heavily mulched, preferably with oak leaves. Azaleas are less likely to mature their wood properly when mulched in late autumn; removal of the mulch for several weeks at that time of year will help them do so.

All woody plants survive winter best when the cold weather approaches gradually. When there is a long, warm autumn and suddenly the weather changes abruptly, the thermometer dropping 20 or 25 degrees in a single night, there is certain to be plant injury, regardless of hardiness. Sometimes woody stems split open. Some plants that ordinarily survive winter with ease are killed to the ground, but usually grow again from the roots in spring. All sorts of unusual injury may occur when the weather changes suddenly and there is little the gardener can do to prevent it.

There also is little you can do to counteract a sudden drop in temperature in spring when buds already are unfolding and bloom may be lost because they are nipped by a cold snap.

But these two freaks of nature are part of the hazards of gardening and happen only rarely.

A landscape of both evergreen and deciduous shrubs looks spectacular with a light dusting of snow.

6
REJUVENATING OVERGROWN SHRUBS

Quite often, the problem we face is not so much selecting new shrubs to plant around our property, but figuring out what to do with the existing plantings we've inherited from the previous owner.

Sometimes it is best to just take a chain saw and remove the unsightly mass of twigs, trunks and branches. In other cases shrubs can be reshaped and rejuvenated relatively easily. Presented here are several easy ways to put new life into old, forlorn-looking shrubs and small trees.

Figure 1 shows a typical suburban ranch house where foundation shrubs have been neglected and allowed to grow too large. Beside the door is a mock orange (A) that has grown a thicket of twigs and branches so dense that air circulation is restricted; the bush has no vigor and flowering is sparse. The first step in this case would be to thin out the tangle of multiple stems, especially any that are dead, reducing the number of main branches by at least half. The shrub also needs shearing along the top to reduce some extra-long branches and trim-

ming along the sides to stop branches from encroaching into the doorway. Lilacs and viburnums that become overgrown like this can be rejuvenated in the same manner.

Around the corner from the door is an overgrown forsythia (B). The arching canes have extended so far up and out that they obscure the window. In this case, thinning out the canes would not achieve much. The entire plant must be cut back to within a foot of the soil and the stumps allowed to sprout new growth. Each year thereafter the plant will need to be pruned to keep it low and cascading, and to prevent it from obscuring the window. To maintain heavy flowering, feed a forsythia immediately after flowering in spring.

Next, in a space between two windows, an evergreen yew (C) has become overgrown and untidy. It will require drastic pruning to create a spire shape. Though yews are not classified as flowering shrubs, they are almost always used in foundation plantings to complement shrubs that do flower.

An azalea (D), originally planted below a window, has

Figure 1

grown upwards. It is obscuring the view and blocks light from coming into the house. Azaleas are quite attractive pruned or sheared into "mounds" or "cushions." It may be necessary to shear every year, soon after the flowers have faded, to maintain the low profile.

A pair of Japanese maples (Acer palmatum) *are planted as sentinels on either side of a front door.*

At the corner of the house a needle evergreen (E)—a juniper—has become untidy from lack of pruning. A neat, pyramid shape brings it into scale with the house.

Around the corner, a rampant rhododendron (F) has grown too tall. Long branches should be cut back, but the plant might be allowed to maintain an informal appearance as a good contrast to the more formal shapes of the evergreens and the azalea.

Figure 2 illustrates the results of pruning.

After any heavy pruning of shrubs to force new growth, rake a general purpose fertilizer into the upper soil surface at the rate recommended on the label. Then apply a layer of mulch to restrict weed growth. It is generally advisable to avoid pruning during drought.

A beautiful specimen of lace-leaf Japanese maple (Acer palmatum 'Dissectum Atropurpureum') *helps to soften the hard architectural lines of the house.*

Figure 2

REJUVENATING AN OVER-MATURE SHRUB

In figure 3, a shrub has been left to its own devices and has grown too large and dense. It is out of proportion to other plants nearby and does not flower well because its top growth is more than the root system can cope with, and the many dead twigs create poor air circulation inside the bush. There are two possible remedies. The first one is shown in figure 4. The tangle of branches can be pruned to leave only a few strong structural stems and a canopy of flowering branches on top. Figure 5 shows the other remedy. The tangle of branches can be thinned, leaving a cluster of healthy main stems, which are then cut back to about 12–36 inches above the soil. With fertilizer, soil conditioner and regular watering, the pruned stems will be forced to produce a mass of side branches that will create a compact, bushy plant controlled by pruning.

Figure 3

Figure 4

Figure 5

REJUVENATING A HEDGE

In figure 6, a hedge has grown so tall that it is restricting views from the house and is vulnerable to damage from ice and snow. The remedy, shown in figure 7, is to shear the hedge back to below the height of the gate, forcing side shoots and bushier growth. Feeding, watering and soil conditioner will ensure rapid branching and a dense, luxurious "knit." Frequent shearing will keep the hedge low and compact, as shown in figure 7.

Figure 6

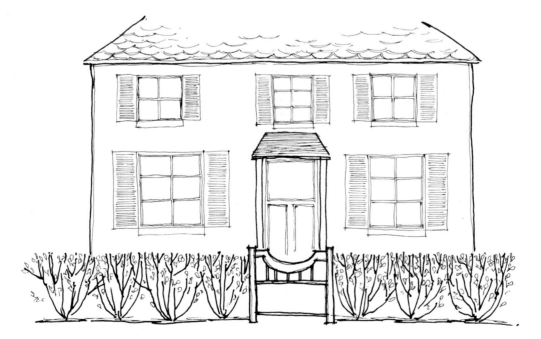

Figure 7

Illustration by Anne L. Meskey

REPAIRING A SPLIT TRUNK

Accumulations of ice and snow and wind storms can damage branches and even split a trunk, especially of shrubs that have brittle branches, such as the smoke bush (*Cotinus* species). When a bush stands alone in the middle of a lawn, as shown in figure 8, it is especially disheartening to see a once symmetrically shaped plant suddenly look as though it has been torn asunder.

However, before you take out the chain saw to put the poor thing out of its misery, there are two ways you might be able to save it. The first, shown in figure 9, is to pull the split parts together with rope and create a clamp with a steel pin and bolts to hold them together. Drill a hole through the split trunk and insert the pin. Most tree experts also recommend coating the sides of the tree with wound dressing to resist decay.

If the split is severe, there may be no choice but to cut the smallest part of the split away and discard it. Pull the remaining part of the plant into an upright position and keep it erect using strong wire or rope, as shown in figure 10. Where the wire or rope encircles the trunk make a cushion with a piece of plastic, rubber garden hose or cloth. Use a peg to secure the line. Smear tree wound dressing around the split.

Illustration by Anne L. Meskey

Figure 8

Figure 9

Figure 10

SAVING A FALLING DOWN TREE

After heavy rains and high winds, when the ground is soggy and unable to maintain good anchorage for roots, tall, top-heavy shrubs and trees may lean over and be in danger of falling, as shown in figure 11. If the plant cannot be pulled back into an upright position easily, it may be possible to build a wooden brace to stop the trunk from leaning further. Then the branches can be pollarded. Pollarding, shown in figure 12, is a pruning technique whereby branches are cut back to within about 12 inches of the top of the trunk, eliminating the problem of a top-heavy foliage canopy, and forcing slender new branches from the stubs. Weeping trees such as weeping cherries can be particularly attractive when pollarded. Whenever the new branches become too long and heavy they can be cut back to the stumps in the autumn of each year to force new growth the following spring.

Figure 11

Figure 12

7
WHEN SHRUBS CHANGE

When a gardener buys a shrub, grows it, and sees its leaves and flowers add their beauty to the garden, he expects both foliage and bloom to continue in the same manner year after year. When a change occurs in either leaf or flower, it startles and alarms him. This results in letters like these to the local garden editor:

1. "One part of my lilac is blooming beautifully, but the rest of the bush isn't blooming at all and the leaves look different. They look like those on my neighbor's hedge."

Or 2. "Something is wrong with my lilac. Some of the leaves at the tips of the lower branches are all sort of scalloped at the edges and a different shape from the rest."

Or 3. "My snowball bush has different flowers from those it used to have. They used to be like little snowballs and now they are wider and flatter."

Or 4. "My daughter planted a beautiful red-flowered Blaze climbing rose; this year there is a white bridal wreath where the rose was."

Or 5. "Would you please tell me how it is possible for my rosebush to have buds that look all the same, but when the flowers open they may be pink or rose color or even white or yellow?"

Or 6. "My son gave my mother and me each a blue hydrangea for Mother's Day last year. We planted them outdoors later in the season. This year both are flowering, but the flowers on mine are pink while those on hers are blue. How can this be?"

Each one of these six gardeners is troubled because of a change in either the leaves or the flowers of a shrub. And there are four entirely different reasons for the changes described in these six letters.

The first reason (letters 1, 3, and 4) is reversion.

The second reason (letter 2) is injury by a weed-killing chemical.

The third reason (letter 5) is "sporting" by the plant.

The fourth reason (letter 6) is response to soil reaction.

REVERSION

Let's go back to the first reason and see just how a plant "reverts." My dictionary gives the following as the biological definition of the word revert: "to return to or toward or show

some of the characteristics of an ancestral, primitive or earlier form." This is a good definition, because that's what plants sometimes do.

They may return to the original form of the plant if they are selections from or hybrids of that plant. Suppose you have a small-flowered polyantha rose that bears, ordinarily, orange flowers. One day you find, to your surprise, that one flower or flower cluster is red, rather than orange. The orange-flowered rose was bred from the red, so when it bears a few red flowers it may be said to be reverting.

Sometimes a double-flowered shrub will have one branch that bears single flowers. This happens occasionally with double-flowered mock oranges. This, too, is reversion.

There is another more common occurrence with shrubs, also called reversion, but that is really quite different and should be called by a different name. This pseudo-reversion happens when a shrub is made up of parts of two different plants.

Hydrangea macrophylla *will change color according to the soil pH. Blue coloring occurs in acid soil, pink coloring in alkaline soil.*

Sometimes these are of the same plant group, as roses or viburnums. Sometimes these are of different plant groups, as lilac on privet. In either case a strong-growing genus or variety is deliberately chosen to be the understock or rootstock of the new plant. Onto this rootstock is budded or grafted the more desirable (often a cultivar) top. Thus the plant you buy is composed of parts of two different plants.

Let us suppose that this plant is a lilac, as in letter number 1. When lilacs are not grown on their own roots, as they really always should be, they usually are budded onto a rootstock of privet. Privet is very strong growing and sometimes outgrows the lilac top. If the owner of a lilac does not realize what is happening and keep the privet shoots cut off below the ground surface, next thing he knows he'll have a nice, cheap privet bush instead of a nice, expensive lilac.

Now, let's consider letter number 3. The plant in this case is a snowball, known more accurately as a viburnum. In this case a fine-flowering variety, such as *Viburnum carlesii*, was budded onto a strong, fast-growing variety, such as *Viburnum lantana*. The *lantana* has outgrown the *carlesii* or perhaps the *carlesii* has been unknowingly pruned off or has been injured, leaving only the lantana to grow.

Many viburnums, such as Chinese snowball bush (Viburnum macrocephalum) *have green flowers that change to pure white.*

Letter number 4 concerns a rose—a climbing rose, so a vine rather than a shrub. (However, the same thing happens with shrub roses.) The reason I have used this particular letter is that it tells an impossible story: presumes that a climbing rose has changed into a spirea (bridal wreath is the common name of several species of spirea).

What actually has happened in this case is that a fast-growing, strong-rooted species, *Rosa multiflora*, has been used

Roses are extremely susceptible to color variation, depending on climate, soil fertility, and other factors of their environment.

for a rootstock. A bud of the red-flowered, named variety rose, Blaze, has been inserted into a multiflora cane and thus we have the two-parted rose that was purchased. It is obvious that somehow the Blaze top was lost. Perhaps it was killed by a too-cold winter. Or it was pruned off or injured. Or it just died. At any rate, the white non–bridal wreath blooms are those of the multiflora rose understock.

These last three cases are all commonly called reversion and, of course, in a sense they are reversion, but different types than that of the dictionary definition (the actual growth of a plant in the manner of one or another of its ancestors).

It isn't really necessary for you to endure this type of reversion. By insisting on being supplied with "own root" plants when you are buying them, you avoid a two-part plant.

CHEMICAL INJURY

The second reason for a change in the form of a plant, or rather the form of its leaves, is chemical injury. When gardeners spray lawns with potent weed killers or run over them with a fertilizer spreader filled with a dry formulation of the same weed-killing chemical, leaf injury and change in leaf form may result.

The gardener need not have been careless in applying the chemical. He may have been very careful. In fact, the gardener next door may be the one who, all unknowingly, caused the change. For the minute amount of chemical that may be carried by the wind to nearby shrubs is enough to make leaves look different if it drifts on them. This is the cause of the trouble described in letter 2.

SPORTING

The change in the flower color of a plant, as described in letter number 5, is due to a bud mutation commonly called a "sport." The change itself is known as "sporting."

The way in which a plant sports was a matter of conjecture for generations. Recent developments have made it possible to know accurately how sporting occurs. Sporting "is closely tied to the development of the *growing point* of the *shoot*" and is "brought about principally by a genetic change (mutation, sporting) in one or more genes or chromosomal changes occurring originally in the nucleus of a single cell at the very center of a growing point of a bud or shoot."

To explain the paragraph above, the nucleus is the central, denser part of a cell (and all living things are made up of cells). The nucleus is composed of chromosomes, which are thread-like objects that bear the genes. The genes determine the heredity of a plant or animal. Thus, when there are changes in the genes or chromosomes these are inherited by the new

Here is an example of sporting on an azalea. The solid orange group of blossoms is called a branch sport.

plant part. For when there is new growth (caused by cell division) the chromosomes contract by coiling, first gather together near the center of the cell, then split lengthwise, and then half of each moves to the opposite ends of the cell. After that a new cell wall forms between the two groups of chromosomes and the single cell has become two cells. Thus each new cell inherits the changes in the genes or chromosomes that were in the single cell from which the new ones formed.

The paragraph above is, of course, an oversimplification of a complicated process. However, it is all the explanation that I feel is needed to explain to a gardener what happens when a plant sports. Anyone who wishes to know more can obtain a copy of the article cited.

Now you can see how it happens that a rose bud may open into a bloom of a color different from those on the rest of the plant. Or, a rose shoot may suddenly grow much, much taller than those on the rest of the plant, so that it is a climbing shoot.

Some plants seem to be especially prone to sport. Chrysanthemums often have some shoots that bear flowers of a different color than those on the rest of the plant. Some roses, like the old variety Ophelia, are quite likely to have white, pale pink, and deep rose flowers on a plant all at the same time.

Plant breeders use these sports to produce new varieties. By taking off the top of the climbing shoot of a rose, and rooting it, a climbing type of the parent rose variety may be produced. Variegated-leaved varieties of shrubs and vines often are produced by propagating shoots that have sported with variegated rather than plain green leaves. New rose varieties also may be grown from sports.

So if you see any unusual variation on a shrub, don't be too upset by it. Perhaps it means that you, too, will have a chance to produce a new variety.

Soil reaction can change, so a Hydrangea macrophylla *may produce pink flowers for a few years, then change to blue flowers, then go back to pink, and so forth.*

SOIL REACTION

Letter number 6 is just one example of thousands of letters written each year telling about an unaccountable (to the average gardener) change in flower color of a hydrangea.

This change is due to the chemical reaction of the soil. When the soil in which a hydrangea is growing is acid in reaction, the flowers on that plant will be blue. When the soil reaction is alkaline, pink flowers are produced.

Not only that, but since soil reaction changes, there may come a year when a hydrangea will produce blue flowers on one side of the plant, pink on the other. Or the plant may have blue blooms for a few years, then pink for two or three, then shift to blue again.

Since soil and its reactions are covered in Chapter 4, How to Plant Shrubs, no further details will be given here. If your hydrangea blooms blue and you want it to bloom pink, add a handful of lime to the soil around it. If it blooms pink and you want blue flowers, give the plant a handful of garden sulphur in the fall. Simply sprinkle either chemical on top of the soil around the plant, mix it into the top inch or two and water thoroughly.

White hydrangeas do not change flower color. You cannot make them have pink or blue flowers.

MINOR VARIATIONS

Minor variations in color of flower often occur because of variations in soil. Your neighbor's weigela may be a shade pinker than yours, even though one was grown from a cutting taken from the other. These little variations are quite common and no cause for excitement.

There also are minor variations in foliage color, usually due to exposure to sun. Thus, if you enjoy arranging foliage indoors, and you admire the corkbark euonymus (*Euonymus alata*), and if you have room for two plants, be sure to set one in full sun and the other in semi-shade. The fall color of the leaves of the one in sun will be brighter and redder; while the leaf color of the one in shade will be deeper and more purplish. The two shadings form an interesting contrast.

If you haven't room in your garden for two such large shrubs as *E. alata*, grow instead the dwarf form, *E. alata* 'Compacta.' It has the same corky bark, so pleasing for winter interest, the same handsome fall foliage coloration, but will take up far less room in your garden.

Burning bush (Euonymus alata) *undergoes a beautiful autumn leaf change, turning from emerald green to fiery red.*

8
HARDINESS

If we are going to talk about hardiness, the first thing to do is to decide what hardiness is. It is the ability of the plant to thrive in the climate in which it is growing. All plants have a set of growing conditions that they prefer. When one or several of these are changed, the plant cannot be expected to grow as well; in fact, it even may die.

Plants growing wild are growing under the best conditions for them or they would not be growing in that area. The more closely the conditions in your garden approximate those under which the plant normally grows, the more hardy the plant will be with you and the better it will grow for you.

Hardiness of a particular plant in a particular area depends on a number of factors: the lowest temperature in winter, the amount of water it has received during the growing season and receives during winter, the humidity of the air around it, the type of soil it is in and the drainage conditions surrounding it, the degree of protection from drying winds and the amount of sun it receives during the year.

MICROCLIMATES

In considering these factors, microclimates must be taken into account. Even though your garden is in a certain hardiness zone the lowest temperature in winter may be higher than those given for that zone because your garden may be protected by your house and garage, by nearby houses, or by evergreens in a windbreak more than others in the area. Or, if you are near the center of a city, it may be warmer by a degree or two in your garden than in the suburban gardens outside the city. Even within your own garden, there are always varying degrees of temperature and of protection that may make it quite possible for you to grow plants that people gardening only a block away cannot grow.

MINIMUM TEMPERATURE

Minimum temperature in winter determines where it is too cold for a given plant to grow and also where it is too warm for a given plant to grow. Many gardeners do not realize that some plants cannot thrive where winter temperatures are too high, just as others die where winter temperatures are too low. Peonies cannot be grown in New Orleans because winters are not sufficiently cold to give them the rest period they need.

To guide you in your choice of plants hardy in your area,

as far as minimum winter temperature is concerned, the northernmost zone in which the plant grows well is given in the plant descriptions in Chapter 12. If your garden is sheltered, or you have sheltered areas in it, as described above, then you may be able to grow plants recommended for one zone south of you. There is little doubt that you can grow plants recommended for at least one and possibly two zones north of you.

WATER

The amount of water a plant has received during the growing season determines the state of its health about as much as any other factor. Shrubs that have grown well during the season are more likely to be hardy in your garden. Broad-leaved evergreen shrubs need copious watering in late fall because their leaves will be on them all winter and it is better for wet soil than dry soil to freeze around their roots. Deciduous shrubs do not need special watering in fall unless they were transplanted then. After their leaves have fallen their need for water decreases markedly.

To prevent damage to flower buds on forsythia branches covered in snow, sweep snow from the branches before it has a chance to freeze.

AIR

Some shrubs grow naturally where air is damp. They will not thrive under other conditions, so don't attempt to grow them unless your garden is in an area where such conditions prevail.

DRAINAGE

Most shallow-rooted plants winter best when they are in well-drained positions. Only the plants that naturally grow along the banks of streams or lakes will come through the winter unscathed under those conditions. A few of the moist soil–loving shrubs, like *Ilex verticillata*, will adapt themselves to drier soils, but they never grow quite as tall or quite as robust as in damper ones.

SOIL

As is explained in Chapter 4, How to Plant Shrubs, some plants must have acid soil, while most plants grow best in soil that is slightly acid to slightly alkaline. The plant that is growing in suitable soil is more likely to winter well than the one that is not.

No matter where you live, there are shrubs that will be hardy in your climate or in the microclimates that you either have in your garden or can create if you wish. If you have little time for gardening, but want a garden anyway, choose your shrubs carefully, both for hardiness and minimum care, and you'll have a garden you can sit back and enjoy.

Azaleas pruned into mounded shapes decorate a shrub border.

Alternating red and white azaleas form an unusual screen.

9
SHRUB TROUBLES

Like all other living things, shrubs have their troubles. For most shrubs these troubles are so minor that the gardener need pay no attention to them. For other shrubs, troubles are, for all practical purposes, non-existent. Since these two groups of shrubs comprise the vast majority, there are left comparatively few shrubs that need a little of the gardener's time to control whatever the trouble may be.

In almost every case, however, controlled or uncontrolled, the shrub will survive the trouble. This statement is the premise on which this chapter rests—for if shrubs weren't tough and practically without troubles, I never would have specialized in woody plants, I wouldn't be growing shrubs in quantity and, therefore, I certainly wouldn't be writing this book.

Should anyone ask me what has been the worst trouble my shrubs have had during the many years I've been growing them, I can answer in a single word—rabbits. Some gardeners undoubtedly would substitute mice or deer for rabbits, but the eating habits of certain animals, which can consume an entire large shrub during several months of a severe winter, so that only stubs are left, are certainly the most devastating shrub trouble.

Even when we lived in a city of 50,000 inhabitants, rabbits came into the yard and ruined shrubs. In our present 6-acre garden, despite the fact that hundreds of shrubs are ringed with fine-mesh chicken wire or hardware cloth, rabbits take their toll. We somehow unknowingly leave unprotected each fall a few shrubs, such as flowering quince, that rabbits dote on; and, when the winter is snowy, drifts pile up so high that rabbits eat over the tops of the 2-foot-high wires. Furthermore, while nothing will convince me that rabbits cannot read the price tag on a shrub, by wire-guarding the new and expensive ones and those known to appeal to rabbits, the creatures merely are encouraged to eat other shrubs that they do not like quite so well.

Thus, in a hard winter, when snow is on the ground from mid-December to late March, getting deeper and deeper as the season progresses, rabbits will eat even barberries and buds from young lilacs, shrubs they do not ordinarily touch.

A man who lives down the road from us told me that, in one such hard winter, 20-year-old forsythias in his garden were eaten clear to the ground by rabbits. I have had what was a 5-foot-high *Prunus tomentosa* in the fall reduced to a 3-inch stub by spring.

Exbury azalea 'Golden Sunset' likes the cool environment along a stream bank.

Short of a campaign to trap and transport elsewhere all the rabbits or other shrub-loving animals that visit your yard, or systematic destruction of them, all you can do is put wires around favorite plants each fall—the animals' favorites as well as yours. Then you can spray the unguarded plants with one of several repellents on the market and hope for the best. The only bright spot in this dark picture is that, even when eaten to the ground, most shrubs will grow again from the roots. Shrubs are really tough.

If the gardener's time is considered, it is relatively easier to control the shrub troubles caused by insects and diseases than by predators. Many troubles from these causes can be avoided.

AVOIDING SHRUB TROUBLES

If you have no desire to control shrub pests, you can avoid the work simply by not planting shrubs known to be highly susceptible to certain diseases or extremely attractive to certain insects.

For instance, anyone who has grown lilacs can practically guarantee to you that they will be attacked by scale insects at least once or twice in their lives. If they are, the scales will suck juices from the stems to which they have attached themselves and these stems will die an untimely death unless you spray once very early in spring to kill the scales. If this once-a-year or every other year spraying is too much trouble, don't plant any lilacs and you won't have to do it. (Of course, only the scale-infested stems will die—the rest of the shrub will go on growing well until the scales move to other stems. It will be years before you lose the lilac, but the plant probably won't bloom as much or perhaps won't bloom at all during certain of those years.)

Just as some shrubs are favorites of certain insects, some shrubs and small trees are prone to attack by certain plant diseases. For instance, some species of hawthorn (*Crataegus*) and some species of flowering crabapples (*Malus*) may be alternate hosts for certain rusts. Rusts are diseases that make the leaves look rusty, usually in distinct spots.

The two rusts referred to above—cedar apple rust and hawthorn rust—pass part of their lives on a member of the apple family, to which both hawthorns and crabapples belong, and the other part usually on red cedar (*Juniperus virginiana*) and its varieties. Both alternate hosts are absolutely necessary for the rust to complete its life cycle.

If you yearn for hawthorns or crabapples, then, you can either: (1) make certain that red cedars are not growing in your neighborhood and avoid planting them in your yard; (2) plant only varieties of hawthorns or crabapples that are resistant to rusts; (3) suppress your yearnings: don't plant hawthorns or crabapples; or (4) plant whichever varieties of the two you like best and prepare to spray the plants should rust attack. (It may never do so and the plants will live even if it does.)

WHEN TROUBLES ARE SLIGHT

The gardener who does not make it a practice to look over his shrubs periodically never sees the minor troubles that his shrubs have and they flourish despite these troubles. As an example, lilacs often get mildew in the fall, especially if the weather is damp. Since the leaves will drop shortly because of the lateness of the season, the lilacs are not really bothered by this disease. Most gardeners never notice it, though it can be unsightly when the white coating gets heavy on the leaves. Unless your lilac is placed where it is conspicuous and the appearance of mildew annoys you, this is a shrub trouble to ignore.

Obviously, if you don't see insects on your shrubs, you won't know about them. For instance, caterpillars may feed on leaves of one branch of a shrub and, since they stop in due course of time (though you cannot tell in advance just how many branches they will defoliate before they stop) you may never notice their depredations. In a small garden, where the appearance of each shrub is important, it would be sensible to spray or dust that small part of the shrub on which caterpillars first are seen to prevent its disfigurement, provided you see the caterpillars.

This deck looks beautiful with crabapple blossoms hanging over it.

In a large garden like mine, I am more likely to hold a paper bag under the branch and cut it off. At the end of each tour of the garden the bag, with whatever pest is in it, goes into the burner and usually that marks the end of the pest.

In precisely the same way, aphids, if seen when just starting to attack the tips of shrub branches, can be controlled by dunking those tips in a pail of nicotine sulphate (Black Leaf 40) solution or spraying with the same insecticide. A few aphids may be washed off with water from a hose. Or, if no hose is within easy reach, the cut-and-burn method is effective.

When first observed, the troubles described above usually are minor. Control them then and they are not likely to become serious. But, regardless of whether or not the troubles are controlled the shrubs still will be with you for many years.

It would, of course, be ridiculous for me to pass off shrub troubles from insects or diseases as all minor or all needing little or no attention on the part of the gardener. Yet, before I go on to tell you about the commonest troubles that you are likely to encounter sooner or later if you grow shrubs, I would like to tell you a few plain facts:

1. We owned our former garden for 21 years. About 100 shrubs were included in its plantings. In all those years the only spraying for a specific pest was to control scale on lilacs, and a few times branches of various shrubs were dunked to kill aphids on them.
2. Our present garden is 14 years old now. Some of the shrubs in it were moved, full size, from our previous garden. They never have been sprayed or dusted in this garden any more than in our previous one.
3. We now have over 1000 shrubs in this garden. During the past 14 years I have sprayed 3 times for lilac scale—that is, I have looked over the 63 lilacs to see whether or not scale insects were attacking and have sprayed the branches that had scales on them. A few times I have seen aphids on the tips of branches of an assortment of shrubs and have cut off and burned those tips. We have no such thing as a general spray program, in fact we simply leave the shrubs alone to grow big and produce the quantities of flowers for which I grow them.
4. Sometimes I know I should spray, but can't. For instance the big American holly outside the window my typewriter faces has been attacked by leaf miner for the last three years, but I have not done anything to control it because in the first place it is growing so well that no insect is going to stop it and in the second, how can I spray when at the proper time for doing so the silliest, flightiest female I ever have known, a female cardinal, builds her nest in it? Since the leaf miners aren't seriously harming the holly, I haven't taken control measures to avoid disturbing the cardinal.

This is a close-up of the handsome berry clusters on hybrid holly.

I know also that I should have sprayed several springs ago the three pyracanthas back of the lily pool, which we see below the dining room window because they have scab, which coats stems and berries with black soot. But I seem never to be home at the correct time for spraying and, furthermore, even if the disease overlays the berries with unsightly soot, it makes little difference. I'm not going to enjoy them anyway, for the warblers stop at our garden on their southern migration just when the berries turn orange and they strip off every berry, then move to the huge female yew under the south windows of my office and do the same.

Postscript: We forgot to protect these pyracanthas with wire last winter so the rabbits ate them to the ground. Of course they grew again from the roots and were soon as large as ever but there were no signs of soot this year on either leaves or berries. So even rabbits have silver linings!

If you have gathered from the above that my attitude toward insects and diseases is to leave well enough alone, you have gathered correctly. Usually I am far more interested in seeing whether or not a shrub will survive an attack than I am in controlling it. After all, should a shrub die from insect or disease attacks (and none ever has in all these years) I could always buy another one.

From the thousands of letters I have received from readers, I am convinced that people do more harm to their shrubs by coddling them and fussing about every little pest that comes along than they do good. If your attitude and feelings about shrub troubles differ from mine, and you wish to know what they are and what to do about them, here are the commonest of the shrub troubles.

This is an example of bagworm infestation. Each bag contains a hungry caterpillar.

The adult Japanese beetle has a ravenous appetite for tender green leaves.

Aphids (plant lice)

When you see colonies of tiny insects concentrated at the tips of new shoots with succulent leaves, these are aphids. They come in several colors and many species. They injure a plant by sucking its juices, thereby reducing vigor and sometimes causing malformations. They secrete a substance called honeydew, which in turn attracts a black sooty mold and this makes a plant unsightly. Aphids also act as carriers of virus diseases. Ants use aphids much as humans use cows, placing them on plants to feed and then themselves feeding on the honeydew of the aphids. Thus ant control contributes to aphid control.

To control aphids use nicotine sulphate (Black Leaf 40) in soapy water (the soap serving as a spreader and sticker), or rotenone, pyrethrum or Malathion. Insecticidal soap will also control aphids.

Bagworms

These are not found on shrubs as often as they are on evergreens, but since they are the homes of caterpillars, they should be cut off and burned when seen. If this cannot be done, spray the foliage where the caterpillars are feeding with any stomach poison.

Beetles

While Japanese beetles have not yet spread to some parts of the United States, other areas have had to live with them for years. They are chewing insects, and do enormous damage. These beetles are half an inch long, coppery green in color with tufts of white hair extending out from under the wing covers. They appear about the end of June and are not to be confused with rose chafers, which they resemble.

Since the grub stage in the life cycle of Japanese beetles is passed in the soil, where they feed on grass roots, one good way to control them is to treat lawn areas with milky spore disease dust, which carries a disease fatal to Japanese beetles.

Beetles feeding on leaves and flowers may be controlled by spraying with Sevin, Methoxychlor, Diazinon or other substances. Sprays must be regular and frequent, for it is almost impossible to control beetles feeding on flowers that have opened between sprays.

Borers

These are one of three classes of insects that most gardeners never see. Borer signs are: (1) holes in the stems or branches of shrubs; (2) little piles of frass hanging onto the riddled stem or

Anthracnose disease (also called lower branch dieback) on a flowering dogwood.

"black spot," which appears on roses, are serious troubles. Black spot can cause all the leaves on the plant to drop, thus weakening the plant for future years.

As you already know, the only roses included in this book are those commonly called shrub roses. Most of them are tough; though they may be attacked by black spot and even completely defoliated by it, they will grow new leaves later in the season and will continue to survive such attacks year after year. You may also control the disease.

A shrub rose that can be guaranteed to get black spot in every year that weather conditions are favorable for the disease is *Rosa foetida* 'Bicolor,' the Austrian Copper rose. Its flowers are so beautiful that you may wish to grow it despite its propensity for this disease, but, if you do, plant it apart from other shrub roses so the disease does not spread from it to other nearby plants.

As previously indicated, you do not need to spray or dust shrub roses because they happen to be attacked by black spot. You can ignore the trouble and the plants will survive. If, however, you wish to control it, use sulphur, starting when the leaves unfold and continuing every 10 days through the growing season. Sulphur will control powdery mildew at the same time it controls black spot.

Rose spot anthracnose might be included here under leaf spots. This disease, however, is more common on climbing than on bush roses. It shows on leaves as round brown or blackish spots that turn grayish with a dark red border. Sometimes the quarter-inch spots merge into larger discolored areas. If they appear on canes, spots may be either spindle shaped or round, purplish or brownish but characterized by sunken centers that are gray. Bordeaux mix is the usual control.

Mountain laurel, when it is planted in a damp or too-shaded place, especially where moisture from trees drips on the plants, is subject to a leaf spot that is hard to control. The best thing to do is to move the plant to a drier or less shaded spot, though spraying with Bordeaux mix when new leaves are appearing, and repeating the spray two or three times at two-week intervals, will help control it.

If you feel you must control leaf spots on other shrubs, try first a copper fungicide like the old Bordeaux mixture, which has the advantage of being widely available in garden supply stores. If this does not help, then try sulphur or fungicidal soap. Since the fungi that cause most leaf spots are of various kinds, the type of fungicide that controls one fungus may not control another. A mixture of several types of fungicides may be your best bet.

Mildew disease on a lilac.

Mildews

There are two distinct types of mildews: powdery and downy. Powdery appears on plants as a whitish coating that looks like felt, covering buds or stems or leaves, especially young ones. Downy mildew appears as white, gray, or sometimes purplish down, usually on the undersides of leaves.

Powdery mildews grow best when the air is damp and the weather humid (but do not grow during rain). Poor air circulation, plants set too close together and warm days followed by cool nights all predispose plants to attack by powdery mildew. Bordeaux mix, copper fungicides and sulphur all control this trouble, which attacks many, many plants.

Downy mildews grow best in wet weather. Bordeaux mixture or sulphur will control them.

As has already been noted, powdery mildew often attacks lilacs in late summer and, while it may be unsightly, doesn't do any harm, so may be ignored. The same remark applies to the same mildew that sometimes appears on privets, viburnums, blueberries, azaleas, and euonymus at the same time of year.

Powdery mildew on roses may be controlled with fungicidal soap or sulphur.

Rots

When the tissue disintegrates into either a hard, dry mass or a soft, wet mass, the term used for the trouble is rot. Since rots are most common in plants set in low, damp areas, avoid planting shrubs unadapted to such areas in these places.

The most devastating rot in shrubs is blueberry mummy berry (also called brown rot) caused by a fungus that invades tips of shoots and the flowers when they appear in spring and later affects the young berries. These turn color, usually tan or cream, and fall off. Thus the crop is materially reduced. Best control is to cut off and burn the affected parts when seen. Or, spread paper under the berry bushes so you can clean up rotting berries as they drop, before they can overwinter and allow the disease spores to reproduce in spring.

Rusts

The term rust is not necessarily properly applied to every rusty-appearing area on a plant. Such areas may or may not be true rusts, which are microscopic fungi and damage many plants. Some of these are important crop plants, and one of these (black stem rust of wheat) has as its alternate host *Berberis vulgaris*, the common barberry. Alternate hosts were explained earlier in this chapter under Avoiding Shrub Troubles, therefore, it is necessary to note here only that it is illegal in many wheat-growing states to grow *Berberis vulgaris* (an attractive shrub) and that it is illegal to import this shrub into these states or into the United States.

The Japanese barberry (*Berberis thunbergii*) and its varieties and other barberries commonly grown in gardens are considered resistant varieties so may be grown in any state.

Cedar-apple rust, such as previously explained, alternates during its life cycle between red cedar (*Juniperus virginiana*) and its varieties (and sometimes other junipers such as *Juniperus horizontalis* and *Juniperus scopulorum*) and members of the apple family, notably the native crabapples and particularly Bechtel's crab. Best control is elimination of one or the other alternate host from your garden and those of your near neighbors. The next best control is to examine any of the susceptible junipers in early spring, particularly if weather is wet, and to take off and burn the galls, which then are formed but have not yet grown horns or discharged spores.

Other possible controls are spraying junipers in early spring with wettable sulphur, and spraying alternate hosts in the apple family in dry weather with the same material two or three times beginning in early spring and extending into early summer.

The same remarks apply to control measures for hawthorn rust and quince rust. Hawthorn rust galls on junipers usually are dark reddish and smaller than those of cedar-apple rust and those of quince rust usually are mere swellings on branches and twigs (which often die completely). Alternate host for hawthorn rust is usually hawthorns, but mountain ashes and flowering crabapples as well as crabapples grown for fruit, apples, and pears may also act as hosts; buds, twigs and fruits may be distorted and leaves caused to drop prematurely. Quince rust may have as its alternate hosts apples, crabapples, pears, quinces, mountain ashes, chokeberries, and amelanchiers, as well as hawthorns. This disease is especially noticeable on English hawthorn. Fruits are covered with clusters of bright orange spores that are surrounded by white projections.

Currants (*Ribes* species) are alternate hosts of white pine blister rust. The European black currant is considered most susceptible and it is illegal to grow these fruits in many states and to import them into the United States and Canada. However, the ornamental currants commonly grown in gardens, as well as the red currants grown for fruit, are not considered susceptible, so may be grown anywhere.

There are other rusts of minor importance to shrubs but most of them may be ignored except if they mar the appearance of an important specimen. In this case try sulphur or Bordeaux mix. A badly infected plant is, perhaps, better dug up and burned, though this is hardly likely to be necessary.

Wilts

When foliage of a plant becomes limp and wilts it is probably because the plant hasn't had enough water and the soil is dry. Try a thorough soaking of the soil around the plant before you jump to the conclusion that a disease is troubling it. If the plant responds you know what caused the trouble.

Wilting also may be due to water loss from plant tissues because of too much fertilizer. Do you remember from your high school course in biology an experiment demonstrating the process called osmosis? This showed the movement of liquids as it occurs within a plant and from soil to plant and vice versa. The conclusion was that there is movement of fluids both in and out of a plant cell, through the cell wall, but that the *greater* movement always is from the less dense liquid to the more dense. Normally, the cell sap is more dense than the soil water. However, when a plant is over-fertilized, the soil water becomes more dense with chemicals from the fertilizer than the cell sap and thus the normal movement of liquid from soil to plant is reversed, more fluid moves from plant to soil instead and the plant wilts.

This type of wilting usually can be corrected by soaking the soil with water so that excess fertilizer is washed out of the soil. When a plant wilts shortly after being fertilized, suspect this reverse movement of liquids rather than a disease, and act accordingly.

When a specific organism, like a fungus, clogs some of the cells in the conducting vessels or destroys them, obviously the plant wilts. If wilt occurs in just one branch, cutting it off below the infection may stop the trouble, but sometimes the entire plant wilts because of soil-borne fungi. Saving that particular plant is hopeless and soil sterilization outdoors often impractical, especially if other plants are growing nearby. Better sacrifice the one affected plant.

There is, of course, one precaution you can take and that is to grow wilt-resistant cultivars of plants subject to a wilt disease.

FIRST AID TO SHRUBS

It must be obvious to all but the most inexperienced gardener that this one short chapter just hits the high spots of possible shrub troubles. However, it is quite possible that you'll never need more information about them than this chapter gives, for all of them are not going to appear in your garden at one time, most of the attacks will be slight and easily dealt with, and, to repeat once more, most shrubs are not affected by troubles.

If one of your shrubs has symptoms of a disease or is attacked by an insect for which you find no description here, contact your local county agent for information on how to send a sample to a laboratory, normally located at your state land grant university.

This flowering dogwood is badly infected with anthracnose disease.

Japanese beetle damage.

Leaf scorch on a flowering chestnut.

HORSE SENSE

If you had answered all the letters I have answered from people whose plants (not necessarily shrubs) were troubled by some pest, you'd know that most people go off half cocked at the first sign of trouble. This is not the way to react.

It doesn't make any sense at all to grab a sprayer or duster, fill it with the material closest at hand and cover the shrub with that material. This probably won't do any good and may do incalculable harm.

Instead, first examine the extent of the trouble. If it is slight and is in form of an insect, try washing it off with water from the hose or a pail. Watch the shrub and if the insect does not reappear, forget it. If trouble is slight and seems to be from a disease and the shape of the shrub won't be ruined if you remove the affected part, cut it off, burn it and forget it.

If the trouble is greater in extent, take a look at it from all sides of the leaves, stems or whatever part is affected. If it seems to be from an insect, what is the insect doing? Eating holes in leaves? Then it's a chewing insect and any stomach poison sprayed on the leaves will cause it to commit suicide as it eats. Are there no visible holes, but signs of wilting leaves? If it isn't drought then it's a sucking insect and any insecticide that comes in contact with its body and either clogs the pores or burns it, like nicotine sulphate, will kill it. And so on.

If the trouble is definitely not from an insect, look through the common diseases in this chapter and see if what is attacking the plant fits one of those descriptions. If so, get one of the remedies advised, then read the directions on the label and follow them precisely. No precise quantities are given in this chapter because manufacturers sometimes change formulas. If they do, they also will change directions on the package.

Keep firmly in mind that an insecticide will not control diseases and that a fungicide will not control insects. You need a specific kind of chemical for a specific kind of pest (and the chemicals are getting more specific all the time). Timing is extremely important in control of some pests and even the right spray applied at the wrong time may be ineffective and therefore a waste of time and money. Since almost all pesticides are poisons, take all precautions printed on the label. Never disregard them thinking "it can't happen to me." I could tell you stories of things that have happened to nurserymen!

Never use a sprayer or duster in which a weed killer has been used for anything but weed killers. Keep one sprayer for pesticides, one for weed killers and mark each clearly with a tag on the handle and a sign painted on the side of the container, so that no one can possibly use the wrong one.

While it is true that a sprayer or duster may be cleaned so that little or no weed killer remains in it, the process is so lengthy that it is hardly practical. Furthermore, even if thoroughly cleaned, and then stored for some time, the next use still may prove lethal to the plant involved.

TROUBLE FROM WEED KILLERS

Even if you never accidentally spray a shrub with a weed killer, the use of one of these chemicals on your grounds, near shrubs or quite far from them, or even the use of one by your neighbor, still may show up as trouble on your shrubs. I remember the year the lilacs along our lilac lane had some leaves with scalloped edges. This turned out to be injury from weed killer that had been used in granular form on the grass of the path between the lilacs the previous fall. Fortunately only a few leaves were affected on each plant and all plants survived. Sometimes shrubs are not so fortunate. A breeze blowing from a weed killer being sprayed on a lawn nearby can transport sufficient weed killer to injure, and sometimes kill, a valuable shrub. So use weed killers with greatest caution at all times and in all places. Remember the chemicals cannot differentiate between a broad-leaved weed and a valuable ornamental shrub.

LOOKING FORWARD

New chemicals for control of plant troubles appear on the market each season. Some of them soon replace older ones. And still others offer a new approach to the control of pests. Such a one is Cygon. This is the first systemic insecticide available to the home gardener. Other systemics are so highly poisonous that their use has been confined to commercial plantings. Cygon, while still poisonous and not used by organic gardeners, is less so than others.

Cygon is used as a spray on leaves or as a soil drench and is absorbed by the plant through either its leaves or its roots. It enters the plant's system (hence the name systemic) and stays

Gummy sap oozing from members of the Prunus *family of trees and shrubs is usually an indication of borers.*

The chlorosis on this Pieris japonica *is caused by iron deficiency.*

there in the sap. When certain types of insects attack the plant they get a dose of the poison and die.

When used as a soil drench, Cygon usually has to be applied about once in eight weeks. Foliage applications must be repeated every two or three weeks to be effective. As is evident, Cygon is available in liquid form only. It is said to control such plant troubles as euonymus scale, boxwood and holly leaf miner and other sucking and burrowing insects.

Development of dry or granular forms of new systemic insecticides make possible one-application control of the sucking, boring or mining insects that hatch only one brood a season. Lessened numbers of applications are possible to control insects of similar kinds that have several broods a year. For instance, scientists at the University of Maryland have found that a single application of a granular systemic insecticide will control azalea lace bug for the season.

These granular chemicals are applied to the soil to be taken up by plant roots and translocated or moved within the plant to other parts, to be ready for the insects when they attack. They are easier to use than soil drenches or foliage applications and, furthermore, said to be safer than the former systemics.

They have been tried against and reported to control aphids (including snowball aphid) holly, boxwood and azalea leaf miners and other insects. As an example of their ease of use, a single treatment in early April is recommended for all-season control of the snowball aphid, which is an annual visitor to the snowball (*Viburnum opulus* 'Roseum') and also frequently attacks the American cranberry bush (*V. trilobum*).

The development of systemic insecticides presages more complete control of certain pests with considerably less work. However, it must be borne in mind that while systemic insecticides will be effective against any insects that suck plant sap (like aphids), or burrow or tunnel within the plant (like scale insects or leaf miners), and therefore come into contact with the sap within the plant, they will not control insects that feed on the layers of leaf tissue (epidermis) because the systemics are carried in the sap, not in the tissues.

Part Three

Acquiring Shrubs

10

HOW TO BUY SHRUBS

Have you ever visited a nursery sales lot on a fine, sunny Sunday afternoon in May and listened to a family buying nursery stock to plant around the house? If you have, you must know that few families come to the nursery adequately prepared. If you haven't, follow an actual family of four—Mother, Father and two children and observe, as I did, what they buy and why they buy it.

Remember that the month is May and in the nursery sales lot there are hundreds of plants of azaleas in full bloom. Mother promptly selects several with flower colors a rosy-lavender. These she thinks may fit under the picture window at the front of the house even if it is rather close to the ground.

Father makes a beeline for the spruces because they look so sturdy, and decides he'll buy two of them, one for each side of the front door, close to the 3-foot-wide path from the sidewalk to the house.

The kids think the red-leaved barberry is such a pretty color and want their parents to buy some plants to place under the picture window at the front of the house—the same picture window for which Mother has selected the azaleas. So a compromise is reached and the family decides to buy some azaleas and some red-leaved barberries, both for under the same window.

This is a true example of what one family did and if it seems to you that they did a good job, consider the following: Since Mother lives in the Detroit area, the chances are better than even that the soil around her house is alkaline or circumneutral. Azaleas, with certain notable exceptions, must have acid soil to survive. She doesn't know this, so probably won't own the azaleas very long. Furthermore, she has not considered whether or not azaleas will tolerate the exposure at the front of the house, where she intends to plant them. In the hot summers of the climate in which Mother lives, azaleas grow best on the north or east side of a building. If the picture window that she bought them to plant under faces south—this exposure would be another reason why she probably will not own the azaleas for long. And, of course, she has not armed herself with the exact measurement of the distance between that picture window and the ground.

Father's spruces, selected for their sturdiness, are sturdy indeed. They are forest trees that will grow so high they will dominate any but a very tall house (and the one Father lives in is one story high) and will spread so wide that both the 3-foot-wide front path and the front doorway soon will be obscured and unusable.

The foliage color of the red-leaved barberries, though beautiful with the azaleas while they are clothed only with foliage, will clash with the flower color when they sport blooms and, if the house against which they are placed happens to be red brick, both red foliage and rosy-lavender flowers will battle the house color. Furthermore, barberries are poor plants to use in a house planting for this usually is the planting that the family wants to see best kept. The barberry thorns will make weeding between the plants an unpopular chore, which will not add to the chances of the house planting looking neat at all times.

This family, visiting the nursery without adequate measurements, also bought too many plants for the space they have unless their house is 100 feet long, and I'm willing to bet they also planted what they bought too close to the house wall. How do I know all this? I've made a practice of standing to one side and watching and listening to what goes on in nurseries (and other sales places for horticultural and allied products). It's an excellent way for a garden writer to get ideas for articles.

This family, of course, furnished a perfect example of the wrong way to buy woody plants, shrubs included.

Oakleaf hydrangea (Hydrangea quercifolia) *cascades from a raised planter over a patio.*

THE RIGHT WAY

Then what is the right way to go about such an enjoyable task as selecting plants for your own grounds? Stated briefly, to be elaborated upon further; you should: (1) first know the area for which you want to buy and (2) if the space is limited, as it usually is, have measurements with you that will help you to buy only as many plants as are needed of correct ultimate heights and spreads to fit your space.

(3) You should have some idea of how you wish this area to look and which shapes of plants will best assist the architectural lines of your house to look their best or, if they are not pleasing, to conceal them.

(4) Next, you should have some background knowledge of how the nurseryman sells shrubs, and (5) of course you should know something about the plants you are considering buying. If you know nothing about the plants, you'd better (6) know something about your nurseryman.

OBSERVING AND MEASURING

Going back to points 1 and 2 above—it is easy to measure the footage you cover in one pace as you walk. You can use this figure to pace off the important distances in your yard. Putting these down on paper needn't be a chore either: cross-section paper, available at any stationery store, makes it simple. Depending on the size of the paper and the size of the squares, assign a foot to a square, or more, or less, and after that just count squares.

House measurements should be accurate—use a steel tape, or lacking that, a yardstick or a tape measure. Be sure to measure the distance from ground to windows as well as the wall space between windows and doors, and between these features and the house corners.

PICTURING

If you own a camera, take pictures of your house from various angles. These are extremely helpful when planning the landscaping. If you have an enlargement made of a snapshot, ask that it be printed faintly, so you can draw right on it, if you wish. Or, you can draw on a piece of thin paper placed over it, if the picture is printed at normal darkness.

What to draw? Just the shapes of plants that will be most suitable to the type of architecture of your house or to the areas you wish to plant. For any shape and height you draw, there's surely a choice of plants that will meet your requirements. Just doodle a bit and see how you can make your house and lot look their best. For instance, suppose one wing of your house is higher than another and dominates the scene. A horizontally branched tree or large shrub planted at that end of the house will visually lower its height. A tall, slender plant of any type will accent the height.

Flowering dogwoods carry color above the roof line of a house and also help shade a lean-to greenhouse.

Wisteria vines smother an arbor with decorative blossoms.

Walk back and forth across the street from your house, looking at it as you do so, and you'll be much better able to judge the ultimate heights and the shapes of the plants you should acquire to enhance the picture.

After you have a good idea, not only of the shapes of the plants you wish to buy, but also the sizes to which they should ultimately grow to fill the areas in those sketches, these, together with the measurements you have taken, will help you and the nurseryman determine which kinds of plants and how many plants you actually need to buy.

It will help, at this stage of planning, if you will write down your positive likes and dislikes. If you detest plants with yellow or red foliage, write it down. If both husband and wife are concerned with the planning, it is just as well to avoid plants disliked by one or the other.

If you do not wish to do this planning yourself, you may want to have a nursery send a person, preferably one trained in landscape design and architecture, to your home to draw a simple plan, including the specification of the plants to be used. Usually, if you buy the plants from that nursery, there is no charge for the plan. However, there is a moral obligation implied, and you lay yourself open to the possibility of getting a stereotyped plan or else one that is drawn up to suit the convenience or the stock of the particular nursery.

When you do the planning yourself, you are free to visit several nurseries and buy plants where you see fit. Furthermore, if you do not wish to visit nurseries, you can buy from a mail order source.

Before you go further in planning, figure precisely how much money you can afford to spend for the planting. Decide whether you will do it all in one year or spread the cost over several years. Will you set out the plants yourself or have the nursery do it? If the nursery does the planting, there will be a charge for it. If you do it yourself you must include in your price estimate the cost of the necessary shovel and garden hose (unless you already own them) and the cost of peat moss or some other type of organic matter to improve the texture of your soil, which hardly is likely to be perfect. Fertilizer cost need not be included since no fertilizer should be used at planting time.

Should you decide to have the nurseryman plant, decide also whether or not you wish the plants guaranteed to live. Then ask the nurseryman how much he charges for this guarantee that the plant will live a year or the nursery will replace it at no charge.

Now you are ready to think about buying plants, including shrubs, from either a local nursery or a mail order concern. So, now you need some background knowledge about the nursery business.

BACKGROUND KNOWLEDGE

Sizes and Price

Plants are available in many sizes. In general, the smaller the size, the cheaper the plant. However, this rule does not apply to certain dwarf plants. In these cases you are paying a higher price for a plant that grows slowly, takes more time to reach a saleable size, and never will outgrow the space you plan for it.

If you will remember that plants grow—an obvious fact, but one that isn't always recognized—just look at all the houses overgrown by plants—you will know that you can buy the smaller sizes if you haven't enough money to buy the larger ones and that the plants will eventually grow to the size you can't afford to buy at the start.

For Pieris japonica *to bloom like this, an acidic soil is required.*

Spacing

This leads us to the matter of spacing. Plants should be set out sufficiently far from the house wall (at least 2 feet for a small plant, at least 3 feet for a medium-sized one and more for one that will grow very large) to allow for the ultimate spread of the plant. Thus the side of the plant towards the house will grow as full and beautiful as the side away from the house. Plants also should be set sufficiently far apart to allow for their spread, whether they're to be placed near the house or away from it in a shrub border.

There is no specific rule for spacing plants according to their ultimate size, so I'll tell you a general principle I've found useful. If the plant will ultimately grow 10 feet high, allow the same footage for the ultimate width. If it will ultimately grow from 5 to 10 feet high, allow three quarters of the ultimate height for the width. If the plant will some day be from 2 to 5 feet high, allow 3 feet for the ultimate spread. Plants lower than 2 feet often grow as wide as or wider than their heights, so the distance to plant them apart depends on the individual plants.

Hedge planting is another matter. Plants always are set so they are closer together than in other plantings and thus will form a tight screen as they grow.

The reason you should inform yourself about spacing of plants is so that you avoid overbuying. This also is the reason you should plan first and keep in mind that plants grow.

Background shrubs should be spaced so the viewer, from a distance, can see their individual beauty.

Flowering saucer magnolia (Magnolia *x* soulangeana) *blooms early in spring. See page 75 for the same scene several weeks later.*

Home Nursery

Realizing that plants grow awakens the possibility of planting a home nursery of plants you cannot buy or cannot afford to buy in large sizes. Mail order firms often offer plants that your local nurseries do not carry, but mail order sizes usually are small because shipping charges are lower when plants weigh less. See the source listing in the appendix.

The canny gardener makes a nursery bed somewhere on his lot and plants small plants before he builds a house, while the house is being built, or whenever he can buy the plants he desires. In this way, in just a few years, he has plants the sizes he wants, can move them into his landscaped area, and has saved the money he otherwise would have had to pay for a larger size of the same plant.

Packaging

Woody plants may be purchased with their roots bare of soil, sometimes packed in damp sphagnum moss or excelsior (or some other material that, moistened, will keep the roots damp) and sometimes not. These are known in the nursery trade as bare root plants.

Woody plants also may be purchased with their roots encased in the ball of earth in which they grew, this ball wrapped in burlap, pegged with nails or wound about with twine to hold it in place. Such plants the nurseryman calls B & B, meaning balled and burlapped.

Most deciduous shrubs, those that drop their leaves in winter, are sold bare root. Some nurseries plant these bare root shrubs in early spring in tar paper or other similar pots or cans, so that you can buy them, if you want, long after the regular planting season is over. If when you plant them, you slip them gently out of the containers and into prepared holes, their

roots will not be disturbed and they will continue to grow. Shrubs available in containers are referred to as container stock or sometimes as potted shrubs. The former name also is used, and more properly belongs, to plants grown in containers from the time they were rooted cuttings. When you see the term container-grown stock, it refers to these plants grown with roots confined for easy transplanting.

The shrubs (and trees and evergreens) sold B & B are those of varieties that do not move well bare root, or are too large to move with bare roots. Nurserymen have had years of experience with plants, so they know which kinds tolerate transplanting with roots first bared of earth and which will not.

Because of labor charges, container stock costs more than bare root stock and B & B stock usually costs more than either of the other two.

Mail order nurserymen usually ship bare root shrubs with moist wrappings around the roots. This is satisfactory for the purchaser since mail order sizes are not large. Mail order nurserymen also offer small sizes of evergreens, both broad and narrow-leaved, with small balls of earth around the roots, or in small containers in which the plants have been grown in sphagnum moss rather than soil. Shipping charges are a little higher for these plants, but by no means excessive.

Flowering crabapple (Malus sargentii) *blooms with pansies in early spring.*

The shady site and stream at the bottom of a hill creates a cool, humid microclimate in which rhododendrons thrive.

Sizing Standards

Sizing of bare root, deciduous shrubs or B & B, broad-leaved evergreen shrubs is reasonably standardized. The sizes are expressed in terms of feet and/or inches of height if the shrub grows higher than wide. If it grows wider than high, the same terms of feet and/or inches refer to the spread rather than the height.

Smaller sizes of shrubs, up to 24″ in height, usually are sized in 3″ steps, as 12″–15″ or 15″–18″. Shrubs larger than 24″ are sized by half-foot steps, as 2′ to 2½′, 2½′ to 3′. Still larger shrubs are sorted according to one-foot steps, for instance, 4′ to 5′, 5′ to 6′. Shrubs that are more than 6′ high are sold in sizes that vary from one another by 2′. For example, 8′–10′, 10′–12′.

The American Association of Nurserymen has published a leaflet for its members that sets forth in explicit detail size standards for woody plants. Since these have been approved by the American Standards Association, Inc., they are likely to remain unchanged for some years.

With regard to shrubs the standards state the minimum number of canes of a minimum height that a shrub of a given size (height or spread) and a certain type (seven types of deciduous, five of broad-leaved evergreens are delineated, with examples given of each) should have to be acceptable in the trade. All of these size standards are subject to certain grading tolerances.

Such further pertinent information also is included in the leaflet as recommended widths and depths of earth balls considered satisfactory for balled and burlapped stock, whether nursery grown or collected.

Collected Plants

Plants offered for sale in nurseries, nursery sales lots and some catalogs are not always nursery grown. Some are collected, which means that they are dug from the woods or fields where they grow wild. Because their roots usually spread wider and deeper than any reasonably sized earth ball can encompass and because they have not been repeatedly root pruned as are plants grown in nurseries, such plants are harder to reestablish in your garden. Additional care is needed in order that collected plants survive.

The extra work involved and the lessened chances of survival should be taken into account and weighed against the probably lower price of collected stock when you are considering such a purchase. Since many native plants are becoming endangered from wild collection, it is better to avoid buying collected stock.

It is not usually worthwhile to collect plants yourself. Unless they are very small and you can dig them with an extra-large ball of earth around their roots, they are not likely to survive transplanting for the reasons given in the paragraphs above. Should you be considering collecting plants, make certain that you collect them from land you own or have permission from the owner of the land from which you dig them. Check with your state department of agriculture to see if an inspection certificate is required before transporting plants.

Handling

Nursery stock that is dug while you wait at the nursery, or has just been dug, or plants that have been properly packaged and refrigerated, are worth far more than the same size plants of the same kind that have been handled improperly or allowed to dry out after being dug. Carefully handled plants reestablish their roots more readily, grow better and grow larger in a shorter time.

Buying from Farther South

Another bit of background knowledge that you should have is that plants normally hardy in your climate may be purchased from nurseries in other climates and will thrive in your garden if only you give them a reasonable chance to do so.

For instance, a shrub grown in a nursery two hardiness zones south of where you garden is not likely to stand the shock of being moved to a much colder climate in late autumn. There will be either a dead shrub or one with far smaller tops when spring rolls around.

On the other hand, if you buy that same shrub in early spring (having ordered it the previous fall, specifying the earliest date on which you can plant it immediately or heel it into a large pile of peat or compost until weather permits planting), it has a long growing season ahead of it. During this it can reestablish its roots and, as the weather gradually cools, its wood will harden. While it might be sensible to protect a shrub spring-moved from the south the first winter after planting, it certainly should not be necessary to do so during any successive winter if, as I said above, the shrub is of a kind normally hardy in the hardiness zone in which you live.

I am speaking from experience in this matter and I realize that what I am telling you is the opposite of what garden experts have been preaching for years—never to buy from farther south than one hardiness zone. This, I think, is silly, and I have umpteen shrubs in the garden to prove it.

Bargains?

Low priced plants are bargains only when they come from a good grower and have been carefully handled. It sometimes happens that such an establishment is overstocked on one kind of plant and can, therefore, offer it at reduced prices. These plants are bargains, but plants left over at the end of the season at an ordinary sales lot are worth precisely what you pay for them and no more.

An example that comes to my mind whenever bargain plants are mentioned is that of a now defunct (bankrupt, and no wonder) plant sales lot—not a nursery—that followed the interesting practice of laying bare root rose plants on the roof of a shed. These were invisible to a person standing on the ground in the sales lot, but clearly visible if one were driving on a nearby elevated expressway. When more bare root roses were needed to supply customers' demands, someone simply used a ladder to reach a supply of the poor plants, which then had their dried-out roots wrapped in damp sphagnum moss and were packaged in water-proof paper before being sold. At the end of the season these plants were offered at a very special (and widely advertised) sale for only $1.00 each. By that time they weren't worth even a quarter.

KNOWING ABOUT SHRUBS

Way back at the beginning of this chapter I suggested that there were five different types of knowledge that you should have in order to buy shrubs intelligently. Point 5 was knowing something about the plants you consider buying. Since the greater portion of this book is devoted to descriptions of the shrubs available to you in the nurseries of the United States and Canada, you have only to read and look at the pictures in order to gain a modicum of knowledge about the shrubs you may wish to purchase. However, I do not consider such knowledge a substitute for actually seeing the plants. Places where you may go to see them are described in Chapter 2.

Washington hawthorn (Crataegus phaenopyrum) *produces showy white flowers in spring and red berries in autumn.*

The compact, rounded shape of this azalea is maintained by light pruning after the flowers fade.

KNOWING YOUR NURSERYMAN

How does one go about knowing one's nurseryman? From hard experience gained through walking nursery rows several months of every year for many years, and visiting what by now must be thousands of nurseries and their garden centers, here are the points I look for when I judge a nursery and, therefore, its owner. First of all, I try always to look over the sales lot and part of the nursery before I meet the owner. As I walk, I ask myself the following questions:

Does the place look clean and well kept? I don't mean that the nursery must be weedless, because sometimes when weather is extremely hot and dry, it is better to leave weeds in place for a mulch. But it usually is easy to tell whether the proper work has been done around the nursery rows. Plants in the sales lot should definitely be weed free, well watered and generally well kept.

Are the plants well spaced? I don't like to buy plants that have been growing crowded together since too many roots usually are lost when digging one plant, because of the need for saving the roots of the ones on either side.

Are many plants in the nursery overgrown? If so, I always wonder why they weren't sold long ago. Of course every nursery has a few very large plants. That is normal, but too many are too many.

In reverse, are there too few holes visible from which plants have been dug? If so, I always wonder if the prices of the stock have been set so high that sales are few.

How about signs of insect pests? Or plant diseases? One thing a good nurseryman always does is keep his plants well sprayed to control these pests.

Are the rows labeled? Now I realize that it is next to impossible to keep labels in place over the entire nursery (I have seen children and even adult customers take labels out of the ground) but certainly most of the labels should be in place and legible. If a label is missing, a good nurseryman should not show signs of worry, because he should have a map of his nursery, with each kind of plant indicated on it. The plants in the sales lot certainly should be labeled and the more information on the labels, the better the nursery is likely to be.

Is the nursery growing only the commonest kinds of plants? Perhaps I should not include this point because you may be a new gardener, quite uninterested in any but the most common plants. However, this is an important point for me to notice, since I am interested in buying only the unusual shrubs I don't already own (and it gets harder to find these every year). But I do think that a nursery growing only the commonest plants is not progressive.

After all this walking and looking I have a fair idea of what is being grown in the nursery and an overall impression of it. So will you if you walk and ask yourself the same questions that I do. Now it's time to go to the office, but first, if there is a garden center, I walk through it and look around. Is it neat? Is the stock well displayed with instructive signs and prices? Are there interesting items as well as the usual pesticides and fertilizers? Is there literature to help the customer? (This does not necessarily mean free literature.)

Now it's time to meet the nurseryman.

Perhaps it is not fair for me to tell you what I look for in a nurseryman, for I've been in some phase of the plant business since age 13, I've met many, many nurserymen and count some of them among my best friends. But the first and most important thing I look for in a nurseryman is knowledge of the plants he grows. If he doesn't know his plants, how they grow and why he is growing them the way he is, then he is not a person I trust and therefore I do not wish to deal with him.

It is not necessary that he be able to "out-Latin-name" me—this is hard to do. He needn't know more about every plant he owns than I do, though he certainly does about many of them, but he should have a good general knowledge of plants and not be flabbergasted by a botanical name.

A great many nurserymen, of course, are as plant crazy as I am and we have a wonderful time together, discussing plants. Most of the people who deal in plants have to be plant crazy or they'd never be in a business that deals with living things that require such a great deal of time, effort and care to help them survive and grow.

If, about now, you are asking yourself what difference it makes whether or not you know your nurseryman, let me try to tell you. He can give you the benefit of his years of experience as to which plants will thrive in your particular climate and soil. He can tell you the sizes to which these plants will eventually grow and their idiosyncracies if any. He can tell you how to modify your soil to suit the plants you buy, if this is necessary, and how to plant and care for them. That is, if he is a reliable nurseryman.

Because I know how much a reliable nurseryman can do for you, especially if you are an inexperienced gardener, I feel that, when you figure the price of the plants you buy, you ought to take into account the advice you get from your nurseryman, or from the nursery catalog in which you find the plants you desire. Assistance of this kind is not forthcoming when you buy low-price plants from a fly-by-night operator of a seasonal sales lot.

This professional advice is one of the most important things a nurseryman or cataloger has to offer. He wants to keep you as a customer, so that the prime ingredient of his sale to you is your success with the plant you have bought from him.

Finally—if you feel that knowing how to buy woody plants is just too much bother—consider this. The cost of landscaping a building is generally considered to be approximately 20 percent of the cost of the building. Thus the cost of the planting around your house—whether you put in your own time or pay for that of the nurseryman—is a big part of your investment. This means (or should mean) that any time you spend learning how to buy plants and how to select plants is well justified if only to protect the investment in money and in planting time that you are about to make.

Cotoneaster horizontalis *creates a dense, impenetrable, but attractive ground cover.*

11
PROPAGATING SHRUBS

GROWING YOUR OWN

The next best thing to finding the shrub you want in your lo-cal nursery or listed by a reliable mail order firm is to know a friend or neighbor who owns that shrub. For then, if the laws of your state permit moving a piece of a plant with roots on without requiring the plant first to be inspected, and if the plant is of the type that grows with numerous stems from the ground, your problem is solved.

Division

Assuming the owner of the shrub is amenable, for most shrubs you need only dig from the outer edge of the plant a group of stems or shoots, with roots attached, take them home and plant them, and that's that. This should be done in early spring or after the leaves drop in fall. You now own the shrub, unless it happens to be one of the few kinds that are grafted on an understock that is a different kind of plant.

This process is called, in nursery parlance, division. You di-vided your friend's shrub and took a piece or portion or divi-sion of it home. Since your shrub is actually a part of the par-ent plant, it will produce growth and blooms exactly like the parent. Kerrias, spireas, mock oranges and lilacs are among the shrubs that are easily divided. Just be sure you take a division of such size that it need not be nursed along for years. If you want more plants of the same shrub, you'll soon be able to grow them from this division you have just acquired.

It would be convenient, since division is the easiest possible way of propagating shrubs, if all shrubs might be propagated by this method. But most of them do not send out many shoots from their bases, so to get a new shrub from these you must use other methods.

Layering

If the shrub that you want and someone else owns has supple stems that may be easily bent to the ground without breaking, then it probably is possible to layer it. This process is akin to division since you make the plant grow its own offset or new plant, then divide or remove that from the parent after it has grown its own roots.

With shrubs that root readily, like forsythias or rose

Kerria japonica *presents attractive yellow flowers in early spring.*

daphne, layering may be done in spring or early summer and often the young plant will be sufficiently rooted to be cut from the parent and transplanted in fall. Shrubs that take longer to form roots still may be layered in spring and the young plant removed early in summer of the following year. Or they may be layered in fall and the young plant removed the following fall. A few shrubs are so slow to form roots that it will take two full seasons of growth before the young plant can be separated from its parent.

Layering is an excellent method for the home gardener to use because it is easy and requires no special equipment. The number of layers that may be made from one shrub is limited only by the number of supple branches around its perimeter. Layering is widely used in European nurseries and is used in America for plants that do not come true from seed and that are hard to propagate by other methods.

Simple Layering

Select one slim, young stem or slender branch that is long enough to reach the ground and is on the outer edge of the plant for ease in handling. Bend it to the ground, noting ex-actly where it touches the soil. Using a clean, sharp knife, wound the stem at this spot, on the side of the stem next to the ground when it is bent down.

Stems may be wounded in one of four ways: (1) by remov-

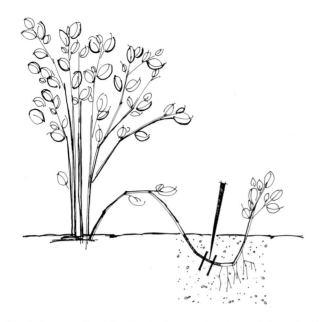

Simple layering: Bend the stem to the ground and wound the underside where it touches the soil. Bend it to the ground once more, anchor it in place, and heap soil over the wounded stem. Keep soil moist and roots will grow from the wound.

Serpentine Layering

When branches are especially long and pliable as on some shrub roses, and you want several more plants of the same shrub it is possible to wound a long branch in several places, always, of course, on the side of the branch that touches the soil when it is bent down. Wounds should be so spaced that there are several leaves or leaf buds between them. The wounded areas are bent to the ground and anchored as previously described. The portions of the branch between cuts are arched slightly and allowed to remain above ground. Since this means that the finished layer looks rather like a snake, the name of this type of layering becomes obvious. It is possible to sink pots into the ground under each wounded area so that the roots grow into the pots. This makes it even easier to transplant the young plants later, when cuts are made along the branch between each layer to allow the youngsters to be moved.

Mound Layering

When shrubs have stiff branches like deutzias and mock oranges that do not lend themselves to bending to the soil, another method of layering can be used to propagate them. This process starts one year and finishes two years later, the long time being the reason it is not more generally used.

The first year the plant to be mound layered is cut back severely to encourage it to grow many shoots from the base. The next year, in spring, soil is mounded around the base of the plant. New shoots, as they grow from the roots, will root in this soil mound, the additional roots forming at the nodes of the shoots. If you will look at a branch of any shrub, you will see that there are distinct places from which leaves or buds grow and areas between these places where no leaves or buds grow. Leaves or buds grow from a branch at a node. The areas between nodes are called internodes. Roots usually form most readily from nodes—a convenient fact, useful in any type of propagation.

ing a narrow strip of bark all around the stem; (2) by making a cut into the stem, almost halfway through it, and inserting a pebble in the cut to keep it open; (3) making a slashing cut upward in the stem, almost halfway through it; (4) making a V-shaped notch in the stem, extending almost halfway through it. This last method is the one I prefer.

After the cut has been made, dust into it a minute amount of root-inducing hormone powder such as Rootone (available at any garden supply store). This promotes rooting of some shrubs. On others, it seems to have no effect, but since it costs only a few cents and often helps, its use should be routine. Remove the leaves for a few inches either side of the wound. Bend the branch to the ground again and anchor it in place, using a forked stick, a stone, or a U-shaped piece of wire turned upside down with ends thrust into the ground either side of the stem. The idea is to keep the rest of the branch, that portion between the wound and the tip, above ground, only the wounded area underground. Heap soil, preferably sandy soil or a mixture of soil, peat and sand, over the wounded area to a depth of 3 to 5 inches. If the soil under the wounded area is not light and does not have plenty of organic matter in it, it also will help root growth if you mix sand and peat with it.

The soil both above and below the wounded area should be kept moist, always. In time roots will grow from the cut into the soil. When these have grown sufficiently so that they can support the tops of a new plant, cut the branch between the parent plant and the youngster and move the latter wherever you want it to grow.

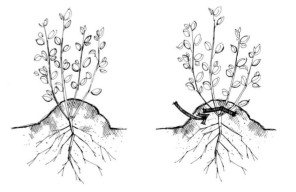

Mound layering: Severely prune the shrub. The next year, mound soil around the base. New shoots will grow from roots and form their own roots in the soil mound.

Illustrations by Anne L. Meskey

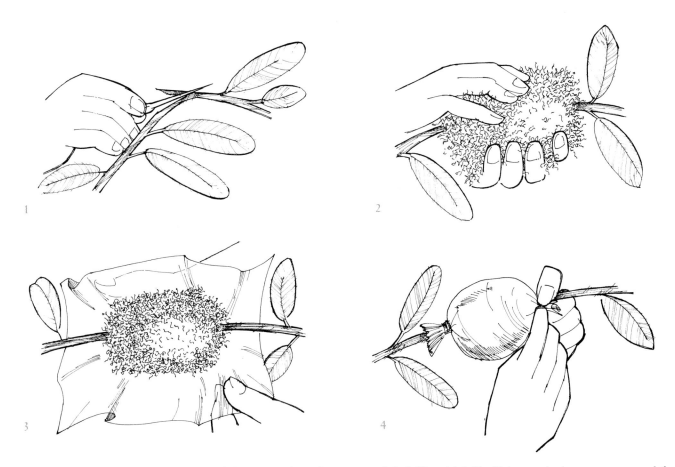

Air layering: (Top left) *First, wound the stem of the growing plant where roots are desired.* (Top right) *Mould dampened sphagnum moss around the wound.* (Lower left) *Wrap a sheet of polyethylene plastic around the moss;* (lower right) *and fasten firmly to branch or stem so no moisture will be lost from moss. Roots will form in time from wound and will grow in moss.*

Air Layering

A fourth type of layering is called air layering because it is done up in the air instead of bringing stems in contact with the soil. This method is used to propagate plants with very tall, almost rigid stems or plants hard to reproduce by other means. The same type of wound is made as in simple or serpentine layering, wherever you wish roots to form, the hormone powder is dusted into the wound, and then a little damp sphagnum moss is molded around the wound and a handful is tied to the branch over the wounded area. A sheet of polyethylene plastic is placed over the moss and wrapped to overlap so that no moisture can evaporate from the moss inside and no rain can penetrate to soak the moss. Sphagnum moss is available from bogs (if you have one handy), from greenhouses, florists, or nurseries. Garden supply stores sell a kit that contains all necessities for air layering, including sphagnum.

Bind the ends of the plastic with strips of plastic tape or electrician's tape to hold the plastic to the branch as well as to seal the covering over the moss. Thus, while the polyethylene permits passage of air, the moisture in the moss remains constant and very little after-care is required. Air layers have been known to need no care for a year when polyethylene has been correctly applied. If you are worried about the state of affairs, open the plastic occasionally to see if all is well, adding a little water if it is needed.

Air layering may be done during spring or summer, but is best done in spring as then roots usually will be formed by fall. Air layers made in summer usually do not root until the following spring, though much depends on the kind of plant being air layered. No additional protection of the layered area is necessary during winter.

In due course of time roots will grow from the wound into the moss. Sometimes you can see them through the plastic covering. Other times you must loosen the plastic to see if they have grown. When the moss ball is well filled with roots, cut the young plant from the parent, removing the plastic but leaving the moss in place. Plant the youngster with the moss still around its roots. Water well and give the usual care that you would give any shrub after planting.

All of these methods, as well as other methods of layering, will produce plants with characteristics identical with the parent plant because, as in division, the new plant is actually a part of the parent plant. A portion of the parent plant also is used for another method of propagation—by cuttings.

Cuttings

Types

There are several different kinds of cuttings, named for the part that is removed from the parent plant, as stem, root, or leaf cuttings. Shrubs are most frequently and usually most satisfactorily propagated by stem cuttings so this is the only type that will be considered in this book.

Stem cuttings, that is pieces of the stems of the parent plant, may be removed from the parent at various times of year, when the parent is in various stages of growth. Early in the season, when the new growth on the parent plant is still soft and easily manipulated with the hand, the cuttings are called softwood or green since they are taken from immature, green or succulent parts of the plant.

Later in the season, in July and August, when branches have hardened somewhat, the cuttings taken then are called half-ripened or semi-hardwood. Still later, in the fall, when the season's growth is mature, hardwood cuttings may be taken from the parent plant.

The best time of year to take cuttings depends on the particular genus and species of the parent plant. In general, the harder the wood of the plant, the earlier in the season the cuttings should be taken. The lists of ways to propagate shrubs in the appendix indicate the season or seasons at which cuttings may be taken advantageously from various shrubs. Sometimes cuttings may be taken at several different seasons from the same kind of shrub.

There is no set length for a cutting, other than the irreducible minimum of one node for root formation, one node for top growth and, of course, the internode between them. A cutting this short may be made when only one small branch of the parent plant is available. But usually three to four or four to five nodes are used for a single cutting.

Softwood Cuttings

There are two requirements for a parent from which softwood cuttings are to be taken. The first is that the shrub be in vigorous growth and excellent health. The second is that the wood be at such a stage of growth that the top of a branch will snap off like a snap bean (break off cleanly all across) when bent over. If it bends rather than breaks, the wood is too old for softwood cuttings.

Assuming the parent plant meets both requirements, take pieces from tips of branches, from wood that grew during the current season and that has leaves unfolded and mature. Take the branch tips to a cool, shaded place and here make the cuttings, meanwhile keeping the branches covered with moistened burlap.

Cuttings will vary in length according to the length of the internodes of the plant you are propagating. Unless you are short of cutting wood, cuttings should have three or four nodes when finished. You can make one cutting from the tip of each branch or make several from one branch. Use a clean, sharp knife to make cuttings of any kind: sharp so it does not leave irregularities in the cut, clean so it does not transmit disease. Usually, with softwood cuttings, it is a good idea to cut just under a node but this is not absolutely necessary, except with plants having hollow stems like philadelphus. Softwood cuttings usually root easily from almost any part placed underground. Make the cut at a 45 degree angle across the stem.

Remove all leaves from the lower third of the cutting so that they will not be in the rooting medium and decay there. If upper leaves are very large, reduce their size by cutting off part of each. Except for removing what is necessary, remember, at this time, that the more foliage you can leave (without having leaves wilt), the better. Any flower buds on a cutting should be removed. The best time to make cuttings is in early morning. After each is made, wrap it in damp paper or cloth or pop it into a polyethylene plastic bag so that it keeps fresh. Under no circumstances allow cuttings to dry out.

When you have made all the cuttings you wish, plus a few extra to make up for those that do not root, it is time to plant them. For this you need a special rooting medium and a special place. Both of these are discussed under Rooting Mediums on the next page.

Cuttings: This stem of holly is being made into a tip cutting; be sure to cut directly under a leaf.

Semi-Hardwood or Half-Ripened Cuttings

These are taken when wood is partly matured, during summer (July and August) and even sometimes into early September. The exact time will depend on the growth stage of the plant you are propagating. The wood should still be brittle enough to snap across when you bend it double. Cuttings from branch tips should be taken 4 to 6 inches long, with a clean cut made just below a node.

Because softwood or semi-hardwood cuttings of some species seem to root more readily when a bit of the branch is left attached to the cutting, such heels often are left. To take a cutting with a heel, select a side shoot and pull it downward to separate it from the branch. As it comes off, a bit of the branch will adhere to it, both above and below. This adhering part of the branch is the heel. The letter "H" following the name of a shrub in Part III of the appendix indicates that a heel is a desirable addition to cuttings of that shrub.

Handling Softwood and Half-Ripened Cuttings

Rooting Mediums

Rooting mediums should have the following properties: be able to hold cuttings upright, be as sterile as possible so as not to support disease, be loose so that there is good aeration around the rooting cutting, yet hold moisture. These mediums (and some others) meet these requirements: sharp, clean sand (mason's or builder's #2 grade); vermiculite (exploded mica); Perlite, a mixture of 50 percent vermiculite and 50 percent perlite; and sphagnum moss. In some cases sphagnum is used as it comes from the bale, merely shredded with the hands; in others it is milled (ground) before using.

A good rooting medium to use for broad-leaved evergreen shrubs that grow best in acid soil is composed of 75 percent peat moss and 25 percent granular styrofoam.

Probably the best place to put whichever rooting medium you decide to use is in a cold frame. In the case of half-ripened cuttings a cold frame is almost a necessity because of the time of year the cuttings are taken. They must be protected from the winter cold in some way, since it will take 5-15 weeks for them to root and sometimes more than that.

An inexpensive cold frame may be made from a window frame and sash bought at a second-hand lumber yard.

If you do not own a cold frame and wish to root just a few cuttings, try a "double flowerpot." For this propagator you need a 3-inch pot (measured across the top of the pot), and a larger, flattish pot, called a "pan." Plug the drainage hole in the bottom of the 3-inch pot with a small cork. Hold the small pot in the center of the larger one so that the rim of the little

Pot-within-a-pot: Insert cuttings in rooting medium and place it in a large, flat flower pot (called a bulb pan). Set a small pot in the center of the large one (plug the drainage hole with a cork). Put water into the small pot, allowing it to gradually seep into the growing medium.

one is level with that of the big one. Fill the space below and around the little pot with whichever rooting medium you have selected.

The idea of the pot within a pot is that the small one is kept filled with water. Since the hole in the bottom is plugged with a cork, there will be only gradual seepage of water into the rooting medium. Thus it will be kept evenly moist yet never too wet.

The double pot must be set in a shaded place. A tent-like cover of polyethylene plastic may be set over it to keep moisture in. Make this by cutting several wire coat hangers and re-bending them into a U-shape, like croquet wickets. Stick the ends of these Us into the ground over the pot and drape the plastic over these supports, anchoring the ends with soil. If it gets too hot and humid under the plastic, slit it here and there for additional ventilation, and cover the plastic with burlap or newspaper between 11 A.M. and 2 P.M. You can buy a kit that includes a wooden framework large enough to hold two flats or several pans, wire to curve over, and a plastic cover complete with vents.

For more than a very few cuttings, you can make a propagating bed in a shady, sheltered place outdoors by simply digging out the soil to a depth of 4 inches and replacing it with vermiculite or another rooting medium. Plant the cuttings in this, spacing them half an inch apart, and put a plastic tent over them. Just before you insert the cuttings into the rooting medium, it is a good idea to treat the base ends with a root-inducing hormone powder.

Water the rooting medium just before inserting cuttings. Push a third of their length into the medium if rooting them where humidity is high; half of their length if rooting outdoors. Water again when they have been inserted. This second watering settles the medium around the cuttings. Don't forget to label cuttings with the name of the plant from which they were taken and the date on which you made them.

Aftercare

For the first ten days at least, the cuttings need to be shaded and the rooting medium should be kept always moist, never waterlogged. After this, though broad-leaved evergreen cuttings may continue rooting in the shade, those of deciduous shrubs will need a little sun. Adjust the light accordingly.

You can usually tell when roots are forming by the appearance of new top growth. It is also possible to investigate root growth by pushing a bit of the rooting medium aside with a finger and looking at the roots.

Softwood cuttings usually root quicker and easier than other types, though they do require more attention to prevent leaves wilting. They take from 2 to 12 weeks to root and will respond more to higher temperature than other types of cuttings taken later in the season.

When roots are at least an inch long, softwood cuttings may be potted into separate pots or planted in flats or cold frames. This must be done soon after rooting takes place since rooting mediums have little or no nourishment in them, depending on which medium you use. If a peat-styrofoam mixture is used, even softwood cuttings can be left in it over winter. Half-ripened cuttings are left in the frame during winter and transplanted in spring. Some may take that long to root. The more mature the wood from which these cuttings were taken, the longer it will take for roots to form.

If you have only a few cuttings, make a little bed in a protected corner of the garden and transplant cuttings to this, spacing them 6 to 8 inches apart. Or pot them and sink the pots to the rims in such a bed. Keep cuttings well shaded for at least two weeks after transplanting.

If roots are well established in late autumn, the cuttings may be left as they are for the winter and protected from heaving and thawing of the soil by a straw covering, placed after soil is frozen. In early spring you can move them to their permanent positions in the garden.

Rooting Cuttings under Mist

State universities and nurserymen have been experimenting with the use of a constant or an intermittent mist of water to keep leaves of cuttings (especially softwood cuttings) from wilting and to help rooting. With these systems no shading is necessary and plants may be rooted outdoors with great ease even some kinds formerly thought difficult to root.

The gardener who wishes to try propagation under mist needs: (1) a mist nozzle; (2) a place where water is available so the nozzle may be used; (3) a propagating bed that is perfectly drained; (4) polyethylene plastic.

To make the propagating bed, level the area and put coarse

A quiet area to sit and relax is created with an enclosure of shrubs and small trees.

drainage material (coarse gravel or crushed stone) over it to a depth of at least 2 inches. Over this put the rooting medium selected. Box the bed in with boards and peg them in place. Enclose the bed on three sides with polyethylene film supported on a wooden or metal framework. When enclosing the bed, consider the direction of the winds prevailing in your area, for wind can carry the mist away from the cuttings. A shield of plastic properly placed will prevent this.

Install the mist nozzle either in the bed or just outside it, so placed that the mist covers the bed area. The nozzle should use low pressure and may be connected by hose to the water supply. The nozzle is turned on only during the hot part of the day, during which time it may run either constantly or intermittently. Intermittent mist is even more satisfactory than constant mist but requires either a person willing to turn the water on and off or an electric time switch that will do the job.

Unless the nozzle has a very small opening and is carefully adjusted the propagating bed will be drenched and the cuttings will not thrive.

Hardwood Cuttings

These are taken from the plant when wood is mature or hardened after the leaves fall and up until mid-winter, but while the plant still is dormant or resting. A list of shrubs that may be propagated from hardwood cuttings is in the appendix.

Select branches from wood of the current season's growth that are about as thick as a lead pencil. Make cuttings with at least three to four nodes. Since the cuttings should be tied in little bundles and it is easy to confuse which end is up, make your top cuts straight across (square to) the stem, an inch or so above a node, and your bottom cuts just under a node and slanting across the stem. Thus the top and bottom of the cuttings will be marked in a way easily distinguished. Arrange cuttings of each kind of plant in your hand with tops up, level the bottoms against a table top or other surface, and tie the cuttings into bundles. Label each bundle with the name of the shrub from which the cuttings were taken.

The bundles now must be stored for the winter so that a callus will have time to form over the cut ends. This takes at least six to eight weeks, so cuttings must be made at least this long before planting time.

To store indoors one needs a dark cool cellar where temperature can either be controlled or will remain between 40 and 45 degrees F. If temperature can be controlled, store cuttings at 50 to 55 degrees the first month to promote quick callusing, then reduce temperature to between 40 and 45 degrees for the remainder of the winter.

Lacking a cellar, the cuttings can be buried outdoors in a well drained place, in a hole dug to below the frost line.

When cuttings are to be stored indoors they should be buried in a box (preferably wooden) filled with sawdust, soil, sand, or peat, any of these materials being slightly moistened. When cuttings are buried outdoors, they are set into the hole either vertically or horizontally and slightly moistened sand, peat, sphagnum moss, sawdust, or light, sandy soil is packed around them.

As soon as ground can be worked in spring, take the cuttings from storage and plant them in rows in a place in full sun and near a water supply. Dig a V-shaped trench for the cuttings. If you wish them to remain in this place for several years, plant 9 inches to a foot apart and dig trenches 2 feet apart; if you intend to transplant them in fall or the following spring, plant 6 to 8 inches apart and dig trenches a foot apart. In any case, set cuttings so only the top bud or node is above ground, regardless of how many nodes the cutting has. Use sand or sandy soil to fill in around the cuttings. Firm the soil, leaving a slight depression at the top to hold water.

Except for watering as necessary (which will, of course, depend on the weather), no further care is necessary. By fall the cuttings should have sufficient roots to be transplanted where you wish them to grow. Or, you can, if you wish, leave them in the row over winter and transplant them in spring. And you also can leave them in the row for several years.

A line of pink dogwoods (Cornus florida 'Rubra') along a fence row in spring.

Grafting

There are still two other ways to increase shrubs by using a piece of the shrub you want to own. These are grafting and budding. They are similar to one another in that you apply a piece of the plant you want to a plant that is usually less desirable. They differ in plant parts used and in methods.

In grafting, the piece of the desired shrub is made to grow on another shrub by bringing together the growing layers of their stems and holding them until they grow together.

The plant on which the graft is to be made usually is chosen because of its strong growth. It is called the "stock" or "understock" or "rootstock." This plant supplies roots and sometimes part of the stem of the new plant you are going to make. The piece of branch you take from the shrub you want is called a "scion." This will become the top of the new plant.

It is essential that the understock and scion be closely related botanically; otherwise their growing layers will not knit together. Thus you graft holly on holly, rose on rose, and so on. The more closely they are related, the more compatible they will be.

The plant to be the understock should be a strong seedling (which you probably will have to grow yourself since these are virtually unavailable) or a rooted cutting from one to three years old. It is best to decide which plants you will use for understocks in fall, since grafting is done in very early spring, just as the buds start to grow.

Scions are taken from the shrub you wish to multiply while that shrub is dormant (resting, minus leaves or flowers), in very late fall or during winter or in earliest spring. Unless you are bringing scions from a distance, it is easier to cut a few scions in early spring and store them in a plastic bag in the refrigerator. However, if you must take them well ahead of time, tie them in small bundles, label them and bury them in sand or sawdust, using the same procedure as for hardwood cuttings.

In taking scion wood, select that which grew the previous season, because young wood unites more readily with the understock. Twigs that grew a foot or more during the past season are best. You can trace back from the top of the twig to the first growth ring, readily visible on the twig, and thus measure how much growth was made during the season past.

There are numerous types of grafts, such as splice, whip, side, tongue, cleft, bridge, etc., but only two will be discussed here: splice grafting because it is most used with shrubs and is easiest; and bridge grafting because it sometimes offers the only way to save a shrub that has been girdled by rodents.

Splice Grafting

This is one of the easiest ways to graft and is used, usually, when stock and scion are about the same thickness. Both scion and understock are prepared by making, with a razor-sharp knife, diagonal cuts from an inch to two inches long, the stock being cut off at whatever height you wish to graft. The scion should have a matching cut made across the bottom. These

Golden privet (**Ligustrum** x **vicaryi**) *keeps its colorful leaves all year.*

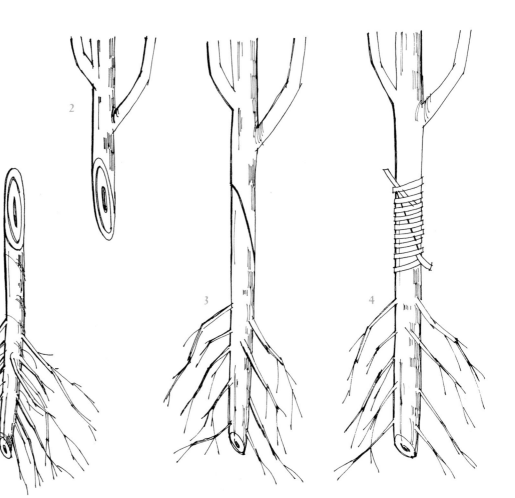

Splice grafting: (From left) Select a plant for rootstock and cut it off at an angle. Cut a scion of the shrub at the same angle. Fit the two together. The closer to the same diameter they are the easier the cambium or growing layer of each will fit together. Fit the scion to the rootstock and bind the two together. Grafting wax may be used to cover the area.

cuts should be made as nearly alike in angle and in diameter as possible, the better to fit one to the other. The cut edges should be carefully fitted together so that the growing layers of stock and scion touch one another as far around the circumference of each part as possible.

The growing layer or cambium is the green layer, usually directly under the outer bark or skin of a branch. It grows between bark and wood. Cut across a branch and you'll see it plainly. This is the only part of a branch that grows and, in order to have the graft take, the cambium of the scion must unite or grow together with that of the stock. This knitting together of stock and scion will take place only when scion buds are dormant.

It rarely is possible to have cambium layers touching all around the circumference of both stock and scion because the stock usually is thicker than the scion, but a substantial part of each must touch.

Once you have stock and scion correctly placed, bind them together so they stay in that position. Raffia, a dried grass from Italy, which comes in hanks and is available from nursery suppliers and seedmen who carry sundries, is the time-honored

material to use. It is soft but not too soft, easy to handle, and will in time disintegrate by itself. Rubber bands or special grafting tape or waxed thin twine will do as well since they will break under pressure as the branch grows larger.

After stock and scion have been tied together, you may wish to cover the entire area of the graft with grafting wax obtained from a garden supply store, or ordinary paraffin from the kitchen. Either of these must be melted over hot water, allowed to cool so that it won't injure the plant but not so much that it begins to solidify, and then applied to the area. This waxing seals the graft from air, infection, and mechanical injury—but it is not absolutely essential to the graft.

In due course of time, exact time depending on the species, the cambium layers of stock and scion will unite and growth of the scion will show when this has happened. Watch to see that the material used for binding stock and scion together does not stay intact and strangle the plant. After the scion has grown a foot or more you may loosen the ties if you wish. Otherwise no special aftercare is necessary, unless growth appears from the understock. As soon as you see it, remove it at the point of origin.

Flowering crabapples and flowering cherries are prominent features in Claude Monet's Garden, at Giverny in France.

Bridge Grafting

When you discover, in early spring, that rabbits, mice, or deer, have girdled (stripped and eaten bark all the way around) your favorite shrub, first aid is in order. If done as soon as you find the injury, bridge grafting may save the shrub.

In this type of grafting you actually bridge the gap where the bark no longer exists with several scions, splicing the cambium layer below the girdling with that above and thus allowing continued flow of nutrients and water within the plant. The number of scions used will depend on the circumference of the girdled plant. Use enough so that eventually they will grow together and replace the bark of the girdled portion. Even one scion used as a bridge may save the shrub. Two or even three may be used on a fair-sized shrub.

Scions should be taken while still dormant (though in an emergency they may be taken when buds have started to grow if these developing buds are immediately removed). Wood used should be from growth of the previous year that is from ¼ to ½ inch in diameter. Naturally the scions must be from a compatible or related species. Be sure, when making them, to mark which end of each scion is up by the same system as previously described under Hardwood Cuttings.

Before grafting, prepare the injured area on your shrub by trimming off any loose or wounded bark until you have only healthy, undamaged tissue. Cut this back until there is a straight line of bark around the plant at both upper and lower edges of the girdled area.

Cut slots in the bark just above and just below the girdled area, each from 2 to 3 inches long and precisely the width of the scion to be inserted in each. Cut only through the bark, leaving a ½ to ¾ inch long flap of bark at each end of the slot and removing bark from the rest of the vertical area you are preparing. Now, having tailored each slot to a specific scion, tailor scions to fit the slots, making each just long enough to

fit into one pair of slots, plus enough extra length so the scion will be slightly bowed when inserted. This bowing is for two purposes: to allow for good contact between cambium layers of stock and scion, and to allow for necessary movement when the branch or trunk sways in the wind.

To tailor a scion, make long, smooth, slanting cuts on the same side of the scion, at both top and bottom of it, each cut the same length so the scion will fit smoothly when inserted into the slot. On the opposite side of the scion from these cuts, make ½-inch slanting cuts so that a scion actually will be wedge-shaped at either end. Trim off any buds on the scion, as these are not desirable.

Insert each scion in the slot made for it, pushing the top wedge of the scion under the flap of bark left for it at the top of the girdled area, with the long, slanting cut against branch or trunk. Then insert the bottom of the scion the same way. Check to make sure scions are right side up. Nail scions in place, using very small, flat-headed, wire nails. Use a nail through each flap of bark and more if necessary, so the scions will stay as you have placed them and not pull out of place. Cover the places where scions meet branch or trunk and the entire girdled area very carefully and thoroughly with grafting wax or paraffin. It is as important to keep air from the girdled area as from the places where scions touch branch because dried wood is not conducive to good growth of the shrub.

There is no reason to remove nails later, when scions have grown in place. But, if growth starts from buds on scions, be sure to remove these shoots.

These beautiful blossoms are from a flowering crabapple (Malus 'Radiant') in early spring.

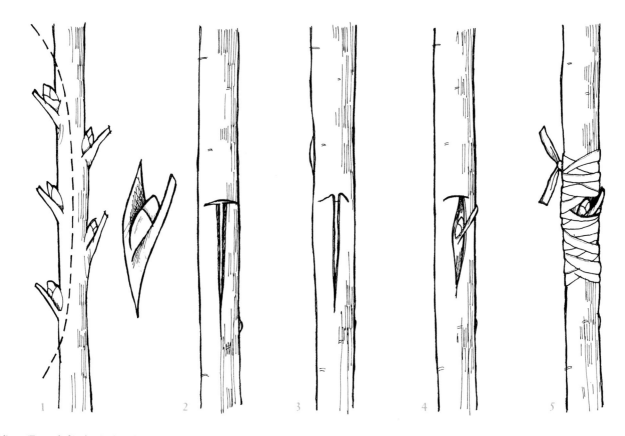

1   2   3   4   5

Budding: (From left) A "bud stick" (indicated with dotted line) is a piece of the desired shrub with many buds on it. Remove the leaves but leave parts of their stems as "handles." Cut one of the buds from the bud stick leaving a small bit of bark on it above and below and one leaf-stem handle. Make a T-shaped cut through the bark of the understock only. Lift the bark gently and insert the bud. Push it down until it fits snugly against the cambium layer under the bark. Replace the bark over the bud, and bound it in place.

Budding

Budding is a kind of grafting in which a single bud of a desired variety, with a bit of bark attached, is inserted into the stem of an understock. This operation is performed during late summer (late July to early September) when the bark slips easily—in other words may be readily separated or peeled from the wood of the stem or trunk.

Because of this timing, the bud scion material (called by the nurseryman "budstick") always is of the current year's growth. To make a budstick, first select a stem about the diameter of a pencil on the plant you want to propagate. Cut off all the leaves except a portion of the leaf stems (petioles), which you leave on to serve as handles. Then cut a thin segment from this stem that includes the bark and the buds with their handles intact. This is your budstick.

Under normal circumstances you will cut a budstick from the plant you wish to own and then perform the budding operation. If, however, the plant you wish to own is at a distance and you are going to transport budsticks, put them in water or wrap them in polyethylene plastic bags to carry them. If you must store them, they will keep for several days in plastic bags, in a refrigerator at about 40 degrees.

The budding operation consists of cutting a single bud, with its attached bark above and below it (called a shield) from the budstick, making a T-shaped cut in the bark only, not into the cambium of the stock, lifting the bark, and inserting the bud right side up under the bark and on top of the cambium layer of the stock. Since you can gently lift the bark with the tip of a budding knife and expose the cambium only when the bark slips easily, the reason for budding when this is possible (in late summer) becomes clear.

The bud, once it has been inserted in the T-shaped cut, must be gently pushed down until it fits snugly against the cambium. Some budders remove any wood in back of the bud before inserting it, to get a better fit. The bark is allowed to settle back in place and then the bud is tied into place, using rubber bands, special grafting rubbers, or grafting tape or raffia or similar materials. Rubber strips or tape may be cut in three weeks.

Early in the following spring, the top of the stock is cut off just above the bud you inserted, and the ties that held the bud in place are removed. By this time the bud should have grown firmly in place and the growth from it will become the top of the plant. If you wish to grow the plant in tree form, instead of as a shrub, cut off the top of the stock 6 inches above the bud and tie the stem that grows from the bud to this stub so it will grow vertically and straight. Watch budded plants to see if the understock tries to grow. If so, take off any growth at point of origin from the stock.

If, at this point, you wonder why anyone would graft or bud a plant when it is so much simpler to divide it, or to grow it by layering or from cuttings, the answer is that certain plants cannot be reproduced easily by those methods (and many plants will not come true from seed) so the best way to propagate them is by grafting or budding. These two processes also are used when plants do not grow strongly on their own roots, or to make weeping forms of shrubs or trees.

Grafting or budding also may be used to solve the problem of pollination, as when a female holly plant is not producing berries and obviously needs pollen from male flowers. In such a case one or several branches of a male holly may be grafted or buds budded onto the female plant.

Larger Plants Sooner

The nurseryman uses grafting or budding for another purpose, which is important to those who buy shrubs. He uses it to make a saleable sized plant more rapidly than he could by any other method. Most of the time this is satisfactory to the purchaser of the shrub, though a grafted or budded plant always needs an extra bit of supervision lest the understock produce shoots. If the graft or bud is close to where the soil line was where the plant grew previously, setting the plant so that the union is several inches below the soil line will discourage the understock from growing shoots.

A hardy pink-flowering hybrid rhododendron was created by crossing a hardy American species with a less hardy Himalayan species.

In some cases, however, as in the grafting or budding of lilac on privet, this practice by nurserymen is decidedly undesirable. For one thing a disease may develop. For another, privet is a stronger grower than lilac and even though privet leaves are very different in appearance from lilac leaves, the uninitiated gardener may not notice that the understock has grown until the privet has outgrown the lilac and he sees the undistinguished white flowers of privet where before he had large, beautiful lilac blooms.

This type of undesirable growth is not restricted to privet. My *Viburnum carlesii*, since it was allowed to grow for picture purposes, is now a dual shrub—the lower part *Viburnum carlesii*, the upper and much larger part, *Viburnum lantana*. *Carlesii* was budded onto *lantana* because *lantana* is a strong-rooting shrub while *carlesii* is not. However, I would much prefer the less sturdy growth of *carlesii* on its own roots than the chore of hacking back and keeping back the *lantana* growth.

These examples are given to show you that more than one kind of shrub is grafted or budded on an understock by the nurseryman and that, in every case, the understock may become a problem to the gardener who owns the shrub. Thus the gardener must be ever watchful.

In the case of roses, the most popular outdoor plant in America today, this problem becomes acute, for roses are grown in innumerable localities where winters are sufficiently cold to kill the named variety top that has been budded onto a rootstock. In this case, unless plants are carefully protected, the gardener will be shocked to find that the big, beautifully colored flowers of the named variety he bought have been replaced by the smaller, definitely less desirable, flowers of the understock.

Before leaving this interesting subject of growing a new plant from a piece of an existing one, an important point must be made. Cultivars of shrubs always must be propagated by one of the methods previously described for any of these will produce a plant resembling the parent, whereas propagating by seed will not, as you will see when you read on.

Seedage

Shrubs may, of course, be grown from seed. Some that grow very easily in this way will present you with "volunteer" seedlings each year, under or near the female parent plant. If you grow these to flowering size, you will often find that their flowers do not exactly resemble those of the plant you found them under. This is because they probably had two parents, not just one as did the plants reproduced by the methods already described. Therefore they have inheritance that is far wider than the one-parent plants and often do not come true from seed, that is, resemble either parent. Of course the female

A mass planting of hardy rhododendrons cascades down a hillside at Longwood Gardens, Kennett Square, Pennsylvania.

parent is the only one of which you are certain, unless you yourself have applied the pollen that produced the seed and have kept away all other pollen and thus are familiar with the flowers of the plant from which it came.

It is precisely because of this wide variation in plants grown from seeds that nurseries or people interested in new varieties grow shrubs from seeds. Among thousands of seedlings there may be one that has foliage or flowers or form noticeably different from any shrub of that genus or species already in commerce. This seedling may be named by the nursery or person propagating it and, in time, become a popular new cultivar.

If you will examine closely the flower of almost any shrub, you will see first the conspicuous parts, the petals, which are usually white or brightly colored. Around the outsides of the petals at their bases are shorter, green or greenish or sometimes other colored parts called sepals. These two groups of parts, the petals collectively called corolla and the sepals collectively called calyx, are held in a thickened part of the flower

stem, which is called the receptacle. The flower stem itself is called the peduncle. All these parts you will see at a glance.

But, in the center of the flower, usually surrounded by the petals, there are smaller, less readily visible parts. These are of two different kinds. Near the center there is usually one, but sometimes several thickened parts; and around this or these are more slender parts that vary in number. The thickened part is called the pistil and is the female organ; the slender parts are the stamens, the male organs.

The stamens produce the pollen that, when deep yellow and ripe, may be deposited on the tip of the pistil. This tip, when ready for pollination, is sticky and thus holds the pollen deposited on it. The pollen grain then germinates, grows a pollen tube downward, through the style (stem part of the pistil) to the ovary below. Reaching the ovary, the pollen grain unites with one of the ovules in the ovary, and fertilizes it. From this fertilized ovule a seed gradually develops. The ripened ovary becomes the fruit.

Scarlet honeysuckle (Lonicera sempervirens) *decorates a picket fence.*

Flowers of a few shrubs lack some of these flower parts: petals in *Fothergilla*, pistils in *Alnus* or alder. In flowers of other shrubs, parts are more or less united (petals in *Lonicera* or honeysuckle, stamens in *Baccharis*, pistils in Rhodoendron). However, most of the shrubs you may wish to grow from seed will have all the flower parts clearly visible.

There are two types of flowers in flowering plants, called perfect and imperfect. The perfect flowers have both stamens and pistil or pistils, that is both male and female organs, in the center of the flower. Most shrubs have this kind of flower. The imperfect flowers have either stamens or pistil but not both.

Imperfect flowers are borne sometimes on the same plant as perfect ones; sometimes male flowers are borne on one part or several branches of a plant, female flowers on another part or branches of the same plant; and again, male and female flowers may be borne on separate plants.

When they are on separate plants it is obvious that, in order to get seeds, the gardener must own plants of both sexes (or graft or bud a part of a plant of one sex onto that of another) since the female flowers produce fruit and therefore seeds but not without pollination by pollen from a male flower. Holly (*Ilex*) is an excellent example of this type of plant—male flowers are borne on one plant, females on another. The gardener who wonders why his holly does not bear red berries should examine the flowers when they appear in May and see if they are male or female. If he then purchases a plant of the opposite sex, it should be set within 40 feet of the first one to insure good pollination.

Under normal circumstances, the wind, the bees, butterflies, or sometimes simply gravity will carry pollen from one flower to another on the same plant or from a flower of one plant to a flower on another plant and so seed is set.

Plants with perfect flowers usually will fertilize themselves or each other but occasionally the pollen from flowers of one plant will not fertilize flowers of the same plant. Such is the case with many varieties of fruit trees. Pollen from another tree of another variety is necessary to fertilize flowers of the first tree and produce the fruits that contain the seeds.

Controlling Parentage

When you want to control the parentage of the seed you wish to grow, you can select both parent plants. Remove the stamens as soon as the flower or flowers open on the plant selected as female parent, so that they cannot ripen pollen, and cover the flower or flowers with small plastic bags to prevent wind or insects from depositing pollen on the pistil. When the pollen is ripe on the plant selected as male parent, use a soft brush to remove a bit from the anther (tip) of a stamen, remove the cover over the flower on the female parent, and deposit the pollen on the sticky apex of the pistil. Then replace the cover over the pollinated flower. Under normal circumstances this flower will produce seeds and you will know the immediate parentage of that seed.

This still does not necessarily mean that the seedlings will resemble either parent, because ancestors also contribute to their appearance. But a percentage will resemble one parent or the other.

Assuming that you have made a cross of pollen from one parent onto the pistil of a flower of another parent, you next must wait for the fruits to ripen. This you also must do if you wish to collect seeds from naturally fertilized plants.

Ripeness usually is told by the changing color of the fruit. Holly berries change from green to red (sometimes first to yellow or orange). Drying and splitting of seed coverings also is a sign of ripeness. When these signs show you it is time, gather the fruits and, if necessary, treat them to extract the seeds. This is a very simple matter with such shrubs as Roses because you need only split open the fruits (hips) and harvest the seeds.

It is a little harder with shrubs that bear fleshy seeds like currants (*Ribes*) or honeysuckles (*Lonicera*) because you have to remove the flesh in order to get the seed. By soaking these seeds in water you can reduce the flesh to a soft mass. Then, with your fingers, you can separate seeds from flesh. Sometimes fleshy fruits are merely dried, then the seeds with dried flesh attached are planted. The same thing may be done with seeds that have appendages adhering to them, as maple (*Acer*).

With the seeds ready for planting, recall to your mind those volunteer seedlings that grew so well under and near the mother plant. This recollection gives you the right idea as to the environment you should try to reproduce in order that the seeds germinate (sprout) and grow well. A great many amateurs simply plant the seeds under the parent plant, but care for them by giving them water when needed until they have sprouted and grown. This works well with seeds that are ready to sprout soon after they are planted, like ornamental horse-chestnuts (*Aesculus*). They can be either planted right after they are harvested or stored outdoors, in a container, for the winter, then planted in spring.

But there is a little matter of individuality with seeds. Many of them do not sprout readily. Some don't because they are not chemically ready to sprout, others because the conditions necessary for growth are not satisfactory. Still others have hard seed coats that resist the penetration of the air and moisture necessary for sprouting.

An arbor of Chinese wisteria (**Wisteria sinensis**) *forms an alcove against a stone wall.*

Dormancy

Those seeds that are not yet ready to germinate are said to be dormant, which means resting. There are a number of reasons for dormancy, the first being the hard seed coat that will not permit penetration of the necessary oxygen and water. For the same reason, the bud inside the seed may not be able to penetrate outward. The temperature outside the seed may not be right (some seeds sprout only at certain temperatures). Or the light may not be right (some seeds need light to sprout, others will not sprout in light). Then again, there are times when the conditions inside the seed itself are not right for germination to take place. When two of these factors affect the seed dormancy, it is said to be doubly dormant.

Breaking Dormancy

Something has to be done to break the dormancy if the seed is to be sprouted and grown. If the seed has a hard coat, there are two commonly used methods of circumventing it: (1) Put it in water that has just stopped boiling and let it soak in that water as it gradually cools for about 12 hours. (2) Use a small file to open the seed coat in one place. This method requires patience and a delicate touch.

Which one of the two methods you use will depend on the hardness of the coat of the particular seed. Seeds that have the hardest coats will require the second method.

Stratification

When dormancy is caused by conditions within the seed, the seed may merely need a period of after-ripening during which it is supposed that chemical changes take place in the seed that allow it to germinate. This period of after-ripening may be speeded up by a process known as cold stratification. While the word cold still belongs in the name, since seeds are exposed to low temperatures as well as given moisture and air, the stratification usually does not belong since seeds are routinely mixed with whatever medium is selected to hold them rather than placed in layers between layers of the medium, as used to be the practice. Yet cold stratification is the term still commonly used.

Select the medium you prefer to mix the seeds with from sand (best for seeds that have pulp remaining around them), granulated peat moss (acid peat if plants are those requiring acid soil like rhododendrons), or shredded sphagnum moss.

Find a container that will hold some of the medium plus the seeds. This could be a glass jar, a plastic bag, or a tin can. Mix the seeds with the moist (but not saturated) medium, or put them in layers between layers of the medium if you wish. Cover the jar or can to keep moisture in so that seeds will not dry out, but not so tightly as to keep all air out. Closed polyethylene plastic bags permit passage of air while retaining moisture. Store the containers in the refrigerator. A temperature of 40 degrees is an ideal one during stratification, but most refrigerators are set at about 45 degrees, a deviation too slight to cause any trouble. Look at the seeds occasionally and, if any show signs of sprouting, take them out and plant them. If it is winter, plant them in pots indoors.

Some seeds, like American hollies' (*Ilex opaca*), do not seem to be mature enough to sprout until about two years after they have been harvested. Do not despair when seeds you have fussed over do not respond in what seems to you a reasonable length of time. Maybe they just aren't ready to grow yet. Be patient!

The seeds that are doubly dormant may need several of these treatments before they will sprout. Try this treatment for them: mix seeds with the medium, store in a polyethylene bag at room temperature for four months, then in the refrigerator for another four months.

Planting Seeds

Select a half-shaded place in the garden where soil is good. Prepare a bed by removing stones, mixing peat or sand with the existing soil if necessary, and tilling the soil until the texture is fine. Make the bed narrow enough so you can weed it by reaching in from either side. Sow the seeds by broadcasting over the surface of the bed, or make rows and sow in those. Cover lightly with sand. Keep the soil evenly moist but not wet. If it dries rapidly, put a piece of burlap over the surface to keep moisture in. The burlap, however, must be removed at first signs of growth.

If you make the bed in spring, keep weeding and watering it as needed. In about 30 days quite a few seeds should have sprouted. These should be kept in this seedbed until large enough to transplant. If you make the bed in fall, plan to protect seedlings from rodents. Bend a piece of wire screening so it will cover the bed. After planting the seeds and covering them with sand, put on the screening cover and leave the bed alone for winter. By spring many of the seeds will have grown and you may be able to transplant some.

Very fine seeds like those of rhododendron are stored for the winter and are sown in spring over the surface of flats or pots filled with sieved, moist, acid peat moss. They are not covered, just watered with the finest possible mist spray. The flat or pot is covered with glass or plastic, set in a warm, semi-dark place where the temperature is 65 to 70 degrees F, and moved to a light, airy one when sprouting starts. Young seedlings are then moved into flats filled with 50 percent granulated Dutch or German peat and 50 percent Michigan peat. After ten months, move into the nursery row.

Transplanting

When seedlings are large enough they may be transplanted to a nursery row, where they are spaced from 6 to 9 inches apart, and grown there for a year or two (depending on the size of the plant), after which it is time to move them wherever you want them to grow to full size.

Most shrubs may be moved to a nursery bed made in the same manner as the seedling bed, though the soil need not be as fine and the bed should be in full sun. The acid soil–loving plants, sprouted in peat, are transplanted into a mixture of 1 part sand, 2 parts each of very acid peat and mildly acid or neutral peat. In this they can be grown for almost a year, after which they are transplanted again to a cold frame or a bed raised above the surrounding soil level, into a mixture of half garden soil and half granulated acid peat.

A grassy path wanders through plantings of shrubs and small trees in a woodland setting.

Rhododendrons and Spanish bluebells are perfect companions in this woodland garden at Winterthur Museum, near Wilmington, Delaware.

Winter Protection

All small seedlings require some protection from winter's cold. Covering the seedling bed with granulated corn cobs or straw or some other light mulch material is sufficient protection, but this covering should not be placed until after the soil is frozen, otherwise rodents may make their winter homes in it. The covering is intended to keep the soil frozen and thus avoid the alternate freezing and thawing of soil that might heave the seedlings out of the soil entirely. Chicken wire around the bed will protect seedlings from rodents.

SUMMING UP

It is easy to grow some shrubs from seed; not so easy to grow others. With these it may be a long, fussy process. But growing shrubs from seed can be an interesting hobby.

Many gardeners find the other methods of propagating shrubs equally interesting as a hobby and are thrilled to see—several years from the time cuttings, layers, or grafts were made—first blooms on a shrub they have grown from a bit of the parent plant. Occasionally, a shrub is propagated by one method or the other because of sheer necessity—it is absolutely the only way to acquire that particular variety of plant.

It should always be borne in mind that many woody ornamental plants are patented. These may not be vegetatively propagated (that is, increased by any method other than seeds, which may not reproduce the desired plant) without the permission of the owner of the patent.

And, should you be one of the lucky ones to produce a shrub different from all others (which should be carefully checked with authorities at your nearest state university before you jump to conclusions), please take the trouble to name it correctly and thus avoid thwarting botanists, nurserymen and many others.

Part Four

Shrubs and Trees to Know and Grow

12

SHRUBS TO KNOW AND GROW

The purpose of this chapter is to tell you, in quite a bit of detail, about the shrubs that are available for your garden. The descriptions are of the shrubs as I know them, through presently growing over a thousand, through previously having grown hundreds more, through observations in countless nurseries and thousands of gardens, including all major botanical gardens, in many parts of the world.

The heights given are those of the largest shrubs of each kind I ever have seen or, if the shrub was immature when I saw it, the height to which the nurseryman or the director of the botanical garden (if he knew) said it grew. In the case of the comparatively few shrubs that I have neither grown nor seen growing, the height given is that shown in standard reference books.

Flower sizes, where they are indicated, were measured by me in my own garden, several times in several different years, using a transparent ruler.

Sometimes a flower form is described as pea-shaped. By this I do not mean that it is round like a pea, but is shaped like the flower of either a sweet pea or an edible pea.

Single flowers have one row of petals. Semi-double flowers have several rows of petals, while double flowers may have so many petals that their form is ball-like. The reason that double flowers do not produce fruits is that the pollen-producing stamens (seen in the centers of single and semi-double flowers) have developed into petals. Without pollen there can be no fruit or seed production. Thus double-flowered shrubs must be propagated by some vegetative means.

The zones of hardiness, or areas in which a given shrub will survive, are numbered according to those shown on the Plant Hardiness Zone Map. This map is in the adapted version, which is small and suitable for reproduction (see Appendix Part V). A much larger map, with zones shown in colors, with finer gradations of zones into *a* (northerly) and *b* (southerly) and with all counties and large cities indicated, is part of Miscellaneous Publication Number 814. The larger version is the one you probably will wish to use to find the plant hardiness zone in which you live. Both maps were compiled by a commission of the then American Horticultural Council.

Degrees of shade that a plant will tolerate without ceasing to bloom are defined at the top of the list of shade tolerant plants in Part I of the Appendix.

The shrub listings are alphabetical by botanical names, because the only way you can be sure of buying the shrub you want is by using these names. If you know only a common name, look first in the index where such names are given followed by the correct botanical name. Older botanical names, no longer correct, and incorrect catalog names are all listed as synonyms in parentheses following the currently correct botanical name. "Syn" has been used as an abbreviation for "synonymous with."

The " × " between genus and species names of a shrub (e.g. *Abelia × grandiflora*) indicates that it is a hybrid and its parents are those given in parentheses after the botanical name of the shrub (*A. chinensis × A. uniflora*). This information will be of value to nurserymen and gardeners hoping to propagate, for it means that seeds taken from the shrub are not at all likely to produce one identical with it.

Our cultivar designations do not have " × " in front of them to designate that they are hybrids but, in most cases, any binomial, that is a two-word name, of which the second name represents a cultivar is a hybrid.

I have followed the common practice of using only the initial of a generic name in discussions after the genus already

Rhododendrons are popular, hardy shrubs where soil is acidic in North America.

An avenue planted with Golden-chain tree (Laburnum × watereri) *creates a bright canopy over a walkway.*

has been named. Thus *Abelia grandiflora* is followed by *A. chinensis*.

In addition to as many synonyms as possible, I also have listed, following the botanical name of each shrub, as many common names as I have been able to find. Those used in standard reference books and in catalogs have been augmented by names of woody plants collected over a period of 30 years by R. Milton Carleton, compiler of *Index of Common Names of Herbaceous Plants*.

As you will see, if you examine the common names listed for each shrub, these vary widely. In fact they may not be the same from state to state or from locality to locality, as explained in Chapter 2. Furthermore, if you will look at the variety of common names after, for instance, *Calycanthus floridus*, you will see why it is impossible and, in fact, downright silly to attempt to designate a shrub by a common name. Even if it has only one that is widely used, that one cannot be depended upon to be the only one. Step over the border into Canada or fly to London and the common name may change. The botanical name usually is identical in any country (the word "usually" is a disclaimer, to cover the times when the person from one country is using the currently correct name and the person from the other country is using an older name).

If you wish to know which plant is a variety and which a cultivar, with a view to determining a method of propagation, look at the way the name is written. All cultivar names are enclosed by single quotation marks and the first letter of the cultivar name is a capital. Varietal names are not set off and not capitalized. Names that are enclosed by double quotation marks are those not yet recognized by botanists—called invalid. The shrub bearing such a name may vary from others and the nurseryman naming it realizes this, but botanists simply haven't gotten around to recognizing it.

When I refer to the species in Chapters 12, 13 and 14, I mean the species to which the particular shrub belongs. For instance, *Kerria japonica* is the name of a species of shrubs. *Kerria japonica* 'Picta' differs from the species, that is *K. japonica*, by having green and white leaves instead of plain green ones. It resembles the species in having single flowers. *Kerria japonica* 'Pleniflora' differs from the species because of its double flowers, although it resembles the species in growth habit and foliage color and form.

In order to make clear my descriptions of the forms of shrubs, I had sketches made from the shrubs in my garden and drew the outlines on the right. Thus, you always can refer to them if you wish to reconcile my words with your mental picture of what they mean. There are, of course, other shrub forms, but these are the most common ones you will meet and I shall describe most often.

The natural habitat of as many native shrubs as possible is

An array of flowering shrubs adorn a simple, flagstone garden path.

given to serve as a guide to whether a shrub will survive your climate. This information also should make you swell with pride that the northern part of the continent has so many natives worthy of cultivation in gardens.

Should you regard the planting of "native" plants with derision, may I remind you that all plants, except those known as cultivars, are native to some part of the world.

Blooming times, given as early, mid-, or late in a certain month, are the times the shrubs bloom in my garden in hardiness Zone 5b. You can adjust the blooming time given to that in your garden by adding or subtracting a week for every 100 miles that you live north or south of Detroit. This is on the theory that frost moves northward at the rate of 15 miles a day and that flower bloom depends on the time frost disappears—a theory that will not stand close analysis but that at least furnishes you a guide.

In order that you get the most information from this chapter, I would suggest that you read the general discussion of a genus if there is one under the genus heading. This covers characteristics shared by members of the genus or, sometimes, ways in which they are used in the landscape.

Then go on to read the description of the particular species, variety or cultivar of shrub that interests you.

For more ready reference the main listing of each genus is capitalized in boldface type. Species of a genus are paragraphed. Varieties and cultivars of a species are arranged in alphabetical order.

1. Narrow, upright

2. Horizontal

3. Few stems, widely spreading

4. Upright and arching or fountain forms

5. Irregular

Illustration by Anne L. Meskey

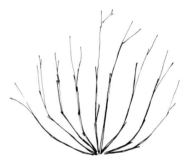

6. Upright and spreading

7. Upright with curving branches

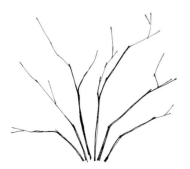

8. Upright, widely spreading

9. Tree form or standard form with single stem

10. Dense and compact

Abelia 'Edward Goucher' (A. grandiflora × A. schumannii).

Not as vigorous in growth as *A. grandiflora* and not as hardy (only to Zone 6), this semi-evergreen hybrid looks much like *A. grandiflora* but has larger flowers, more lavender or purplish pink in color.

Abelia × grandiflora (syn A. rupestris) (A. chinensis × A. uniflora) (Glossy abelia, Bush-arbutus or, sometimes, just Arbutus)
Zone 5b; 6′ in the south, 3′ in Zone 5

This is a pretty and useful densely growing shrub with small, glossy leaves that are evergreen further south, but deciduous in Zone 5. Beginning in late June it has pale pink tubular flowers, ¾″ long, in clusters, which it continues to bear until frost. After they have gone, the rose-colored calyxes (the plant parts that surround the petals) remain on the plant and are effective for weeks. The leaves turn bronzy in autumn, deep bronzy-purple as winter approaches, and remain that color for as long as they stay on the shrub, which depends on the weather.

In Zone 5b this shrub needs a protected situation, for even in such a place it kills to the ground in severe winters, but it grows again from the roots each spring. Usually there is some winterkill even when the winter isn't severe. This means a slight pruning job in early spring, to cut out the dead wood. In milder climates, as on Long Island, New York (Zone 7), abelias are sometimes cut to the ground each spring in order to keep them from getting leggy. This drastic pruning is possible because the flowers are borne on wood of the current season's growth.

Abelia likes best a light, peaty soil but will grow in any reasonably good soil with no special preparation needed.

Abelias are prettiest combined with broad-leaved or needled evergreens because their glossy leaves show best then. South of Zone 5 abelias are used for pruned or unpruned hedges and are well adapted to this use because of the many fine twigs.

Abelia × grandiflora 'Prostrata' (Prostrate glossy abelia)
Zone 6 to southern part of Zone 5 (in a protected place); 2′

This plant is just what the Latin name says it is—a prostrate or almost prostrate form of glossy abelia. Flowers are white, growth is dense, and the plant is an excellent ground cover where it is hardy.

Aesculus parviflora

AESCULUS

Aesculus parviflora (Bottlebrush buckeye)
Zone 5; 8′–10′

The height of this shrub does not give a true idea of its size because, in time, it may grow twice as broad as it does high or even more.

This means that when planting it, space must be allowed for the shrub to spread. This it does by means of underground suckers.

The flowers appear in late July and August when few other shrubs bloom and, partly because of the long pink stamens of the white flowers (the clusters of which look not unlike candles) and partly because of the gray undersides of the leaves, the effect of a shrub in bloom is feathery.

The seeds that follow the blooms are deep brown, enclosed in capsules ¼″ long, ⅜″ wide at the widest point, which first are bright yellow then turn brownish orange. Stems with capsules on them are widely used in Japan in flower arrangements.

Foliage turns from green to yellow in autumn, giving a second season of interest.

Aesculus parviflora will grow in any reasonably good soil. It tolerates slight shade but grows better in full sun. It is a handsome shrub when well grown; native from South Carolina to Alabama.

Abelia × grandiflora

Aesculus pavia (syn *A. pavia rubra*)
(**Red buckeye**)
Zone 5
In its native habitat, from Florida to Virginia and westward to Louisiana and West Virginia, this buckeye may grow either as a shrub or as a small tree. It may be as small as 4' or as tall as 20'.

It is similar to *A. parviflora* in its horse chestnut–like leaf and in the fact that it usually grows broader than it does high. Flower clusters are the same shape as those of *A. parviflora* but the flowers are bright reddish-rose and appear, not in late summer, but in May and June. Oddly, they rarely open fully.

Do not prune leader. Prune away dead branches as needed.

A. pavia also is tolerant of many soil conditions, though it too responds to good soil. This plant rarely is listed by nurseries and the few that carry it may not always have it in stock when you want to buy it.

Aesculus pavia

ALTHEA

(see HIBISCUS)

AMELANCHIER

(Shadbush, Shadblow, June-berry, Service-berry, Bilberry, Canadian medlar, Maycherry, Sugar-pear, Showy Mespilus)

The chief reason for growing any shadblow is the white flowers that open in late April or early May before the leaves fully expand. Should the weather at that time of year turn warm, these blooms will last only two or three days, but if the weather is first sufficiently warm to allow the flowers to open, then turns cool and stays cool, the blooms may be in good condition for as long as ten days.

All shadblows are suitable for woodlands or along the margins of streams or lakes, especially when there are taller trees back of them. The sight of a shadblow in flower against black water is one to remember.

After the flowers have finished blooming, there still is some interest to the gardener in amelanchiers in the coloration of the new leaves of some species, but after leaves are fully grown, an amelanchier is just another shrub until the fruits color. Most gardeners never see this stage for birds eat fruits as soon as the first bit of color (other than green) appears. In autumn, some amelanchiers have outstanding yellow foliage color.

Amelanchier alnifolia
(**Saskatoon**)
Zone 1; 10'
Native in Canada from the Yukon southward to Ontario and in the United States from Oregon eastward to Iowa, this shrub is used in the north for its early white flowers, usually appearing in May. Edible, blue-purple to blue-black fruits ripen in July.

The common name of this shrub is that of a city in Saskatchewan, named for the shrub.

Amelanchier stolonifera

Amelanchier stolonifera
(**Creeping service-berry**)
Zone 3; 4'
This is one amelanchier that is not normally found in moist places. Instead, it grows in poor, dry soil and exposed areas, often in rocky sites. Upright growing, but creeping by underground stolons, this shrub forms patches of growth that will hold loose soil in place. For this reason, it is useful on banks or in wild areas where soil needs holding. It blooms in late May to early June and the almost black, juicy, edible fruits ripen in July to August. This is one of the best species for fruits. A bloom like that on plums overlays the fruits. Do not prune leader. Prune away dead branches as needed.

AMORPHA

(Bastard-indigo, False-indigo, Indigo-bush)

Amorpha fruticosa
(**Bastard-indigo, False-indigo, Indigo-bush**)
Zone 4, possibly Zone 3; 12'
This usually is seen as an awkward shrub because it has been allowed to grow without pruning. Fortunately,

whenever it grows too widespread and open, it may be cut to the ground in early spring and will grow again from the roots. Since the flowers are borne on wood of the current season's growth, there will be no lost season of bloom.

Leaves of this amorpha are on the gray side of green, but not gray like those of *A. canescens*, a close relative. The flowers are tiny, borne in long spikes, opening in July. The false-indigo rarely has a spike of blooms that are all open and perfect at the same time. A notable feature of the flowers, pretty when seen at close range, is their golden stamens against their violet-purple petals.

False-indigo, because it grows wild along streams from Florida to Wisconsin, is said to prefer a moist soil. In both this garden and my former one, the plants have done well in dry, sandy soil. Seed pods of false-indigo, which are purplish-brown, stay on all winter, giving winter interest.

ARALIA

Aralia spinosa
(Hercules' club, Devil's walking stick, Angelica-tree, Tearblanket, Monkeytree, Prickly ash)
Zone 5; 20'–30'

This tree-like shrub is exotic in appearance and might be suitable for use as an accent plant in an Oriental-style or perhaps a Mediterranean-type landscape, but in the average landscape it sticks out like a sore thumb. Flowers are white; small, but grouped in large clusters; open in August. Leaves are very long, sometimes to three feet. Fruits, which ripen in September and are popular with birds, are small black berries on red stems. Branches are thick and spiny. This shrub tolerates almost any soil; will grow in the light shade of tall trees as well as in sun. Plants pruned to the ground will normally sprout new shoots.

ARONIA
(Chokeberry)

These hardy shrubs usually are recommended for use because of their colorful berries, but I think the white flowers in late May are just as pretty as those of many other shrubs grown chiefly for flowers. The leaves of some aronias are shining and are attractive all season.

Aronias grow best in moist soil, but will tolerate dry places too. They do well in full sun or light shade. They may be used at the edge of a woodland or in a shrub border. All are upright and slightly spreading in growth, easy to move and to grow.

Aronia arbutifolia
(Red chokeberry)
Zone 5; 6'

Native from Ontario and Nova Scotia to Michigan and Missouri and southward to Florida and Texas, this aronia has the showiest fruit of any—bright red, but only ¼″ in diameter. It usually is produced in abundance. If the shrub is not in too-deep shade, the leaves turn red in fall and contrast beautifully with the berries.

Aronia arbutifolia 'Brilliantissima' has even more abundant, glossy, red berries. Apparently birds do not like them and the berries therefore hang on the shrub until late in winter.

Aronia arbutifolia

Aralia spinosa

AZALEA

Botanists classify all azaleas as rhododendrons. A few progressive nurserymen follow the botanists but most nurseries continue to list these plants as azaleas in catalogs and call them azaleas in sales lots. In order to reconcile the names, I have listed below the name given in most catalogs for each azalea in this book and, in the second column, the proper botanical name.

In an effort to bridge the gap between the thinking of botanists and nurserymen, I am discussing the rhododendrons called azaleas under the heading of Azalea, but they are listed under their proper names (that is under Rhododendron) in the Bloom Time Chart in the appendix.

Hybrid groups widely available in the catalogs are listed below the proper names of the plants.

Hybrid groups: Exbury hybrids, Gable hybrids, Ghent hybrids, Girard hybrids, Glenn Dale hybrids, Kaempferi hybrids, Knap Hill hybrids, Linwood hybrids, Mollis hybrids, North Tisbury hybrids, Robin Hill hybrids, Southern Indian hybrids, Vuyk hybrids.

Azalea flowers are among the most brilliantly colored of any group of shrubs in existence. It is for these bright, gay, prettily formed flowers that these plants are grown. They also are the reason why gardeners in regions where azaleas are not native want so desperately to grow them, even if soil and climate are not precisely suitable.

For, to grow azaleas (and other rhododendrons), the first point you must consider is that most of them need acid soil in order to thrive. They prefer pH 4.5 to pH 5.5, and need this acidity not just at the soil surface but for a full foot of depth, if not a foot and a half.

If you live in an area where the soil is naturally acid, you will have little concern over this point—in fact you may wonder why it is stressed. The gardener who lives where soils are neutral (pH 7) or slightly alkaline (above pH 7) will know, for he must replace existing

Southern Indian hybrid azaleas

soil with a more suitable acid soil mixture in order to grow most azaleas.

This is not as difficult as it sounds, because all azaleas are shallow-rooted and even an extra-large, extra-deep hole need only be 18″ deep to contain the root system and allow for root growth in acid soil.

Furthermore, a few kinds like Mollis hybrids and *R. schlippenbachii* will grow in neutral or slightly acid soil and may not need soil replacement in order to thrive.

Therefore, if you are not blessed with acid soil and wish to grow azaleas, you have a choice of restricting the ones you grow to those that will thrive without soil replacement or of replacing soil for any that will grow in your hardiness zone.

Soil preparation and replacement for acid soil plants is discussed in Chapter 4.

There are two types of azaleas— evergreen and deciduous. Most evergreen azaleas are not hardy north of Zone 6. As you saw in Chapter 8, I am a firm believer in trying to grow plants generally considered hardy in the zone

south of the one in which one lives—on the theory that perhaps, in certain microclimates in one's garden, one may be able to grow an especially beautiful or rare plant.

Therefore, some years ago, I started trying various evergreen azaleas, knowing perfectly well that my garden is in Zone 5b (the southerly part of Zone 5). A variety of evergreen azalea that shows no signs of injury, either to plant or to flower bud, despite temperatures of −12° F for three days and nights at a time, is Fedora. Some other evergreen azaleas have proven hardy below the line of snow which covers them some winters, though the part above that line will die. If you too are of an adventurous spirit, try evergreen azaleas, one variety at a time, and see if you too can make them at home in your garden.

Although a well-drained sub-soil is essential, for azaleas cannot stand wet feet, dry soil should be avoided because the shallow roots of azaleas dry out easily. For this reason, a mixture of acid peat moss and soil is ideal for azaleas. Even when growing in this mixture, azaleas must be watered if the summer is dry. Soaking the plants once a week is plenty. If the water used, city or well water, is alkaline in reaction, as it often is, and much of it is needed to keep the plants alive, there is danger of changing soil reaction because of the alkaline water. Your community probably has an analysis of its water available from city hall. It might be well to provide yourself with a copy since the pH will be indicated.

Mulching often is recommended for azaleas to keep their roots cool and moist. However, the United States Department of Agriculture, while advocating mulching for the rest of the year, warns that mulching delays the hardening of wood in autumn and thus makes the plants more sensitive to freezing in winter cold. Therefore, the gardener who mulches his azaleas is advised to remove the mulch in early autumn for three weeks to a month and then replace it for the winter.

Oak leaves have been recommended for a mulch for azaleas because, when they decompose, they are acid in reaction. Lacking oak leaves, pine needles or ground corn cobs provide a good mulch. Peat is a poor mulch because it absorbs so much water that rain or watering must be extremely heavy in order to penetrate the mulch *and* get to the soil below to give the azalea roots needed water. In summer the surface of peat dries, cakes, and becomes impenetrable. Cocoa bean hulls also are a poor mulch for acid soil plants because potassium salts are leached from the hulls in too great quantity for the well-being of the plants.

Use your common sense in selecting a mulch material. Whatever you apply should be loose to admit water, yet cover the soil sufficiently to keep it cool and moist.

In addition to proper soil, the site chosen for an azalea should have conditions as much as possible like those in which it grows naturally. These will vary with the species. For instance, *R. viscosum*, the swamp azalea, grows naturally in low, damp places and will thrive in your garden if you can provide such

Wild North American azaleas

conditions. If you can't, grow it anyway and give it extra water. The scent of its white flowers will repay you for the extra effort.

R. calendulaceum, on the other hand, delights in light shade on a dry ridge or high land, so, if you have such a place, light it up with this azalea.

If you haven't such a place, then select the northeast side of a tree or building, where there is morning sun but afternoon shade—enough sun to make flowering certain, but not sufficient to scorch—and grow azaleas like *R. calendulaceum* (the flame azalea) there.

The spot to avoid planting any azalea is a hot, dry corner in full sun, for no azalea will grow under this combination of adverse conditions.

The best time to plant azaleas is in late spring or early fall—late April or mid-September. They can be moved bare root if plants are very small, but otherwise should be purchased only with a ball of earth around their roots. They may be moved with no injury

while in full bloom providing you water them weekly during the following summer. In fact, if you are selecting azaleas to carry out a specific color scheme, it is best to buy them in bloom so that you can see the flower colors.

Only the azaleas commonly listed in the catalogs and hardy from Zone 6 northward are described here. These are mostly species but several groups of hybrids also are included. It is impossible in this book to attempt to describe the numerous cultivars.

Rhododendron arborescens (syn *Azalea arborescens*)
(Sweet or smooth azalea)
Zone 5 and part of Zone 4; 6'–9'

This species is native from New York and Pennsylvania to Georgia and Alabama; westward to Kentucky and Tennessee. It grows along mountain streams and in cool mountain meadows; is tall, upright, but becomes wider than it is high. It flowers in mid-June (one of the last azaleas to bloom).

Rhododendron calendulaceum

Buds are pinkish and flowers, which smell like those of heliotrope and are 1½″ to 2½″ in diameter, vary in color according to the individual plant bearing them. Sometimes they are white, flushed pink or red; at other times they are blotched yellow, with or without the flush. Always they have red stamens.

Because of the color variation and because many wild plants are straggly in form, you should buy only plants you've seen growing in a good nursery.

Foliage is glossy, bright green, turning dark red in autumn. It is easy to tell this azalea from *R. viscosum*, which usually blooms a bit later, because *viscosum* has hairy leaves and branches while in *arborescens* these are smooth.

Rhododendron calendulaceum (syn *Azalea calendulacea*) (Flame azalea) Zone 5 to part of Zone 4; 6′–8′, sometimes taller

This colorful azalea is native from Pennsylvania to Georgia; westward to Ohio and Kentucky. It grows in open woods on hills or mountains and, when it is in bloom, with flower colors ranging from yellows through oranges to scarlets, it is easy to see how it acquired its common name, for truly the woods seem aflame and stay that way for several weeks as the blooms are long-lasting.

Flowering time is early June; flowers of some plants are more fragrant than those of others. If you select your plants while they are in bloom, you can not only select those with more fragrant blooms, but also can best arrange them in your planting to show their colors to advantage. Plants with darker colored blooms will bloom slightly later than those with paler coloring, a point to consider in color scheming. In autumn the foliage turns yellow to bronze.

Rhododendron canadense (syn *Rhodora canadensis, Azalea canadensis*) (Rhodora) Zone 3 to part of Zone 2; 3′

Native from Newfoundland and Labrador to New York, Pennsylvania and New Jersey, rhodora grows well only where the soil is very acid and moist and the air is moist and cool. Rhodora has dull, bluish-green leaves, rose-purple flowers in mid-May, and is best used in a mass planting in a boggy place.

Exbury hybrids Zone 6 and some probably in Zone 5. Some are being grown at the University of Minnesota Arboretum, which is in Zone 4.

The Exbury group is listed as one of four subgroups of Knap Hill hybrids (described subsequently), all named for the places in which they were developed. This particular group was developed at Exbury, Southhampton, England, by the late Lionel de Rothschild, who started hybridizing shortly after World War I, using Knap Hill hybrids developed by the late Anthony Waterer in his nursery.

There are numerous selected cultivars and these hybrids also are sold in mixed colors. All are beautiful, but form and flower color vary with the cultivar so that it would be sensible to see in bloom what you're buying before you buy it.

Exbury hybrid 'Golden Sunset'

Gable hybrids

These were bred by Joseph B. Gable, Stewartstown, Pennsylvania, and are intended to be a group of very hardy evergreen azaleas. The Korean azalea (*R. yedoense poukhanense*), a very hardy evergreen azalea, which becomes deciduous but survives in Zone 5a, and the Kaempfer azalea (*R. kaempferi*) were used as parents for many of this group, though a wider range of parentage is found. Gable hybrid azalea 'Stewartstonian' is probably the most famous cultivar from Joe Gable, who was propelled from obscurity to overnight fame by an article in the *Saturday Evening Post* entitled "The Flaming Forest of Joe Gable." The word flaming is perfect to describe the color of 'Stewartstonian', which almost smothers itself in brilliant red flowers. Plants can be kept low and compact by heavy pruning, but left alone they grow tall and erect, their oval pointed leaves turning molten bronze in autumn.

There are a number of other cultivars ranging widely in form and in flower color. Most of them are hardy in Zone 6; a few in Zone 5b. If you live in these zones or south of Zone 6; it will pay you to try these hybrids.

Rhododendron × gandavense (Ghent hybrids, Pontic or Pontica hybrids)
Zone 4; heights vary according to the cultivar—generally 6' to 10' at maturity

This group of azaleas has an extremely mixed parentage, including the species *calendulaceum*, *luteum* (syn *A. pontica*), *molle*, *nudiflorum* and *viscosum*. It is, therefore, only to be expected that these hybrids will vary greatly.

Flowers of the Ghent hybrids may be single or double; white, pink to red, yellow or orange and often are combinations of two colors as in the cultivar 'Daviesi', which is white with a yellow blotch.

The most important single fact about these azaleas, as far as the gardener is concerned, is their hardiness. This, coupled with the wide color range in the group, gives the gardener in the north a chance to combine them with various species for a first-rate azalea garden. The Ghents seem to grow best in light shade.

Ghent hybrids (see *R. gandavense*, above)

Rhododendron kaempferi (syn *R. obtusum kaempferi*, *Azalea kaempferi*) (Torch azalea, Kaempfer azalea)
Zone 5; to 7' and sometimes more, broadening with age

Like the flame azalea, this one got its common name of torch azalea because of the brilliance of its flower colors. These range from salmon through orange-red to brick-red and the plants do not necessarily bloom all at the same time—some, regardless of color, will bloom much earlier than others. They are upright growing, bear single, semi-double or double flowers from 1¾" to 2½" in diameter. Plants are deciduous in the north, evergreen in the south.

In Japan, where it is native, this azalea grows all over the mountains and makes a blazing mass of color when in bloom. It does the same in the Arnold Arboretum, which has large plantings on hillsides. In order to maintain the flower color at its brightest, this azalea should be planted in shade. It will tolerate deep shade and still flower.

Girard hybrids

Developed by nurseryman Peter Girard, Sr., from Geneva, Ohio. Girard's evergreen azalea hybrids, such as his 'Hot Shot' (a reddish orange) and 'Purple Robe' (a beautiful clear purple variety), are especially exceptional.

Glenn Dale hybrids

This hybrid originated from an aggressive breeding program undertaken by Ben Morrison, former director of the National Arboretum. Though developed in the Washington, DC area, they are hardy to −10 degrees F, and some 450 cultivars are available, mostly with large flowers. The varieties 'Ben Morrison' (a spectacularly large flowering pink and white bicolor) and 'Buccaneer' (an early flowering reddish-orange) are especially good for home landscapes.

Kaempferi hybrids

This group is not for very cold climates. Most cultivars are hardy in Zone 6, a few in Zone 5b. Plants usually are tall and upright, some cultivars eventually

Gable hybrid 'Stewartstonian'

becoming 6' and more high. Blooms of most are single, range from 1"–1½" in diameter and range in color from white through rose and red and orange red to red violet and purple.

Knap Hill hybrids
Zone 5a, but some are being grown at the University of Minnesota Arboretum in Zone 4
This is a group of azaleas that started with hybridizing by Anthony Waterer in England and was continued after his death by Knap Hill Nursery, which he had owned. Parents of the group were *Rhododendrons molle*, *calendulaceum*, *occidentale*, and *arborescens*. The resulting hybrids were not widely disseminated until after World War II.

There are so many gorgeous azaleas in this group that it would be a chore to decide which to buy first. I spent a long morning walking and photographing at Knap Hill and came away with a mile-long list of azaleas I must own.

Mr. Waterer told me that he has bred cultivars that bloom in July but that the flower colors are pale and he now is breeding for deeper colors with the same late blooming habit.

Knap Hill hybrids are characterized by flowers of huge size, 2" to 3" across, mostly wide and flat in form, most single, but a few with double blooms. In addition to the huge flowers, many cultivars bear them in enormous trusses. I counted 28 flowers in a single cluster, and I do not doubt that there were larger groups on some plants. Some of the plants bear flowers in rounded clusters, others in wider, flatter clusters. Flower colors range from creamy whites and creams through many pinks, roses, reds as well as yellow, salmon, and orange.

Most of the plants grow upright in form but some are wider than high and, apparently, are dwarf. Most of the cultivars bloom in late May or early June.

As already explained, the Exbury hybrids come under the classification of Knap Hill hybrids since they started with Anthony Waterer's older hybrids.

Rhododendron molle

Rhododendron × *kosterianum* (**R.** *molle* × **R.** *japonicum* **and, more recently, other species)**
(Mollis hybrids)
Zone 5, though some are being grown in Zone 4; 3' to 5'
R. molle, with yellow flowers, and *R. japonicum*, which occasionally has yellow flowers but usually has blooms of orange or red, have given these hybrids a color range from pale yellow through gold and orange-yellow to salmon, orange, and many shades of red. Many sales lots offer plants grown from seeds, some of them practically pure *R. molle*, and nurseries offer these plus numerous cultivars, so it is best to buy plants while in flower. If you must buy in fall, it is possible to tell which plants will have light-colored blooms simply by observing the bud color, which is pale in those plants and dark in plants that will have darker colored flowers.

Mollis hybrids bloom in late May with the late tulips and beautiful color combinations may be devised using these two together. Bloom clusters are usually 5" or more in width. Flower sizes of the hybrids vary with the cultivar but many are 2" to 3" or more in diameter. The commonest orange flowered sort has 3¼" blooms of strong red-dish orange; the commonest yellow flowered is colored closest to pale orange yellow, but yellower.

Mollis hybrids are not as hardy as Ghent hybrids, and they are not, generally speaking, long-lived. They will, however, thrive in circumneutral rather than acid soil and in full sun.

Linwood hybrids
Named for a town on the Jersey shore where Dr. Charles Fischer developed an extensive collection of greenhouse forcing azaleas that was later extended to include hardy landscape quality plants. The varieties 'Linwood Blush' (a light yellow-pink) and 'Linwood Lavender' (a lovely light purple) are widely available.

Rhododendron molle (syn **R.** *sinense*, **A.** *mollis*)
(Chinese azalea)
Zone 5; 3'–4'
Blooming in late April to early May, *R. molle* has golden-yellow flowers blotched with deeper color (sometimes green), and 3½" in diameter. They are borne on upright plants. However, most of the plants sold in the United States under this name probably are hybrids since the species rarely is found in the trade.

Rhododendron mucronulatum (syn
A. mucronulata)
(Korean rhododendron)
Zone 4 to part of Zone 3; 4'–5'
One of the few deciduous rhododendrons, this plant blooms with the later
forsythias, with single, light pinkish-
lavender or rosy-lavender single-flowers
in mid-April to late-April before the
leaves appear. It has one weakness—
because it blooms so very early, its buds
and sometimes its flowers may be
nipped by a late frost. A plant in full
bloom may be frosted and ruined in a
single cold night. Though this happens
only about once in five years, it would
be wise to set the plant where too much
sun does not make the buds open even
earlier than they would normally.

North Tisbury hybrids
The work of gardening enthusiast Polly
Hill, on Martha's Vineyard, Massachusetts, these hybrids are primarily low,
spreading plants suitable as ground covers or for cascading from balcony
planters, hanging baskets and retaining
walls. The cultivar 'Joseph Hill' is a particularly fine dwarf, with glowing red
flowers, frequently seen planted in rock
gardens with a little shade and moisture
to keep it comfortable.

Robin Hill hybrids
These are generally late blooming azaleas developed by hybridizer Robert
Gartrell, involving crosses between Sat-
suki and Kurume azaleas, but generally
hardier than either parent. The cultivar
'Betty Anne Voss' has incredibly large
purple-pink double flowers that open
out like a floribunda rose.

Southern Indian hybrids
Not many of these large-flowered azaleas are hardy in the Northeast. They
are a group of relatively vigorous plants
common in the South, suffering severe
winterkill at temperatures below 10 degrees F. A delightful exception is 'Delaware Valley White', a large, mounded,
spreading plant with dazzling white
blossoms, hardy to 0 degrees F.

Rhododendron mucronulatum

Rhododendron nudiflorum
(syn *A. nudiflora*)
(Pinxterbloom, Pinxterflower azalea, Honeysuckle, Honeysuckle
azalea)
**Zone 4 with protection, Zone 5
without; 4'–5'**
A deciduous shrub, this azalea is native
from Massachusetts to North Carolina
and westward to Tennessee and Ohio.
It has 10 RP 8/5, moderate pink or
white flowers, 1½" in diameter, in
May before the leaves start to grow. It
grows in open woods and along streams
and is one of the azaleas that will grow
in full sun. It also is native in Germany
and, when I was a youngster, following
a European custom which sets aside a
special Sunday for picking these
flowers, my father and I used to walk
to the woods in northern New York
state and come home with armsful of
blooms.

Rhododendron obtusum
'Amoenum'
(Amoena azalea)
Zone 6; 4'–5'
This has magenta flowers of the hose-
in-hose type, blooming in mid-May.

The plant is spreading, usually becoming wider than high, and is dense in
form.

Rhododendron obtusum × *arnoldianum* (*R. amoenum* × *R.
kaempferi*)
Zone 6 to Zone 5b
Hardier than *amoenum* and slightly
taller growing, this has 1¼" wide
flowers colored 7.5 RP 6/12, deep purplish pink.

Rhododendron roseum
(Roseshell azalea)
**Zone 4 to part of Zone 3; 4'–5',
but may become taller.**
Native from New England to the high
mountains of Virginia and westward to
northern Ohio and northern Indiana,
this azalea often is confused with a similar native species, *R. nudiflorum*, which
it resembles so much that it formerly
was considered a form of *nudiflorum*.
Its bright pink flowers are fragrant
while those of pinxterbloom are not.
Individual flowers are about 1½" in
diameter and they appear in late May.
Leaves are bluish green.

**Rhododendron schlippenbachii
(syn *A. schlippenbachi*)
(Royal azalea)
Zone 4; 10′ or even more.**
This is a beautiful azalea in both spring
and fall, for in mid-May it has 3″ wide,
single, flattish, purplish pink (5 RP 8/5)
or sometimes white, fragrant flowers
with brown dots in the throats. Blooms
appear just as the leaves are unfolding
and in autumn these leaves turn yellow,
orange and crimson. The plants grow
upright, yet eventually spread to be
wider than they are high. There is sufficient variation in flower color among
plants of this species to make it sensible
to see in bloom the plant you intend to
buy. This is one of the few azaleas that
does not demand highly acid soil.

**Rhododendron vaseyi (syn *A. vaseyi*)
(Pink shell azalea)
Zone 4; 8′–10′**
Native in the mountains of western
North Carolina, this lovely azalea forms
tall, upright plants, blooms in mid-May
before its leaves unfold, with single
flowers that may be white (in variety *album*), or pale pink. They are graceful
and give an airy effect; are particularly
pretty when seen reflected in water.
The plant will grow in either moist or
dry soils and in full sun as well as in
light shade. The leaves turn red in autumn, giving it another season of color.

**Rhododendron viscosum (syn *A.
viscosa*)
(Swamp azalea)
Zone 3; to 15′**
Because this azalea grows in swamps
and along streams from Maine to South
Carolina and Tennessee, it is a prime
choice for that damp spot in your garden. It is among the last of the azaleas
to flower, blooming usually just after *R.
arborescens* (though sometimes opening
while *arborescens* still is in flower) in
early to mid-July.
    The flowers are single, white to
cream, 1″ to 1½″ wide and extremely
fragrant. How many blooms appear on
your plant depends on the care with
which the nursery that propagated it se-

lected the parent stock and the particular season. Some years a plant will be
laden with flowers and others produce
only a few blooms.

**Rhododendron yedoense (syn *R.
poukhanense yedoense*, *R.
poukhanense* 'Yodogawa', *R.
Yodogawa', *Azalea poukhanensis
yedoensis*)
(Yodogawa azalea)
Zone 4; 3′ to 4′**
This double-flowered form was found
first in gardens and given the specific
name of *R. yedoense*. Later, when the
single-flowered form was found in the
wild, it was given a varietal name, *R. yedoense poukhanense*. This is confusing, to
put it mildly, but a few other plants also
are named backwards. Blossoms are
2¼″ in diameter, closest to strong reddish purple in color.

Form is low and spreading, the
leaves evergreen in the south, the plant
becoming deciduous in the north.

**Rhododendron yedoense poukhanense
(syn *R. poukhanense*, *Azalea
poukhanensis*)
(Korean azalea)
Zone 5 to part of Zone 4; 3′, but
growing taller in shade**
This is a low, spreading evergreen azalea
in the south, though deciduous in the
north. It has fragrant, single, 2½″ wide,
strong reddish purple flowers with red
markings. It blooms reliably in mid-
May, which its double-flowered variety
often does not. It seems to me well
adapted to semi-shaded situations as it
grows so well for me in such a place. I
cannot say the same for the double-
flowered form.

Rhododendron schlippenbachii

BERBERIS

(Barberry)

People tend to regard barberries solely as hedge plants. While it is true that many species make excellent hedges, it also is true that there are species worthy of planting as specimens. The difficulty is that most gardeners, when they think of barberries, think only of *Berberis thunbergii*, the Japanese barberry. This is an attractive and extremely useful plant but it is not by any means the only barberry to grow.

In addition to having foliage that blends well with that of other plants and that often furnishes beautiful fall color, barberries produce attractive yellow flowers, especially pretty when viewed at close range, and handsome berries, which may be red, purplish or black. Some barberries are evergreen, certainly in Zone 6 and most winters in Zone 5b.

All barberries will grow in practically any kind of soil and in full sun or light shade, though they will not have as brilliant foliage color in autumn when growing in shade. They all are easy to move, so it is quite possible to transplant a full-size plant or a full-size hedge. Diseases and insects trouble them but little.

Some barberries, however, notably *B. vulgaris*, are alternate hosts to a disease of wheat called black stem-rust. In the interests of healthy wheat, such barberries are not permitted in states that grow wheat, nor are they permitted to be imported into either the United States or Canada.

Berberis julianae
(Wintergreen barberry)
Zone 5; 5'–6'

As hardy an evergreen barberry as can be found, *julianae* is sturdy and strong, erect in growth, with handsome, dark green leaves and long, sharp spines growing from them. The twigs, too, have thorns.

This barberry has clusters of yellow flowers, each ⅓" in diameter in mid-May, and blue-black berries in autumn. It may be used as a specimen or in a house planting (not near the doors) or in a shrub border, but it should be borne in mind that weeding near it is no joy unless the hands are covered with leather gloves. Those spiny leaves and branchlets blow off in winter, and spring cleanup time finds them on the ground.

Berberis koreana
(Korean barberry)
Zone 4; 5' or 6'

This is, to my way of thinking, the most beautiful of the barberries that can be grown in the north. It is deciduous, growing erect while young, later spreading more, with upper branches arching gracefully. The twigs are thorny, the leaves bright green in spring, becoming veined with red later in the season and deep orange-red in autumn. Vivid yellow, ¼" diameter flowers in mid-May become berries hanging in drooping clusters 1¾" long. These ³/₁₆"-long fruits are first greenish yellow, later bright scarlet-red. They remain in good condition for some time.

Korean barberry may be used as a hedge, clipped or unclipped, but is prettier when unclipped. It also has a place in a shrub border or may be used as a specimen or in a house planting. It should be placed where it may be enjoyed all year.

Berberis thunbergii 'Atropurpurea'

Berberis thunbergii

Berberis thunbergii
(Japanese barberry)
Zone 5 to part of Zone 4; 6'–7'
The most adaptable of the barberries, this is the one most often seen in hedges. It will thrive in any type of soil, will grow in semi-shade as well as in sun, and tolerates dry conditions with no apparent difficulty.

It grows upright, is densely branched, thorny, has yellow flowers, tinged reddish on the outsides, to ½" in diameter, blooms in the middle of May. Oval, brilliant red berries follow and these, against the scarlet autumn color of the deciduous leaves, make the plant especially attractive at that time of year. Birds dislike the berries so they stay on the plant all winter to become red contrasts for the next spring's yellow flowers. This barberry is a good specimen plant, a first-rate hedge, and is acceptable in the planting around a building or in the front row of a shrub border.

Berberis thunbergii 'Atropurpurea'
(Red Japanese barberry, Purple-leaf Japanese barberry)
Zone 5 to part of Zone 4; 5'–6'
This red-foliaged form is not quite as hardy as the species. While a hedge entirely of this barberry is bright enough to knock one's eyes out, the plant combines well with green barberry and may be used to accent the corners where a hedge turns or the ends of a hedge of green barberry. It also is a good specimen and may be used in the foreground of narrow-leaved evergreens. Plant it only in sun as in shade it loses its bright foliage color and leaves are green.

Berberis thunbergii 'Atropurpurea Nana' (syn B. thunbergii 'Crimson Pigmy')
Zone 5 to part of Zone 4; 2'
Dark red leaves and a dwarf, very compact habit of growth are characteristics of this little shrub. It may be used as a low hedge (providing the leaf color is not objectionable), as a specimen in a rock garden, as a "facing down" plant for taller shrubs or evergreens.

Berberis thunbergii nana 'Crimson Pigmy' (see B. thunbergii 'Atropurpurea Nana')

Berberis thunbergii 'Rose Glow'
An introduction from Holland, this barberry has unusual rosy pink young leaves with deep reddish-purple patches. A real novelty.

Berberis thunbergii 'Sheridan Red'
An introduction of Sheridan Nurseries Limited of Ontario, this barberry is described by the nursery as "vigorous grower with deep, dark red foliage. Makes an excellent tall hedge."

Berberis verruculosa
(Warty barberry)
Zone 6 to part of Zone 5; 3'–4'
Glossy, dark green evergreen leaves, white underneath, turning bronze in autumn; ½" diameter golden-yellow flowers late in May, followed by deep violet-black berries; plus a neat, compact growth habit and spreading form are the characteristics of this barberry. The twigs are thorny and warty, hence the common name. Where it can be grown, this makes a beautiful specimen .

Berberis thunbergii 'Atropurpurea Nana'

BUDDLEIA
(Butterfly bush)

Buddleias or butterfly bushes are grown for their spikes of flowers, which, in the most popular *B. davidii* cultivars, are borne throughout the summer months when not too many other shrubs are in bloom. The only hardy buddleia is *B. alternifolia* and the word hardy is not too accurate in describing it. Even in Zone 5b the shrub occasionally dies to the ground, not necessarily in a severe winter. That is, it may survive several severe winters only to die to the earth during a winter that does not have particularly low temperatures but during which some other factor or factors kill this buddleia. *Buddleia davidii* cultivars all die to the ground each winter or should be pruned to ground level in spring if they do not winterkill entirely to the ground. Since they all bloom on wood of the current season, this annual dying back makes no difference. Even *B. alternifolia* will grow again from the roots, though a season's flowers will be lost since it blooms only on wood produced the previous year. Soil may be hilled around the roots of all buddleias in autumn for protection from severe cold and this sometimes will save a bush from complete death. But buddleias, at best, are not long-lived plants.

Perfect drainage and a protected spot often help keep buddleia roots alive even without protection. These shrubs need full sun and will grow and bloom better when soil is rich.

Buddleia alternifolia (Fountain butterfly bush, Hardy butterfly bush)
Zone 5 and occasionally, with some die-back each winter, in Zone 4; 10'–12'
Shaped just as one of its common names implies and spreading wide so that it must be allowed plenty of room in the garden, this butterfly bush is a beautiful sight when in flower. Long spikes of fragrant ⅛" wide florets, light purple in color, arranged in ¾" wide

Buddleia alternifolia

clusters, appear in mid-May to June and their very numbers make this shrub a bouquet of bloom.

Leaves are small and gray-green and keep the shrub attractive when it is not in flower.

Buddleia davidii (Orange-eye butterfly bush)
Zone 5, occasionally in Zone 4; 6'–12'
Lilac-purple flowers with a not-too-conspicuous orange eye distinguish this shrub; it is rarely seen in comparison with its cultivars, which are widely grown.

These cultivars are commonly called "summer lilacs" because the flower col-

ors of most are similar to those of lilac blooms.

There are many cultivars available in a color range from white (as in 'White Bouquet'), through pink (as in 'Charming' or 'Fascinating') through lilac, lavender, deep purple, and reddish violet. All cultivars have fragrant blooms that are attractive, so you can allow your taste to dictate the flower color you want to buy. Blooms continue to appear until frost on most cultivars.

Buddleia davidii magnifica
Blooming from the middle of August onward, this variety is stronger-growing than *davidii*; has rose-purple or violet-purple flowers with dark orange eyes and the outer edges of the petals are rolled or reflexed. Blooms are larger than those of *davidii* and borne in dense clusters.

Buddleia × farqubari (B. asiatica × B. officinalis)
Zone 6 to Zone 5b; 5'
Fragrant, lavender flowers in drooping clusters start to open on this plant in mid-July and continue until frost. They seem rarely to open fully and therefore are not nearly as conspicuous as those of *B. davidii* cultivars. The plant on which they are borne also is much smaller than the other buddleias.

Buddleia davidii 'Burgundy'

BUXUS

(Box, Boxwood)

Boxwoods are the glory of southern gardens, where tiny plants are used to edge rose beds and where enormous older plants form handsome specimens put to numerous uses in the landscape. In the northern states only a few boxwoods thrive and huge plants are practically unknown.

Boxwoods are grown for their foliage and their form, not for their inconspicuous flowers. All are evergreen and, in the warmth of a sunny day, their foliage gives off an unusual and unforgettable aroma—not precisely a fragrance. If you visit the boxwood garden at Mount Vernon or any other estate where there are boxwood plantings on a warm, sunny day, stand still near the plants and treat yourself to a sniff. Ever afterward, the unmistakable scent will tell you if you are near boxwoods.

Boxwood plants should preferably be moved in early spring and, if of any size, should always be purchased with a ball of earth around the roots. Plants should be set where drainage is good and the soil texture is open. Where soil is reasonably good, no special preparation is required; nor need holes be especially deep, for the plants are shallow-rooted. A hole a foot wider on each side than the earth ball will, however, be appreciated.

Plants should be set at precisely the same depth as they grew in the nursery (look for a dark line around the stems of the plant, which marks this place)—never deeper. On the other hand, they should not be set shallower than they grew in the nursery lest the roots be exposed to air.

Boxwood thrives in either full sun or light shade. In northern climates it is best to set the plants where they will be sheltered from drying winter winds, as well as hot sun in late winter and early spring. As far as low temperatures are concerned, if you choose the kind of box that will survive in your climate, winterkill will not be one of your wor-

ries. There is nothing but extra work in store for the gardener who ignores hardiness and therefore must build shelters of burlap and wood to help his box plants survive the winter.

Boxwood needs additional water if the summer is dry, but do not wait until there is a drought as boxwood is slow to show the effects of lack of moisture. Never mound soil up around boxwood plants, for then water will run away from the roots. Deep mulching is inadvisable because it excludes air from the roots, as is cultivation on top of the root area because of the possibility of injuring the shallow roots.

If boxwood is planted for a low hedge, plants should be set 10″ apart. If the hedge is to be formal, it must be pruned as needed to keep it shapely. Once a year any dead twigs should be cut out from the plants. A good time to do this is late spring, before new growth begins, but after you can see which parts are dead.

There are two species of boxwood that will survive winters in the north: *microphylla* and *sempervirens*. Of the two, *microphylla* is the hardier.

Buxus microphylla
(Littleleaf box)
Zone 6 to Zone 5b; 3′–4′

Littleleaf box, as previously stated, will withstand lower temperatures than will *B. sempervirens*, which may have tips of branches injured by cold even in Zone 7.

Littleleaf box has leaves to an inch long, is compact in form, low and slow-growing. Unfortunately leaves sometimes turn brown in winter and for this reason some of the cultivars may be preferable to the species.

Buxus microphylla 'Compacta'
(syn Buxus microphylla nana compacta)
(Kingsville dwarf box)
Zone 5; 1′ but many times wider than high

A very dense, naturally low-growing form, this has good, green leaves.

Buxus microphylla koreana, also listed in some catalogs as koraensis (Korean boxwood)
Zone 5 to part of Zone 4; 2′–3′, but occasionally to 5′

The hardiest box, this forms a nice looking plant, broader than high, even though it has not the billowing form or the height of the beautiful southern boxwoods. It has withstood 18 degrees below zero in my garden with absolutely no injury while two cultivars of *B. sempervirens*, not 30′ away, in the same general part of the garden but in a slightly more protected place, have browned to the snow line.

The only criticism that can be made of Korean boxwood is that the foliage often turns tannish or yellowish or brownish-green during winter so as to refute the description of "evergreen." The browned leaves are alive and well and will turn green again in spring. A cultivar named 'Wintergreen' stays green all winter.

Buxus microphylla 'Compacta'

Buxus sempervirens (Common Box)

CALLICARPA
(Beauty berry, Jewel berry)

Callicarpas are deciduous and are "die-back-to-the-ground" shrubs in Zone 5, although the tops often survive the winter in Zone 6 and southward. Where tops do winter, they should be pruned severely in early spring for vigorous growth and many fruits later in the season, since flowers and fruits are borne on wood of the current season's growth.

Callicarpas grow in any soil; prefer full sun but tolerate light shade. They are all upright growing, have inconspicuous flowers, and are grown only for their colorful fruits. These are berries that are borne at the tips of the new wood and, while they are perfectly beautiful in color, they remain on the plants for only 2 or 3 weeks after the leaves have turned yellow and then fallen.

Callicarpa japonica

Buxus sempervirens (syn B. s. ar-borescens)
(Common box)
Zone 6 and protected places in Zone 5b; 6′–8′
The shiny, dark green leaves grow to 1¼″ long, the form of the plant is dense and billowy, and specimen plants or hedges have a charm all their own. This is the boxwood commonly used throughout the south, where it grows to 25′ high and almost treelike.

Most of the varieties of *B. sempervirens* need winter protection, which is easily given by sticking evergreen branches into the soil near the plants on the windward side and the side from which the hottest sun comes. Wooden and burlap screens also may be built on these sides to keep off wind and hot sun.

Buxus sempervirens 'Vardar Valley'
Zone 5a; 2′–3′
The Vardar Valley is in the Balkan

Mountains and the original plant of this cultivar was found growing there. Plants are flattish on top, may grow twice as wide as they grow high.

Buxus sempervirens 'Newport Blue'
Zone 6 to Zone 5b
Bluish-green leaves that are small and round, slow growth and the ability to stand shearing to shape are characteristics of this cultivar.

Buxus sempervirens 'Suffruticosa'
(sometimes listed in the catalogs as B. suffruticosa)
(Edging box)
Zone 5b; 2′–2½′
The smallest boxwood, a true dwarf, this is the kind to use to edge flower beds or garden paths. It has roundish leaves about ¾″ long, is very slow-growing, and has a dense, compact form. Foliage is more fragrant than that of other boxwoods.

Callicarpa dichotoma (syn C. purpurea, syn C. koreana)
(Korean jewel berry)
Zone 6 to part of Zone 5; 4′
Upright in growth, this shrub has inconspicuous pink flowers, but the berries are lilac-violet, coloring in September, October, and November.

Callicarpa purpurea
(see C. dichotoma)

Callicarpa japonica
(Japanese beauty berry, Japanese jewel berry)
Zone 5; 4'
White or pink inconspicuous flowers in early June are followed by ³/₁₆″ diameter, violet colored berries in October to November. These show off well against the leaves, which turn pale yellow.

CALLUNA
(Scotch heather, Heather)

In Europe you can see heather plants covering thousands upon thousands of acres of poor land where apparently nothing else will grow, and when they are in bloom they look like a sea of color. I have seen and photographed them singly and in vast numbers in Scotland, Holland, and Greece and these acres of color are a joy to remember.

These same heather plants can be grown in the garden provided they are supplied with the same perfect drainage, poor, acid soil and sunshine that they have in their native habitats. These conditions are not hard to duplicate. Choose a slope or the top of a wall for your heather planting, replace the existing soil with half sand and half acid peat, adding a handful of sulphur to each bushel of soil as you mix it, and plant heathers in this. If they have good soil the plants will grow vigorously, become leggy, will flower sparsely or won't bloom at all. They just cannot stand luxury.

The soil should not be allowed to dry completely during the summer heat and the easiest way to accomplish this is to mulch over the soil and under the plants after they have had time to re-establish their roots. Buckwheat hulls make a satisfactory mulch.

To keep plants compact and to force plenty of new growth, which means plenty of bloom, heather plants may be pruned as needed or even sheared if necessary, but this must be done in early spring or not at all.

Because the plants must be in full sun to bloom, their evergreen foliage may become burned in late winter and very early spring. For this reason, save boughs from your Christmas tree and lay them over the tops of the heather plants, leaving them in place until the cold weather is past.

Heathers may be used to cover banks, as ground covers in sunny areas, in rock gardens and on tops of walls. They vary in height, most hugging the ground in mats, but the tallest growing to several feet in height.

Calluna vulgaris
(Scotch heather, Heather)
Zone 5 to part of Zone 4; 1½'–2½'
Scotch heather is an evergreen shrub with tiny, needle-like leaves and small spikes of bell-shaped purplish pink flowers. There are many cultivars of Scotch heather with different flower colors, foliage colors and growth habits. Given below are short descriptions of the cultivars most frequently found in the catalogs.
• *Calluna vulgaris* 'Alba' is just like the species but has white flowers.
• *Calluna vulgaris* 'Alba Erecta' has a more upright form and white flowers.
• *Calluna vulgaris* 'Atrorubens' (syn *C.v.* 'Alportii') (Red heather). Crimson flowers against grayish foliage are the distinguishing features of this dense, erect-growing heather.
• *Calluna vulgaris* 'Aurea' sports pink flowers against golden yellow foliage.
• *Calluna vulgaris* 'Cuprea' has purple flowers against golden yellow leaves.

Calluna vulgaris

Calycanthus floridus

CALYCANTHUS

Calycanthus floridus
(Strawberry shrub, Sweet shrub,
Carolina allspice, Bubbly blos-
soms, Sweet Bubbie, Peat shrub,
Peat tree, Sweet Betsy)
Zone 5 to parts of Zone 4; usually
4′, but may grow to 6′ or 7′
Although this shrub is native from Virginia to Florida, it is hardy in the north.
In an especially severe winter it may die
to the ground but it will grow again
from the roots. The form of the shrub
varies from dense to open and straggly
depending on the soil in which it grows.
In clay soils the shrub tends to grow
more open in form.

The branchlets give off an odor like
camphor. The shiny green leaves are aromatic when crushed. They turn yellowish in autumn and the large seed
pods turn brown about the same time.
Pods are borne, usually, only once in
several years.

This shrub, however, is really grown
for its 1¼″ to 1¾″ diameter reddish-
brown flowers, which open from June
to July. These have an unusual fragrance, at first rather like a spicy strawberry but, when older, more like that of
a spicy, ripe apple.

For generations, these flowers have
been used in bureau drawers as substitutes for sachet and carried to church to
perfume the owner. The fragrance is
most noticeable on a warm, sunny day
or when your hand has warmed a
flower.

Sad to say, the fewest of strawberry
shrubs on the market now have fragrant
flowers. Propagation should be from
fragrant plants only, but unfortunately
this is not the case. Search out a nursery that sells plants with fragrant
flowers if you want to grow this shrub
for its chief attraction.

Strawberry shrub grows in any soil,
in sun or light shade, but thrives best in
a rich, moist soil, in part shade and a
protected place. It requires little pruning
save for removal of dead branches and
thinning crowded stems.

Calycanthus floridus in fall foliage

CARAGANA
(Pea tree, Pea shrub)

Very hardy, deciduous shrubs or small
trees, these are natives of the Soviet Union and China that will grow in any
soil, even almost pure sand. All of them
prefer sunny places and start to flower
when very young. They are inclined to
be straggly in growth, so should be
heavily pruned every few years. If necessary, any of them may be cut to the
ground and will grow anew from the
roots.

Caragana arborescens
(Siberian pea tree)
Zone 3 to part of Zone 2; 20′
This often is used in shelter-belt plantings on the Great Plains. It is a native of
Manchuria and Siberia; an excellent
plant for a tall hedge, when planted 18″
apart, or may be used to give height to
a shrub border. Growth is upright, bark
gray and young twigs yellow-green. The
flowers, which open in May, are vivid
yellow, and shaped like those of peas.
The pods, which contain the seeds, also
are shaped much like those of peas but
are flatter. They are 2″ long, ⅛″ wide,
and are strong yellow green before they
turn tan.

There are half a dozen cultivars of
the Siberian pea tree available in Canada, all having the same hardiness and
resistance to drought as the species.

Caragana pygmaea
(Dwarf Russian pea tree)
Zone 4, probably to parts of Zone
3; 2′–2½′
Slender, arching branches give this low,
spiny shrub its character. The young
twigs are colored red-brown, the older
ones dark gray. Flowers are two-toned,
the lower petals brilliant yellow, flushed
vivid yellow, which is the color of the
top petals. Blooms are ⅞″ long and
⁹/₁₆″ wide across the top petals (widest
part of the flower). They are borne singly and are marked reddish on the outsides. This shrub may be used as a specimen in a rock garden or where a small
accent is needed or in the front of a
shrub border. It often is grown in tree
form, especially in Canada, and is effective as a specimen when so grown.

CARYOPTERIS

Caryopteris × *clandonensis* (*C. incana* × *C. mongholica*) (syn *Spiraea caryopteris*)
(**Bluebeard, Blue spirea, Chinese beardwort, Verbena shrub**)
Zone 6 to Zone 5b; 2′–3′
Grown for its blue or bluish flowers in late August and early September, this is a delicate little shrub with slender branches and gray leaves. The following cultivars, each with a different shade of blue flowers, are listed in the catalogs: 'Azure', 'Blue Mist', 'Dark Knight', 'Heavenly Blue'.

Of the cultivars listed above, I have grown the two most widely available: 'Blue Mist' and 'Heavenly Blue'. The latter has strong violet flowers and never lives through even a mild winter, though I've tried growing it half a dozen times. 'Blue Mist', with flowers of light violet, grows well, surviving even severe winters without protection.

Set these plants only where they have good drainage and full sun. If they die to the ground during winter, they usually will grow again from the roots in spring. In milder climates they should be pruned to the ground each spring to encourage new growth and shapeliness.

A single shrub is not particularly effective in the garden unless planted with another shrub having flowers of a contrasting color or placed in a perennial border next to perennials of contrasting hue that bloom at the same time. However, a group of three or more of the same cultivar, planted 3′ apart, will give an airy gray and blue effect at a time of year when it is needed.

Caryopteris incana (syn *C. mastacanthus*)
Zone 7 to part of Zone 6; to 5′
Dull green leaves, violet-blue (and occasionally white) flowers, which appear in October to November, are the characteristics of this species.

Caryopteris mastacanthus (see *C. incana*)

Caryopteris × *clandonensis*

CEANOTHUS

Ceanothus americanus
(**New Jersey tea, Mountainsweet, Redroot**)
Zone 4; 3′
Native from Canada to South Carolina and Texas, this little shrub is a poor substitute for the gorgeous, blue-flowered ceanothuses that grow so well in California and states with similar climates. However, since this is the only one I can grow, I grow it, though it frequently dies to the ground in winter. It always comes up again in spring and, since it blooms on wood of the current season's growth, no flowers are lost.

This shrub has tiny white flowers in dense clusters at the tips of the branches, produced most heavily in July but with a few appearing now and then during the rest of the growing season. The reddish fruits in September are interesting in shape and of some garden interest.

In a spot where the soil is too poor for other shrubs, this one will thrive with no care at all. It has formed large colonies along the roadside near our lakeside cabin where it is in the poorest possible soil and is covered with dust from the road all summer.

Ceanothus americanus

Chaenomeles japonica

CHAENOMELES

(Flowering quince, Japanese flowering quince, Japonica)

The flowering quinces furnish brilliant color in the garden in early spring. In addition to their bright flowers, they have shiny, dark green leaves, bronze or reddish on some varieties and cultivars when first open. The flowers appear with the leaves or after the leaves unfold. Growth habit of the different varieties and cultivars varies; some grow upright and dense, others low and dense and in still others growth is so open as to be straggly.

This is one genus in which most catalogs are years behind in proper nomenclature. This is due, in part at least, to the number of times that botanists have

changed its name. First it was *Pyrus*, then *Cydonia*, and now *Chaenomeles*.

One reason for all these changes is that originally a botanist gave an incorrect description of the fruit, which temporarily confounded later botanists. Another is that the dried herbarium specimens made by early botanists were incomplete and were collected at the wrong time of year for correct identification.

In the genus *Chaenomeles* (still called *Cydonia* in some catalogs) there are two species that account for the flowering quinces grown in northern gardens. Of these *C. japonica* is from Japan and is a low-growing shrub, usually to about 3′ in height. The second species, *C. speciosa* (formerly *C. lagenaria*), is from China and is a big shrub, to about 6′ high and sometimes more.

Because they flower so early in spring, flowering quinces should be transplanted or moved in autumn. They move easily, are undemanding as to soil, but should have full sun to bloom their best. Most varieties have thorns, so should be placed elsewhere than along a narrow path. Occasional pruning is required but only for renewal of growth or for better form.

Chaenomeles japonica (Japanese quince, Firebush) Zone 5, occasionally to Zone 4 where usually it is not flower-bud-hardy; 3′

If you will notice the height to which this shrub grows you will immediately recognize its usefulness. Here is a plant with excellent foliage (though lacking autumn color) that requires little care and has brilliant orange-red, single flowers 1¼″ in diameter in late April or early May. It may be used under many windows without any worry about its growing so tall as to obscure them, or anywhere else where a low shrub is required. The quince-like fruits are excellent for jelly.

Chaenomeles japonica alpina (Dwarf Japanese quince) Zone 5; 1′–1½′, usually the lower figure

An even smaller form of the species, this can be used in house plantings where windows come practically to the ground, or as a ground cover for a bank or level area, or to face down higher shrubs. It spreads widely. My aunt used to have one of these shrubs in her garden that was fully 8′ in diameter. Flowers are strong reddish orange, 1¼″ in diameter. New foliage is bronze to reddish bronze.

Chaenomeles 'Maulei' Zone 5; 2′–2½′

A small plant, therefore useful in many places, this has single, salmon-pink, but sometimes orange, flowers against dark green leaves. Usually each plant bears an abundant crop of fruits.

Chaenomeles speciosa

Chaenomeles speciosa (syn *Chaeno-meles lagenaria*, syn *Cydonia ja-ponica* of the catalogs)
(Flowering quince)
Zone 5, occasionally to Zone 4; 6′
Tall, generally upright growing plants with dark green leaves, sometimes glossy, which unfold with or before the scarlet flowers, these have large quinces that turn from green to yellow when ripe and make excellent jelly. If you will combine these quinces with apples, half and half, the jelly is not so heavily flavored and in my opinion is more delicious. Several plants are needed for cross pollination in order that fruit be produced.

CLEMATIS

Clematis paniculata
(Sweet autumn clematis)
Zones 5 to 8; 20′ and more
Sensational late summer–flowering fragrant white flowers cover the slender stems from top to toe, followed by gray, fluffy seed heads that persist after the small, oval leaves have fallen. Good

for covering arbors, trellises, and fencing. Plants thrive in a wide range of well-drained soils in full sun. Native to the northeastern United States, plants re-seed readily, bloom the first year from seed.

CLETHRA

Clethra alnifolia (syn *C. paniculata* of the catalogs)
(Summersweet, Sweet pepper bush)
Zone 4 to part of Zone 3; 3′–8′
White, sweet-scented flowers in erect clusters appearing in July and August when few other shrubs are blooming are certainly the outstanding characteristic of this genus. The shrub itself also is attractive with its shining green

leaves. Its height depends on how well it likes its environment. It grows naturally in wet woods or swamps, though sometimes in drier places, usually along the eastern coast from Maine to Mississippi. The closer you can duplicate its accustomed habitat, the taller it will grow. Even in dry places it will be about 4′ high. It does equally well in full sun or semi-shade, but in full sun the foliage takes on a deeper yellow to orange coloring in autumn. It is tolerant of many soils though it grows best in acid, peaty soil. Increasing by underground stems, it soon forms clumps; so adequate space for these should be allowed when it is planted. This shrub may be used in a border, by a pool or stream, or in a wild garden, and is most effective in groups of three or more plants.

Clethra alnifolia

Clethra alnifolia 'Rosea'

The pink-flowered form of *C. alnifolia*, this starts to bloom about a week later than the species, and the flower spikes are a bit heavier than those of the species. Nurserymen have complained to me that the plants they bought for re-sale as pink-flowered had pinkish buds but white flowers. Our plants have deep purplish pink buds and flowers pale purplish pink inside and light purplish pink on the outsides of the petals. Fore-warned is forearmed, so they say; evidently the plants you buy should be seen when in flower.

Clethra paniculata
(see *C. alnifolia*)

Clethra paniculata rubra
(see *C. alnifolia* 'Rosea')

COMPTONIA

Comptonia peregrina (syn *C. as-plenifolia*)
(Sweet fern)
Zone 2; 4'

Even though this grows naturally in an acid peat or dry acid sand, it will grow well in any acid soil where nothing else will thrive. It is native from New Bruns-wick to Manitoba, southward to Vir-ginia, westward to northern Indiana and northeastern Illinois.

Its merits are the graceful habit of growth, the form and the aromatic fra-grance of its leaves, which are fern-like,

quite different from those usually found on woody plants. This plant is said to be difficult to transplant, though many people say they do not find it so. If you intend to try moving it from the wild, wait until it is dormant in fall, take a good-sized piece of the sod in which its roots are contained, and move the en-tire piece of sod to a place where the soil is poor and acid.

Sweet fern may be used in a wild garden or as a ground cover for banks where soil is poor.

CORNUS

(Dogwood)

This large genus contains plants that are trees, others that are shrubs and even one species (*C. canadensis*) that is a low-growing ground cover. The tree forms commonly used with shrubs are de-scribed in Chapter 13. It is these trees that are most spectacular when in flower. The shrubby dogwoods usually are grown more for the color of their twigs and branches or their fruit or even their bright leaves in autumn than for their flowers. These blooms, while not spectacular individually, usually are borne in such large quantities that a shrub is conspicuous while in blossom.

The dogwoods grown primarily for their twig color should be pruned heav-ily every year or two, whether they otherwise need it or not, because the younger twigs have the brighter colors. Some professional gardeners cut these

Cornus alba 'Sibirica'

particular dogwoods to the ground about every 5 years in order that new and more colorful growth start from the roots.

There is one dogwood, grown as a shrub or sometimes as a tree, that is spectacular in bloom—*Cornus kousa*, the Korean dogwood. Read the description on page 128.

Cornus alba
(Tatarian dogwood, Siberian dog-wood)
Zone 2; 3'–9'

While the young twigs are greenish early in the season, they are bright red by the end of it and, with branches of the same color, this shrub is grown be-cause of their brightness. It is particu-larly lovely in winter against snow. Leaves are yellow-green, flowers white, borne in flat clusters in May. Fruits are white, grayish-white or bluish-white. The shrub is upright in growth habit.

Cornus alba 'Argenteo-marginata'
(syn *C. elegantissima* of the cata-logs)
Zone 2; 6'–7'

This form is a less vigorous-growing shrub than *C. alba*. It has red branches and the leaves, which may grow to 5" long, are edged with white. Flowers are white, arranged in 2" diameter clusters. Because of the foliage a planting of these shrubs gives a striking green and white effect, impossible to reproduce adequately in a photograph. This shrub

Comptonia peregrina

Cornus canadensis

is especially effective when used in a border in combination with green-leaved shrub or tree dogwoods.

Cornus alba aurea
(see *C. alba* 'Spaethii')

Cornus alba elegantissima
(see *C. alba* 'Argenteo-marginata')

Cornus alba 'Gouchaultii' (also spelled Gouchalti and Gouchatti in the catalogs) (Gouchault dogwood)
The foliage of this dogwood is yellowish and pink or red or yellowish white and pink or red, in streaks. It makes a good specimen where such a color combination is desired or may be combined with green-leaved dogwoods or shrubs.

Cornus alba 'Kesselringii'
The characteristic that distinguishes this dogwood from others is the branch color—very dark purple, nearly black. The unfolding leaves are red.

Cornus alba 'Sibirica' (Siberian dogwood, Coral dogwood)
Zone 2; 9'
Because of its coral-red twigs, this is an even more colorful dogwood than *C. alba* to use when winter color is the aim. Flowers are creamy-white, small, and arranged in the usual flat clusters. They are effective in May and are followed by berries that usually are white but may be blue-white. Fall foliage color is red. One possible advantage of this dogwood is that it is not as rampant in growth as the species.

Cornus alba 'Spaethii' (Yellowedge dogwood, Spaeth dogwood)
The leaves of this cultivar, which grow to 5″ in length, are yellow green (closest to moderate yellow green bordered with brilliant greenish yellow, a most effective combination).

Cornus amomum
(Silky dogwood, Redbrush, Squawbush, Swamp dogwood, Blueberried dogwood)
Zone 4; 9'
Native from Massachusetts to Georgia and westward to New York and Tennessee, this dogwood has reddish winter twigs but they are duller red than those of 'Sibirica', so for winter color 'Sibirica' is superior. However, *amomum* has a point in its favor, which is that the blooms appear later than those of most red-twigged dogwoods—mid-June. Plants of this dogwood tend to grow more tree-like than those of other dogwoods with red twigs. This plant needs room to spread and grows particularly well in damp soils. Fruit is blue, but shades vary, so that it may be pale blue, deeper blue and sometimes is almost white. Leaves turn red in autumn. It is easy to distinguish this species from others. Just break off a stem and look at the pith in the center. It is dark in this dogwood.

Cornus canadensis
(Bunchberry)
Zone 2 to 8; 8″
Native to Alaska and cool, moist forested areas of the Northeastern United States, (also high altitude parts of New Mexico and California) this variety is probably the most beautiful of all shrubby groundcovers and excels in shady areas—especially under pines, camellias and rhododendrons. It has a low-growing, spreading habit, rarely more than 8 inches high, creating a dense, uniform green mat in acid soil, and it has pointed, oval leaves arranged in fours. In May, a dainty white four-petaled flower composed of bracts appears at the center of these leaf whorls. The leaves turn red in fall. The flowers are followed by showy red oval fruits that ripen in late summer and persist into fall if not eaten by birds.

Plants are slow growing and demand a humus-rich soil and plenty of moisture to get established. Superb groundcover for woodland gardens and as an edging for shaded paths.

Cornus elegantissima
(see *C. alba* 'Argenteo-marginata')

Cornus flaviramea
(see *C. sericea* 'Flaviramea')

Cornus kousa
(Japanese dogwood, Kousa dogwood)
Zone 5; 20′
Cornus kousa is the shrub I chose to plant next to our front door.

Slow growing when small, and with rather upright growth when young, the branches become more horizontal with age. The bracts are white, pointed at the tips, unlike those of *C. florida*, and minus the notches of *florida*. Green at first, the bracts begin to change to white in early June after the leaves have grown and gradually enlarge until the diameter of a group of bracts is 1¾″. After several weeks pink or rose spots dot the bracts. These spots spread and the rose color gradually suffuses the bracts until the effect is of pink bracts. Unless the weather turns hot, the bracts remain in good condition for a full month. *Kousa* flowers about three weeks later than *C. florida*.

The true flowers are greenish yellow, appear in the center of the bracts, and are inconspicuous. The fruits that fol-

Cornus mas

Cornus kousa

low them look like pink or rose raspberries. Birds love them so they do not last long. The foliage color in autumn is dull red.

Cornus kousa chinensis
(Chinese dogwood, sometimes called Korean dogwood by nurserymen)
Zone 5; 20′
There are two differences between this variety and *kousa*. The bracts are larger than those of *kousa* and they are shaped differently. They are longer, start to narrow when halfway to the tip and are sharply pointed at the tip. This variety does not bloom reliably in my garden while *kousa*, except when an unusually severe winter kills the flower buds, blooms every year. However, I have seen, in a sheltered situation between two houses in Ithaca, New York, a plant of *chinensis* so laden with bracts that the leaves scarcely were visible. Evidently this is how *chinensis* can perform when sufficiently protected.

Cornus mas **(also written *mascula*)**
(Cornelian cherry)
Zone 5; 20′ or sometimes a little taller.
Blooming before the forsythias, usually in early April, this dogwood shows off the true flowers since it has no bracts. Each yellow flower is tiny, only ⅛″ in diameter, but the clusters of blooms may be 1″ in diameter and often are so profusely borne that the entire shrub appears yellow since it has no leaves as yet.

The shrub is rounded in form, dense in habit, with shining green leaves. The ½″ long, ¼″ wide, plum-shaped fruits turn from strong red to dark red, but, since they are hidden by the leaves, are not effective in the landscape. They are edible and excellent jelly may be made from them.

Cornus mas will grow in any soil and in light shade or full sun. It blends well with many other shrubs and is a good border plant or a specimen at the end of a border.

Cornus officinalis
(Japanese cornel)
Zone 5; 30'

Similar to *Cornus mas*, this dogwood blooms a week earlier; also has yellow flowers borne before the leaves unfold. Flower petals are narrower and more pointed than those of *C. mas* and there are other minor differences, but the effect of the two plants is much the same. The fruits, scarlet in color, borne from August to September, are thinner than those of *C. mas* and more nearly oblong in shape. Leaves are shiny green, turning red in autumn. Older plants have interesting bark that hangs in thin strips.

Cornus racemosa (syn *C. paniculata*)
(Gray dogwood, Panicled dogwood)
Zone 4; 3'–15'

A native dogwood that grows from central Maine to Ontario, Minnesota, and Manitoba, south to Delaware, West Virginia, Kentucky, Missouri, and Oklahoma, this is a good plant to use for a screen planting. It can be sheared or allowed to grow naturally with equal success. It grows easily, is upright in form with many branches, and has long, narrow leaves. Small creamy-white flowers in the usual flat clusters, in this case 1½" wide, are followed by little white berries in early summer, borne on bright red stems that remain on the shrub after the birds have eaten the berries, thus making it colorful late in the season. It is because these berries appear before those of most other shrub dogwoods that they are so popular with the birds. Foliage color is purplish when autumn arrives; twig color is gray, so the plant is not particularly effective in winter.

Cornus sanguinea
(Bloodtwig dogwood, Red dogwood)
Zone 4; 12'

While the common and botanical names of this dogwood would lead one to believe that it has the brightest red twigs and branches of any shrub dogwood, such is not the case. Their color

Cornus sericea (Red osier dogwood)

is duller than that of the same parts of *C. alba* 'Sibirica'. The growth of this shrub is more upright than that of the Siberian dogwood, however, and the leaves are hairy on both sides. The flowers are the usual small, white florets arranged in flat clusters, but the white in this case is tinged greenish. Blooms appear in late May or early June; fruits that follow are black, ripening in September. The foliage is a dark blood-red in autumn.

Cornus sericea
(Red osier dogwood)
Zone 2; 3'–9'

This shrub grows in swamps, along the shores of lakes and in moist thickets from Labrador to the Yukon, south through New England to West Virginia and west to Ohio, Illinois, Iowa, Nebraska, and New Mexico. Kinnikinnik, which is one of the common names sometimes applied to either *C. amomum* or this dogwood, is given because the Indians used the bark of *C. sericea* to make the kinnikinnik that they smoked.

The characteristic that a gardener must remember about this dogwood or its varieties is that they all spread by means of stolons or underground stems. Therefore they should be planted only where they have room to expand, otherwise there will be a constant pruning problem. Since the red osier grows especially well in moist situations, it is

sensible to use it in these, though it will tolerate drier soils. Its place is definitely in a naturalistic planting.

The branches often are prostrate, rooting where they touch the ground, though most of them grow upright. Their color is blood red or purplish red and the winter twigs are bright red. Leaves are dark green on the tops, whitish underneath. The small flowers are dull white, borne in rather loose clusters starting in late May, but continuing to appear intermittently for several months. Fruits, borne in summer, are white; autumn foliage color is reddish.

This dogwood may be distinguished from *C. alba* because the disks in its flowers are red and conspicuous while those of *C. alba* are yellow.

Cornus sericea 'Flaviramea' (syn *C. sericea lutea*)
(Goldentwig dogwood)
Zone 2; 5'

Lower growing than the red osier dogwood, this also spreads by means of underground stems. The branches are yellowish and the twigs bright yellow. Flowers are white in 1¼" clusters and fruits also are white but are not effective for any length of time as the birds eat them as soon as they whiten. It may be used wherever the yellow color of its branches and twigs is desired.

Cornus sericea lutea
(see *C. sericea* 'Flaviramea')

Cornus sericea 'Flaviramea'

Corylopsis spicata

CORYLOPSIS
(Winterhazel)

Relatives of the witch hazels, these shrubs have clusters of yellow blooms in mid-April and these early flowers are the reason for growing them. They are not as husky or as hardy as witch hazels. *C. glabrescens* is considered the hardiest and will bloom fairly often in Zone 5b, regularly in Zone 6.

Winterhazels prefer to grow in sun but will do well in light shade. Moist, but well drained, peaty or sandy soil is best for them. They should be pruned in summer if it is necessary to make them grow more compact.

Corylopsis glabrescens
(Fragrant winterhazel)
Zone 6 to Zone 5b; 15′
A compact, rounded shrub with fragrant, pale yellow flowers in drooping clusters before the leaves unfold, this is a native of Japan.

Corylopsis spicata
(Spike winterhazel)
Zone 6 to Zone 5b; 4′–5′
Handsomer and hardier than either *pauciflora* or *sinensis*, this species is not quite as hardy as *C. glabrescens*. It has showier flowers than the three species just mentioned and more of them. They also are fragrant, are bright yellow and have purple anthers.

CORYLUS
(Hazel, Filbert)

Ranging in height from 9′ to 30′, depending on the precise species or varieties, hazels are grown for their interesting catkins early in spring and for the bright colored foliage of certain varieties, the unusual form of others. All those named below are easy to grow in any fairly good soil and require practically no care.

Corylus americana
(American hazelnut or hazel)
Zone 4; 3′–8′
Found growing from Maine to Saskatchewan, southward to Florida and Georgia, westward to the Dakotas, this shrub usually grows in hillside pastures and thickets. The catkins appear in April and May and the edible fruits ripen in August and September.

Corylus atropurpurea
(see *C. maxima* 'Purpurea')

Corylus avellana
(European hazelnut)
Zone 5 to part of Zone 4; 15′
A large shrub, rounded in form, with big, coarse-appearing, roundish leaves, this grows in full sun, light shade, or even quite deep shade, in almost any soil short of clear sand.

The male catkins expand before the leaves open in early spring, but since they have been noticeable all fall and winter, they also give interest at those seasons. This shrub suckers badly, so must be placed where it has room to spread or the suckers kept cut. It makes a good clipped hedge where suckers do not matter or can be controlled. Otherwise it is best used in a naturalistic planting. Many cultivars of this hazel are used for commercial crops of nuts.

Corylus avellana 'Aurea' (syn C. maxima aurea)
(Golden filbert)
Yellow leaves early in the season and yellowish branches distinguish this variety and are the reasons for growing it. Some selections have far better yellow coloring than others, so buy this from a good nursery and see it before buying.

Corylus avellana 'Contorta'
(Contorted hazel, Harry Lauder's walking stick)
In the United States I never have seen this plant growing taller than 6′, but in Europe, in the north of Holland, it was a small tree with a single trunk and about 20′ high.

The only reason for growing this shrub is for its curiously contorted branches. These form a pattern against a wall, particularly effective in winter. It has the usual catkins early in spring and

Corylus avellana

Cotinus coggygria 'Purpureus'

the foliage, while not as large as on some hazels, looks like that of the others.

This shrub usually has the top of the contorted hazel grafted or budded onto an understock of the European hazel. As a result it must be watched so that the understock does not outgrow the less vigorous contorted variety.

Corylus maxima atropurpurea (see *C. maxima* 'Purpurea')

Corylus maxima aurea (see *C. avellana* 'Aurea')

Corylus maxima 'Purpurea' (syn *C. maxima atropurpurea*) Zone 5; 10'
This cultivar is the best of the purple-leaved hazels and should be purchased in preference to others. The foliage color will be deepest if the plant is grown in full sun. Leaves are rounded, flowers the usual catkins, and nuts (if any form) have a red or pinkish husk and are edible.

COTINUS

Cotinus coggygria (syn *Rhus cotinus*) (Smoke tree, Smoke bush) Zone 4, though sometimes dies back in winter in this zone; usually 10'–12', but may reach 15'
While this shrub has been used for enough years to call it old-fashioned, it still is extremely popular today. It is entirely different in effect from any other plant while it is in bloom because the fruiting panicles, which most plants bear in quantity, look like fluffy smoke. In this species the smoke is pinkish or grayish at first, later the pinkish smoke turns brown while the grayish smoke remains much the same color as it was at the start. The seeds are found in the midst of the smoke.

The flowers of the two sexes are found on different plants. It therefore becomes important to buy a female plant since the male plants do not produce the smoke. Also, because plants grown from seeds vary greatly in their production of the fruiting panicles, they should be seen before purchasing. The smoky effect lasts for many weeks.

The leaves of smoke trees are unusual in shape and handsome in their brilliant yellow and orange autumn colors.

Cotinus coggygria 'Purpureus' (syn *C. c. rubrifolius*) (Purple-leaved or Red-leaved smoke tree) Zone 5 to part of Zone 4, though it may die back in the winter in this zone
If anything, this variety is almost more beautiful than the species, for in it the young foliage is purple and the smoke gives the same color effect. The leaves remain purplish green all season.

There are several selected types of the purple-leaved smoke tree. 'Notcutt', a British selection, is said to be hardy and to grow 10' to 12' high, with leaves of a deep bronzy-purple and dark purple fruiting panicles. 'Royal Purple' is said to grow 6' to 8' high with dark, shiny red to purple leaves, turning to green, edged pink all summer. Dark maroon smoke is said to appear in June and July.

Cotinus coggygria rubrifolius (see *C. coggygria* 'Purpureus')

Cotinus coggygria (Smoke Bush)

COTONEASTER
(Rockspray, Quinceberry)

This is a large genus of shrubs and occasionally trees, some evergreen, some half-evergreen, others deciduous. They are grown for their glossy green foliage, their various interesting growth habits or their beautiful fruits. Sometimes they are grown for their flowers, but only occasionally, as in most species these are small, even though numerous. Most cotoneasters (pronounced ko-toe-nee-a'ster, not cotton-easter) are easy to transplant, though the evergreen forms should be purchased with balls of earth around their roots. Cotoneasters grow well in full sun, tolerate light shade, but do not thrive in deep shade. They are happy in any fairly good soil, but need good drainage and dislike moist places or moist soils.

Cotoneaster acutifolia
(Peking cotoneaster)
Zone 4; 12'

A dense, upright-growing shrub with slender branches spreading as they grow upward, this is widely used for hedges in the far north and makes handsome ones. It also may be used in shrub borders or wherever its glossy leaves and upright habit are needed.

Not only are the leaves shiny, but they have a firm texture. They are 1" to 1½" long. Flowers are almost white, only very faintly purplish or pinkish, and ³/₁₆" in diameter. The fruits that follow them are black.

Cotoneaster adpressus
(Creeping cotoneaster)
Zone 4; 6"

A prostrate shrub that presses itself to the soil and often roots where it touches earth. It is irregularly branched. The leaves are glossy green, slightly undulating or wavy at the margins, the flowers are small and pink, the fruits bright red. The plant is at its best when fruits are on it and one can see the contrast in color between them and the shining leaves.

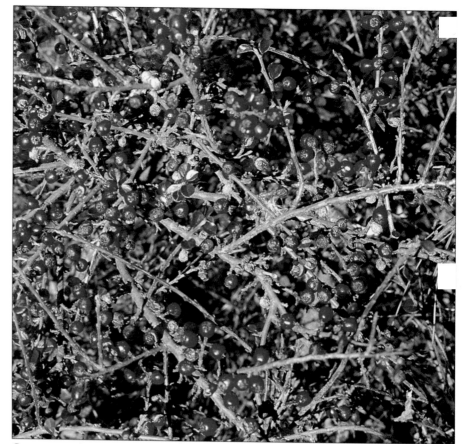

Cotoneaster adpressus

This is a shrub to be used in very special places, perhaps in a rock garden or on top of a wall where the long branches can trail downward.

Cotoneaster adpressus praecox (syn C. praecox)
Zone 4; 15"–2'

Forming a low mound with a dome-like shape, this variety is useful in front of taller shrubs, as a specimen in a rock garden, or wherever its unusual shape will make it useful. It has dark green, shiny leaves, ³/₁₆" wide, pale pink flowers flushed deep purplish red, followed by bright red fruits.

Cotoneaster apiculatus
(Cranberry cotoneaster)
Zone 4; 3'–4'

This shrub has horizontally spreading branches that, when they reach a suitable place, will fan out flat to the ground or a wall, much in the manner of those of *C. adpressus*. For this reason it may be planted on top of a wall where it first will grow upright, then send out the branches, which droop and finally grow flat on wall or ground. We have one plant set at the top of a wall that has first spread itself across the wall and then across a flight of several steps. Two other plants, set at the side and top of another short flight of steps, have billowed onto the steps, then fanned out across them. This unusual growth habit can be used to advantage in landscaping certain areas, sometimes as a ground cover.

The foliage of this cotoneaster is glossy, dark green; flowers are ¼" in diameter, deep purplish pink flushed strong purplish red. The berries are larger than those of many other cotoneasters and look like cranberries, hence the common name of the plant. They are ½" long, ⅜" in diameter, shining and strong reddish orange in color. Chipmunks dote on them and soon strip the bushes.

Cotoneaster dammeri (syn *C. humifusa*)
(Bearberry cotoneaster)
Zone 5 to part of Zone 4; 1'
A prostrate, evergreen shrub with long, trailing branches that frequently root where they touch the soil, this differs from many other cotoneasters because of the odd habit of growth. It is a good plant for use as a ground cover or possibly in a rock garden to trail over rocks.

Flowers are small and white, appearing in early June. The berries, ripening in fall, are bright red against glossy, dark green leaves.

Cotoneaster horizontalis
(Rockspray cotoneaster, Rock cotoneaster, Quinceberry, Plumed cotoneaster)
Zone 6 to Zone 5b; 2½'
In the north this is deciduous, in the south it is evergreen, but in Zone 5b it is semi-evergreen, the leaves remaining on the plant until winter is well along. The outstanding feature of this shrub is its horizontal branching habit, which is beautiful and useful.

The plant may be used as a ground cover on sloping or level ground or on top of a wide, double wall with earth between the two walls, or even as an espalier by inducing the horizontal branches to grow vertically against a wall.

The bright green leaves are ½" long; turn red and orange in autumn. Flowers are small, pink and appear in mid-June. The bright red fruits are small and there are rarely many of them, at least on my plants. Apparently a milder climate is needed for heavy berrying, for I have seen plants laden with fruits in Zone 7.

Cotoneaster horizontalis perpusilla
More depressed in growth than the species, this variety has more small branches and many more, larger berries than the rockspray cotoneaster.

Cotoneaster humifusa
(see *C. dammeri*)

Cotoneaster horizontalis

Cotoneaster microphylla
(Small-leaved cotoneaster, Wall cotoneaster, Rockspray)
Zone 6; 3'
This plant grows into a sort of tangled mound if left untrained. In that form, it is useful only in between rocks in a rock garden or place in which there naturally are rocks. However, with a little training and pruning it forms a mat instead of a mound. It is dense in growth, has glossy, dark green leaves, more evergreen than those of the Rock cotoneaster, small white flowers in June and scarlet berries in fall. Its leaves are the smallest of any cotoneaster.

Cotoneaster multiflora
Zone 5 to parts of Zone 4; 8'
This shrub and its variety *calocarpa* are exceptions to the general rule with cotoneasters, for they definitely are grown for their flowers as well as their fruits. The plants flower profusely in May, with upright clusters of white blooms borne all along the branches. These are followed by equally profuse, large, red fruits in autumn. The forms of the plants are spreading and 10' to 12' must be allowed for either shrub to reach its full size. Branches are slender and arching, leaves oval, bluish-green and deciduous. Both *C. multiflora* and *C. m. calocarpa*, either in bloom or in berry, are gorgeous shrubs by any standards.

Cotoneaster horizontalis (Rockspray Cotoneaster)

Cytisus × praecox

Cotoneaster multiflora calocarpa
Slightly larger flowers and fruits distinguish this variety from the species.

Cotoneaster praecox
(see C. adpressus praecox)

CYDONIA
(see CHAENOMELES)

CYTISUS

(Broom, a common name applied also to the genus Genista)

These slender-branched, sometimes almost leafless shrubs have value in the garden for their bright colored flowers and for the fact that the branches stay bright green during the entire winter. However, even in Zone 5, where many of them are supposedly hardy, they sometimes die to the ground in a severe winter, growing again from the roots the following spring.

They like full sun, most of them dote on poor, sandy soil, and all must have perfect drainage. They are not easy to transplant even when young and rarely can be moved when mature. The best way to buy them is grown in pots or, if this form is unavailable, then with earth balls around the roots. It is best to move them in spring.

Flowers of all are shaped like those of peas (they belong to the same plant group) and, in the hardy brooms, almost all are some shade of yellow.

Cytisus andreanus (see C. scoparius 'Andreanus')

Cytisus × praecox (C. multiflorus × C. purgans)
(Warminster broom; Some catalogs list other brooms as Warminster broom)
Zone 6 to part of Zone 5; 4' to 5'
Blooming from mid-May to early June, this is the earliest broom to flower. The ⅜″ to ½″ wide blossoms are borne all along the arching branches and are two-toned, the 2 lower petals brilliant green-

ish yellow and the 2 upper petals such pale yellow that they are almost white. A plant in bloom is literally covered with flowers.

Cytisus × praecox 'Albus'
The same as the Warminster broom, except for white flowers instead of yellow.

Cytisus × praecox 'Hollandia'
(Warminster broom)
Zone 6 to part of Zone 5; 6'
This is a cultivar of *praecox* with a red eye in the yellow flowers, which are the same shade as the species.

Cytisus purgans
(Provence broom)
Zone 6 to part of Zone 5; 3'
A dwarf shrub with a dense habit of growth and stiff, upright branches, this has brilliant, deep yellow flowers in mid-May.

Cytisus scoparius
(Scotch broom)
Zone 5; 4'–6'
Upright-growing, this shrub is laden with comparatively large, to 1″ long, bright yellow flowers in mid-May. These are usually borne singly or in pairs in the axils of the leaves.

Cytisus scoparius (Scotch Broom)

Cytisus scoparius 'Andreanus'

Cytisus scoparius 'Andreanus'
Zone 5b

More erect growing than the Scotch broom, this variety has yellow flowers with crimson "wings" and is well worth trying to grow for the bright flower colors.

DAPHNE

Daphnes are considered cantankerous shrubs to grow. This is because their requirements so often are not met and they simply will not grow unless conditions suit them. Perfect drainage is requirement number one. Loose, sandy soil is requirement number two, and full sun is requirement number three. A cool "root run" is the fourth and last requirement. No protection is needed in winter if temperatures do not go below minus 10 degrees. If they do, then throw straw or a few evergreen branches over the daphnes after the ground is frozen. These plants should be watered in summer only if the soil has been dry for 10 days or more, as they do not like wet soils. They should be purchased with balls of earth around their roots and are best moved in spring. They are worth any additional trouble it takes to grow them for the scent of their flowers if nothing else—and I say that about very few shrubs.

Daphne × burkwoodii 'Somerset'
(D. caucasica × D. cneorum)
Zone 4; 5' to 6'

For all garden purposes this daphne is identical with the species, *burkwoodii*. If the two are not the same plant, they certainly have the same parentage and are treated as one in this book.

Originating in England, this daphne is an upright-growing shrub that, in May and early June, has star-shaped, fragrant, pale pink to white flowers in great quantities. Individual florets measure ⅜" across and the clusters in which they are arranged are 1½" in diameter. The plant is almost evergreen in Zone 5b, dropping its leaves for only a few weeks in spring. It is effective when planted at the front of a shrub border or may be used as a specimen near a sitting-out area. It should be purchased as a potted plant for ease in transplanting and also because larger sizes are expensive.

Daphne × burkwoodii 'Carol Macki', a variegated variety

Daphne cneorum
(Rose daphne, Garland flower)
Zone 4 in well-drained soil; 6" to 8'

When this shrub is in flower its fra-grance pervades the area near it, so that visitors search for the source. It has evergreen, gray-green foliage, makes a low, flat mound in the garden, so is best used on top of a wall, in a rock garden or as a ground cover.

When it is in bloom, in late May or early June, this mound of foliage is almost obscured by the ¾" wide clusters of strong purplish pink flowers. Since large plants of this daphne may be a yard across, a plant in bloom is quite a sight. Plants that are happily situated will bloom a little now and then during the summer, but particularly about September. The plant has sufficient foliage to furnish coolness for its own roots, but many gardeners mulch under the leaves and over the soil with stones in an effort to insure a cool area for the roots.

Daphne mezereum
(February daphne)
Zone 4; 3'

This is a small, upright-growing, deciduous shrub planted for its extra-early rosy pink flowers, which are intensely fragrant. These are borne in clusters along the branches and appear before the dark green leaves unfold. Whoever gave this shrub its common name must have lived in a milder climate than I do, for I can depend on flowers on April 10 to April 14 from the pair of these daphnes in a protected place under one of the west windows of my office. Vivid red, oval, ⅜" long berries follow the flowers, clustered along the steams. Although these are attractive, they are poisonous.

Daphne mezereum should be moved only when very small, as it is difficult to move when larger, should always be purchased with a ball of earth around its roots and should not be set in a prominent position for it has a disconcerting habit of dying with no apparent cause. When two or three plants are set side-by-side and all appear to be growing equally well, one may be dead in spring while the others are in full bloom. There seems to be no sensible explanation for this behavior.

Daphne mezereum 'Alba'
This is the white-flowered variety of the plant described above and is identical with it except for more vigorous growth, the flower color, and the color of the berries, which are yellow. Regardless of color, they are still poisonous.

DEUTZIA

A group of shrubs grown for flowers, which in most are white or white tinged with pink, rose, or purple. Only one, *D. gracilis*, has particularly pretty foliage. None have any autumn coloration and none have fruit of any significance.

Furthermore, since they bloom on branches grown the preceding year and start growth with the first warm weather, they lose some twigs every year and these brown areas must be removed or the shrubs look unsightly.

On the other side of the balance sheet are the facts that deutzias will grow in any soil, like full sun the best but will tolerate light shade, and when they flower, some are so laden with blooms that the branches hardly can be seen. They have little or no trouble from insects or diseases. All deutzias can be moved with bare roots but, because some of them have a tendency towards tenderness, are best moved in spring.

Deutzia crenata
(see *D. scabra*)

Deutzia crenata rosea, D. rosea plena, or D. rosea floriplena
(see *D. scabra* 'Plena')

Deutzia gracilis
(Slender deutzia)
Zone 5; 3'–4'
A slender-branched, graceful, delicate-looking shrub, with narrow leaves of pale green, this is the first deutzia to flower. It bears a wealth of white, scentless, ½" to ¾" wide blooms in upright clusters 2" to 4" long in late May.

Deutzia gracilis

If you can have but one deutzia, this is the species to grow. It may be used at the front of a shrub border, for edging a walk or as an interesting unclipped hedge. If a small specimen shrub is needed, it even can be considered for that use. It will grow well in light shade.

Deutzia gracilis rosea
(see *D.* × *rosea*)

Deutzia × lemoinei (D. parviflora × D. gracilis)
(Lemoine deutzia)
Zone 5 to part of Zone 4; 5'
In late May this shrub bears white flowers in upright clusters. It is a good, compact plant, a parent of a group of hardier hybrid deutzias.

Deutzia × lemoinei 'Compacta'
Even hardier than *D.* × *lemoinei*, this is a smaller plant with even more compact form.

Deutzia × rosea (D. gracilis × D. purpurascens) (syn D. gracilis rosea)
(Rose-panicle deutzia)
Zone 6 to Zone 5b; 4'–5'
The flowers of this shrub are differently formed from those of most deutzias. They are bell-shaped and white, tinged pink on the outsides of the petals. They appear in late May to early June.

Deutzia × *lemoinei*

**Deutzia × rosea 'Pink Pompon'
Zone 6 to Zone 5b; 3'–4'**
If you are looking for a pink deutzia and live where this one is hardy, buy this first. The flowers are double, ⅝" in diameter, borne in tight clusters 1½" in diameter and almost that in depth. The overall effect of the blooms is of light purplish pink but the outsides of the petals and the buds are striped with deep purplish pink. The petals are not white, they are definitely pale pink, on the lavender side. The flower color fades as the blooms age, the first effect being more pink than the effect a week later, which is more lavender. Blooms appear in early to mid-June. The shrub needs a place in full sun for best color.

**Deutzia scabra (syn D. scabra crenata, syn D. crenata)
Zone 6 to Zone 5b; 8'**
In late June this handsome deutzia bears single white flowers, sometimes tinged purplish on the outsides. It is better known for its double-flowered varieties.

Deutzia scabra crenata (see D. scabra)

**Deutzia scabra 'Plena' (syn D. scabra roseaplena)
Zone 5b; 8'–9'**
The double, ¾" wide, white flowers, tinged moderate purplish red on the outsides of the petals, are borne in 4½" long spikes. They appear after the middle and usually towards the end of June.

ENKIANTHUS

**Enkianthus campanulatus
(Redvein enkianthus, Necklace shrub, Bell-flower tree)
Zone 5 to parts of Zone 4; 8' or 10' in the north, to 20' in the south**
While in general this shrub needs the same soil and environment as do azaleas and rhododendrons, it will grow in soil that is less acid and in a drier situation than most of them, though it grows more compact under these circum-

Erica carnea

stances than it normally would. It will grow either in full sun or quite deep shade. Its growth is unusual because of its lateral branches, which are arranged in whorls. This is not particularly noticeable as long as the tufts of leaves are green, but comes into view when they turn brilliant scarlet in autumn. The flowers appear in mid-May, before the leaves unfold, looking like little bells in long-stalked clusters. They are yellowish or orangish in color; are pretty but not exactly showy. The capsules that follow them are inconspicuous.

Enkianthus campanulatus

ERICA
(Heath)

These plants are related to *Calluna* (heather) and require the same general conditions of growth. See *Calluna* for directions for growing them.

**Erica carnea
(Spring heath)
Zone 6 to Zone 5b; 6" to 1', depending on growing conditions**
The rose-colored flowers in early April against the fine, evergreen foliage are the chief reason for growing this plant. It is compact if pruned occasionally, is pretty even without the flowers, and the buds that form in mid-summer to open the following spring are light green and interesting much of the year. There are numerous cultivars of this heath in the catalogs, far too many to list here.

Erica × darleyensis

Erica × darleyensis (parentage uncertain)
(Darley heath)
Zone 6; 3′

The advantage of this hybrid over other heaths is twofold: its vigorous growth and its ability to survive poor conditions—even to thriving in a soil that contains lime (that is, not acid in reaction). It flowers from late autumn, about November, through the winter providing it is in a sheltered place.

The foliage is evergreen and fine in texture, the flowers are lavender-pink and small.

Erica vagans
(Cornish heath)
Zone 6 to part of Zone 5; 1′ to 1½′

Pink or pinkish purple flowers from August to October, dark green, needle-like foliage and a spreading form distinguish this shrub. There are several varieties and cultivars available with flowers of different colors.

Erica vagans 'Alba'

White Cornish heath has white flowers; it is otherwise like the species.

EUONYMUS
(Spindle tree)

The botanical name, so often mispronounced, is U-on′-uh-muss with the accent on the second syllable. The genus *Euonymus* is a large one with many species, varieties and forms. Some of this group are vines, some are prostrate and best used as ground covers, others are shrubs many of which become vines if support is near them. Some may be grown as vines or as shrubs, depending on how they are pruned. Some are evergreen or nearly so. None have showy flowers; all are grown for their foliage color in autumn, their interesting bark or shape, or their bright fruits. So, if you are looking for a flowering shrub you can skip this genus entirely.

Euonymus tolerates almost any soil, though it grows best in good soil. All kinds will grow in sun and a good many will tolerate light to quite heavy shade.

An important pest that attacks most often the evergreen vining types is euonymus scale, which can ruin a plant. See Chapter 9 for a discussion of scale insects. This scale is more of a pest in some parts of the country than in others. There are localities in which it hardly is known.

Euonymus alatus
(Winged spindle tree)
Zone 4 to part of Zone 3; 8′ or 9′ and eventually about as wide as high

An extremely useful shrub because of the autumn coloring of its leaves, which turn first pink, then scarlet. Best color is obtained when the plant is in full sun but, since a plant in shade will have different and deeper coloring than one in sun, the gardener interested in foliage for flower arrangements should grow at least one plant in each situation.

The shrub form is dense, rounded at the top; the branching stiff with the branches spreading horizontally. Branches and twigs have from two to four broad, corky wings attached. Flowers are ⅜″ across and are insignificant because they are not only small but strong yellow green in color so hardly are visible. The fruits are small and red, often lost against the bright autumn foliage. Winter silhouette is interesting because of the branching habit and the wings.

This shrub may be used in a border, as a specimen, or for a hedge.

Euonymus alatus

Euonymus alatus 'Compacta'
Zone 5 to parts of Zone 4 where it
is a borderline shrub; 4′–5′
A dwarf form of the species described above, this is even more useful because it is smaller. It is rounded in form, has the same bright autumn foliage coloration as the species, but often lacks entirely the corky appendages to the branches. These always are smaller than those in *alatus* and, as stated above, often are non-existent, especially in mature plants.

This plant is useful in many ways—as an unclipped or lightly clipped hedge (it is so compact that it needs clipping but rarely), as a specimen shrub where bright fall color is needed in a landscape design, or as a foreground shrub in a border.

Euonymus americana
(Strawberry bush, Hearts-a-
bustin'-with-love, Bursting heart,
Fish wood, Brook euonymus,
American spindle tree, American
burningbush)
Zone 6 to Zone 5b, though it will
kill to the ground line in a severe
winter in Zone 5b; 5′ to 6′
Upright in growth with slender branches, this has delicate, pale pink flowers with dark purplish red stamens, beautiful especially when seen at close range. These are followed by fruits that are pinkish-red and warty, quite different from those of other species. While these are on the plant, the foliage is dark red. Strawberry bush will tolerate shade and grows especially well in damp spots, though it also will thrive in dry soil.

Euonymus atropurpureus (see
Chapter 13)

Euonymus europaeus (see Chapter 13)

Euonymus fortunei
(Wintercreeper)
Zone 5
This species is a clinging vine that sends out little protrusions that look like roots but actually hold the vine to its support.

Euonymus fortunei 'Gold Edge'

This vine is listed in this chapter about shrubs because it is the most variable of any species of woody plants and, before its assorted shrubby varieties and cultivars are discussed, an explanation is needed.

First of all, it must be borne in mind by every gardener who reads this that *E. fortunei* is the hardiest of evergreen vines. If you were a nurseryman, you too would be on the lookout for any evergreen vine (or its shrub forms) hardy in the north because these would be excellent plants to offer your customers, who have not too many hardy plants from which to choose. (This is the reason why nurserymen have selected far too many forms.)

Next, it must be recognized that the variability of the varieties of this species because of sporting (see explanation in Chapter 7) is so great that only the varieties of *Euonymus kiautschovicus* (a species formerly called *E. patens* and still so listed in many catalogs) comes near to rivaling it in variability.

And, finally, these varieties of *E. fortunei* vary depending on whether the plants are mature or juvenile in form. As an example of these two forms and what happens to make one cultivar change from one form to the other, I shall use a vining type of euonymus, *Euonymus fortunei* 'Colorata'. This vine

normally is used as a ground cover and is a splendid plant for this use. Its cultivar name comes from the color of the leaves in late autumn and all winter—a purplish red.

Now as long as 'Colorata' is grown as a ground cover vine, it will remain juvenile in form. Just let it reach and climb a support and it will become mature in form. When the nurseryman (or you) takes cuttings (see Chapter 11, on propagation by cuttings) from a juvenile form of 'Colorata' the plants grown from these cuttings will retain the juvenile, vining form. If cuttings are taken from the mature form, shrubby plants will result. These are referred to in nursery catalogs as *E. fortunei colorata erecta* and in this book as *E. f.* 'C', erect form.

The variability does not end here, for both large and small-leaved types of the erect form are listed in nursery catalogs and I own plants of both types, purchased at the same time, in the same lot of plants. These erect forms of 'Colorata' are easily distinguished from other erect forms of euonymus by that reddish-purple winter foliage color.

There is one more point to be made in this discussion and that is that the mature form of 'Colorata', like the mature form of *E. fortunei* 'Vegetus', will eventually bear fruits, while the juvenile forms of both of these plants never fruit.

Euonymus fortunei 'Emerald'

Euonymus fortunei 'Carrierei' (syn *E. radicans carrierei*)
Zone 5; 4'

This euonymus normally is a shrub but if supported it will revert to the vining form and become *E. fortunei*. You see, this cultivar is a selection from *fortunei* that is one of the first sports to appear on a mature plant of *fortunei*. It is one of the two cultivars (the other being 'Vegetus') that can be depended upon to bear fruits at a reasonably early age.

The leaves are glossy, dark green and semi-evergreen. Fruits, which are bright orange, remain on the plant for a long time.

Euonymus fortunei 'Emerald' (or Corliss) selections
Zone 5

Corliss Bros., Inc. of Gloucester and Ipswich, Massachusetts, have introduced a number of shrub forms of *E. fortunei*. All are hardy in Zone 5. All of their names start with the word "Emerald" and, while all are evergreen, their heights and widths vary according to the particular selection. All are patented.

Euonymus fortunei, erect form

There are so many, many selections that could be described by this name that it is impossible to tell what a nursery offers under this listing. Some nurseries give this erect form as synonymous with the selection 'Sarcoxie' described below. At any rate, if you are interested in buying an erect form of *fortunei*, it probably would be sensible to see first what you are buying.

Euonymus fortunei radicans, erect form

Euonymus fortunei radicans is a vining euonymus with semi-evergreen leaves about an inch long, usually with pointed tips and slightly heavier or thicker texture than those of *fortunei*. They often are not glossy. The erect form carries these characteristics into a shrub.

Euonymus fortunei radicans vegetus or *vegeta*
(see *E. f.* 'Vegetus')

Euonymus fortunei 'Sarcoxie'
Zone 6 to part of Zone 5; 4'

Introduced by the Sarcoxie Nurseries, Sarcoxie, Missouri, this has shiny green leaves about an inch to an inch-and-a-half long. Even if planted in full sun, this selection holds its foliage far into the winter. It will grow in partial or even quite heavy shade as well as in sun and is easy to shear to any desired form. However, it kills to the ground in a severe winter and does not grow again from the roots.

Euonymus fortunei 'Vegetus' (Evergreen bittersweet)
Zone 5 to parts of Zone 4; 4'

A semi-evergreen cultivar in Zone 5 and northward, this plant will grow as a vine if set next to a support, but will be an irregularly shaped shrub if not given a place to climb. It piles up its branches since each branch grows more or less horizontally. It may be trained to any desired shape, although I think its natural form is artistic. It sometimes is used as a clipped hedge.

Leaves are rounded, thick-textured, often described as leathery, and range from 1″ to 1½″ in diameter. The bright orange fruits have earned it its common name. These remain in good condition for months until the birds finally eat them, sometimes as late as early spring. The plant is easy to grow, easy to transplant.

Euonymus fortunei radicans, **erect** form

Euonymus kiautschovicus (syn E. patens)
Zone 6 to Zone 5b, where it kills completely in a severe winter, but may live for years if set in a sufficiently protected place; 7' or slightly more and spreading almost as wide

This shrub is semi-evergreen in the north, evergreen in the south. While the general growth habit is upright, some stems run along the ground, rooting where they touch, then turning upward. In this manner large clumps often are formed.

Leaves are deep green, narrow, and leathery in texture. Flowers, which are the usual yellowish-green or greenish-white, appear in early September and, since the plant is literally covered with them, they give it a light, airy appearance. Pinkish or red fruits follow these blooms but only where the growing season is sufficiently long, which is not usually the case in Zone 5b. In that zone fruits ripen only about once in ten years.

This is a beautiful, almost evergreen shrub that combines well with broadleaved evergreens or narrow-leaved evergreens. It also may be used as a clipped or unclipped hedge.

There are several cultivars of this species in the catalogs, some said to be improvements on it, others much lower-growing and therefore well worth investigating.

Euonymus nanus turkestanicus (syn E. nanus koopmannii)
(Fernleaf euonymus)
Zone 5 to part of Zone 4; 4'–6'

The species, *E. nanus*, is half-evergreen and low growing, only to 2', and procumbent in form. This has the common name of Dwarf euonymus. The variety, *turkestanicus*, is more vigorous in growth, and taller, 4' to 6'. It has narrow leaves that turn bronze-purple in autumn and stay on all winter in Zone 6, much of the winter in Zone 5b. Fruits are bright orange-red in late summer.

Euonymus kiautschoviais

Euonymus patens
(see E. kiautschovicus)

Euonymus planipes
(see E. sachalinensis)

Euonymus radicans
(see E. fortunei radicans)

Euonymus sachalinensis (syn E. planipes)
Zone 5 to parts of Zone 4; 7' to 8'

It is the pendant fruits of good size that make this euonymus different from the others. They are bright red, handsome, and most years there are plenty of them. The new leaves are bright red, turning bright green as they unfold.

Euonymus vegetus
(see E. fortunei 'Vegetus')

Euonymus yedoensis
(Yeddo euonymus)
Zone 4; 10' or more

A big shrub with stiff, upright form, flattish or slightly rounded at the tip, this has leaves often 5" long. They turn bright red in autumn when the plentiful dull pink or pinkish-purple fruits appear. These remain on the plant for a long time after the leaves have fallen.

EXOCHORDA
(Pearl bush)

The two species of pearl bush most frequently grown are large shrubs, erect and broad when older, inclined to be leggy when young, therefore occasionally needing hard pruning directly after flowering. They are grown for their beautiful strings of white, pearl-like buds and the flowers that open from them in late April to early May.

Pearl bushes grow easily in any soil; prefer a sunny spot. Both may be used in the back row of a shrub border. Neither of the large species needs to be grown in a small garden since 'The Bride' takes up so much less space, while still contributing the same pearl-like buds and white flowers.

Exochorda giraldii wilsonii
(Wilson pearl bush)
Zone 5 to parts of Zone 4; 8'–10'
This variety has slightly larger flowers (1½" in diameter) than *E. racemosa* and usually is a larger, more shapely plant. Leaves are more gray-green than those of *E. racemosa* and the plant flowers about a week earlier.

Exochorda grandiflora
(see *E. racemosa*)

Exochorda × macrantha
'The Bride'
(*E. korolkowi × E. racemosa*)
Zone 6 to parts of Zone 5; 3'–4'
A dwarf pearl bush of much more compact form than the two larger ones, it has the same strings of white buds and flowers but blooms are larger, sometimes to 2" in diameter. This is a valuable addition to the group since it takes up comparatively little space. It may be used in the front of a shrub border or in a grouping of low-growing shrubs or even as a specimen.

Exochorda racemosa **(syn *E. grandiflora*)**
(Pearl bush)
Zone 5 to parts of Zone 4; 8'–10'
This is said to be hardier than either of the other two pearl bushes described above, but since I've never had any trouble with any of them, even after a severe winter, I cannot say whether this is true or not. The flowers of *E. racemosa* are slightly smaller than those of the Wilson pearl bush (to 1¼" wide), but not enough to make any real difference in the garden picture. They are white, centered with green. The plants definitely are leggier than the Wilson pearl bush.

FONTANESIA

Fontanesia fortunei
Zone 5, a borderline shrub in Zone 4 where it may kill to the ground in winter but grows from the roots in spring; 15'
It seems a shame that this shrub is available from so few nurseries for it is drought resistant, grows well in any soil in full sun or light shade, and is a real toughy.

Growth is upright, vigorous and graceful. Foliage is much like that of a willow but very shiny. The ⅛" diameter, greenish-white flowers are arranged in 3"-long pendant clusters and appear in June to July. This shrub has very small (about ¼" long), flat, oval fruits; creamy-tan in color, born in clusters. These have no ornamental value.

This fontanesia is an excellent hedge plant, clipped or unclipped, and should make a welcome change from the more common privet since fontanesia is more graceful. It may be used also at the back of a border with lower growing shrubs in front.

FORSYTHIA
(Golden bell)

In most gardens forsythias signal the arrival of spring, though in our garden they are among the second-round of shrub bloom, the witch hazels and other extra-early shrubs having already finished flowering.

Widely planted for their bright yellow, scentless flowers, forsythias are a welcome note in the garden after a dreary winter. For this reason, if for no other, every garden ought to boast at least one forsythia. Their flowering season starts, depending on the year, usually in late March or very early April and continues for three full weeks if proper selection of species and varieties is made.

Forsythias are easy to transplant, easy to grow, tolerate almost any soil (though a long, severe drought in summer will have a deleterious effect on a plant in dry soil), and thrive in sun or light shade. The plants will grow in deep shade, but will not bloom to any extent.

Books on plant pests say that forsythias may be attacked by several, but in all the years I've been growing forsythias I've never seen any sign of dis-

Exochorda × macrantha

ease nor have I noticed any evidence of insects—a fact worth remembering.

There are several different forms of forsythias—dwarf and compact; upright and spreading, but still fairly compact; and widely spreading, usually arching. Due consideration should be given to the ultimate size of a forsythia since the larger-growing sorts need plenty of room. If crowded, they will require constant pruning.

Forsythias bloom on wood grown the previous year. For this reason the proper time to prune them is immediately after flowering. However, as long as the flower buds already are formed, it seems to me more sensible to do any necessary pruning a month to six weeks before flowering time and use the pruned branches for forcing indoors. By doing this, pruning is accomplished without loss of a year's bloom and the forced branches provide indoor beauty long before blossoms are possible outdoors.

Forsythias never should be given a "crew haircut" as they so often are in parkways or around public buildings. Their natural form is gracefully arching or stiffly erect and whichever it happens to be, it should be followed and not modified in pruning. Cutting the older branches to the ground every year is good practice as new shoots will grow from the roots and renew the shrub.

The only forsythia that will bloom reliably in the north (Zone 4) is *F. ovata*. Several others will grow well, but since flower buds are killed each winter, rarely if ever will bloom. 'Arnold Dwarf' may be used as a ground cover in Zone 4 and makes an excellent one since no flowering is involved.

Forsythia 'Beatrix Farrand'
Zone 4; 6'–8'

Plentiful golden yellow flowers, darker than those of *F. intermedia* 'Spectabilis' and 2" to 2½" in diameter, plus extremely vigorous growth are the hallmarks of this triploid forsythia. Originated at the Arnold Arboretum, Jamaica Plain, Massachusetts, it is named for the late landscape architect.

Forsythia × intermedia 'Lynwood'

Forsythia × intermedia (F. suspensa × F. viridissima)
(Border forsythia)
Zone 5; 8'–9'

This plant shows signs of its hybrid nature by displaying, on occasion, traits from both parents. Some plants will be found that have purplish red and gold autumn color, inherited from *F. viridissima*, and also, on some plants the generally upright growth habit of the border forsythia will be modified by arching branches, like those of *F. suspensa*.

Border forsythia is a vigorous-growing shrub that, when older, may grow as broad as it is high. It is best known in gardens for its cultivars.

Forsythia × intermedia 'Arnold Dwarf'
Zone 5 to parts of Zone 4; 2'–3'

Growing at least as wide and often twice as wide as it is high, with branches that droop and root where they touch the ground, this plant is a fine ground cover. Its disadvantage is its almost complete lack of flowers. If flowers are desired on a low-growing

plant, use *F. viridissima* 'Bronxensis' instead of 'Arnold Dwarf'.

Forsythia × intermedia 'Arnold Giant'
Zone 5; 8'

A tetraploid forsythia with an upright growth habit, thickish leaves and large, dark yellow flowers, this cultivar does not seem to me as good a plant as many others.

Forsythia × intermedia 'Lynwood' (syn 'Lynwood Gold')
Zone 4; 5'–7'

A branch sport of *F. intermedia* 'Spectabilis' found in Ireland, this cultivar has deep yellow flowers almost evenly spaced along the straight, erect stems. I have been told by southern nurserymen that it will grow and bloom better if cut to the ground directly after flowering. I have hesitated to copy them for where I live I do not believe there would be sufficent growth during the remainder of the growing season to produce flowers the next spring. The blooms are slightly lighter in color than those of the species and of good size.

Forsythia × intermedia 'Spectabilis' (syn *F. spectabilis*)
(Showy border forsythia)
Zone 4; 5′–6′

The most floriferous of any forsythia, this has vivid yellow blooms, from 1¼″ to 1¾″ in diameter. A plant in bloom is like a living bouquet. Although I own plants of all of the species listed here and all the newer cultivars, I would rather grow this forsythia than any of the rest. People who do not like bold flower colors should grow 'Primulina', for 'Spectabilis' is certainly bold and brassy in bloom.

Forsythia × intermedia 'Spring Glory'
Zone 4; 6′–8′

A bud sport of *F. intermedia* 'Primulina' found in Ohio, this shrub has the paler yellow flowers of its parent but they are larger, to 2″ in diameter, and they are more evenly spaced along the upright branches. A well-grown plant usually has more flowers than one of its parents growing in similar soil and light.

Forsythia 'Karl Sax'
Zone 4; 6′–8′

A tetraploid forsythia, this is more graceful in growth habit than 'Arnold Giant'. It bears a profusion of inch-wide, deep yellow flowers, darker than those of 'Beatrix Farrand'. It is said to be hardier than that cultivar.

Forsythia ovata
(Early forsythia, Korean golden bell)
Zone 3; 6′–8′

If you live in the north and want to grow a forsythia, try this species first. If it will not flower for you, no forsythia will. The flower buds are the most winter-hardy of any forsythia.

People often compare the early forsythia with the showy border forsythia and say that the early sort is not as beautiful. I do not agree with this at all. In the first place the showy border forsythia is not in bloom until the early one is almost finished flowering, so there is no direct comparison in the garden. In the second place, I find the early forsythia quite as lovely in its own way. It is true that its blooms are individually smaller than those of some other forsythias and that it does not have quite as many blossoms as many others, but it still is an excellent garden plant and delightful in flower. For these reasons I commend it to gardeners who love forsythias and wish to extend their blooming season.

F. ovata is upright and spreading in form, more compact than many other forsythias and, for that reason, often more desirable. Flowers are ½″ to ⅜″ in diameter and brilliant yellow in color.

Forsythia spectabilis
(see *F. intermedia* 'Spectabilis')

Forsythia suspensa
(Weeping forsythia, Weeping golden bell)
Zone 5, flower buds winter kill in Zone 4, although the plant survives; 6′–7′

A graceful forsythia, this has slender, arching or drooping branches that touch the ground and root where they touch. It has golden yellow flowers. It may be used to cover banks, be planted on top of a wall to droop over it, or be espaliered against a fence or wall because its branches are so flexible.

Forsythia suspensa fortunei (syn *F. fortunei*)
(Fortune forsythia)
Zone 4; 8′

The growth habit of this variety differs markedly from that of the species. Branches first grow erect to almost the full height of the shrub, then those around the outer edges droop downward. Flower color is the same as that of the species.

Forsythia suspensa

Forsythia suspensa sieboldii
(Siebold forsythia, Siebold's weeping golden bell)
Zone 5; from 3' up

A low-growing, spreading shrub, this is a first-class ground cover for sunny banks, or anywhere that a downward-growing shrub is needed. It grows upright to a few feet in height, then the branches, which are almost procumbent, arch over to touch the ground, rooting where they touch. Flowers are darker yellow than those of *F. suspensa* and therefore contrast with them. Thus, where a long bank needs to be covered, the two may be used together for variety in yellows. The Siebold forsythia also may be used almost as a vine, to grow flat against a fence or wall or be trained and pruned to form patterns against any solid surface.

Forsythia viridissima
(Greenstem golden bell)
Zone 6 to Zone 5b in protected places; 9'

Upright in growth, then with branches arching, this forsythia is distinguished from the others by its olive-green branchlets. Flowers, too, are tinged greenish and are darker yellow than those of some forsythias. They start to show color just as those of the Siebold forsythia are passing their prime. Because of this later flowering habit, this species may be used to extend the forsythia season in a large garden; but a more important reason for growing this plant is for the purplish-red color of its leaves in autumn. It is the one forsythia with dependable fall color, though leaves of some others turn gold or purple and gold some autumns.

Forsythia viridissima 'Bronxensis' (also listed as 'Bronx')
Zone 5; 2'

This plant grows into a low mound, more than twice as broad as it is high. Because of this growth habit it may be used for a low accent or in front of a shrub border as a facing down shrub. This is the only dwarf forsythia that flowers.

Forsythia, tree forms

Some nurseries train forsythias to a single, long, straight stem, allowing the plants to branch only at the top. Thus the shrub is made into a tree. This tree form is usable on either side of a flight of steps or an entranceway, but you had better see it to make certain that you like it before you buy.

FOTHERGILLA
(Witch alder)

Fothergillas are relatives of the witch hazels, with similar fruit capsules, but entirely different flowers. They are all native to the southern Appalachian Mountains, mainly to Virginia and Georgia, and are useful in the garden because they have two seasons of interest. In spring, as the leaves are unfolding, the odd, thimble-form, petal-less, white flowers appear; and in autumn, providing the plants are not in deep shade, the leaves turn yellow, orange or scarlet. Flower buds are formed in autumn, so plants should be pruned (if this is necessary, which it is only rarely) after flowering.

All fothergillas are slow growing, preferring light shade and moist, but well-drained soil. However, they will grow in full sun and dry soil if watered well during dry weather. Fothergillas are pretty when planted in woodlands, but even prettier in house plantings or

Fothergilla major

when placed in front of or with evergreens.

Two species are available; two additional species only rarely appear in nursery catalogs.

Fothergilla major
(Large fothergilla)
Zone 5; 8'

Stiff in branching, upright in growth, becoming a rather large plant, pyramidal in shape, this has flowers in late April to mid-May. Clusters may be 2" long, midway in size between those of *F. gardeni* and those of *F. monticola*.

Fothergilla monticola
(Alabama fothergilla)
Zone 5; 5'–6', sometimes taller

Growth habit is more spreading than that of *F. major* and branches are less rigid. The flower spikes also are longer, 2½"

Fothergilla monticola

Genista tinctoria

GENISTA

(Whin, Woadwaxen, Broom)

Genistas should come to mind when the place in which you want to plant has poor, dry, sandy soil. This genus loves these conditions and all members prefer full sun. All genistas are hard to transplant so should be purchased grown in pots if at all possible.

Genista tinctoria (Dyer's greenweed) Zone 2; 3′

The common name of this shrub indicates its former use in dying cloth. It has erect, angled branches, blooms in early June and is the hardiest member of this genus. There are single-and double-flowered forms, both with bright yellow flowers. In winter the twigs remain bright green. Where soil and exposure are suitable, this genista may be used for holding dry banks or in a rock garden.

HAMAMELIS

(Witch hazel)

Witch hazels have the distinction of being the last shrubs (or small trees) to bloom in autumn and, with the possible exception of pussy willow, the first to bloom in spring in the north. It is because they thus prolong the flowering season at both ends that they are grown in gardens.

They are natives, growing along streams, in low land or on banks, from Wisconsin east to Quebec and south to northern Georgia and Missouri. The bold leaves have large, rounded teeth and turn gold in autumn. The flowers of all witch hazels have long, slim petals. Blooms appear while the brown, wood-like seed capsules from the year before still are on the plants.

Witch hazels are useful both in wooded areas and in city gardens, for they tolerate smoke, dust and dry air better than most shrubs. They are upright and spreading in form.

Hamamelis × intermedia

Identifies a number of hybrids between *H. japonica* and *H. mollis,* the best of which came from a Belgian nurseryman at the Kalmthout Arboretum. The best varieties are 'Jelena', a rich coppery-red, and 'Primavera', a bright yellow. An American-bred hybrid in this group is 'Arnold's Promise', from the Arnold Arboretum.

Hamamelis japonica (Japanese witch hazel) Zone 5; usually a shrub, 10′–12′, but may be a tree to 20′

One of the early spring–flowering witch hazels, this prefers a drier, sunnier situation than the other species. Small leaves, at most 4″ long, turn bright orange-yellow in fall. The flowers have bright yellow petals with purplish sepals and are not as fragrant as those of other witch hazels.

Hamamelis japonica

Hamamelis japonica flavopurpurascens (Red Japanese witch hazel)

The difference between this variety and the species is that in this the flower petals are red or reddish, sometimes entirely so and sometimes only at the base. Sepals are deep purple.

Hamamelis japonica rubra (see *H. j. flavopurpurascens*)

Hamamelis mollis
(Chinese witch hazel)
Zone 6 and the southern part of Zone 5; usually a shrub to 12', but may be a tree to 25'

With the largest and most fragrant blooms of any witch hazel, this should be more widely grown than it is. The plant has a neat, compactly rounded form, hairy branches and top leaf surfaces. The lower leaf surfaces are covered with gray "wool." Leaves turn bright yellow in late autumn.

Flowers are golden-yellow, the bases of the petals often red. Petals are an inch-and-a-half long and slender. Blooms are fragrant. If you have space for but one witch hazel, choose this one.

Hamamelis mollis 'Brevipetala'

A fast-growing, vigorous cultivar with flowers of orange-yellow in early spring and the shorter petals suggested by the cultivar name.

Hamamelis vernalis
(Vernal witch hazel, Spring witch hazel)
Zone 6 to southern part of Zone 5; 6', but sometimes to 10'

Usually the first shrub to bloom in spring, this witch hazel is native from Missouri and Arkansas southward to Louisiana. In a protected spot, like a corner between house walls, this shrub is quite likely to have flowers in January

Hamamelis mollis

or even earlier. In an unprotected place it will bloom, depending on the weather, in late February or early March. Because weather usually is cool to cold at that time of year and witch hazel flowers close on a cold day to re-open again when weather warms, they remain in good shape for weeks.

Blooms of the spring witch hazel are not nearly as large as those of *H. mollis*, being only ½" in diameter, but there are many of them on a shrub and they are fragrant. Color range is from yellow to two-toned reddish and yellow.

Because it sprouts from the base and spreads by means of suckers, this witch hazel makes a dense clump in time. Leaves turn yellow in autumn.

Hamamelis virginiana
(Virginian witch hazel, Common witch hazel, American witch hazel, Monkey faces, Pistachio, Tobacco-wood, Winter bloom)
Zone 5 to part of Zone 4; 15'

The witch hazel that is used as an astringent is made from the branches of this shrub distilled and mixed with alcohol. Its branches also have been used for centuries and still are used by water dowsers as divining rods.

Native to the woods from Quebec westward to Minnesota and southward to Georgia and Tennessee, this hardiest witch hazel blooms from late September onward. I have seen it still in bloom in Michigan, in a sheltered spot in the woods, on Christmas day. It is the last shrub to bloom in the north.

Growth habit is open, rather straggly; leaves are large for a witch hazel and turn bright yellow in autumn. This shrub does not sucker, but often is found in colonies in the woods because its seed capsules, when they are dry and ripe, pop open with a sharp sound and shoot the black seeds out for several to many feet. The record shot seems to be 36'. This habit is disconcerting when it happens with pods on a branch that has been brought indoors.

Flowers are bright yellow; sepals brownish. The shrub will grow in light shade but blooms more freely in full sun. It is an excellent plant, not only for the edge of a woodland, but also in the background of a shrub border.

Hamamelis vernalis

Hamamelis virginiana

HIBISCUS

(Shrub althea, Rose-of-Sharon)

Hibiscuses are narrow-growing shrubs with almost vertical branches. Their chief use in gardens is for their late summer bloom. In August and September, when few other shrubs flower, their bright blossoms are most welcome. Their secondary use is in seaside gardens for they will tolerate growing conditions by the seashore.

Foliage is not outstanding and leaf buds do not unfold until late in spring. Because of this, many gardeners are certain that their plants are dead. Patience usually will prove otherwise. Hibiscus plants are not easy to establish. They should be moved only in spring and the soil over their roots mulched for the first two winters. Once they are well established they should need no protection.

Hibiscuses grow well in many soils but prefer one with plenty of organic matter that holds moisture. They wilt easily when summers are dry and should be watered during drought. They survive city conditions, tolerate some shade (but bloom better in full sun) and are useful in narrow places where wider-growing shrubs would need constant pruning. They sometimes are used for unclipped hedges.

Heavy pruning in spring results in larger flowers but an unsightly shrub. Unelss there is a reason for wanting these larger blooms, it is simpler to let nature take its course, which means a plant will produce many more, but smaller, blossoms.

Hibiscus syriacus
(Shrub althea, Shrubby althea)
Zone 5; 6′–8′
This plant is known in gardens through its cultivars, many of which are listed in nursery catalogs and available in nursery sales lots. The flowers of some are mediocre, of others beautiful. If I could choose but one cultivar it would be 'Blue Bird', with clear blue blooms centered with a dark eye.

You will find that there are three flower forms in hibiscus: single, semi-double and double. Most cultivars have flowers with dark centers or centers of rose or rose-red, but a few have unmarked blooms.

Work at the National Arboretum has produced some spectacular large-flowered hybrids, the best of which are 'Diana', a triploid hybrid with extra large pure white flowers that remain open at night, 'Helene', a white with red eye and 'Minerva', a lovely large lavender flowering cultivar.

Tree forms are available, trained to a single stem with branching allowed only on top of this, as are also hibiscuses with variegated green and white leaves and hibiscuses sold as 'Tricolor' with branches of three different cultivars grafted onto a single plant.

HOLLY

(see ILEX)

HYDRANGEA

Hydrangeas are particularly useful in the garden because they bloom during summer. Most of the species are easy to grow but the more tender kinds often are difficult to flower. After a mild winter, plants may be loaded with blooms but often after a severe winter there will be no flowers.

Hydrangeas are not particular about the soil in which they grow. Some of them, notably the oak-leaved hydrangea (*H. quercifolia*), will thrive in shade.

Hibiscus syriacus

Most hydrangeas have white flowers. On some species these turn green or greenish as they age and merge with the foliage. On others they turn from white to pink or rose as they grow older, thus prolonging their effectiveness in the garden. The more tender hydrangeas have handsome pink, rose, blue, or lavender flowers, depending on the acidity or alkalinity of the soil in which they are growing. (See Chapter 7 for an explanation of this phenomenon.)

Hydrangea flowers have three distinct forms that vary with the species. One is conical, as in *H. paniculata* 'Grandiflora'; another is practically flat, as in the lacecap varieties and cultivars; and the third is a globe, as in *H. arborescens grandiflora*.

There also are two different flower cluster forms, one composed of small fertile flowers in the center with large, showy sterile flowers around the outside and the other of practically all sterile blooms. The lace design in the lacecap hydrangeas is due to the placement of fertile and sterile flowers in the flower cluster.

Hydrangea arborescens
(Wild hydrangea, Seven bark, Bissum, High geranium)
Zone 5 to part of Zone 4; 9′
Native from southern New York, Indiana, and Illinois south to Florida, Missouri, and Oklahoma, this hydrangea is not as showy nor is it as widely seen in gardens as its variety, *grandiflora*.

For garden purposes, the difference between them is that almost all of the flower head of *grandiflora* is of large, sterile flowers whereas that of *arborescens* often is composed of all small, fertile flowers, therefore it is not nearly so effective in the landscape. For this reason, *arborescens* might be used in a wooded area, while *grandiflora* would be more likely to be used in a cultivated garden. Flowers of both are white, turning greenish with age.

Hydrangea arborescens 'Annabelle'

Hydrangea arborescens 'Annabelle'
Zone 6; 3′–4′
A selection of Prof. J. C. McDaniel at the University of Illinois, this has larger heads than the Snowhill hydrangea, up to 8″ across and even larger. These are effective in June and continue to color until August. Like the Snowhill hydrangea, this will grow well in part shade or on the north side of the house. It does not thrive in the southern part of the country.

Hydrangea arborescens grandiflora
(Hills of Snow or Snowhill hydrangea)
Zone 5 to part of Zone 4; 3′
The dwarfness of this variety, the large creamy-white blooms, plus the fact that it flowers in early July, make this an extremely popular shrub. It flowers so profusely, most years, that it seems truly a small hill of snow. Form is upright and usually quite dense. The heart-shaped leaves are attractive but do not turn color in autumn. The white blooms turn greenish, then brown as they get old.

This shrub is not absolutely hardy in some of the northern parts of Zone 5 and in Zone 4. If winters are severe it may kill to the snow line but, since it flowers on new growth, no blossoms will be lost. The plant simply grows smaller than it would elsewhere.

Snowhill hydrangea grows in almost any soil, prefers full sun and is easy to transplant and grow. It is widely used in foundation plantings, in rows to mark the property line and in shrub borders.

Hydrangea hortensis
(see H. macrophylla hortensis)

Hydrangea macrophylla (syn H. hortensis, H. opuloides, Hortensia opuloides)
H. macrophylla hortensis
(Hortensia, French hydrangea, Blue hydrangea, Florists' hydrangea)
Zone 6 to protected places in the southern part of Zone 5; About 3′ in Zone 5b
These two hydrangeas, *H. macrophylla* and *H. macrophylla hortensis* are listed here together because the catalog nomenclature is so hopelessly confused that it is impossible to guess which one is meant by the catalog listing. Catalog names used for this group or members of it include: *H. domotoi, H. hortensis, H. otaksa* and *H. mariesii* and, in addition to these, just the word "Hydrangea" in front of any cultivar name.

To a gardener this confusion of names should mean that he should see either the plant he wishes to purchase while it is in bloom or a good picture of it. This is the only way he can be certain of getting what he wants.

None of the hydrangeas in this group is hardy in the far north. A few cultivars, notably 'Nikko Blue', will live and bloom annually if they are set in protected places in Zone 5b. 'Nikko Blue' flowers on wood of the current year's growth so that any dieback during winter does not lessen the amount of flowering.

The lacecaps and many others of the cultivars bloom from buds at the tips of branches grown the previous year, so that there are no buds left to bloom if these branches winterkill.

If these hydrangeas demand sheltered places and winter protection, is it worthwhile to grow them? I think so, because their bright blooms certainly help the garden picture to be beautiful in July and August.

The best way to protect plants of the tender hydrangeas is to bend their branches downward as far as they will grow without breaking and to heap soil over them. Some gardeners top this mound with a bushel basket turned upside down. This holds all underneath it firmly in place. It also is possible to lift the plants and move them into a cool basement for the winter, but to me this does not seem worth the effort.

Flower color of these hydrangeas depends on the reaction of the soil in which they are growing. If they are in acid soil, the plants will produce blue flowers; in alkaline soil the blooms will be pink or rose. It is possible to control flower color by adding lime to the soil to make flowers pink or sulphur or iron sulphate to the soil to make flowers blue. I do not advocate the use of alu-

Hydrangea macrophylla

minum sulphate as an acidifier because, sooner or later, a residue of free aluminum will be left in the soil (it shows as a white coating on top of the soil) and this may kill the plants.

I would advise anyone who wants to grow these hydrangeas to try one or two plants to see how well they bloom before buying more. Start with 'Nikko Blue' and, if you live in Zone 5b, set it in a protected corner. (In Zone 6 you need not bother.) If this thrives, it does not mean that another, less hardy cultivar will do the same. Try another and see what happens under your conditions.

Varieties and cultivars in the catalogs include: 'Blue Boy', 'Blue Prince', 'Blue Wave', 'Bouquet Rose', 'Domotoi', 'Mariesii', 'Nikko Blue', 'Otaksa', 'Parsival', 'Pink Monarch', 'Royal Blue', 'Veitchii', and *Hydrangea serrata* 'Grayswood'. Most have globe-shaped flower heads and single blooms.

'Parsival' and 'Domotoi' have double flowers. 'Blue Wave', 'Mariesii', 'Veitchii', and 'Grayswood' are all lacecaps. A variegated, green-and white-leaved form of 'Mariesii' also is offered.

Hydrangea paniculata (syn *H. p. praecox, H. p. tardiva*)
Zone 4; 12'–15' as a shrub, to 30' as a tree in Japan, but may be kept to any size by drastic pruning early each spring
Hardiest of all the hydrangea species, this rarely is seen in species form. The people who would prefer a smaller flower head than the peegee hydrangea has should grow the species instead. It has a dense, rounded form, is tolerant of many soil conditions and light shade. However, it grows best in full sun and in good, rather moist soil. It has escaped from cultivation in some places in Massachusetts.

The panicles are composed mostly of sterile flowers plus a few fertile ones. They are creamy-white and change to pink and rose as the season advances. Flowering starts in August. The plant may be used as a specimen or at the back of a shrub border.

Hydrangea paniculata 'Grandiflora'

Hydrangea paniculata 'Grandiflora' (Peegee hydrangea, P. G. hydrangea, for the initials of its specific and varietal names)
Zone 4; 20'–25', but may be kept a more reasonable height by severe pruning in early spring
The chief difference between this variety and the species is the flower form. Bloom clusters are larger in the peegee hydrangea and practically all the flowers are sterile. A well-grown shrub may have panicles a foot-and-a-half long and a foot through. The flowers, which are first green, turn white and then, as they age, pink, rose, or sometimes purplish. They remain on the plant well into the winter. They may be cut and dried at any of their color stages and often are used for winter bouquets.

Blooming time, like that of the species, is August and the flowers remain in good condition for weeks, if not months.

This hydrangea often is seen trained to tree form, that is to a single main stem or trunk. When nurseries list "tree form," they mean a plant so trained. There are, occasionally, places in a large garden where such a plant is well situated, but this does not happen often.

Hydrangea paniculata praecox (see *H. paniculata*)

Hydrangea paniculata tardiva (see *H. paniculata*)

Hydrangea quercifolia
(Oak-leaved hydrangea)
**Zone 6 to Zone 5b, worth trying
further north in a protected place;
5' or 6'**
Growing wild in Georgia, Florida, and
Mississippi, this plant is as much at
home in the garden as in its native habitat. Its handsome leaves are reason
enough for growing it, but its autumn
foliage color and lovely flowers, as well
as its ability to thrive in dense shade,
are additional reasons.

As the botanical name (and, for
once, also the common name) implies,
the leaves are shaped rather like those of
an oak. They are, however, of softer
texture than those of oaks. Medium
green on top, leaves are white underneath, effective when the breeze blows
and the undersides show. They turn
dark red and reddish-purple in autumn.

Shrub form is upright and dense.
Flower panicles also are upright, with
white florets turning purplish as they
age.

Florets are 1¼" in diameter, the
clusters 6" long and 4" across.

HYPERICUM

(St. Johnswort, Touch and heal)

Hypericums are of various sizes. Some
may be classed as ground covers; others
range in height from 2' to 4'. All are
able to thrive and grow in hot, dry
places and poor, sandy soil. Most also
will grow well in light shade.

A few are extremely hardy; others
will grow only in Zone 6 and southward. Any that are doubtfully hardy in
your area should be moved in spring
only and preferably purchased with an
earth ball around the roots.

All have yellow flowers, most with
prominent yellow stamens in their centers. The taller-growing varieties make
good additions to shrub borders because
they bloom during summer when there
are not many other shrubs in flower.
The lower-growing ones are excellent
ground covers, spreading rapidly. One
or two even might be used in a border
among perennial flowers.

Hypericum calycinum

Hypericum aureum
(see *H. frondosum*)

Hypericum calycinum
**(Aaron's beard, Rose-of-Sharon [in
England], Aaron's beard St. Johnswort)**
**Zone 6 to southern part of Zone
5; 1'**
Set 18" apart, plants of this species
make a fine ground cover for a hot,
sandy, sunny, steep bank. This plant,
spreading by means of underground stolons, fills in between the plants rapidly,
and discourages weed growth by its
denseness. What more could you ask in
a ground cover except that it also thrive
in semi-shade, which this one does?

It is hardy certainly as far north as
Ithaca, New York, and in my garden.
However, it is not evergreen in either
place. In more southerly climes it is
evergreen. Leaves are leathery in texture, gray underneath. The four-angled
stems are reddish in color.

2½" blooms appear in late July or
early August and usually continue to
open at least until mid-September.
Bright yellow, they are borne at the tips
of the stems and are centered with several anthers that, until pollen is shed,
are bright red.

Hydrangea quercifolia

Hypericum frondosum

Hypericum frondosum (syn *H. aureum*)
(Golden St. Johnswort)
Zone 5; 3′

Native to South Carolina and Tennessee, Georgia and Texas, this St. Johnswort can be grown successfully further north. It is upright-growing, dense, and has heavy branches for so small a shrub. Sometimes there is but a single stem. Foliage is bluish-green. The 2″, single, bright yellow flowers, borne singly or 2 or 3 together, start to appear the middle of July and continue through most of August.

Hypericum patulum henryi (Henry St. Johnswort)
Zone 6; 3′

In the southern states this plant is evergreen. It is semi-evergreen in Zone 6 but becomes deciduous in Zone 5b. It also dies to the ground in severe winters in Zone 5 but grows again from the roots in spring.

It is a pretty plant with very long leaves, sometimes 3″ long. Flowers appear in July and are single, yellow and 2″ to 2½″ across.

Hypericum patulum 'Hidcote'
Zone 6 to southern part of Zone 5; 18″ and about the same in width

This cultivar is from the Hidcote estate in England. While it freezes to the ground every winter in Zone 5b, it comes up from the roots in spring. Since flowers are produced on new wood, this freezing back does not mean that bloom is lost.

The 2″, fragrant, bright yellow, cup-shaped flowers start opening in late June and there are some on the plant until frost. Where it can be grown, this is a shrub well worth growing.

Hypericum prolificum (Shrubby St. Johnswort)
Zone 5 to parts of Zone 4; 4′

Native from Ontario to Iowa and southward to Georgia, upright and dense in growth, this shrub becomes mounded in shape. Branches are thick with peeling, light brown bark. Leaves are narrow and shining dark green. Flowers, which appear from July through September, are only ¾″ in diameter, bright yellow and single. They are borne in clusters of a few flowers each.

Hypericum 'Sun Gold'
Zone 6 to southern part of Zone 5; 2′, may be more than that in diameter

This cultivar winterkills to the ground in Zone 5b but grows again from the roots in spring. However, it blooms on wood of the current season's growth so flowers are produced despite the freezing back.

Leaves are medium green. Blooms are 2½″ in diameter, in 4″ wide clusters, vivid yellow and are produced from July through August and part of September. This is a handsome hypericum that should be grown where it is hardy.

ILEX

(Holly)

The most beautiful hollies are evergreen trees. Their berry-filled branches frequently are used for Christmas decorations. The hardy tree hollies are described briefly in Chapter 13. In this chapter both deciduous and evergreen shrub hollies are described if they are hardy from Zone 6 northward and are listed in nursery catalogs used in this book.

All evergreen hollies are best moved in spring. Sometimes, when transplanted in fall, they drop all their leaves. Usually these grow again in spring, but sometimes the plants simply die during winter. Evergreen hollies should always be purchased with earth balls around their roots, never bare root. On the other hand, deciduous hollies may be moved in either spring or fall and with bare roots.

Good garden soil, preferably one retaining moisture and acid in reaction, will grow good hollies. The situation in which hollies are planted must be well drained, except for those that often grow wild in swamps, noted in their descriptions below.

It is important for the gardener who wishes to grow hollies to realize that, with few exceptions, male and female flowers are borne on separate plants. Of course the female plants bear the berries, but a male plant is needed within about 40′ to pollinate the flowers of the female plant.

Many people who grow hollies set plants of both sexes in the same hole to insure pollination. Then they keep the male plant pruned so that it is small compared with the female but produces enough flowers so that their pollen, when carried by bees or wind, will pollinate the female flowers and berries are produced. Since foliage of male and female plants of the same species is identical, the two plants can be pruned to appear as one to the casual observer.

Ilex cornuta 'China Boy' and 'China Girl'
Zone 5 to 9; 8′–10′

This handsome species of holly is normally associated with the South, but these two are the first hardy types suitable for the northeast. 'China Girl' bears a good crop of red berries and has lustrous, dark green spiny leaves. Excellent hedge material.

Ilex crenata (Japanese Holly)

Ilex crenata
(Japanese holly)
Zone 7
Plants in this zone are not described in this book. However, some of its varieties and cultivars are hardier than the species, so are listed below.

Ilex crenata bullata
(see *I. crenata* 'Convexa')

Ilex crenata 'Compacta'
Zone 6
A particularly compact form of *I. crenata*, this has the same small, deep green leaves, dense growth habit and black berries as the species.

Ilex crenata 'Convexa' (syn *I. bullata, I. convexa, I. crenata bullata, I. convexa bullata, I. buxifolia* of the catalogs)
(Convex-leaved holly, Box-leaved Japanese holly)
Zone 6 to southern part of Zone 5; 3′ but may grow twice as wide
An evergreen holly with small leaves, convex on top, which makes them concave below, this is an extremely useful holly. It makes an excellent low hedge; may be used in place of boxwood where box is hard to grow. It is pretty with needled evergreens or deciduous shrubs in house plantings and may be used as a specimen where a low, wide evergreen plant is desired.

It will grow in part shade as well as in full sun. It should not be given a protected spot. I know this sounds odd, but in a planting of 22 of these hollies, my only losses were among the plants more protected than others. When I complained to the nurseryman from whom I had bought the plants, he said he had noticed the same thing—that plants in the open field survived winters during which plants in more sheltered locations succumbed.

This holly is grown for its foliage. The blooms, like those of all hollies, are inconspicuous and the black berries are borne some years and not others; are not particularly beautiful in any case.

Ilex crenata 'Green Island'
A dwarf form that is flat topped, spreading, and almost horizontally branched. It has little twigs and light green foliage, sometimes tinged purplish-brown. It has a solid appearance, rather like a cushion. As for size, the pair of plants Frank Styer, the originator, gave me years ago when he first selected this holly grew only 7″ high but over 2′ wide in the six years I owned them.

Ilex crenata belleri
Zone 6 to southern part of Zone 5; 3½′
Because it is so compact and slow-growing, this holly might be used as a specimen in a rock garden. It is an evergreen dwarf with tiny leaves, very dark green. So thickly do these leaves cover the plant that you hardly can put your finger between them.

Ilex crenata 'Hetzi'
Zone 5; 3′
Another dwarf holly with the convex leaves described under *I. crenata* 'Convexa', this holly seems to be even hardier.

Ilex crenata 'Latifolia' (syn *I. crenata rotundifolia*)
(Round-leaved Japanese holly)
Zone 6
This is a form of holly distinguished by its large, round, shining leaves, which are evergreen.

Ilex crenata 'Microphylla'
(Little-leaf Japanese holly)
Zone 6
Excellent for a low hedge because it is compact and twiggy, responding well to pruning, this holly has black fruits and the tiny leaves indicated by its botanical name.

Ilex crenata 'Repandens'
Zone 6
As its botanical name suggests, this plant grows flat, very compact, and slowly. It has narrow, pale green leaves.

Ilex crenata belleri

Ilex glabra (Inkberry)

Ilex crenata 'Stokes' (also listed as 'Stokes Dwarf')
Zone 6, about 1'
A tiny, compact holly useful for edging rose beds or for tiny hedges.

There are many other varieties and cultivars of *I. crenata*, but these are most widely listed in the catalogs.

Ilex glabra
(Inkberry, Gallberry)
Zone 5; 6' or more
Useful as a hedge plant or near the house, this holly may be evergreen or it may drop its leaves, depending on the severity of the winter. Leaves may be 2" long, are usually light, but sometimes dark green and also sometimes have glossy surfaces. Fruits are black, and ⅜" in diameter. They follow tiny white ¼" wide flowers that are greenish yellow in the center, the color turning to brown as the flowers age.

While this holly is not nearly as handsome as many of the Japanese holly varieties and cultivars, it is much hardier. It is native from Nova Scotia to Florida and westward to Missouri, growing in low, damp places. It will, however, succeed in dry soil in the garden. It spreads by means of stolons and forms a dense clump. Growth habit is upright.

Ilex glabra 'Compacta'
Growing only 3' high, this has dark green, glossy foliage that may not be as pleasing in color when the plants, which are all female, bear their abundant fruits.

Ilex × meserveae
(Blue hollies)
Zone 5; 6'–12'
Interspecific hybrids between *I. rugosa* and *I. aquifolium* first produced by a New York gardening enthusiast, Mrs. F. Leighton Meserve. They possess lustrous, blue-green leaves and make handsome lawn accents or hedges. Berry production in the females is abundant. 'Blue Princess' (female) and 'Blue Stallion' (male) are two outstanding cultivars.

Ilex serrata
(Japanese winterberry)
Zone 5; 6'–7'
The saw-toothed edges of the leaves are responsible for the botanical name of this deciduous holly. The flowers are ³/₁₆" in diameter in ⅜"-wide clusters and are pale pink. The red berries stay in good condition for some time.

Ilex verticillata
(Michigan holly, Virginia winterberry, Swamp holly, Winterberry, Coonberry, Black alder, because leaves turn black after the first frost)
Zone 4 to part of Zone 3; 10' but sometimes 18'
This deciduous, widely spreading holly grows in swamps from Newfoundland to Minnesota, southward to Missouri and Georgia. However, it also will grow, but never as tall, in dry soil, so may be used in any ordinary garden situation.

Its smooth, gray branches are conspicuous in winter; the dark green leaves are virtually lost in the summer landscape, but the shrub is outstanding in autumn when the bright red, quarter-inch berries ripen while the leaves still are in evidence. After the leaves fall the berries remain on the plants and often are cut for Christmas decorations by commercial florists.

Ilex × meserveae

Ilex serrata

Ilex verticillata

The cultivar 'Sparkleberry', an introduction from the National Arboretum, is an especially good variety for heavy berry displays.

Like other hollies, *Ilex verticillata* needs a male and female plant for berry production. However, any male plant of the common American holly will act as a pollinator, so it is not always necessary to buy two plants for a heavy set of fruit.

KALMIA

(Laurel, American laurel)

Laurels are evergreen shrubs that need acid soil to thrive. One is outstanding in flower—mountain laurel (*K. latifolia*).

The foliage of several species, including the one named here, is poisonous to cattle when eaten in quantity. It also would be poisonous to humans but, since it is thick and leathery in the species most often planted, it hardly is likely that humans would try to eat it.

Laurels are pretty when combined with narrow-leaved evergreens or with rhododendrons and azaleas.

All laurels should be purchased with earth balls around the roots and preferably moved in spring.

Kalmia latifolia
(Mountain laurel, Calico bush, Big-leaf ivy, Bush ivy, Poison ivy, Spoonwood, Wicopy, Clamoun) Zone 5; 25' in the wild, but about 6' under cultivation.
This is one of the loveliest of American natives and when it flowers in the middle of June the woods from New York and New England south to Florida, westward to Louisiana, Ohio and Indiana become a glory.

Flower color varies from plant to plant. Blooms on some are pure white, on others varying shades of pink, mostly moderate pink. The inch-wide

Kalmia latifolia

florets are borne in 5″ diameter or larger clusters and are most beautifully detailed inside each floret. The buds, too, are exceptionally pretty. Both buds and blooms appear against dark, glossy evergreen foliage. Growth habit is upright and spreading.

Mountain laurel is found at the edges of woods in which soil is gravelly or in clearings. Sometimes it is found growing in swamps, which indicates the wide range of soil conditions in which it will grow. However, the soils in which it is found always are acid and, in order for it to thrive in gardens, soil that is not naturally acid must be acidified for it.

After the flowers have faded, the evergreen leaves remain for interest the rest of the year. The seed pods are not pretty nor are they interesting. Furthermore, in the interests of more flowers another year, they should not be allowed to develop but should be removed from the plant as soon as they form.

If you are buying mountain laurel, be sure to ask if the plants are nursery grown or collected. Those collected have been dug from the wild and are not as likely to survive transplanting as those grown in nurseries.

Mountain laurel often is used in plantings near the house or at the edges of woodlands and on banks. It also may be used in front of evergreens in a position not too far from the house, so its flowers may be enjoyed, or with other broad-leaved evergreens. It looks particularly effective when massed.

A great deal of plant breeding effort has been spent to improve the number of Kalmia varieties available. Dr. Richard Jaynes, at the Connecticut Agricultural Experiment Station, has produced some of the best color breakthroughs. Plantsmen in the Pacific Northwest have also done much good work to expand the color range. Some of the best new varieties include 'Ostbo Red', a rich red in the bud stage, 'Bullseye', a red and white bicolor, and 'Olympic Fire', a dark red in bud opening to appleblossom pink.

KERRIA

(Kerria, Kerrybush, Corchorus, Jews-mallow)

Kerrias are upright-growing shrubs with many small twigs that often winterkill, necessitating some pruning each spring. Branches are slender, leaves attractive and the double flowers on one variety particularly so. The kerrias described below bloom in mid-May.

Kerria japonica
(Japanese kerria)
Zone 5; 4′–6′

This shrub can be kept to the lesser height by pruning one or two old branches to the ground each year.

This is a rather temperamental plant because while it may be alive in autumn it quite often is dead by spring. This single-flowered form is far more often winterkilled than the double-flowered. But the single-flowered has one great advantage—it will thrive and flower in quite heavy shade.

The plant is upright-growing, with thin branches that remain bright green all winter, many fine twigs, medium green leaves with prominent veins and coarse teeth. The flowers are 1½ to

1¾″ in diameter. They are more yellow than strong orange-yellow and more gold than medium orange-yellow. Unfortunately the flowers do not remain on the plant for more than five days to one week, while those of the double-flowered form are in good condition for two to three weeks. There may, however, be occasional blooms during summer and usually a fair show of them in early fall. This plant is best used in a shrub border.

Kerria japonica floriplena
(see K. j. 'Pleniflora')

Kerria japonica 'Picta'
(Silver kerria, Variegated kerria)
Zone 5; 2½′

This is not only a much lower-growing kerria but, on the same bright green, slender branches as the species, it has green leaves edged with white and single, ¾″ to 1″ diameter flowers, closest to strong orange yellow.

Care must be taken to suppress ruthlessly any shoots growing from the ground that have all-green leaves or these will outgrow the branches with variegated leaves.

The plant is particularly suitable for use as a specimen.

Kerria japonica 'Pleniflora'

Kerria japonica, 'Pleniflora'
(Globeflower, Japanese rose)
Zone 5; 6′

This shrub looks the same in form and everything else except bloom as the species previously described. It is different in hardiness, surviving winters during which the single-flowered species is killed. Because of the double, rose-like flowers, the blooms are far more effective in the garden than the single-flowered form. These little "roses" are 1½″ to 1¾″ in diameter, are so full of petals that they are practically ball-shaped and are sufficiently conspicuous to have both common names refer to them. Use this kerria as a specimen or in a border.

KOLKWITZIA

Kolkwitzia amabilis
(Beauty bush)
Zone 5 to part of Zone 4; 12′ high and spreads to 8′ in width

This big shrub has upright branches that arch over all around the outside of the plant, creating a fountain-like effect. The leaves are small and not remarkable except in autumn when they turn reddish. The thousands of small tubular, ½″-wide flowers are the reason for the shrub's common name.

These occasionally are white and equally occasionally deep pink, but usually the 2 upper petals are light purplish

Kerria japonica

pink, while the paler throats are veined and marked with strong orange.

These flowers remain in good condition for at least 2 weeks if the weather is cool in early June. They are followed by gray, feathery seed heads that are interesting for additional weeks.

Of easiest culture, this shrub needs only a well-drained, sunny situation with plenty of room around it. It is indifferent to soil types and takes care of itself.

It is best used as a specimen, but is also a fine choice for the corner of a large house or the back of a shrub border.

Kolkwitzia amablis

LAVANDULA

(Lavender)

Lavandula officinalis (syn *L. spica, L. vera*)
(True lavender)
Zone 6 to southern part of Zone 5; 2′

When and where winters are mild, this little shrub is evergreen; during cold winters the leaves drop to appear again in spring. These gray-green leaves, more gray than green, and the lavender flowers are the part of the plant that are dried for sachets to place among linens. They also are used in making perfume and oil.

The flowers appear late in June and blend with the leaves so that they do not spoil the overall effect of gray. Two strains are listed in the catalogs.

'Hidcote', also listed as 'Hidcote Blue', is hardier than the species. It grows 15″ high and the flower spikes may add another 15″. Foliage is silvery; purplish-blue flowers open from early July until frost.

'Munstead' (also listed as 'Munstead Dwarf') grows only 1′ high and, because of its compactness, makes an unusual hedge around herb or rose beds. Flowers are deep heliotrope in color.

Lavenders are used as hedges in herb gardens and in perennial borders, but wherever they are used they will profit by pruning to just above the growth of the previous year. This should be done in early spring. While lavenders may be moved in either spring or fall, spring is best, especially in cold climates. They prefer a warm, sunny place, in a dry, not-too-heavy soil.

Lavandula spica
(see *L. officinalis*)

Lavandula vera
(see *L. officinalis*)

LEUCOTHOË

The name of this genus has a dieresis over the final e and is therefore pronounced loo-coh′-thoh-ee.

The leucothoës described below are broad-leaved evergreen shrubs grown for their attractive forms and foliage and for their white, wax-like flowers. They need an acid soil and prefer one that has plenty of peat mixed with it and thus holds moisture. They should be purchased with earth balls around the roots and moved only in spring.

Leucothoë axillaris
(Coast leucothoë)
Zone 6 to part of Zone 5; 2′

This is a useful leucothoë where it is hardy. As you see from the height given above, it is low, its form is dense, it has arching stems, the usual dark green, shiny leaves and tiny bell-shaped flowers in May. It prefers to be placed in semi-shade.

In an area where soil is acid, this plant makes a splendid ground cover, if a 2′ high one is desired, and it also may be used as a facing-down shrub in front of mountain laurel, rhododendron (the lower growing sorts) or pieris.

Leucothoë axillaris

Leucothoë catesbaei
(see *L. fontanesiana*)

Leucothoë fontanesiana (syn *L. catesbaei*)
(Drooping leucothoë, Fetter bush, Dog laurel, Dog hobble)
Zone 5b; 2'–3'
Although this shrub grows wild from Virginia to Georgia and Tennessee, usually in the mountains, it is hardy in the southern part of Zone 5. It is a graceful plant with spreading and arching stems and thick, shiny, dark green leaves, lighter green underneath. These turn bronze in autumn and remain that color during a mild winter, though in a severe winter they drop. The flowers are bell-shaped, ¼" long and ¹/₁₆" wide, creamy-white and fragrant. They hang in little clusters from the undersides of the stems, often along almost the entire length of the stems.

This plant spreads by means of underground stems and, if in an ideal location, will prove that it is satisfied by gradually forming a clump. Because of this growth habit it is hard to use

drooping leucothoë as a specimen plant —one never can tell how large it will get eventually. However, along a woodland path or at the edge of a rhododendron planting, the edge of woods, or with narrow-leaved evergreens in a house planting, leucothoë is quite at home and blends perfectly.

Leucothoë fontanesiana **'Girard's Rainbow' (also listed as 'Rainbow' and called that by nurserymen)**
Originated at the Girard Nursery, Geneva, Ohio, this leucothoë with variegated leaves colored white to cream, pink to rose and green is marginally hardy. While several plants in my garden have survived two winters, one Michigan nurseryman lost a large planting the first winter after setting them out. So, unless you live in Zone 6 or southward, try one plant on the north side of a building before you buy more. Except for a more upright growth, 'Girard's Rainbow' appears to be similar to *L. fontanesiana*. I have yet to see a plant over a foot high.

Leucothoë fontanesiana (Drooping Leucothoë)

(Privet)

Privets are used, if used at all, for hedges although many of them make outstanding specimen plants. Grown primarily for their foliage, some of them also have attractive flowers if the plants are not clipped to hedge form.

The leaves may be evergreen (on privets grown in the south) or deciduous; they may be variegated light green, yellow or white. The flowers of all privets are white, of a few species fragrant and most sorts bloom in June or July. Florets are small but the clusters are, in some privets, large and showy. Privet berries, usually black or blue-black and shiny, often are handsome. Of course they mature only on plants that have not been pruned.

Privets are fast, strong growers or they would not make good hedge plants. Except for the European or common privet they are exceptionally free of pests. They are extremely tolerant of soil variations and of city growing conditions.

Ligustrum amurense
(Amur privet, Amur River privet)
Zone 4; 15'
A dependable privet for the north, this species is semi-evergreen when grown sufficiently far south but deciduous in the north. If left unpruned it forms a pyramidal-shaped plant. Leaves grow 1" long and are glossy on the tops. Blooms appear about the middle of June and are followed by small, dull black berries. This is not as good-looking as either *L. ovalifolium* or *L.* × *ibolium* but is much hardier than either.

There are two distinct types of Amur privet listed in the catalogs. These are designated as "Amur north" and "Amur south." By "Amur south" nurserymen mean *L. sinense*, which is not hardy in the north.

Ligustrum californicum
(see *L. ovalifolium*)

Ligustrum × *ibolium* (*L. ovalifolium* × *L. obtusifolium*)
(Ibolium privet)
Zone 5; 6′–8′
California privet, described below,
probably is the prettiest of the privets
grown in the north. The Ibolium privet
most closely resembles the California
and should be used instead of it in the
north because California privet is not
reliably hardy under northern conditions. In zones where Ibolium privet is
not hardy, Amur privet should be tried.

Ibolium privet is an upright-growing,
deciduous shrub. The foliage is dark
green and glossy. Flowers open in mid-
June and black berries, which remain
on the plants well into winter (unless
the birds strip them from the shrub),
follow the flowers.

Ligustrum ibota
(see *L. obtusifolium*)

Ligustrum ibota vicaryi
(see *L.* × *vicaryi*)

Ligustrum lodense
(see *L. vulgare* 'Lodense')

Ligustrum obtusifolium (syn *L.
ibota*, which is the name usually
listed in the catalogs)
(Border privet)
**Zone 5 to part of Zone 4; 6′–8′,
possibly 10′**
Arching branches make this privet a
graceful shrub and a good looking specimen plant. A further characteristic that
makes it interesting is the autumn color
of its leaves, which may be purplish to
purplish-brown. The flower clusters are
nodding, blooms open from mid-June
to July and, for privet flowers, are
showy. Berries are dull blue-black to
black.

Ligustrum ovalifolium (syn *L. cali-
fornicum*)
(California privet)
Zone 6 and southward
As you can tell from the hardiness zone
stated above, this privet barely comes

Ligustrum obtusifolium

within the scope of this book. However, it is widely sold in more northerly
hardiness zones where it should not be
sold because it is not reliably hardy
there. Sometimes it winterkills even in
the northern part of Zone 6.

What usually happens to the unwary
gardener is that just when his hedge is
high and tight and he is proud of its appearance, a severe winter will cut it to
the ground. If you wonder how often
this happens, exact records show that
both the hedge belonging to our next-
door neighbors (in our former home)
and that across the road from us were
killed to the ground three times in the
21 years we lived in that house. Each
time years were required for the plants
to grow from the roots to useful height.

California privet is handsome, so it
appeals to people looking for a hedge
plant. Where it is hardy it probably is
the perfect choice. But it is not a sensible buy for gardeners in the north, especially since there are hardier privets that
can be depended on to live through severe winters.

California privet is half-evergreen
and upright-growing. Its glossy green
leaves are its most important characteristic. The cream-white blooms in mid-
June and the black berries that follow
them are no more effective than those
of many other privets.

Numerous varieties of this privet are
listed in the catalogs but will not be described here because none of them is
hardier than the species.

Ligustrum regelianum
(see *L. obtusifolium regelianum*)

Ligustrum × *vicaryi* (*L. ovalifolium* 'Aureum' × *L. vulgare*) (syn
L. ibota vicaryi)
**(Vicary privet, Golden privet,
Golden Vicari privet)**
Zone 5; 2′–3′
Because of its vivid greenish yellow foliage color and its comparatively slow
growth (for a privet) this has become an
extremely popular plant. It may be used
for an accent with evergreens or other
shrubs in a house planting, as a low
hedge or edging for a driveway or for
edging a large flower bed in a formal
garden. In fact, it is useful wherever its
foliage color is desirable.

Ligustrum × *vicaryi*

Ligustrum vulgare (Common Privet)

Ligustrum vulgare
(European privet, Common privet, English privet, Prim, Prim-print, Primwort, Print, Skedge, Skedge-with)
Zone 5; 10'–12'
Because in certain localities this privet is subject to a blight that makes it a poor choice, ask to see some hedges of it already growing in your neighborhood before you buy plants of common privet.

It is a wide-growing plant, deciduous, or sometimes semi-evergreen. Although its chief use is for hedges, it also makes a handsome specimen. When grown in this manner the ¼" white flowers in 2" long clusters in mid-June to July and the shining black berries, both against 2½" long leaves, make it attractive over a long period. When the birds leave them alone, the berries hang on well into the winter.

Ligustrum vulgare 'Lodense' (syn *L. lodense, L. lodense nana, L. densi-folium nana*)
A dwarf, compact form of common privet, useful where a lower, thick hedge is needed.

LONICERA
(Honeysuckle)

There are both shrub and vine forms of honeysuckles. The shrubs are upright in growth, are easy to move and to grow in almost any soil. Most prefer to be placed in full sun but many will tolerate a great deal of shade and still flower and fruit. All are vigorous in growth.

Even the evergreen forms of honeysuckles have undistinguished small leaves that do not change color in autumn. Small fragrant flowers are produced in abundance and may be white, yellow, lavender, pink, rose, or red in color. They are followed by equally large masses of berries, beloved by birds. These usually are red, orange-red, or orange, though some honeysuckles have blue or black fruits that are not as conspicuous.

Honeysuckles are of the easiest possible culture. They need no special care, for the shrub forms have no insects or diseases that attack them. They may be used for unclipped hedges, in shrub borders and some kinds make beautiful specimen plants. Many honeysuckles unfold their leaves so early in spring

that it is almost impossible to transplant them while still dormant. For this reason it is better to order them for fall delivery. They may be moved with bare roots.

Lonicera alba
(see *L. tatarica alba*)

Lonicera bella albida
(see *L. bella* 'Candida')

Lonicera bella 'Candida' (syn *L. b. albida*)
(White Gotha honeysuckle)
Zone 4; 6'–8'
This is a large, graceful bush that is covered with large, white flowers in late May. The red fruits ripen in July.

Lonicera 'Clavey's Dwarf'
(see *L. xylosteoides* 'Clavey's Dwarf')

Lonicera fragrantissima
(Fragrant honeysuckle, Winter honeysuckle)
Zone 6 to southern part of Zone 5; 7'
For many years in our former garden we had a plant of this honeysuckle in a corner made by house wall and porch. In this situation it often bloomed in late February and also often was evergreen. When we moved the plant with us to our present larger, more exposed gar-

Lonicera fragrantissima

Lonicera japonica 'Halliana'

den, it changed its habits; it is now deciduous and blooms in early April.

The plant grows upright, then the stiff branches spread outward and arch. Leaves are thick and dark green. Flowers are tiny, creamy-white and so fragrant that even a small spray of them brought indoors will perfume a room. Berries are red but, since they color early, birds eat them as fast as they ripen.

This is a wide spreading shrub that needs room to grow its full size. If not given plenty of space, it will require constant pruning. It blooms on wood grown the previous year so should not be pruned in late autumn or early spring or the flower buds will be cut off.

Lonicera japonica
(Japanese honeysuckle)
Zones 4 to 9; 25' and more

Can be used as a shrub, vine or ground cover for difficult-to-plant slopes. Prune heavily to keep bushy, allow it to twine up support as a vine, or let it creep over the ground as a ground cover. These drought-tolerant plants are vigorous, create a dense weave of vines, and produce masses of yellow and white trumpet-shaped fragrant flowers followed by small, black, fleshy fruit. The oval, pointed leaves are semi-evergreen, persisting all year during mild winters. 'Halliana' (Hall's honeysuckle) is the most widely grown cultivar.

Lonicera korolkowii
(Blue-leaf honeysuckle)
Zone 5 to southern part of Zone 4; 10' or a little more and 8' in width

The reasons for growing this honeysuckle are its blue-green leaves and its bright rose-colored flowers the third week in May. Berries that follow, ripening in July and August, are bright orange-red.

Blue-leaf honeysuckle may be used as a specimen, in the shrub border or for an unclipped hedge. It should be placed only where the unusual color of its foliage is suitable. It is difficult to transplant so should be moved only in spring and purchased with a ball of earth around its roots.

Lonicera korolkowii 'Zabelii'
(Zabel's honeysuckle)
Zone 4; 5'–6'

The same blue-green leaves as the species described above adorn this plant but the flowers are darker and the plant is smaller and neater. Berries are ¼" in diameter, and strong red. Zabel's honeysuckle also is difficult to transplant. They may be moved with bare roots.

Lonicera maackii
(Amur honeysuckle)
Zone 2 to part of Zone 1; 12'–15' and spreading about as wide, making it one of the largest honeysuckles

A full-grown plant of Amur honeysuckle is a gorgeous sight, particularly when in berry. It is pretty when in flower but the fragrant blooms are white, yellowing as they age, so even though there are many of them it is not as showy as some of the honeysuckles with brightly colored flowers.

It blooms in late May and the berries do not color until September in Zone 5b. The leaves remain on the plant until late fall or early winter and so do the berries (if the birds do not eat them). Sprays of this honeysuckle make beautiful table decorations for Thanksgiving.

Lonicera maackii

**Lonicera maackii podocarpa
(Late honeysuckle)
Zone 5 to part of Zone 4; 8′–10′**
This plant is nearly evergreen in Zone 6
and some winters in Zone 5b. It is one
of the last honeysuckles to bloom and
retains its fruits later than the others—
often to late October and November.
Its form is even more widespread than
that of the species described above and
the leaves are even darker green. This
shrub, too, may be grown for berried
sprays to use on holiday tables.

**Lonicera morrowii
(Morrow honeysuckle)
Zone 4; 6′**
Wide-spreading, dense growth, gray-
green leaves, quantities of creamy-white
flowers in late May and early June, yellowing as they age, and followed by
blood red berries in July are the characteristics of this popular honeysuckle. It
thrives in any soil, forms a handsome
specimen plant, though it probably is
best used in groups of three or more
plants in a large area.

Lonicera morrowii

**Lonicera rosea
(see *L. tatarica rosea*)**

**Lonicera sempervirens
(Trumpet honeysuckle)
Zone 4 to 9; 10′–20′**
The flowers are tubular, scarlet-red with
yellow throats, followed by bright red
berries. It can be kept low and bushy

Lonicera tatarica

by pruning, otherwise makes a vine. A
yellow form is also available.

**Lonicera tatarica
(Tatarian honeysuckle)
Zone 4 to parts of Zone 3; 8′–10′**
An extremely hardy honeysuckle, this
probably is the most popular species. It
is upright-growing, tending to become
leggy, especially if planted in deep
shade. Depending on the variety grown,
flowers may be white, pink, or rose.
They open in mid-May, are fragrant,
and are followed by orange-red or yellow fruits. The white flowers in this
group do *not* change to yellow as they
get older as is the case with many other
honeysuckles.

Plants are tolerant of almost any soil,
grow strongly, do not have any pests
that bother them, are trim in appearance and laden with both fruits and
flowers in their proper seasons.

Tatarian honeysuckle may be used as
a hedge (better looking when unclipped), as a specimen, near the back of
a shrub border, or to accent a house
corner in a more intimate planting.

Lonicera tatarica alba
This variety has pure white blooms.

Lonicera tatarica 'Arnold Red'
This variety has flowers of a darker red
than those of any other honeysuckle.
The fruits are large and red.

Lonicera tatarica grandiflora
A variety with white blossoms, twice as
large as those of the species, and larger
leaves.

Lonicera tatarica rosea
This variety has two-toned blooms—
pale pink inside, rose color outside.

**Lonicera tatarica rubra
(see *L. tatarica* 'Sibirica')**

**Lonicera tatarica 'Sibirica' (syn *L.
t. rubra*)**
The blooms on this variety have white
margins and stripes of very deep pink
down the center of each petal. The
leaves are larger than those of the species.

**Lonicera tatarica zabelii
(see *L. korolkowii* 'Zabelii')**

**Lonicera xylosteoides 'Clavey's
Dwarf' (also listed as 'Clavey' or
claveyi)
Zone 4; 6′**
An origination of F. D. Clavey Ravinia
Nurseries, Inc., Deerfield, Illinois, this
is an excellent plant for hedges. It may
be kept clipped or left unclipped with
equal success. Flowers are not particularly noticeable, being brilliant greenish
yellow, nor are the red berries. This
plant is grown primarily for its dense
habit and the many gray-green leaves.

MAGNOLIA

The tree forms of magnolias are discussed in Chapter 13. Here, only one shrub form is described.

***Magnolia liliflora* 'Nigra' (syn *M. nigra, M. soulangiana nigra*)**
(Lily-flowered magnolia, Purple lily magnolia)
Zone 7 to part of Zone 6; 8'
A late-blooming, exceptionally long-flowering, very darkly colored magnolia, this has 5" long purple flowers, darker on the outsides of the petals, lighter, almost white, on the insides. These color in mid-May and are followed in early fall by red fruits shaped like a large-size pod. In the north it is difficult to grow this magnolia to any great height. It kills to the ground in Zone 5b during a severe winter.

Magnolia nigra
(see *M. liliflora* 'Nigra')

Magnolia soulangiana* and *Magnolia stellata
Descriptions of both of these magnolias are in Chapter 13. This is merely a note to say that both of these may be grown with many stems from the ground as shrubs instead of with one stem as trees.

Mahonia aquifolium

Magnolia stellata

MAHONIA
(Hollygrape)

Mahonias are evergreen shrubs with handsome, holly-like leaves and yellow flowers followed by blue or blue-black berries. Unfortunately, in northern climates the foliage browns in spots during winter so that by spring there are many unsightly areas on the leaves. To at least partially avoid this mottling, it is best to place mahonias where they are sheltered from winter sun and wind. These old leaves drop in early spring and new, unmarked ones appear shortly thereafter.

Mahonia aquifolium
(Oregon hollygrape, Oregon grape, Holly barberry)
Zone 5 to southern parts of Zone 4; 3½'
The state flower of Oregon, this mahonia is a native of the West Coast. Its first-listed common name refers to the dark blue berries in grape-like clusters and to the holly-like leaves, shining green and spiny-toothed.

This evergreen is not hard to grow. It prefers some shade, tolerates many soils but does best in one that is moist. It spreads by means of underground stolons and, if it is in the proper location, soon forms large clumps. For this reason it is an excellent ground cover where one several feet high can be used.

Vivid greenish-yellow flowers in late April and early May are borne in dense groups at the branch tips. These are followed by the fruits, which turn color in July.

The plants vary in leaf size, glossiness, and fall color because nurseries grow them from seeds. Thus it is possible to collect varying forms of the same plant.

Oregon hollygrape responds to pruning, so may be kept lower than it normally grows if this seems desirable. It will not be evergreen if placed where hot sun beats down on it in winter. It may be used in front of taller broad-leaved or narrow-leaved evergreens and is a handsome plant for use near a house.

Mahonia beale
(Leatherleaf mahonia, Southern hollygrape)
Zone 6 and protected places in Zone 5b; 12′ in the south, 3′ in the north
Zone 7 is where this shrub shines, but it is not reliably hardy even in the northern part of Zone 6. In Zone 5b, even though it kills back some in severe winters and the flower buds are blasted, it still grows in a northern exposure.

Tall, upright stems, long, stiff leaves that grow horizontally from the stems and are dark blue-green on top, grayish underneath, are characteristics of this shrub. In southern climates the individual leaves may measure 15″ long. They are leathery in texture.

The flowers are paler yellow than those of the Oregon hollygrape and are borne in pyramidal clusters. They are followed by dark, blue-black berries. The plant thrives in semi-shade. Its leaves do not change color in autumn.

Mahonia repens
(Creeping hollygrape, Creeping mahonia, Ash barberry)
Zone 6 to protected places in Zone 5b; 1′ or less
In places where the Oregon hollygrape is too tall for a ground cover, this lower-growing species may be used instead. It spreads in the same manner, by underground stolons, but does not have as shiny leaves as the Oregon hollygrape. They are dull and bluish-green instead of glossy, dark green. The flowers are similar, but like the rest of the plant are smaller than the Oregon species. Berries are black and have a bloom on them like plums have.

Malus sargentii

MALUS
(Apple)

Malus sargentii
(Sargent crabapple)
Zone 5; to 8′, usually less
This is the only crabapple that I will admit is a shrub. It grows wider than high, sometimes twice as wide, and is densely branched in almost horizontal fashion. The flowers are single, 1″ to 1¼″ in diameter, white with golden stamens, and appear in mid-May. They are followed by ⅝″ diameter fruits in small clusters that first are greenish yellow with a red cheek, later turn completely red. Birds love them.

Sargent crab, like most other crabs, is easy to transplant and to grow. Tolerant of almost any soil, it prefers a position in full sun. This is one crabapple that may be planted without any fear that it will act as a host of the cedar-apple rust (see Chapter 9). It is not a native American crabapple, but an Oriental crabapple, which makes all the difference.

MYRICA

Shrubs with aromatic foliage and berries, these grow well in full sun and sandy soil; are widely used in seashore gardens, especially if they do not grow wild in the vicinity, in which case they usually are scorned. However, they will grow well also in heavier soils.

Mahonia beale

Myrica carolinensis
(see *M. pensylvanica*)

Myrica cerifera
(Wax myrtle, Southern bayberry)
Zone 6; 30′
Evergreen in Zone 7 and in parts of
Zone 6, this shrub has dark green, aromatic foliage and aromatic gray berries
as does the bayberry, described below.
The berries remain on the plants during
winter, thus insuring a food supply for
certain species of birds.

Since male flowers are borne on different plants from female flowers, plants
of both sexes must be set out to insure
fruit formation.

Partly because of its size, partly because it spreads widely, this plant is particularly suited for naturalistic plantings.

Myrica pensylvanica (syn *M. carolinensis*)
(Bayberry, Candleberry)
Zone 1; 8′–9′
There is a low, blue-gray stone house in
Cleveland Heights, Ohio, that is landscaped entirely with bayberries. They
are clipped to form a hedge along the
sidewalk and are used in varying heights
for the house planting. The effect is unusual and exquisite.

Although you may not wish to copy
this idea, a bayberry or two in the garden will provide plenty of gray berries
for use indoors in winter.

The plants grow upright and have
stiff, straight branches. Leaves are gray-green and aromatic. The flowers of the
two sexes are on different plants so
both male and female plants must be set
near each other to produce berries. The
blooms are greenish and interesting
when seen close, but not effective in the
landscape. The berries, used to scent
bayberry candles since Colonial times,
are first green, then gray and remain on
the plants all winter and until the Baltimore orioles and catbirds arrive in the
north in spring. Within a few days after
that they are all gone.

NANDINA

Nandina domestica
(Heavenly bamboo)
Zone 6; 8′
Upright in growth this plant has beautiful, fine foliage that turns from green to
red and bronze in autumn. In July the
white flowers appear and are followed
by clusters of berries that turn bright
red in fall. If the birds do not eat them
they stay on the plant until early the
following year.

This is one of the few plants I want
to grow but find impossible to winter.
Three different times I have purchased
three plants each time, setting them in
different sheltered locations, only to
lose them during the first winter that
was not extremely mild.

Nandina does not require any particular soil but grows best in full sun. It is
widely used in house plantings where it
is hardy.

Nandina domestica

OSMANTHUS

Osmanthus heterophyllus
(Sweet holly, Holly osmanthus)
Zone 6; 15′
Suitable for use in house plantings or
for clipped hedges, this evergreen plant
has shining dark green leaves that are
shaped like those of hollies, as the botanical name says. In late summer osmanthus bears tiny greenish-white, very
fragrant flowers that are followed by
blue-black fruits turning color in autumn.

This shrub does equally well in sun
or shade, which increases its usefulness.
Takes heavy pruning.

PAEONIA
(Peony)

The peonies most people know and
love are herbaceous—meaning that their
tops die to the ground each winter and
new ones grow from the roots each
spring. The peonies described below are
not herbaceous—they are deciduous
shrubs. While the leaves fall in autumn,
the tops do not die during winter. Instead, new leaves grow each spring from
the branches as with other shrubs.
These shrubby peonies are no harder to
grow than herbaceous peonies, no matter what you may have read to the contrary. And, borne on them are certainly
some of the most beautiful flowers in
the world. The foliage, too, is exceptionally attractive.

Myrica pensylvanica

Paeonia arborea
(see *P. suffruticosa*)

Paeonia moutan
(see *P. suffruticosa*)

Paeonia suffruticosa
(Tree peony)
Zone 5 to parts of Zone 4; 6' and may spread twice as wide

Someone should long since have given this peony a more realistic name, for it certainly is not a tree, but a shrub. The largest plant I ever have seen is in front of a house outside London, Ontario, and it is 6' high and more than 12' across. This, however, is an unusually large plant as I have seen plenty of mature specimens elsewhere that were not nearly so large.

In addition to not being able to fathom the common name of this shrub, I also do not understand why gardeners everywhere are not growing these plants. When young, they are small enough for the tiniest backyard garden, beautiful enough to suit any connoisseur and as easy to grow as any herbaceous peony. They flower before the herbaceous peonies and are far handsomer with their beautifully shaped gray-green leaves and enormous blooms. The flowers are borne singly instead of in groups as in herbaceous peonies, and may be 6″ to 8″ in diameter, single, semi-double or double in form. Their buds open in late May.

After you have seen tree peonies you will buy as many as your pocketbook will permit. They are not cheap. Because there is little written about tree peonies, I am going to go into more detail about growing them than I have about most shrubs.

See the plants you want to buy in bloom and order them for delivery in mid- to late-October. In September ready the soil by digging out your existing soil (unless it is that gardener's dream soil—a good loam) and replacing it to a depth of 2' with ¾ compost and ¼ granulated peat. If drainage is poor, put 4″ or 5″ of gravel at the bottom of the hole or bed. Just remember that

Paeonia suffruticosa

these plants will be in your garden for your lifetime and that the only time you can give them the best growing conditions is before you plant them.

Space tree peonies widely—6' apart is rather close, 8' or 10' is better, although it will take them many years to spread more than the 6' first suggested. Plant tulips or some other bulbs between the peonies and annuals over the bulbs for the first years until the peonies fill the space between plants. Be sure to set the peonies at the depth marked by the nursery, for the graft (where the cultivated peony, which is the top of the plant, meets the rootstock of the species peony) must be well below ground level.

Protect the plants from heaving out of the soil by placing straw over the ground around the plants for the first winter. Protect from rabbit damage by

chicken wire screens, also for the first winter. After that neither type of protection is necessary.

We keep our plants mulched with buckwheat hulls several inches deep and our care consists of pulling any weeds that appear, pruning any dead branch tips in early spring, and fertilizing after blooming time with 10-6-4 fertilizer, with ureaform, intended for lawns but just as good for tree peonies.

There are many cultivars of tree peonies, some originated in France, some in Japan and some in the United States. The hybrid forms are interesting and different and must be seen to be believed, for some of them have deep yellow flowers, the least usual bloom color in herbaceous peonies.

I will, however, single out one variety for special praise since it is by far the cream of the species.

Paeonia suffruticosa 'Joseph Rock'

Plants grow to 5', produce huge (10") single flowers, a dusky pink with handsome purple markings at the petal centers and lovely ruffled petal edges.

Paeonia suffruticosa 'Joseph Rock'

PHILADELPHUS

(Mock orange, Orange-flower bush, Syringa)

A large group of shrubs that hybridize easily with one another both in the wild and in cultivation, the members are grown for their white or creamy-white flowers, in many cases intensely fragrant. Sometimes mock oranges are grown for their compact form or their foliage color.

Mock oranges will grow in almost any soil but a wet one; do well in semi-shade and in full sun. Once planted, they need little or no care except for occasional pruning of dead wood, unless, of course, a large-growing member of the group is planted where space is limited.

The tall mock oranges may be used for unclipped hedges or screen plantings and sometimes are used for specimens. The low forms may be used in the front of a shrub border or as specimens.

The foliage of most mock oranges is not outstanding, though some, notably the *lemoinei* hybrids, have small leaves and a neat appearance. Leaves of some turn yellowish in autumn and one has yellow leaves during spring and early summer.

Mock oranges range in height from 3' to 20' and include all sizes between these two figures. Their flowers may be single, semi-double or double in form. All are white or creamy-white, a few have colored blotches or are purplish or pinkish when first open, but soon fade to white. The fruits that follow them are brown capsules.

The name "Syringa," used for mock oranges all over eastern United States, was formerly the botanical name of the group but now belongs to lilacs.

Many of the cultivars are the work of one nurseryman, Victor Lemoine of Nancy, France. Some of them have one parent that would not be hardy in the southernmost zone covered in this book —Zone 6—so it should not be taken for granted that all mock oranges are hardy, because many are not.

Two cultivars, 'Frosty Morn' and 'Minnesota Snowflake', are said to live through temperatures as low as minus 30 degrees. These are both well-formed plants and double-flowered. The hardiest single-flowered forms described in this book are *P. coronarius* and *P.* 'Mont Blanc'.

The forms of some mock oranges are far superior to those of others. For example, the widely grown *P. virginalis*, for all the pleasing sight and scent of its blooms, is a leggy shrub that needs frequent pruning.

Philadelphus 'Atlas'
Zone 5; 6'–8'
This cultivar has single, 2" to 3" diameter fragrant flowers.

Philadelphus aureus
(see *P. coronarius* 'Aureus')

Philadelphus 'Belle Etoile' (meaning "beautiful star")
Zone 6 and protected places in Zones 4 and 5; 6'
This exceptionally beautiful mock orange was hybridized by Victor Lemoine. It differs from other mock oranges in its flower form and from most mock oranges by having a rose or purplish blotch in the center of the bloom.

Flowers are fragrant, 2¼" in diameter, single, with pointed petals, borne on plants with a gracefully arching habit.

Plants will survive many winters if in a protected place in both Zones 4 and 5, but may be killed to the ground should the winter be severe. Usually they come up from the roots in spring.

Philadelphus coronarius (Fragrant mock orange, Sweet mock orange, False syringa)
Zone 5 to parts of Zone 4; 10'
This is the plant most people have in mind when they say mock orange. It is upright growing, vigorous in growth, will tolerate drier soil conditions than most shrubs, has ordinary foliage, and single flowers in early June, 1½" in diameter, which have the delightful fragrance suggested by the common name.

Philadelphus coronarius

Philadelphus × lemoinei

Philadelphus coronarius 'Aureus' (Golden mock orange)
Zone 5 to parts of Zone 4; to 6′
Usually much lower growing than *coronarius*, this cultivar has yellow leaves in spring that, if the plant is growing in a sunny place, turn yellowish green later in the season. This color change can be delayed and sometimes warded off altogether by placing the plant where it gets light shade. Otherwise this plant is like the species but its flowers are not so conspicuous against the foliage because it too nearly resembles their color.

Philadelphus 'Enchantment'
Zone 4; 6′
This is a graceful shrub bearing double, 1″ diameter flowers in loose clusters. Flowers have fringed petals.

Philadelphus 'Glacier'
Zone 5 to Zone 4b; 4′–5′
Double fragrant, 1½″ diameter flowers and small leaves characterize this mock orange.

Philadelphus grandiflorus (see P. inodorus grandiflorus)

Philadelphus 'Innocence'
Zone 5 to parts of Zone 4; 6′ high and 5′ wide
One of the most fragrant of mock oranges, this has single, 1¼″ blooms borne in clusters of from seven to nine. 'Innocence' does not bloom well every year but sports a real bouquet of flowers every second or third year. Apparently it needs fertilizer to help it produce sufficent new growth for better and more frequent bloom.

Philadelphus inodorus grandiflorus (syn P. grandiflorus) (Big scentless mock orange)
Zone 4; 10′
Although the botanical name stresses the size of the flowers of this variety, the botanist who named it could not have made adequate comparisons for the blooms are only 1¼″ in diameter, not by any means the largest of any mock orange. As the species name states, they are not fragrant. The plant is upright, handsome, and well covered with flowers, but the gardener who sniffs one gets no reward.

Philadelphus × lemoinei (P. microphyllus × P. coronarius)
Zone 4; 3′–4′
A dense, mound-shaped plant that has small leaves and single, very fragrant flowers from ¾″ to 1½″ in diameter, this mock orange will tolerate light shade and bloom as well there as in full sun.

Philadelphus × virginalis (P. lemoinei × P. nivalis 'Plenus') (syn P. virginalis 'Virginal', P. virginal)
Zone 5 to part of Zone 4; 5′–6′
Semi-double and double, 2″ diameter, intensely fragrant blooms are borne on this upright leggy plant and transform it into a bouquet. This is a coarse shrub that becomes bare of leaves at the bottom and needs frequent pruning to keep it not only looking its best but also within bounds. If such pruning is not possible, then plant a lower growing shrub in front of this mock orange to hide the bare base.

The blooms are so beautifully placed on the branches of this mock orange that they are valuable for cutting.

Philadelphus virginalis 'Minnesota Snowflake' (sometimes listed as 'Snowflake')
Zone 4; 6′ high and 4′ wide
Double, fragrant, 1½″ to 2″ diameter flowers are borne in clusters of eight to ten on a handsome plant that unfortunately becomes bare of leaves at the bottom as it grows older. This mock orange is recommended for its hardiness. Introduced by the same man as was 'Frosty Morn', this plant is said to survive temperatures to minus 30 degrees.

Philadelphus virginalis 'Minnesota Snowflake'

PIERIS

(Andromeda, Lily-of-the-valley shrub, Portuna)

Andromedas are broad-leaved evergreen shrubs, upright in form, with arching branches, glossy leaves and in April fragrant, white flowers in clusters. The flower buds form in autumn, therefore are prominent all winter. After the flowers fade, new foliage grows that is pale bronze, contrasting beautifully with the older, green foliage.

Andromedas prefer light shade and a location sheltered from winter winds. They need a soil that is at least slightly acid and prefer one that is loose and moist, but well-drained.

These shrubs are choice ones for use as specimens or in house plantings or in groupings with other broad-leaved or needled evergreens near the house. They should never be crowded as then their beauty is lost.

Pieris japonica (Japanese Andromeda)

Pieris floribunda
(Mountain andromeda, Mountain fetterbush)
Zone 5; 4'–5'
Upright in growth, this plant often grows wider than high. It has thick, dark green leaves and clusters of fragrant, waxy, white, bell-shaped flowers that grow either upright or nodding. Blooms open in late April, about a week later than those of the Japanese andromeda.

Pieris floribunda

Pieris japonica
(Japanese andromeda)
Zone 6 to part of Zone 5; 7'
Taller than the species described above, this also is more tender to winter cold. It should be accorded a situation near a house wall where warmth from inside tempers the cold or a place protected from winter wind.

It may be planted with the mountain andromeda or with its own variegated form in the foreground. It also looks good against needled evergreens. It shows off best when not crowded.

The leaves are dark, glossy and evergreen. Flowers are creamy-white, fragrant, and borne in drooping clusters. Fruits are brown capsules. A well-grown specimen of Japanese andromeda typifies, to me at least, the perfect broad-leaved evergreen.

Pieris japonica 'Compacta'
6'
High, but compact and dense, this has leaves only half the size of those of the species.

Pieris japonica 'Red Mill'
An extra-hardy variety that produces ornamental red leaves that change to green with age and beautiful white flower clusters.

Pieris japonica 'Variegata' (syn *P. j.* 'Variegata Nana', *P. j.* 'Albo Marginata')
The leaves of this cultivar have narrow, white edges. The plant is dwarf, grows very slowly, and mine never has bloomed during the five years I've owned it. Since the other andromedas next to and in back of it bloom every year and I have seen flowers on other variegated plants, mine must be lacking in some regard.

Poncirus trifoliata

Pieris taiwanensis
Zone 6; 6'

If you live in Zone 6 or south of that zone, this is a lovely pieris to grow. Seemingly more compact in growth than *japonica*, it starts to flower when young and holds its upright clusters well above the leaves.

Other pieris: There are several pink-flowered forms of *Pieris japonica* available and various cultivars are being introduced that have larger flowers or longer bloom clusters or similar variations.

PONCIRUS

Poncirus trifoliata
(Hardy orange)
Zones 5 to 9; 10'–20'

A bushy deciduous shrub or small tree that is armed with thorns as sharp as nails, bearing fragrant citrus-like white flowers in spring, followed by masses of golfball-size yellow fruits that ripen in autumn. These are highly ornamental, smell pleasantly like lemon-soap, and persist long after the oval green leathery leaves have fallen. The fruit is too astringent to be edible. The large seeds—resembling lemon pips—germinate readily all around the parent plant in spring. Needs only light tip-pruning to keep it a tidy shape. Plants are easily transplanted either bare-root or from containers. Tolerates poor soils if drainage is good. Useful for container plantings, hedging and alone as a lawn highlight.

POTENTILLA

(Cinquefoil, Buttercup shrub, Five finger blossom, Five finger grass)

A visiting nurseryman, looking at some of my potentillas, remarked, "An English nurseryman told me that if we'd change the name we'd sell more of them." Isn't it too bad that a name can cheat gardeners everywhere from knowing and growing these shrubs? If the name meant was "potentilla," that comes from the Latin word "potens," which means "powerful" (just like our English word "potent") and refers to the powerful medicine of some species used for medicinal purposes. If the name meant was "cinquefoil," that comes from the French words "cinq" meaning five and "feuilles" meaning leaves and refers to the five leaflets of most potentillas. Are these names really so dreadful that they scare you off? If so, you're missing some carefree shrubs.

Potentillas will grow in any soil but a wet one, tolerate light shade but bloom best when in full sun. They bloom for weeks during summer when not too many other shrubs flower. They have no pests to bother them. They need no pruning, no spraying. What more could you ask?

Potentillas are happy shrubs with varying shades of yellow or sometimes white single blossoms against small leaves that look somewhat like those of strawberries. Blooms are followed by brown capsules that remain on the plants until hidden by the following spring's growth. The plants are all dwarf or of medium height. The foliage of some is gray-green rather than green and, occasionally, silvery.

All are of the easiest possible culture, asking only a sunny place where drainage is good. They may be used for hedges (planted 18" apart), for specimens, or in the front of a shrub border.

Potentilla arbuscula
Zone 5

This variety has a prostrate growth habit and large yellow flowers.

Potentilla davurica (also spelled *daburica*) (Dahurian cinquefoil)
Zone 3; 2'

From northern Manchuria comes this hardy little shrub. Flowers are creamy-white, look like single roses, and are borne all summer.

Potentilla × friedrichsenii (P. fruti-cosa × P. davurica)
Zone 4, possibly to Zone 3; 3′
Sturdy growth, light yellow flowers and continual bloom from mid-June on make this a popular cinquefoil.

Potentilla fruticosa
(Shrubby cinquefoil, Bush cinque-foil)
Zone 1; 3½′
This species is native to most areas of the northern hemisphere but is not appreciated by gardeners. Once planted in dry soil and full sun it will be a joy every year from June until frost. There is a burst of bloom in June, then fewer but some flowers always on the bush until September when there is another, but lesser, burst of bloom. After that occasional flowers may be found until frost. Blooms are single, yellow and 1″ in diameter.

Potentilla fruticosa 'Moonlight'
(syn 'Manelys')
Zone 5; 3′
This cultivar was bred in Sweden where "manelys" means moonlight. It has dark, blue-green leaves and pale yellow flowers, 1⅛″ across. It blooms from June intermittently until frost.

Potentilla 'Lemon Drop'
Zone 5; 2′
A continuous bloomer from June until frost, 'Lemon Drop' has sulphur yellow flowers.

Potentilla 'Mt. Everest'
Zone 5; 3′
Upright and vigorous in growth, this cultivar has dark green leaves and white, 1″ diameter flowers.

Potentilla parvifolia
Zone 5
An excellent rock garden subject, this cinquefoil is a dwarf, with the small leaves its botanical name suggests and, surprisingly, seven leaflets instead of the usual five. The new growth hides the seed capsules. Blooms are lemon-yellow.

Potentilla fruticosa

Potentilla parvifolia 'Gold Drop'
Zone 3; 3′
Has very bright yellow flowers over the usual long blooming period. This is given as synonymous with 'Farreri' by many nurseries.

Potentilla parvifolia 'Klondike'
Zone 5; 2′
A dwarf, compact shrub, this has large, deep yellow flowers. There seems to be a great deal of variation in the plants offered as some people find their shrubs bearing very few flowers, while others speak of the floriferousness of their plants.

Potentilla parvifolia 'Red Ace'
Zone 5
An introduction from England that has proven disappointing in the U.S. Plants are weak, blooms are sparse and easily fade.

Potentilla parvifolia 'Tangerine'
Zone 4; 3′
A cultivar with flowers that open a tangerine-orange color, changing, with age, to golden yellow.

PRUNUS

(Plum, Cherry, Peach, Almond, Apricot, Nectarine)

The genus *Prunus* is an extremely large one and includes plums, cherries, peaches, almonds, apricots and nectarines. In general, members of this genus are tolerant of most soils and, unless they are susceptible to attacks by insects or diseases, are easy to grow. All of the members of this genus prefer full sun. They vary so greatly in growth habit, size, foliage, flowers and fruits that these characteristics cannot be generally described, so are discussed under each species. Tree forms are discussed in Chapter 13.

Prunus besseyi
(Western sand cherry)
Zone 4 to part of Zone 3; 6'–7'
On sandy hills or rocky slopes, even the shores of lakes in the provinces and states from Manitoba to Minnesota, south and west to Wyoming, Nebraska, and Kansas, is found a bushy shrub known as the Western sand cherry, which has nearly black fruit, tiny, but sweet to the taste.

This shrub has ½" diameter, single, white flowers in mid-May.

From this species, by the process of selection, Prof. N. W. Hansen, Brookings, South Dakota, produced what is known as Hansen's bush cherry, which is *Prunus besseyi* with larger fruits and many more of them. If you wish to grow this shrub for its fruits, be certain you are getting Hansen's form as it is hard to tell from the catalog descriptions whether the species or the improved form is meant.

The fruits of either make delicious pies and preserves. In rigorous climates where regular cherries will not grow, these are substitutes.

Prunus × *cistena (P. cerasifera* **'Atropurpurea'** × *P. pumila)*
(Purple-leaved sand cherry)
Zone 1; 8'
The same Professor Hansen who selected fine fruiting forms of the Western sand cherry originated this large shrub. It has so-called "purple" leaves, which are moderate reddish brown on the upper sides and dark red underneath, and retain this color all summer. White or pink, single, ½" diameter flowers with prominent stamens the same color as the foliage open in mid-May and are followed by small cherries almost the same color as the leaves so that they are hard to find without a search. These are edible and may be used for preserves.

The shrub form is upright and quite widely branching. The plant is useful for the back of a border, in a house planting or as a specimen, always provided that its bright foliage color will look well where it is placed.

Prunus glandulosa (Flowering Almond)

Prunus glandulosa
(Dwarf flowering almond, Flowering cherry)
Zone 5 if plants are grafted or budded, Zone 4 if on their own roots; to 5', but usually nearer 3'
Dwarf flowering almond bears single, pink or white flowers in late April or early May at a time when bright flowers are needed in the garden. Red, ½" diameter cherries follow. This shrub, however, rarely is seen in gardens. Instead, its double-flowered forms are the choice of gardeners everywhere.

Prunus glandulosa **'Albiplena'**
(White double-flowering almond)
Slender, straight branches growing from the ground bear faintly pink buds that open to almost ball-shaped, many-petaled, ¾" diameter flowers and the shrub is so covered with them that the leaves, which then are just starting to grow, are barely visible.

This is a beautiful plant when in bloom, though it seems not nearly so well known as the double-flowered pink form. Double-flowered forms do not bear fruit. They are grown only for their early flowers.

Prunus besseyi

Prunus besseyi

Prunus glandulosa rosea
(see *P. glandulosa*)

Prunus glandulosa roseoplena or
rosea plena
(see *P. g.* 'Sinensis')

Prunus glandulosa 'Sinensis' (*syn P.
g. roseoplena* or *rosea plena*)
(Pink double-flowering almond)
Zone 4; to 5', usually nearer 3'
The most popular dwarf flowering almond, this plant is seen in thousands of
gardens. Although it does not bear
fruit, it has attractive foliage, as have
the rest of the dwarf flowering almonds. The flowers, which literally
cover the shrub in late April to early
May, are ⅝" to ⅞" in diameter and
deep purplish red in color. The shrub is
best used in the front of a shrub border
or in a low planting elsewhere.

Prunus laurocerasus schipkaensis
(Schipka cherry laurel)
Zone 6 to protected places in
Zone 5b; 18' in the south, 6' or
less in the north
A broad-leaved evergreen extremely
popular in the south, this is grown for
its horizontal branching form and the
beautiful, shining leaves. In Zone 5b, it
needs the protection of evergreen
boughs in winter to keep it from burning. It looks good at the base of a taller-
growing broad-leaved evergreen like a
rhododendron or with narrow-leaved
evergreens and is sufficiently choice that
it may be used in a house planting or
other intimate setting.

Prunus laurocerasus (Cherry Laurel)

Prunus laurocerasus 'Zabeliana'
Zone 6 to protected places in
Zone 5b; to 5' in the south, 3' in
the north
Smaller in all ways than the Schipka
cherry laurel, it is otherwise similar and
should be protected for winter in the
same manner.

Prunus maritima

Prunus maritima
(Beach plum, Black plum)
Zone 4 to parts of Zone 3; 6'
Along the Atlantic seashore and near it,
especially in the New England states,
this plant grows wild. The first settlers
must have found its small but delicious
fruits a blessing. Nowadays selections
have been made that bear fruits at least
an inch in diameter and these are being
propagated for sale. The fruits make excellent jam.

The chief value of this shrub is for
planting in seaside gardens. It bears
white, single or sometimes double
flowers early in May and the dull purple, or occasionally crimson, ½" to 1"
diameter fruits follow these. It will
grow inland too, if you'd like to try it,
but there are many other more ornamental shrubs for inland gardens.

There is a yellow-fruited variety that
I saw once in Ohio and it is possible
that some nursery is propagating it.
There also is a selected form named
'Autumn'.

Prunus tenella (syn *Amygdalus
nana*, syn *Prunus nana*)
(Dwarf Russian almond)
Zone 2; 3'–4'
Single, rose-red, ½" to ¾" flowers
bloom on this hardy shrub in late April
or early May just as the leaves are unfolding. These are followed by ½"
diameter red fruits in late July. There
are many handsomer shrubs for moderate climates, but this may be grown far
north.

Prunus tomentosa
(Nankin cherry, Nanking cherry,
Manchu cherry)
Zone 1; 9' in the south, 5' in the
north
Upright and spreading in form, this is
one of the welcome, early-flowering
shrubs. Blossoms appear before the
leaves in late April, are pink in bud, and
pale pink to white when open, but are
surrounded by red calyxes and centered
with red stamens so that the overall effect is quite different from that of most
white flowers.

Edible, strong red, ⅜" diameter
fruits ripen in late June and early July.
They may be eaten as they are, since
they are small cherries and very good to
the taste, or they may be made into
jelly or jam.

Some friends of ours have a long
hedge of plants of this shrub and, either
in bloom or in fruit, it is a lovely sight.
The plant also may be used in a border
or as a specimen.

Prunus tomentosa

Prunus triloba

Prunus triloba (syn *P. triloba plena* of the catalogs, *P. t.* 'Multiplex') (Rose tree of China) Zone 5 to parts of Zone 4; 15'

The double-flowered form of this shrub was discovered before the single-flowered form. Botanists, therefore, not knowing there was a single-flowered form, gave it the specific name, *P. triloba*. This means that *P. triloba plena*, of innumerable nursery catalogs, is a name without scientific standing. The shrub that is meant is properly called *P. triloba*.

The many-petaled, double flowers look so much like little roses that it is easy to see why the common name was given this shrub. Blooms are 1″ in diameter, bright pink, and borne before the leaves appear in late April. This shrub is useful in a border.

PYRACANTHA
(Firethorn)

These handsome shrubs are evergreen in the south, almost evergreen in the north, with shining green leaves, white flowers in late May to early June and brilliant orange, red-orange, scarlet, or yellow berries in late September to October.

They should be planted in full sun for most flowers and therefore most fruits. Because they are not easy to transplant, they should always be purchased with balls of earth around their roots and, in the north, moved only in spring.

Pruning may be needed to keep plants compact (they can be sheared to make a hedge).

Pyracantha coccinea 'Lalandei' (also spelled 'Lalandii') (Laland's firethorn) Zone 5b; 6'–7'

This cultivar is hardier than the species, *P. coccinea*, and also more vigorous in growth. It may be used for a hedge, espaliered against a wall or planted with needled evergreens in a house planting.

Its white flowers are as pretty as those of many other shrubs grown exclusively for their flowers and its berries are bright, gay, and showy—brilliant orange-red.

Pyracantha coccinea cultivars (other than 'Lalandei')

There are at least a dozen other cultivars listed in the catalogs, all varying somewhat from one another, usually in berry color, but sometimes in ultimate height or in density of form. All are desirable, but, if hardiness is a prime consideration, 'Kasan' is the hardiest. It is more upright in form than 'Lalandei' and has orange-scarlet berries.

Dr. Donald Egolf, at the National Arboretum, has hybridized a number of new cultivars with Indian names. Two of the best are 'Shawnee' (yellow berried) and 'Mohave', producing enormous quantities of orange-red berries, with built-in resistance to scab and fireblight.

Pyracantha coccinea

RHODODENDRON
(Rhododendron, Azalea)

Both rhododendrons and azaleas are members of the same genus, the genus Rhododendron. Because the nursery catalogs list the two separately, I have attempted to bridge the gap between what the nurseries call the plants and what the botanists call the same plants by describing the rhododendrons known as azaleas under the heading AZALEA. I have, however, given them their correct botanical names, Rhododendrons.

Rhododendrons (as distinguished from azaleas) are mostly broad-leaved evergreens that may be tall or short, so that they may be selected to suit the landscape.

Their form is generally upright and spreading with comparatively few, sturdy branches. The leaves of the hardy sorts are dark green, thick, and leathery in texture. The flower colors vary widely and the blooms include some of the most spectacular in the entire roster of shrubs.

While many more rhododendrons than are listed here grow well in Zone 6, those that will survive from Zone 6 northward are limited to species, varieties and cultivars of unquestioned hardiness. Even though the flowers of these are exquisite in both form and color, it is not fair to judge the entire rhododendron clan by those hardy in the north. Once one has seen hillsides of rhododendrons in Italian gardens or the collection of species in the experimental garden in Boskoop, Holland, one cannot help but be impressed by the enormous range of height, flower color, and blooming time encompassed by this genus. The Pacific Northwest is fast becoming as good a place to see rhododendrons in all their variations as is the south of England: there, the collection at Wisley, the test garden of the Royal Horticultural Society, is outstanding.

Rhododendrons must have an acid soil to survive. Furthermore, the underlying subsoil must not be of heavy clay,

for the water that then would collect around their roots would kill them. They like a loose, sandy, peaty soil mixture with plenty of air in it (because their roots are shallow) but still able to retain moisture. These plants require perfect drainage.

Because of these needs, the best place to plant them is on a slope or in a raised bed and, where the soil is not naturally acid, soil must be mixed especially for them. The preparation of acid soil mixtures is explained in Chapter 4. Fortunately, because of the shallow-rooting habit, replacing soil is not too great a task although deep preparation means better growth. The rhododendrons will repay the gardener many times over with their blooms for making growing conditions suitable for them.

Also because of the shallow root system, it is advisable always to keep a mulch over the soil around rhododendrons. Best materials for this purpose are oak leaves or pine needles, both of which have an acid reaction as they decay. (See the section on mulching in Chapter 5.)

In the north, rhododendrons should be transplanted only in spring. They should be purchased with their roots in earth balls and should be placed in their new positions so that the soil is level with the tops of these earth balls. If the weather is dry during summer, even established rhododendrons need copious watering once in ten days. The mulch, of course, helps keep the sun from drying the soil under it, but will not add moisture to the soil.

When rhododendrons have finished flowering it is a good idea to cut off the faded flowers. Not only does this improve the appearance of the plants, but it avoids the use of nutriment to form seeds and allows the use of these substances for next year's flower bud formation. Rhododendron buds are formed in late summer and early autumn, remain on the plants all winter and open in spring, precise time depending on the kind of rhododendron. For this reason, all pruning should be

Rhododendron catawbiense
'Album Grandiflora'

done right after blooming time, except for broken branches that might as well be cut off when they are noticed. However, pruning rarely is necessary when rhododendrons are grown in the north. They don't grow that fast or that much.

Rhododendrons may be used in house plantings, as unclipped hedges, as specimens, in a border with other broad-leaved or needled evergreens, or in a woodland. They are beautiful in any situation, especially, of course, when in flower.

Most of the ultra-hardy rhododendrons listed in the catalogs and sold in nurseries today are either North American species like *R. catawbiense* or *R. maximum* or hybrids, largely bred in England during the last century by Anthony Waterer, Sr., also responsible for many azalea hybrids. The same careful and extensive breeding work probably would be impossible today because of present high labor costs, which is probably the reason why these hybrids continue to stand at the top of the list of ironclad hardy varieties for the north. Most of them are hybrids between *R. catawbiense* and various Asiatic azaleas brought into England during the last half of the nineteenth century. All of them are beautiful and well worth growing. Those most frequently listed in the catalogs are described below.

Rhododendron 'Album Elegans'
One of Waterer's *R. maximum* hybrids, which grows tall, blooms late and has light mauve flowers that fade to white.

Rhododendron 'America'

Rhododendron 'America'
This plant has beautiful clear dark red flowers, but has a poor habit of growth—rather open and spreading with branches that are inclined to droop.

Rhododendron arborescens (see AZALEA)

Rhododendron calendulaceum (see AZALEA)

Rhododendron canadense (see AZALEA)

Rhododendron 'Caractacus'
Another Waterer hybrid of *R. catawbiense* with an excellent form, but flowers that are dull purplish-red and not easy to combine with other rhododendron flower colors, except white of course.

Rhododendron carolinianum (Carolina rhododendron) Zone 5 to part of Zone 4; 5'–6', usually less
An evergreen rhododendron, this blooms in mid-May. It is an exceptionally dainty species with 3″ diameter flower clusters that may be white or between pale, purplish pink and light purplish pink. The variation in color represents the normal variation in seedling plants. The leaves are narrow compared with those of most rhododendrons and are dotted with brown underneath. The new leaves unfold about the time the flowers are opening. The form of the plant is rounded and compact.

Rhododendron carolinianum album
The white-flowered form of the species just described. It, like the species, is found native in the North Carolina mountains. It has either white flowers or blooms of such pale pink that they are practically white.

Rhododendron catawbiense (Catawba rhodendron, Mountain rosebay) Zone 5 to part of Zone 4; usually to 6', taller in the south
Native to the Allegheny Mountains, chiefly in the states of Georgia and Virginia, this evergreen rhododendron will survive without severe injury a winter temperature of minus 25 degrees F. It will grow better, however, if protected from such severe cold. It is hardier than any of its hybrids.

Its form is upright and spreading. The flowers appear before the new leaves have opened, so are particularly effective. They are freely borne and are red-purple or sometimes lavender-purple (some people call them magenta), spotted with dull yellow-green.

If you live in the far north and would like to try growing rhododendrons, start with this one.

Rhododendron 'Catawbiense Album'
This is not the white-flowered variety of *R. catawbiense* but a Waterer hybrid that is probably the best hardy white that blooms in the middle of the rhododendron flowering season.

Rhododendron catawbiense

Rhododendron carolinianum

Rhododendron 'English Roseum'

Rhododendron 'English Roseum'

This hybrid has the same general color of flowers as 'Roseum Elegans' but is definitely inferior to the true 'Roseum Elegans'. Try not to buy this one, but the real thing.

Exbury hybrids (see AZALEA)

Gable hybrids (see AZALEA)

Rhododendron × *gandavense* (Ghent hybrids) (see AZALEA)

Rhododendron kaempferi (see AZALEA)

Kaempferi hybrids (see AZALEA)

Knap Hill hybrids (see AZALEA)

Rhododendron × *kosterianum* (see AZALEA)

Rhododendron × *laetevirens* (R. carolinianum × R. ferrugineum) (syn R. wilsonii) (Wilson rhododendron) Zone 5; 3½'

Differing from many other rhododendrons in its light green leaves, this evergreen plant is compact in growth with 1″ diameter flowers, pink to purplish-pink, in mid-June. Because of the excellent growth habit it may be used as a specimen, on top of a wall or in a house planting.

Rhododendron 'Lee's Dark Purple'

This is not as hardy as two other purple-flowered hybrids 'Purpureum Elegans' and 'Purpureum Grandiflorum'. It seems, however, to be more widely available. It has dark green, wavy leaves and large trusses of purple blooms.

Rhododendron maximum (Rosebay, Rosebay rhododendron, Cow-plant, Spoon-hutch) Zone 4 to parts of Zone 3; 12′, up to 30′ in the south

Found in the wild from Nova Scotia and Ontario, down the east coast to Georgia and Alabama and west as far as Ohio, this rhododendron grows as a large shrub (or, sometimes, a small tree). It is the tallest rhododendron hardy in the north.

The leaves are long and the new ones are well grown before the flowers open. This is definitely a disadvantage because the flowers thus are partly hidden by the foliage.

They usually are rose-colored, but may be purplish-pink and are spotted with dull yellow-green to orange. They open in late June and look particularly beautiful when seen on a mass of plants. In fact, massing is the best possible use for this plant, along the edge of a wood or a waterway or at the back of a shrub border. The rosebay also is an excellent subject for a hedge.

This rhododendron requires a situation in semi-shade. It is folly to try to grow it elsewhere.

Rhododendron molle hybrids (called *molle* or *mollis hybrids*) (see AZALEA)

Rhododendron mucronulatum (see AZALEA)

Rhododendron nudiflorum (see AZALEA)

Rhododendron obtusum 'Amoenum' (see AZALEA)

Rhododendron obtusum arnoldianum (see AZALEA)

P.J.M. hybrid

P.J.M. hybrid Zone 4; 5′–8′

Named for the owner of Weston Nursery, Hopkinton, Massachusetts, this is probably the most widely planted rhododendron in North America, used in foundation plantings around the house and for mass plantings in commercial shopping malls. The purplish flowers occur in early spring in small but prolific clusters, in sun or partial shade. The shrub will take a lot of abuse. Two companion hybrids are 'Olga', a medium pink, and 'Victor' a light purple-pink. Collectively, they are known as Mezitt hybrids.

Rhododendron 'Purpureum Elegans'

This is one of Waterer's hardy hybrids. It has 3″ wide, blue-violet or lilac-purple flowers with purple centers. These are marked with orange-brown. The plant is compact and has a good growth habit.

Rhododendron roseum (see AZALEA)

Rhododendron 'Roseum Elegans'

Rhododendron 'Roseum Elegans'

One of the hardiest hybrids, dependable in Zone 4, this has mauve-rose flowers with greenish markings almost 3″ in diameter and bears them every spring. The plant has an excellent growth habit and is vigorous.

Unfortunately there are several different plants offered in the trade under this name. So buy it from a reliable nursery and get the true 'Roseum Elegans'.

Rhododendron 'Roseum Superbum'

Once again, this is a Waterer hybrid of *R. catawbiense* that has purplish-rose or purplish-pink flowers. It is not considered as good a flowering shrub as the true 'Roseum Elegans' but, nevertheless, is hardy, vigorous in growth, with a plant that requires a little pruning in its youth for a good form when older.

Rhododendron schlippenbachii (see AZALEA)

Shammarello hybrids

Bred by A. M. Shammarello, South Euclid, Ohio (near Cleveland), these plants are, of course, hardy in that area, which is in hardiness Zone 6. The lowest winter temperature expected in this zone is minus 18 degrees. Some of them are bud hardy to a few degrees lower than this.

Mr. Shammarello bred for "large-leaved, early-blooming plants in pink and red; for later blooming plants in dwarf pinks and dwarf reds; and tall growers exhibiting good plant characteristics in clear pink, red and white."

These hybrids furnish a continuity of bloom from early to late May and are listed in three groups: for early May, mid-May and late May flowering. They certainly should be tried by people living in Zone 6 and some of them probably are hardy in Zone 5, at least the southern part of the zone.

Mr. Shammarello grew the plants in the open field and is one of the comparatively few people with soil too acid for best growth of rhododendrons. He told me he often had to use lime to make the soil more alkaline than it was naturally, so the plants would thrive.

Rhododendron 'Scintillation'
Zone 5; 15′

A very popular large-flowered fragrant pink hybrid from the breeding program of Charles Owen Dexter, Cape Cod, Massachusetts. The upper petal on each flower has bronze spots on a light yellow background, the flowers forming a spectacular truss up to 7 inches wide, with 12–15 flowers to each truss.

Rhododendron vaseyi (see AZALEA)

Rhododendron viscosum (see AZALEA)

Vuyk hybrids (see AZALEA)

Rhododendron wilsonii (see *R.* × *laetevirens*)

Rhododendron 'Windbeam'
Zone 4; 6′

Developed by rhododendron hybridizer, Guy Nearing, small flower clusters cover the plant in great profusion, apricot yellow in bud changing to pale pink. Plants are slow growing, compact, heat tolerant, good for rock gardens.

Rhododendron yakushimanum
Zone 4; 4′–5′

A low-growing, mounded compact shrub with large bell-shaped flowers that are apple blossom-pink in bud, opening up to pure white. A good selection of this species is 'Mist Maiden' introduced by breeder Dr. David Leach. The plants are hardy to cold, but do not like prolonged exposure to heat. Find them a comfortable, moist, shady microclimate around your home.

Rhododendron yedoense (see AZALEA)

Rhododendron yedoense poukhanense (see AZALEA)

Rhodora canadensis (see *Rhododendron canadense*, AZALEA)

RHODOTYPOS

Rhodotypos kerrioides (see *R. scandens*)

Rhodotypos scandens (syn *R. kerrioides*, *R. tetrapetala*) (Jetbead, White kerria)
Zone 5; 5′–6′

Jetbead is an upright, spreading plant with single, white, 1¼″ wide flowers starting to open in mid-May and continuing intermittently all summer. They are followed by shiny jet-black fruits that stay on all winter. The leaves are dark green, remain that color all season, and are on the plant until late autumn, long after the leaves of most other shrubs have fallen.

This is not an outstanding shrub, but it is reliable and makes an attractive addition to any shrub border. The common name, white kerria, refers to a similarity between jetbead and the kerrias. The differences between them are, however, marked. Kerria leaves are alternately placed up and down the branches, while those of jetbead grow from the branches opposite one another. Kerria has green twigs, effective all winter, while those of jetbead are black. Kerria's brown fruits are not at all like the black "beads" of jetbead. And, of course, the flower colors differ, those of kerria being golden yellow. These details are given to show that common names cannot be depended upon at all.

Rhodotypos tetrapetala (see R. scandens)

Rhodotypus scandens

RHUS
(Sumac)

Many people recoil in horror at the mere mention of the name "sumac," because they think only of the scarlet or upland sumac (*Rhus glabra*) that grows along roadsides, in fields and spreads widely where it is allowed to grow as it will. Because of its rapid spread, it frequently becomes a pest in areas where such growth is not desirable.

However, there are other sumacs, and even the scarlet sumac is welcome where a screen is needed or around a summer cottage.

Sumacs vary greatly in height, but all are weak-wooded, so break easily; all thrive in poor, dry, sandy soil and in sunny situations (points in their favor); and all spread by means of underground stems. In autumn their leaves turn bright red and many of them have red fruits, provided plants with flowers of both sexes or plants of each sex have been planted. Otherwise, of course, there will be no fruits.

Sumacs are at home in wild places or semi-wild gardens, although the little fragrant sumac (*Rhus aromatica*) makes an excellent specimen if grown for its foliage and is ideal for covering and holding a steep bank. The shining sumac (*Rhus copallina*) also is good for a specimen because of its beautiful foliage. Other sumacs are grown for their finely divided leaves.

Still other sumacs should be avoided because they are poisonous to touch, especially poison ivy and poison oak. However, the poisonous species can be told from the non-poisonous easily since the poisonous kinds bear yellow, yellowish-white or white fruits while the non-poisonous forms bear red fruits.

Rhus aromatica (syn R. canadense) (Fragrant sumac, Sweet-scented sumac)
Zone 4 to parts of Zone 3; 3′
Growing wild from Quebec to the northern parts of Florida, Alabama, Mississippi, and Louisiana and westward to Texas, this is a first choice for planting on dry banks to hold soil in place. It also may merit a place near the front of a shrub border, provided it has plenty of room to spread, which it will do.

Upright in form, wider than high, with hairy leaves and small yellow flowers in clusters, opening before the leaves unfold in early May, this little shrub has hairy, ¼″ diameter, red fruits in early summer. The foliage turns orange and scarlet in autumn.

Rhus coppalina (Shining sumac, Dwarf sumac)
Zone 5 to parts of Zone 4; 3′–8′
Shining, dark green foliage that turns scarlet in autumn, greenish yellow small flowers in August, and red, hairy fruits characterize this sumac, which may be used for a specimen plant in poor dry soil. It grows wild from New York to Florida and is treelike in growth in the southern part of its range.

Rhus glabra

Rhus cotinus (see Cotinus coggygria)

Rhus glabra
(Smooth sumac, Scarlet sumac,
Upland sumac)
Zone 1; 8'–15'
This is the common sumac of the fields
and roadsides, growing wild over much
of the United States and Canada. It is
useful in gardens only for holding dry,
sandy banks or for screen plantings at
summer cottages. Despite the fact that
it is common and spreads to become a
pest, it is a pretty plant in autumn when
its leaves are bright red and its fruits
scarlet. The flowers preceding the fruits
are greenish yellow and borne in early
July.

**Rhus rubrifolia (see Cotinus coggy-
gria 'Purpureus')**

Rhus trilobata
(Ill-scented sumac, Lemonade
shrub, Skunk bush, Squaw bush)
Zone 5 to part of Zone 4; 3'–4'
Somewhat resembling the fragrant sumac, but with more upright growth,
this shrub is native to the west coast,
eastward to Illinois. It rarely is grown in
gardens. The flowers are not as conspicuous as those of the fragrant sumac,
and, though leaves and fruits are both
red in autumn, this is a shrub only for
the wild garden.

Rhus typhina
(Staghorn sumac, Vinegar tree)
Zone 4 to parts of Zone 3; 30'
The largest of the sumacs that grow
wild in North America, this can be
found from Quebec and Ontario southward to Georgia and westward to Iowa.
It may be either a shrub or a small tree
and, in either case, is upright in form.
The twigs are hairy when young, like
the new horns of the stag, hence the
common name. The leaves turn red in
autumn when the greenish-yellow June
flowers have matured into crimson
fruits. It is for this autumn coloration
that the plant is grown. It is best used
where it has plenty of room to spread
into large clumps. Several of the plants,
set to form a group, then growing together as they spread, are a handsome
sight in autumn.

Rhus typhina (Staghorn Sumac)

Rhus typhina 'Laciniata'
(Cut-leaved staghorn sumac)
Differs from *typhina* by having the leaflets deeply toothed or divided. An unusual plant in appearance, this should be
seen before it is purchased and used in a
garden only where the cut leaves will
show off to advantage, usually as a specimen. This cultivar should not be confused with 'Dissecta', which has leaves
even more finely divided than those of
'Laciniata' and is too often incorrectly
called 'Laciniata'.

RIBES

(Currant)

The currants most people know best
are those grown for their fruits, which
make delicious jelly. There are several
species bearing useful fruits. However,
the currants discussed here are those
grown as ornamentals, either for their
compact form or for their flowers,
rather than their fruits.

Many currants, because they are alternate hosts for a plant disease called
white pine blister rust, are not permitted entry into the United States or Canada, into many of the states, nor even
permitted to be moved from one place
to another within some of the states.
The subject of alternate hosts is discussed in Chapter 9.

Ribes alpinum
(Alpine currant)
Zone 1; 6' but usually about 3'
and slow-growing
The best use for this shrub is as a hedge
plant because it is extremely compact in
form, making almost a solid mass of
fine foliage that does not turn color in
fall. Leaves are small, opening very
early in spring. Flowers are ⅛" in
diameter, borne in 1¼" long clusters,
brilliant greenish-yellow in color and
therefore hardly show among the
leaves. Should you observe them in
early May, you will find them interesting in form. If the plants you own have
female flowers, scarlet berries will follow the blooms. However, it is not a

Ribes alpinum

ever, the leaves are prettily shaped and the clumps never unsightly. The vivid greenish-yellow tubular flowers, centered strong red, cover the plant in early May. Black, edible berries, but not many of them, ripen in late summer provided plants of both sexes are planted. The foliage, which opens with or after the flowers, turns scarlet in autumn.

This currant may be found wild from Minnesota and Arkansas west to South Dakota and Texas.

ROBINIA

(Locust)

Most robinias are large trees, but a tree form is described in the next chapter, and one shrub form here. All have compound leaves, with many leaflets and large, drooping clusters of flowers. The blooms are shaped like those of peas or sweet peas.

Robinia hispida
(Rose acacia, Pink locust, Moss locust)
Zone 6 to southern part of Zone 5; 3'
If this shrub did not have a bad habit of suckering, sometimes near its base and at other times several feet away, it would doubtless be more widely grown because it is tolerant of poor soils. The form is upright and irregular. Long, red bristles cover the branches, accounting for the comon name of moss locust. Great clusters of deep, purplish-pink florets are borne in late May and early June. These resemble the clusters of laburnums or wisterias though they are not as long as either (usually 2¼ to 2½″ long) and the individual florets are larger than those of laburnum. It is for these flowers that the shrub is grown. Odd-looking pods, shaped like pea pods but covered with red to purple bristles, develop in late summer and remain on the plants for some time.

This shrub is wild in the states of Virginia and Kentucky, south to Georgia and Alabama.

good idea to grow female plants as it is the males that have been found not to serve as hosts for white pine blister rust. For this reason, nurseries are propagating the male or pistillate plants almost exclusively.

Ribes aureum
(Slender golden currant, Golden currant)
Zone 1; 6'
Upright in form, this currant is grown for its flowers, which bloom as the leaves unfold and are golden yellow and fragrant, though not as fragrant as those

Ribes aureum

of *R. odoratum*, described below. They also are smaller than those of the clove currant, but there are more of them. Purplish-brown or black fruits follow the flowers.

Ribes diacanthum
(Siberian currant)
Zone 1; 5'
Resembling the alpine currant described above, but more upright in form, this currant has prickles on the branchlets, glossy leaves, greenish-yellow, inconspicuous flowers, followed by small, scarlet fruits. It, too, forms a hedge.

Ribes odoratum
(Clove currant, Fragrant currant, Golden currant, Buffalo currant, Buffalo berry)
Zone 5; 6'
If you have smelled the fragrance of the blossoms of this currant you will not rest until you own a plant. Place it where its habit of suckering will not overrun any plant of value and where you can drink in the scent as you pass back and forth in your garden.

Clove currant is upright and irregular in form. It soon forms clumps because of its suckering habit. These are never dense, but rather sparse. How-

Rosa 'Betty Prior'

ROSA
(Rose)

The roses most frequently grown in gardens nowadays are hybrid tea, floribunda, or grandiflora types that, while technically shrubs, require pruning, spraying and fertilizing to keep them producing flowers. In these days of high-priced garden help and therefore a trend to do-it-yourself gardening, the easy-upkeep plants are coming into their own. High among these are the really shrubby roses for they require comparatively little care. These are the only roses included in this book.

Shrub roses may be one-time bloomers, bearing flowers usually in June, or "remontant" which means you can expect a crop of flowers in June and occasional blooms during summer and autumn. They vary greatly in height and size, as well as in bloom production. The rose species described below all thrive in poor soil and most need full sun, but a few, which are indicated, will flower in light shade. Species roses should not be fertilized and, while the Austrian Copper rose (*R. foetida* 'Bicolor') certainly needs spraying to control black spot, the remainder of the older roses named do not. The newer shrub roses also are trouble free, if not quite to the extent of the species. Most of them profit from light fertilization, few need spraying. In general, shrub rose pruning is confined to removing any dead canes in spring and any canes that are in the way of other plants or traffic.

Shrub roses are sturdy plants. As indicated above, many of them are rose species, found wild somewhere in the world, on this continent or another. Some are varieties or cultivars of these species and have flowers as handsome as those of any rose you care to name.

In this section I have tried to tell you a little about the most widely available of the older shrub roses and indicate some of the modern kinds. If you are seriously interested in the old shrub roses, there are numerous specialty books available through your local library, plus a wide selection of mail-order catalogs. (See sources in the back of this book.)

I would like to add a few words about modern shrub roses. Some of them, to my mind, rival azaleas when they are in flower—and that is certainly a challenging statement. A full grown plant of 'Nevada', for instance, is as beautiful as any shrub that blooms in the garden all season. 'Golden Wings' is hardy into Canada and a simply gorgeous dwarf shrub when it is laden with its single, golden-yellow flowers with their even more golden stamens.

'Betty Prior', while not listed as a shrub, is a good one with flowers throughout the summer and autumn as well as in June. 'The Fairy' (*not* 'Sweet Fairy') is, to my mind, in a class by itself. You will find a brief description later in the text.

Because most of these roses are not widely available, I have indicated them according to hybrid groups in this chapter. You can search the catalogs to find the varieties in these groups as I have done. It's fun to find one you've been wanting to acquire.

In the past, there were only 2 or 3 nurseries in the United States and Canada that listed shrub roses. The number is increasing each year because of the demand for roses that do not require endless care. Some nurseries specializing in shrub roses have much longer lists than others that grow not only shrub roses but other shrubs as well. Only roses widely available are described below.

Rosa
(Climbing roses)
Zones 4 to 9; 10' and more

Climbing roses generally need help in order to climb, usually by having their long whip-like canes tied to a support with twist-ties or string. Some of the best climbers are species roses, like *Rosa banksia* (Lady Banks rose) and *Rosa laevigata* (Cherokee rose), but these are not reliably hardy north of Zone 7. By far the most popular climbers are mutations of hybrid tea roses, such as climbing Peace (a large-flowered pale yellow with magenta petal), or are developed in modern breeding programs, such as Blaze (an extremely free-flowering medium-size red).

Climbing roses are highly susceptible to winterkill unless the canes are pruned back in autumn to leave only four main canes, which should be tied firmly to their support to prevent wind damage.

Climbing roses generally are heavy feeders, prefer a well-drained soil enriched with animal manure and are watered during dry periods.

The following are some of the best climbers for northern conditions:
• 'America'—3½ to 4½"; double coral blooms are fragrant.
• 'Blaze'—2½ to 3"; semi-double blooms are scarlet-red, have slight fragrance.
• 'City of York'—3 to 3½", white, semi-double blooms have yellow centers, good fragrance.
• 'Don Juan'—4½"; deep red double flowers have good fragrance.
• 'Dortmund'—3 to 3½"; cherry-red single flowers have white centers, good fragrance.
• 'Golden Showers'—3½ to 4"; yellow double flowers have good fragrance.
• 'Joseph's Coat'—3 to 4"; double flowers can be red, yellow or a combination of red and yellow, sometimes all three color combinations appearing within the same flower cluster. Slight fragrance.
• 'New Dawn'—3 to 3½"; light pink semi-double blooms are fragrant.

Rosa centifolia

Rosa altaica
(see *R. pimpinellifolia altaica*)

Rosa blanda
(Smooth wild rose, Labrador rose)
Zone 1; 6′

The first common name of this rose refers to the smoothness of the upper parts of the older canes; on the lower parts there are a few thorns or prickles.

This wild rose grows from Labrador and Quebec to Manitoba, southward to New Brunswick, through New England and Pennsylvania, north and west to Ohio, Indiana, Illinois, Missouri, and Nebraska.

The rose is many-branched and spreads into a large clump by means of suckers. Single, rosy-pink flowers, 2½″ in diameter, are found singly or in groups of up to 8 blooms. Round or oval fruits color scarlet in autumn.

Rosa centifolia 'Muscosa'
(Moss rose)

These are all old-time roses that have a green growth resembling moss on the outsides of the sepals that surround bud and flower. This is most noticeable, of course, before the flower is fully opened, for when it unfolds, the flower spread hides the moss. This class of roses has been loved by gardeners for generations. The moss roses now available may be found in the catalogs of specialists in old roses.

Rosa eglanteria (syn *R. rubiginosa*)
(Sweet brier, Eglantine)
Zone 4; 8′

This is the rose with apple-scented foliage that is mentioned in old garden books and in some novels. Its form is arching, it is extremely prickly and, if plants are set 3′ apart, will form an impenetrable hedge, almost as wide as it is high. Eglantine has single, small pink flowers in mid-June sometimes borne in clusters, sometimes solitary. It passes on the apple scent of the leaves to its progeny, for I owned one named 'Lady Penzance', which while entirely different in form and flower color, was delightful to sniff during a warm, moist spell.

Such modern shrub roses as 'Herbstfeuer' (autumn fire) and 'Goldbusch' (gold bush) are hybrids of *R. eglanteria* (although more frequently listed under the former name as "*R. rubiginosa* hybrids").

Rosa foetida 'Bicolor'
(Austrian copper brier)
Zone 5; 9′

Certainly one of the most beautifully and brightly colored roses, this has single flowers, 2¼″ in diameter, their centers vivid yellow and the outer parts of the petals nearest to vivid red. The very edges of the petals are even deeper in tone, but the same general hue. The reverse or undersides of the petals are the same vivid yellow.

Austrian Copper blooms in early June on a tall, upright plant. The hips that follow the blooms are red and most effective in autumn.

The trouble with growing this rose is that it can be depended on to be attacked by black spot, a rose disease that will defoliate the plant unless the disease is controlled by spraying or dusting with Phaltan. The plant will get this disease every single year and will infect other roses around it. Although it will survive for many years regardless of the defoliation, in due course of time it is likely to succumb to the periodic weakening through loss of foliage.

Rosa foetida 'Bicolor'

Rosa foetida 'Persian Yellow'
(Persian yellow rose)

This rose looks especially good when grown with Austrian Copper as the two are similar in height and form. This rose has deep yellow, double flowers that have the unpleasant odor suggested by the specific name. Persian yellow forms a large bush, eventually, and is handsome in flower. It is best; however, to place it away from a porch or other outdoor living room. It is a handsome specimen plant or may be used in a border.

Rosa glauca (syn Rosa rubrifolia)
(Red-leaved rose, Red-leaf rose)
Zone 2; 8' and as wide as high

If you live way up north and want to grow a handsome shrub, try this one. Not only is it extremely hardy, but it also is attractive from spring to fall with its upright growth and bluish green foliage with purplish red undertones and tinges. In early June it produces single, 1½" diameter deep purplish pink blooms tinged in their centers with moderate purplish pink. It is these same tones that tinge the foliage.

The centers of the flowers are almost white and the light yellow stamens set them off beautifully. The flowering continues over several weeks, although there are rarely masses of flowers on the plant at any one time. The hips are an unusual strong red orange.

The coloring of this rose is best when it is growing in full sun. In shade the leaves "gray off" and are not as bright. Because of the height and the foliage color, this rose may be used at the back of a border or as a specimen where its leaves will aid the garden picture.

For the sake of those who wish to garden easily, I might add that my largest bush of this rose is now over 40 years old. It was moved several years ago from our former garden with a ball of earth around its roots. It was not cut back at that time to aid it in reestablishing itself and it kept right on growing and blooming. It never has been fertilized or sprayed, nor has it had any

Rosa harisonii

more pruning than the occasional removal of a broken or dead branchlet.

Rosa harisonii (R. foetida × R. pimpinellifolia)
(Harison's yellow rose)
Zone 5 to part of Zone 4; 6'

Paler yellow flowers than Persian yellow (closest to brilliant greenish yellow), 2" wide and not as double, but fragrant (unlike those of Persian yellow), and nearly black hips characterize this rose. It blooms just before the *R. foetida* trio of *R. foetida*, *R. f.* 'Bicolor' and *R. f.* 'Persian yellow' about the end of May and a bushful of blooms can be counted on every year. Fine for use in a shrub border or as a specimen.

Rosa hugonis
(Father Hugo rose, Golden rose of China)
Zone 5 to part of Zone 4; 3½'–4'

There is no more delicately beautiful rose bud than that of this rose. Add to the exquisite buds finely cut, dainty foliage and brilliant greenish yellow, single 1¾" to 2" diameter flowers blooming with the late tulips in May and you have a rose that everyone who loves beautiful plants should be growing. This rose does not often fruit, but when it does the hips are dark red, almost black red. The plants are upright and spread to form clumps.

Rosa lucida (see R. virginiana)

R. moschata hybrids
(Musk hybrids)
4'–5'

These are listed here because among them are some lovely shrubs, available in a few nurseries. 'Belinda', 'Elmshorn' and 'Cornelia' are just a few of their names. The one most widely listed is 'Robin Hood', especially recommended for hedge use. Its growth is dense and compact and the plant is hardy to below zero. It can be kept to any height over 3' (it naturally grows a bit taller than this). It has cherry red flowers, small, but borne in fair-sized clusters, in June and occasionally during summer and fall.

Rosa moschata hybrid

Rosa moyesii

Rosa moyesii
(Moyes rose)
Zone 6 to parts of Zone 5; 9′, sometimes more

The growth habit of this shrub is positively gaunt, if that word can be applied to plant growth. A few stout, tall stems support branches near their tops. The leaves are small and the flowers are single, 2″ in diameter, and blood red in color. They appear in mid-June. The fruits that follow them are unusual in shape, rather like small flasks, broad at the base, then narrowing to a waist and then widening again. They are orange-red and begin to color in August and September.

Rosa moyesisi hybrids
Here, too, are found beautiful, hardy shrub roses, such as 'Nevada', with large, semi-double, creamy white flowers set off by yellow stamens, and 'Marguerite Hilling', its pink sport.

Rosa multiflora
(Japanese rose)
Zone 5; 12′ and as wide as high

Contrary to many advertisements you may have seen, this is *not* a rose for small gardens. It makes a wonderful hedge to keep cattle confined or to mark the boundaries of a large piece of property and also is an excellent tall ground cover for steep banks along rail-road rights of way where no one wishes children to climb or where soil needs to be held in place. It is an extremely vigorous, fast-growing shrub, beautiful when in flower or fruit, but much, much too large to be planted on a 50-foot lot. In some farming communities local ordinances prohibit the planting of this rose because of its ability to become a pest on pasture land.

Habit of growth is upright with widely arching branches. The leaves are small and the plants very spiny or thorny. Little white flowers, 1″ in diameter, are borne in tremendous quantities in mid-June, literally covering the bushes with bloom. These are followed by little red hips in the same large quantities. They are lovely to look at in autumn and usually stay on the plant during most of the winter, thus are available for use in Christmas decorations.

Rosa nitida
(Shining rose)
Zone 2; 1½′–2′

A wild rose, found from Newfoundland to Connecticut, often in low-lying, marshy areas, this is a very twiggy rose, with many thin prickles or thorns up the reddish stems. It spreads rapidly by means of suckers. The leaflets are narrow, pointed at the tips, glossy green on the upper sides and turning to bright scarlet in fall. It is this autumn coloring that is the shrub's greatest asset. Flowers are single, rose-red in color and, despite the low stature of the plant, are a full 2″ across. The hips are red, covered with bristles, and small, ⅜″ in diameter. They are not long-lasting.

This rose is useful in the front of a shrub border or as a specimen in a rock garden, but in either situation room must be allowed for it to sucker and spread.

Rosa multiflora

Rosa rugosa 'Turkestan rose'

Rosa palustris
(Swamp rose)
Zone 5; 6′

Upright in form, with slender stems, this shrub grows from Nova Scotia to Minnesota, southward to Florida and Mississippi. Its blooms are single and pink, opening in June. The fruits are red in autumn. The only reason for growing this shrub is that it will thrive in wet places, so is useful where these are found. It also will thrive in dry areas but far handsomer species are available for such situations.

Rosa pimpinellifolia
(syn *R. spinosissima*)
(Burnet rose, Scotch brier, Scotch rose)
Zone 4; 3′

Not only is this a low-growing shrub, but it also has a dense, mounded form, which makes it useful in many locations. In early June it bears 1″ to 2″ diameter, single, fragrant white flowers in profusion. These are followed, some years, by black or brownish fruits that are not particularly beautiful.

The former name of the plant was given because the stems are literally loaded with different sizes of thorns and spines.

Rosa pimpinellifolia altaica (syn *R. spinosissima altaica*)
Zone 4; 4′–5′

With larger leaves than the species, fewer thorns, and a strong, upright growth habit, this is a lovely rose when its branches are drooping under their load of blooms. These are cream-white or ivory-white, about 3″ in diameter, and appear but once in early June. The fruits that follow them are reddish-black and unusual in appearance.

Rosa pimpinellifolia hybrids

These are better known under the former name of *spinosissima* hybrids. They are mostly the production of Wilhelm Kordes of Germany and are handsome shrubs, larger than the species. These are not as yet widely available in this country. Look for them in the catalogs. Many of them have names beginning with the word "Frühling," which is German for "spring." Thus 'Frühlingsmorgen' translates to Spring's morning and 'Frühlingsgold' to Spring's gold and so on. These are hardy to temperatures ranging to at least minus 10 degrees.

Most of these hybrids have disease-resistant foliage, bloom only once in May, and need minimum care.

Rosa rubiginosa (see *R. eglanteria*)

Rosa rugosa
(Rugosa rose, Sea tomato, Eatin' rose)
Zone 1; 6′

This is another fine rose for the north. It also is well suited to seaside gardens because it will tolerate salt spray. Add to these advantages a tough constitution, handsome dark green leaves turning almost orange in fall, 2″ wide purplish-red flowers, and tomato-red fruits and you have the reasons why this rose is widely grown. Its faults are that it is very thorny and that both flowers and fruits often are on the plant at the same time, as flowering continues for months and fruits color early. This dual coloration is not an ideal color scheme. However, both colors are tempered by the green of the leaves.

The rugosa rose is useful for clipped or unclipped hedges, for covering banks, or for a place in a shrub border where it has room to spread. There are other flower colors available in its varieties and cultivars that eliminate one of the objections voiced above.

Rosa rugosa 'Alba'

A white-flowered cultivar more upright in growth than the species. The prior remark about the color clash between flowers and fruits does not, of course, apply.

Rosa pimpinellifolia (Scotch rose)

Rosa rugosa 'Frau Dagmar Hastrup'

Rosa rugosa cultivars

The following cultivars of *R. rugosa* are those most frequently found in the catalogs:

• 'Agnes'. Double, pale amber, fragrant flowers. Once-blooming, 6', vigorous and hardy.
• 'Belle Poitevine'. Large, semi-double, rose-pink to magenta-pink flowers 3½" to 4" in diameter. Recurrent bloom. Vigorous growth.
• 'Blanc Double de Coubert'. Double, white flowers.
• 'F. G. Grootendorst'. Small, double, slightly fragrant, bright red flowers with fringed petal edges. Recurrent bloom. Vigorous growth.
• 'Frau Dagmar Hastrup'. Single, silvery-pink flowers. Recurrent bloom.
• 'Grootendorst Supreme'. Deeper crimson-red than Grootendorst.
• 'Hansa'. Large, double, clove-rose scented, reddish-violet flowers. Repeat bloomer. Grows well on the western prairies.
• 'Pink Grootendorst'. Fringed, clear pink flowers in clusters, otherwise like 'F. G. Grootendorst'. Recurrent bloom.
• 'Sir Thos. Lipton'. Double, fragrant, white flowers. Recurrent bloom.

Rosa setigera
(Prairie rose)
Zone 5 to part of Zone 4; 15'

Native from Nebraska, Wisconsin and southern Ontario to the Gulf states, this rose may kill to the ground in winter in the far north but will grow again from the roots in spring, if protected with straw, and make great long canes in one season.

Whether the entire growth is made in one season or not, the canes of this rose are always long and weak. Thus, when the rose is not supported, they arch widely or, if a tree is nearby, they grow up into it and greatly enhance the appearance of the tree when they are flowering. Sometimes the canes lie on the ground and sprawl. Doubtless pruning would give the plant a better form but, if allowed plenty of room, it needs none. It definitely is not a rose for a small garden.

In early to mid-July, when most other rose species have finished flowering, the prairie rose bears single, 2½" diameter blooms in clusters that may be 5" across and 4" in depth. There is no match for the flowers in color. They are between deep purplish-pink and strong purplish-pink, but more rose color. They are fragrant, though many people will tell you that they are not. The foliage turns reddish in autumn and the fruits also are red.

The Detroit Zoological Garden uses this rose as a specimen, next to large buildings, allowed to grow to its full size and kept upright by pruning. If anyone wished to train it flat, it undoubtedly could be used as a climber against a wall or fence.

Rosa spinosissima 'The Fairy'
(see *R. pimpinellifolia*)
Zone 5; 3'

Because I made such a point of mentioning this rose earlier in this discussion of roses, I shall describe it briefly here. It is a low shrub that needs only the dead wood cut off in spring, no spraying at all, little fertilization, yet produces flowers all summer long. It blooms in spurts—that is, there is plentiful bloom in late June in my garden. Then the bushes rest, then form a new set of buds and become laden with flowers once more, and so on throughout the summer and early autumn.

This rose is a sport of one named 'Lady Godiva', which, in turn, is a sport of the well-known rambler rose, 'Dorothy Perkins'. The flowers of 'The Fairy' are the same pink as those of the pink-flowered 'Dorothy' and the same small size but borne in large clusters. In the twelve years that I have owned a dozen plants of 'The Fairy', I have seen black spot on it once, in a very wet season. Would that I could say the same of the hybrid teas, etc., that I also grow.

Rosa spinosissima 'The Fairy'

Rosa wichuraiana

Rosa virginiana (syn *R. lucida*)
Zone 4 to part of Zone 3; 6′
Found from Newfoundland southward to Alabama and westward to Missouri, this rose is vigorous in growth, spreading by means of underground stems. It thrives in sandy soil and forms a beautiful, unclipped hedge.

This is a handsome rose at any season of the year. In spring the shining leaves open and are attractive. In mid- to late-June the cerise-pink, single flowers open, paler at the centers and with yellow stamens showing. The glossy leaves remain in good condition all summer, and in autumn turn first beet red, then orange with sometimes a little yellow added to make the appearance of the plant even more marked. The fruits are red and rounded, ½″ in diameter. They ripen late in the season and are effective against the red-brown winter color of the twigs.

This rose grows too large for a small garden unless restrained by pruning. It is a fine hedge rose if lightly pruned.

Rosa wichuraiana
(Memorial rose)
Zone 5; procumbent
With tiny, semi-evergreen, glossy leaves, this is a rose for covering the ground, especially banks, where it soon will grow so thickly that no weeds can penetrate. It has single, white, 2″ diameter flowers the middle of July and the fruits that follow them are red.

RUBUS
(Raspberry)

Gardeners usually think of raspberries as being grown solely for their fruits. There are, however, several that have such lovely blooms they are grown as ornamentals. They are as easy to grow as any raspberry, needing little or no care except pruning of old canes at the end of the flowering season because, like all raspberries, the old canes do not flower or fruit a second year.

Rubus odoratus
(Flowering raspberry)
Zone 4 to part of Zone 3; usually about 6′
Found wild from Nova Scotia westward to Michigan and southward to Tennessee and Georgia, this is an upright-growing shrub with arching branches and large, hairy leaves. Fragrant, rose-purple, 2″ diameter flowers open early in July, followed by flat, pale red berries that can be eaten. Both flowers and berries often are found on the plant at the same time.

While this shrub grows best in shade, it will grow in sun if it is set in a moist situation or gets sufficient moisture otherwise. It is not a shrub for a small garden as it suckers and spreads. It is best used in a wild garden, to hold a shady bank in place, or in a shady spot in the cultivated garden where there is plenty of room and not many other shrubs would thrive.

SALIX
(Willow)

All willows are easy to grow unless and until they are troubled by borers. Most prefer moist soil but many will grow as well in drier areas. Some have colorful stems or contorted or weeping form, others have beautiful foliage and still others are grown for their ornamental buds and opening catkins. In willows the flowers of each sex are borne on separate plants. The male flowers are the more ornamental and these are the reasons for growing the shrubby willows described below. There are, of course, many other shrub willows listed by specialists in the genus.

Salix caprea
(see Chapter 13)

Rubus odoratus

Salix discolor

Salix discolor
(Pussy willow, American pussy willow, Glaucous willow)
Zone 4 to part of Zone 3; 6' to 20'

Our native pussy willow is found wild from Labrador to Alberta, south to Nova Scotia, New England, Maryland, west to Kentucky, Missouri and South Dakota. It usually grows along streams or in swampy locations, but will grow well in drier locations in the garden. It is hardier than goat willow (*S. caprea*) described in the next chapter.

The leaves of this species are bluish-green on the undersides, which gives the shrub the effect of gray foliage when viewed from a distance. Catkins are gray, the male ones producing bright yellow stamens in March to April. Unless the plants are heavily fertilized and well watered, catkins are smaller than those of goat willow and Korean rose-gold pussy willow. They appear just as those of the latter are dropping.

Salix gracilistyla
(Korean rose-gold pussy willow, but often listed as "Rose-Gold")
Zone 5; 6'–7'

Part of the common name of this pussy willow, the "Rose-Gold" part, was bestowed on the plant by a nurseryman who had a number of these willows on hand and wanted to sell them. It refers to the distinct reddish or rosy under-tone in the coloring of the catkins that, when the stamens are pollen-laden, thus become rose and gold. "Korean" refers to the country of origin, though this willow is more commonly found in Japan and Manchuria.

Much lower growing than either of the other two pussy willows described in this book, this also matures its catkins slightly earlier. They are more elongated in shape than those of the other pussy willows.

Salix purpurea
(Purple osier, Basket willow)
Zone 5 to part of Zone 4; 10'

On low ground, from Newfoundland to Ontario and Wisconsin, southward to Nova Scotia, New England, Virginia, West Virginia, Ohio, Illinois and Iowa, you'll find this willow growing.

When the Indians wove baskets, the supple stems often were their choice. The twigs are purple in winter, which accounts for both the botanical and first common name.

Plants are dense yet graceful, the foliage fine, the catkins very small and gray, appearing in March. This willow is not sufficiently attractive for use in the cultivated part of a garden, but is excellent in a damp place where a practically carefree, but still good-looking shrub is desired.

Salix purpurea 'Gracilis' (syn *S. p. nana* and also sometimes listed as 'Purpurea Dwarf')
(Dwarf purple osier, Dwarf Arctic willow)
Zone 5 to part of Zone 4; 3'–4'

Narrow, blue-green leaves and many slender branches are the important characteristics of this delicate-appearing willow. It is used chiefly for low hedges where dainty appearance is important. Actually the plants are tough and easy to grow.

Salix purpurea nana (see *Salix purpurea* 'Gracilis')

Salix repens
(Creeping willow)
Zone 4; 3'

That low, damp place in your garden where nothing much will grow and you don't want a shrub that will grow tall is the perfect spot to use this low-growing willow. It tolerates poor soil, moisture and even a little shade.

SAMBUCUS
(Elder)

If you have a small garden, there is no reason for you to read about elders. They are too large, too vigorous in growth, for a limited area. They are at their best in wild gardens, especially in moist soil. They tend to grow straggly as time goes on, but can be cut to the ground if too unsightly and will grow again from the roots. Their leaves are large and, while some people consider them coarse in appearance, I think they are beautiful. All elders have tiny white florets arranged in large, delicately designed clusters, and edible fruits. From these some people make wine, some make pies and still others a tart jelly, delicious when served with meat. Birds love the berries so birds and humans often race to see who gets them first.

All elders are easy to transplant if moved when small but hard to reestablish if moved when large. They are not particular as to soil conditions but if moist soil is available they will grow better in it. They require no special care.

Sambucus canadensis **(American Elder)**

Sambucus canadensis
(American elder, Common elder, Elderberry, Bore tree)
Zone 4 to part of Zone 3; 12′
Flower clusters of this elder may be 8″ in diameter and are at their height of bloom in late June or early July. The blue-black berries are borne in just as large clusters as the flowers and make the plants prominent in the landscape in September. Selected forms now are being propagated for finest fruits.

This elder is native from British Columbia to Manitoba and south to New England, Georgia, Louisiana, west to Oklahoma.

Sambucus canadensis 'Aurea'
(Golden elder)
Has brilliant golden-yellow leaves that retain their color all season and is a good choice where such a bright-foliaged plant is needed.

Sambucus nigra 'Aurea'
(Golden European elder)
Zone 5; 30′
This elder may grow as a tree or as a large shrub. It is the yellow-leaved form of the European elder and is not in any way superior to the yellow-leaved form of the American elder. All yellow-foliaged plants should be used with care so that their foliage color does not conflict with nearby surroundings.

Sambucus nigra 'Laciniata'
(Cut-leaved European elder)
The leaves of this elder are deeply and regularly divided. The plant is grown for this characteristic.

Sambucus plumosa aurea
(see *S. racemosa* 'Plumosa Aurea')

Sambucus racemosa
(European red elder)
Zone 5; 12′
Earlier to bloom than the native elder, this has creamy-white flowers early in May. These are followed by scarlet berries in July and August.

Sambucus canadensis 'Aurea'

Sambucus racemosa aurea
(see *S. r.* 'Plumosa Aurea')

Sambucus racemosa 'Plumosa Aurea' **(syn *S. plumosa aurea, S. racemosa aurea*)**
Has leaves deeply cut, golden yellow in color. This does not change during the season, so this plant, often listed as "Golden Plume" in the catalogs, should be considered where a large, yellow-leaved plant is desired.

SPIRAEA

(Spirea)

There are many, many spireas available to the gardener. They fall into two groups for garden purposes—spring-blooming and summer-blooming.

Within these two groups, they might be classified by their flower forms, because the spring-blooming spireas usually are borne in umbels (clusters in which all flower stems start from one point and are about the same length) growing close to the branch or on short, leafy stems. They also may be arranged in looser, flat-topped clusters quite regularly spaced along the branches. Flowers of the summer-blooming spireas are either flat-topped clusters or elongated plumy clusters and, in both cases, are borne at the tips of the branches. In all cases, the individual florets are tiny—the clusters are the noticeable parts, not individual blooms, although they are attractive.

Spireas, as might be expected in so large a genus, vary greatly in height, form, and flowering time. However, practically all of them have undistinguished leaves, only a few have colored foliage in autumn, and none of them have decorative fruits. Because of these facts, the gardener should realize that he is giving most of them space solely for their flowers (or, occasionally, their branching form). All spireas are easy to move and to grow. They need no special soil and have no particular pests. They thrive in sun and many will grow as well in light shade, though their flowers will be fewer. If a spirea should become unsightly through neglect, it may be cut to the ground in early spring and will grow again from the roots.

Spiraea albiflora (syn S. callosa alba, S. japonica alba) (Japanese white spirea) Zone 5; 1½'

One of the summer-flowering spireas, this blooms in July. Flowers are white, as the botanical name tells. It is an excellent low shrub that may be used as a specimen if bloom at that time is required for effect, but is better in the front of a shrub border, perhaps combined with other summer-flowering spireas that have pink flowers.

Spiraea × arguta (S. multiflora × S. thunbergii) (Garland spirea) Zone 5 to part of Zone 4; 5'–6'

This shrub resembles the widely planted Vanhoutte spirea that blooms the end of May, but the garland spirea blooms at the beginning of that month. By planting both species, it is possible to have the same beautifully arched branches laden with flat clusters of white flowers for a longer period of time. The garland spirea may be used as a specimen or in the border. There also is a compact form of this plant, called in the catalogs *Spiraea arguta compacta*, which is extremely useful and very pretty. I am using it for a low hedge.

Spiraea japonica alpina

Spiraea × billiardii (S. douglasii × S. salicifolia) (Billiard's spirea, Billiard spirea) Zone 5 to part of Zone 4; 6'

In late June, and intermittently during the next month or more, the 6″ long, 2″ wide spikes of this spirea enhance the garden picture. They are deep purplish-pink and furnish a welcome change from the earlier white spirea flowers. Billiard spirea should be placed where there is room for it to form clumps, for this it will do. It is a good border shrub and excellent for massing wherever summer bloom is desired.

Spiraea × bumalda (S. japonica × S. albiflora)

This plant is listed only occasionally in the catalogs. It is known through the cultivars described below.

Spiraea × bumalda 'Anthony Waterer' Zone 4; 2'–3'

This plant is named for the same Anthony Waterer mentioned in the discussions of azaleas and rhododendrons. Considering his contributions to the gardens of the world, it is rewarding to know that his memory is kept green by one of the most popular and widely-grown of summer-flowering shrubs.

Starting in late June and continuing intermittently throughout the summer, the strong purplish red flowers open. If the dead blooms are kept cut, flowering will be increased and will continue later in the season. Not only is there handsome flower color, but the young leaves are pink or pinkish, some years only in spring, other years continuing later in the season. The form of the plant is upright and quite compact. It occasionally needs some pruning because one or two branches will grow half a foot above all the others.

All three of the *bumaldas* may be used as specimens or in the front of shrub borders.

Spiraea × bumalda 'Anthony Waterer'

Spiraea callosa alba
(see *S. albiflora*)

Spiraea caryopteris
(see *Caryopteris* × *clandonensis*)

Spiraea japonica alba
(see *S. albiflora*)

Spiraea japonica alpina
Zone 5, possibly Zone 4; 1' or a little less
A fine ground cover for a sunny spot, tolerant of any soil, this little plant grows 10"–12" high and, if plants are set 18" apart, soon will carpet the ground. Little light pink flowers appear in May and occasionally throughout the summer.

Spiraea japonica 'Atrosanguinea'
(syn *S. j. coccinea*)
Zone 6 to southern part of Zone 5; 4'
In spring the new foliage of this spirea is red. In late June to early July, and usually intermittently for a month or more after that, the flowers bloom, strong purplish red in color and in large (to 5" diameter) clusters that are flat.

The plant is taller and more open in growth than 'Anthony Waterer'; and new growth covers dead flowers, a decided asset.

Spiraea nipponica tosaensis

Spiraea japonica 'Atrosanguinea'

Spiraea lemoinei alpestris
Zone 5; 6"
Like *S. japonica alpina*, this spirea is an excellent ground cover, but a lower one, hugging the ground. Plants set a foot apart soon grow together to form a matlike mass—conducive to smothering weeds. Like all spireas this is tolerant of almost any soil. It prefers full sun but will grow in slight shade. Light pink, tiny blooms in May plus one or two at intervals during the rest of the season may be expected.

Spiraea media sericea
(Oriental spirea)
Zone 4; possibly to Zone 3; 4'
Upright in growth, with arching branches, this produces abundant creamy-white flowers in late May, much in the same manner as *S.* × *vanhouttei*. It is hardier than the Vanhoutte spirea, a point in its favor.

Spiraea × *multiflora (S. crenata* × *S. hypericifolia)*
(Snowgarland)
Zone 4; 5'
Blooming in May, this has ¼ to ⁵/₁₆" diameter flowers in clusters several inches across, on branches that arch only slightly. This spirea grows particularly well in the northern part of the midwest.

Spiraea nipponica tosaensis
(Snowmound, Boxwood spirea)
Zone 5; 2½'
Foliage like that of the species, dark green on top of the leaves, but bluish green on the undersides, white flowers in smaller clusters than those of the species, and a moundlike form characterize this pretty and useful spirea. Blooms appear in June.

Spiraea × *pikoviensis (S. crenata* × *S. media)*
(Pikov spirea)
Zone 4; 4'
More upright in form than the Oriental spirea, with stiffer branches, this too has white to greenish-white flowers in May.

Spiraea prunifolia (syn *S. p. plena*, which is the listing commonly given in the catalogs)
(Bridal wreath)
Zone 5 to part of Zone 4; 6'–7'
Botanists gave the double-flowered form of this plant the specific name because it was found first. Later, when the single-flowered form was discovered, it was given the varietal name of *simpliciflora*. This single-flowered form rarely is listed in any catalog. The double-flowered is the one meant, regardless of name.

Round ⅜″ diameter buttons are what the blooms of this spirea resemble. A plant usually is loaded with them in mid-May. Growth habit is narrow and upright and the foliage, glossy green in spring and summer, turns bright orange in autumn, unusual in a spirea.

Spiraea prunifolia

Spiraea × sanssouciana (S. douglasii × S. japonica)
Zone 5; 4½′

This is one of the summer-flowering spireas but it is earlier to start blooming than Billiard's spirea or *macrothyrsa*, sometimes starting in late June. This is its particular advantage because it has rose-colored flowers in pyramidal spikes at the branch tips and is easily mistaken for either of the other similar spireas.

Spiraea thunbergii
(Thunberg spirea, Thunberg's spirea)
Zone 4; 5′

Most years this has the distinction of being the first spirea to flower. It does this in early May, before its leaves have grown. The growth habit is upright and arching, the branches slender, the foliage light green (turning yellow in autumn) and finely textured. Unfortunately, a cold winter will cause some of the branches to die back, necessitating spring pruning. Florets are only ⅜″ in diameter, but are borne in clusters of from two to five.

Spiraea tomentosa
(Hardhack, Hardhack spirea, Steeple bush, Canada tea)
Zone 5 to parts of Zone 4; 4′–5′

From late June to September you will see this plant blooming in damp places from Prince Edward Island to Quebec and Ontario, southward along the Atlantic coast to North Carolina. It is upright in form, spreads into large clumps, has deep rose or rosy-purple flowers set close together in short, upright spikes, pyramidal in shape. It is good to use in the wild garden or for planting by the sides of streams or lakes, but is much too spreading and not sufficiently showy for the cultivated garden.

Spiraea trichocarpa
(Korean spirea)
Zone 5 to part of Zone 4; 6′

Blooming in June, right after the Vanhoutte spirea, this shrub has spreading branches rather than arching ones, and the bloom clusters are larger than those of the Vanhoutte spirea—to 2¼″ in diameter, composed of ¼″ wide white florets with yellow centers.

Spiraea trilobata
(Threelobe spirea)
Zone 5 to part of Zone 4; 3′–4′

The common name and the botanical name refer to the three lobes of the leaf, which make this spirea easy to tell from others. It has slender, arching branches and the flowers, white and formed into large clusters, are spaced all along them in late May to early June. There is a selection named Swan Lake, that is available from a few nurseries.

Spiraea trichocarpa

Spiraea × vanhouttei

Spiraea × vanhouttei (S. cantoniensis × S. trilobata)
(Vanhoutte spirea)
Zone 5 to part of Zone 4; 6′

Once upon a time some traveling nursery salesman must have gone up and down every street in the midwest and sold every householder half a dozen plants of this spirea. This is the only way in which I can account for the vast numbers of Vanhoutte spirea one sees everywhere in this part of the country. It is this overplanting that makes some gardeners shy away from this plant.

If, instead of being influenced by its seeming commonness, you will take a good look at an individual plant, you will see that it is handsome when in flower. The myriad little ⅜″ florets in the flat, 1½″ diameter clusters in late May, borne along the gracefully arching branches, make this one of the best spireas. In some autumns the leaves turn red or orange, giving color at another time of year. The plant is as easy to grow as are all spireas, another good reason why so many gardeners possess one.

Try using this spirea as a specimen or placed in a conspicuous spot in a shrub border.

STAPHYLEA

(Bladdernut)

Staphyleas may be large shrubs or sometimes small trees. They are grown for their smooth, striped bark, bright green foliage, drooping flower clusters, and inflated seed pods.

Staphylea trifolia

Staphylea trifolia
(American bladdernut)
Zone 4 to parts of Zone 3; 15′
Found wild from Quebec and Ontario to Minnesota and south to Georgia, west to Missouri, Wisconsin, Iowa, Arkansas, and Oklahoma, this plant arouses interest when seen in the woods because, whether in flower or in fruit, it is out of the ordinary. It usually, but not always, is found in moist situations and therefore is useful for moist places in the garden, especially in shade.

Growth is upright, the bark grayish, the branches striped and green. The leaves, as the botanical name tells, are three-parted. In May the slender,

drooping clusters of flowers appear. The petals of these are white; the sepals, which are almost as long as the petals, are greenish white and this variation gives an overall effect of pale greenwhite.

The fruits are three-lobed, inflated pods, first green then tan. They mature in October and last a long time when cut. Although the plant is an American native, these pods add an exotic touch to late autumn flower arrangements.

SYMPHORICARPOS

(Snowberry or Coralberry, depending on the color of the fruits; Wolfberry)

Popular shrubs because of their pretty berries and the fact that they transplant easily and grow without care, these may be used for hedges (best unclipped) and for massed plantings on banks to hold soil in place.

Symphoricarpos albus

Symphoricarpos albus (syn S. racemosus)
(Snowberry, Waxberry)
Zone 4 to parts of Zone 3; 3′
While many of the nursery catalogs list this shrub, it is not what they are growing and selling under this name. This shrub is low-growing. The nurseries sell a taller shrub that has smaller leaves than the species, the variety *laevigatus*, described below.

Symphoricarpos albus laevigatus
(Snowberry, Waxberry)
Zone 4 to parts of Zone 3; 6′
Although the cultivated form of this shrub came from the west coast, where it is native to British Columbia and Washington, this variety of snowberry grows wild from the Gulf of St. Lawrence to the Virginia mountains in the east.

It is upright growing with arching branches that may bend to the ground when weighted with fruits. The flowers are tiny, pink and white, and not at all conspicuous. They appear in mid-June and the berries are fully colored in late August. These, as both botanical and common names imply, are white and waxy in appearance, unusual among shrub fruits. The leaves are small, bright green on the upper surfaces, paler green underneath.

This shrub thrives in dry soil where many others will not grow. It is used in gardens as a specimen, in shrub borders, on banks (to hang over them) or as an unclipped hedge.

Symphoricarpos × chenaultii (S. microphyllus × S. orbiculatus) (Chenault coralberry, Chenault's coralberry)
Zone 6 to Zone 5b; 3′
The difference between this shrub and *S. orbiculatus*, described below, is that this hybrid has a neater growth habit, the berries are larger and they are red only on the top sides. The undersides are white. Often each area is spotted with the color of the other. This is a handsome shrub when in berry and may be used wherever soil is not damp. It is pretty in the foreground of a shrub border or used as a ground cover on a bank, but is not sufficiently outstanding for use as a specimen.

Symphoricarpos orbiculatus (syn S. vulgaris, the name under which most catalogs list this shrub) (Indian currant, Coralberry, Buckbush, Snapberry, Turkeyberry)
Zone 2 to parts of Zone 1; 3′–4′, sometimes to 6′
In open woods and on stream banks, this shrub grows from South Dakota to Indiana and Illinois, Pennsylvania, and Ohio, south to Florida and Texas. It suckers, forming clumps as it spreads, so should be planted only where it need not be restrained. State highway departments often plant this shrub by the hundreds on steep banks to prevent soil erosion.

Its growth habit is upright, the leaves dull green and not particularly pretty. Inconspicuous flowers, borne in July and August in small clusters, may be

Symphoricarpos × chenaultii

yellowish-white but often are purplish. Fruits are coral-red, ripening in September and October.

Symphoricarpos racemosus (see S. albus)

Symphoricarpos vulgaris (see S. orbiculatus)

Symphoricarpos 'White Hedge'
This is an upright-growing form with extra large white berries.

SYRINGA
(Lilac)

Have you ever driven along a country road in May and seen a huge old lilac in full bloom by the foundation of what was once a home? Such survivors show not only the toughness and longevity of lilacs but also the regard in which they always have been held. If nothing else in

the line of plants went along in that covered wagon, a few lilac suckers did.

Lilacs prefer slightly alkaline or neutral soil. They are grown for their beautiful, fragrant blooms. Most grow upright and are vigorous, producing large shrubs. Except in certain species, their foliage is not outstanding. Except for one species, they have no bright autumn foliage coloration and their brown seed pods certainly are not attractive. Furthermore, two pests attack almost any lilac in due course of time: lilac scale and borers, both discussed in Chapter 9.

I have written these discouraging words knowing perfectly well that they will deter no one who wants lilacs from owning one or many, but just for the record, so that a new gardener will know, at least, what he or she is up against.

When you are buying lilacs it is most important that you inquire whether they are grafted on common lilac (*S. vulgaris*) or on privet (*Ligustrum*).

If they are, don't buy them at any price. Buy only lilacs grown on their own roots, that is from cuttings of the parent plants. This subject is discussed in more detail in the chapter on planting and it will pay you to read that discussion.

Even though they are gorgeous when in bloom, the hybrid lilacs that are most popular are not really plants for the small garden because of their suckering habit of growth. One of these hybrids may grow as wide as high, increasing in girth yearly by sending up new shoots around the outside of the plant. These may be allowed to grow if you want to propagate from the plants, but otherwise are a nuisance. The easiest way I know of to control suckers is this:

Dig the soil out around the base of the suckers until you can see where they grow from the main part of the plant. Cut them off at these points. Fit a piece of heavy linoleum around the part of the plant you wish to leave growing, right over the places from which the suckers grew and well beyond that area. Fit it tightly to the plant. Then replace the soil you removed and it will hold the linoleum in place.

One advantage of growing lilac species rather than the more popular so-called French hybrids, is that most do not sucker. However, many of them still grow to be huge shrubs.

Before leaving the subject of lilac suckers, there is one more point to remember. A few suckers should be allowed to grow each year so that they may be used as replacements for the older stems, and the shrub constantly is renewed. The method of pruning old shrubs to renew them is described in Chapter 6.

If you keep the suckers under control and also cut the seed clusters from your lilacs as soon as they form, or better yet prune off the dying flowers, the bloom clusters the next year will be larger. This is fact, not fiction.

Lilacs, properly selected, will provide a blooming season of six weeks or more. Should you have room for several plants, bear this in mind and select species and cultivars accordingly.

Syringa amurensis japonica (syn S. japonica of the catalogs) (see Chapter 13)

Syringa × chinensis (parentage not certain)
(Chinese lilac, Rouen lilac)
Zone 5 to part of Zone 4; 12'

Both the botanical name and the first common name of this lilac are misleading. According to them one would think that the plant came from China. Actually, it was found in the botanic garden at Rouen, France, late in the eighteenth century as a chance hybrid.

The plant grows upright and spreading to form a dense shrub. It has slender branches that arch, especially when weighted with blooms in late May. The leaves are smaller than those of the common lilac (S. vulgaris) and daintier. Flowers are small, ½" in diameter, borne in clusters to 6 " long and 4" to 4½" across. They are strong reddish-purple in color and intensely fragrant.

This lilac is beautiful as a specimen plant. It also is a valuable addition to a shrub border of sufficient length so that it does not dwarf the border. It might also be used at house corners if the house were sufficiently large and high for such a big plant.

Syringa chinensis 'Alba'
The white-flowered form, rarely listed in catalogs.

Syringa chinensis rubra
(See S. chinensis 'Saugeana')

Syringa chinensis 'Saugeana' (syn S. c. rubra)
Has red-lilac or lilac-red flowers and, probably because of their color, often is listed in catalogs as 'sanguinea' instead of 'saugeana.'

Syringa, cut leaved
(see S. laciniata)

Syringa French hybrid

Syringa French hybrid 'Victor Lemoine'

**Syringa, French hybrids
(see *S. vulgaris* hybrids)**

**Syringa japonica
(see *S. amurensis japonica* in Chapter 13)**

**Syringa josikaea
(Hungarian lilac)
Zone 1; 12′**
Late flowering compared with other lilacs, usually blooming the first or second week in June, this often is confused with *S. villosa*, the late lilac, which blooms at about the same time. The leaves of the Hungarian lilac resemble those of the late lilac in shape, but are much glossier. The flower color is lilac-violet. Growth habit is upright and slightly spreading.

This species and *S. villosa* have produced a hybrid named *Syringa × henryi* and a selection from this cross is the cultivar 'Lutece', offered sometimes under that name but more often as 'Henry Lutece' or 'Henri Lutece.' This has ¼″ diameter florets in clusters 6″ long and 3¾″ wide, colored light reddish-purple.

There also has been hybridization of the Hungarian lilac with *S. reflexa*. Catalogs of lilac specialists offer the result of this cross as *S. × josiflexa* and at least one cultivar has been selected.

**Syringa laciniata (syn *S. persica laciniata*)
(Cutleaf or Cutleaved lilac)
Zone 4; 6′**
Distinguished by its finely divided leaves on slender branches, this lilac often is planted as a specimen. It blooms in May with ⅜″ diameter florets in clusters to 3½″ long, colored light purple.

**Syringa microphylla
(Littleleaf lilac, Ever-blooming lilac)
Zone 5; 6′**
The first of the two common names given for this lilac is accurate, since the leaves are among the smallest grown by lilacs. The second common name, used by too many nurserymen, is far from accurate since it makes the gardener envision constant bloom. It is true that this lilac, in addition to its normal flowering in late May, has a few flowers in late summer and early fall, but these hardly justify the word "everblooming."

The shrub is upright, with arching branches, eventually grows much wider than high, blooms in late May and has pale lilac flowers. It is useful where the wide form and the small leaves are desirable—as a specimen, in a house planting or a border.

Syringa laciniata

Syringa microphylla

Syringa microphylla 'Superba'
Has single flowers, pale pink in the bud and even paler when open. It is a delightful plant when in bloom, both for its flower color and its fragrance. Nurserymen often call it "daphne" lilac, but whether for its flower color or its fragrance I do not know. It blooms late in May, with smaller, tighter flower clusters than those of many other lilacs.

**Syringa × persica (probably *S. afghanica × S. laciniata*)
(Persian lilac, Persian elder, Persian jasmine)
Zone 5 to part of Zone 4; 6′, often less**
There is an enormous amount of confusion in the nursery trade between this lilac and the Rouen (or Chinese) lilac. Most of the lilacs listed and sold as Persian actually are the Rouen.

The Persian lilac is, with the Korean dwarf lilac, the smallest of lilacs. Its growth habit is upright, the branches are slender, the flowers pale lilac, borne in small clusters in late May at the same time as those of the common lilac open. The most sensible use of this plant is as a specimen because it would be lost in a shrub border or even a smaller grouping of shrubs.

Syringa × *persica* 'Alba'
The white flowered form of the plant described above. The floret is ½" wide, the flower cluster to 8" long and 4" across. Both the tube of the flower and its center are very pale purple.

Syringa × *persica laciniata* (see *S. laciniata*)

Syringa × *prestoniae*, also spelled *prestonae* (*S. reflexa* × *S. villosa*) (Preston lilac)
Zone 1; 10"
The botanical name given above refers to a group of hybrid lilacs originated by Miss Isabella Preston when she was horticulturist of the Canadian Experimental Station, Ottawa, Ontario, Canada. This cross also has been made by other breeders. Far too many cultivars have been named in this group, for a great many, although sold under different cultivar names, are almost identical when they bloom.

These hybrids have two great assets—late flowering and extreme hardiness. Most of them flower in mid-June, which is several weeks after the common lilac and most of its hybrids are past bloom. All Preston lilacs are upright and dense in growth habit, vary somewhat in bulk or size, and have foliage similar to that of the late lilac (*S. villosa*). Their bloom spikes are large, too, comparing favorably with the largest clusters of the common lilac cultivars. The Preston lilacs are not, however, really fragrant, though most of them lack the malodorousness of the blooms of the late lilac and a few are mildly fragrant.

These shrubs are so large and so dense that they even may be used as windbreaks to protect lower-growing shrubs or other plants. They also may be used in hedges or, where space is ample, as specimens.

My favorite of this group is 'Coral', which has coral-pink buds and pale pink flowers. If you wish to buy one or more of these hybrids, you really ought to see them in bloom so you can select the flower color you like best.

Syringa vulgaris (Common Lilac)

Syringa pubescens
(Hairy lilac)
Zone 4; to 15' but usually not more than 10'
The outstanding characteristic of this lilac, as far as the gardener is concerned, is its fragrance, which is spicy. Its small pale lilac or pale pinkish blooms are borne in small clusters but there usually are many clusters on a shrub and, since they are borne in pairs, they appear larger than they are.

The hairy lilac blooms with the first of the common lilacs and is also of value for this rather early flowering time.

Syringa reflexa
(Nodding lilac)
Zone 5; 12'
Upright growing, with sturdy branches, this lilac differs from the others in the fact that the flower clusters are narrow and droop or nod from the branches. They grow to 5" long, with ¼" wide florets. Buds are bright pink, the flowers open pink on the outsides and white inside. This is a late-blooming lilac, usually blossoming the first or second week in June, with the Hungarian lilac. There is a white-flowered form, *S. r.* 'Alba.'

Syringa rothomagensis (see *S. chinensis*)

Syringa saugeana (see *S. chinensis* 'Saugeana')

Syringa × *swegiflexa* (*S. sweginzowii* × *S. reflexa*)
(Pink pearl lilac)
Zone 5 to part of Zone 4; 8'
Blooming in early to mid-June, this lilac has red buds which open to pale pink flowers borne in 6" long clusters. It is a fine addition to the group of late-blooming lilacs.

Syringa velutina (syn *S. palibiniana*)
(Dwarf Korean lilac)
Zone 5 to part of Zone 4; 6' to 8', but usually about 3'
Here is a lilac that will fit into any garden. A small, neat plant with small leaves turning red in autumn and 6" long clusters of light purplish pink flowers with slightly darker tubes, (thus giving an overall impression of deeper flower color), this lilac blooms in early June.

At Wisley, the trial grounds of the Royal Horticultural Society of England, this lilac is used as a specimen plant in the large rock garden. It is small enough (and can easily be maintained that size by a slight amount of pruning) to be used in a house planting. It is well-placed near the front of a shrub border or might be used as a dense, compact specimen wherever such a plant is needed. It is available in "tree" or "standard" form for use in a formal garden.

Syringa villosa
(Late lilac)
Zone 1; 9', sometimes taller

The big drawback to this lilac is that its flowers smell more like those of privet than they do like lilacs—and most people do not like their odor.

Aside from this, it is an extremely hardy lilac, upright and dense in form, blooming in early June to mid-June. Flower colors of this lilac vary because plants usually are grown from seeds (see discussion in Chapter 11). They may be any shade from white to rosy-lilac. My oldest plant of this lilac has moderate pink buds and pale pink florets ¼" in diameter, grouped in clusters to 10" long and 9" across.

Plants produce many blooms so that a blossoming plant is a good landscape subject if only it is not placed where people constantly get the odor of the blooms. This lilac may be used for a windbreak or a heavy screen planting, also makes a fine unclipped hedge and can be used as a specimen.

Syringa villosa hybrids (see discussion under S. prestoniae)

Syringa vulgaris
(Common lilac, English lilac, Blue ash, Blue-pipe privet, Pipe privet, Pipt tree, Roman willow, Celache)
Zone 3; 15'

This old-time, well-loved, fragrant lilac is as popular today as it ever was. Upright in form, with straight, heavy stems, this bears flowers in mid-May. Florets are ½" in diameter, clusters to 4" long and 3" wide. Bloom color is light purple.

This lilac is extremely hardy and thrives with little care, even growing wild in some parts of the world, though it has escaped from cultivation since there are no native wild lilacs in either the United States or Canada.

Syringa vulgaris 'Alba'

The white-flowered form of common lilac, also intensely fragrant.

Syringa vulgaris hybrids

Practically every nursery in the country lists these as French hybrids. Actually, *Syringa vulgaris* is native to much of eastern Europe but the term "French" comes from the fact that a great many of these hybrids (cultivars) grown today are the products of one hybridizer—Victor Lemoine—who also gave gardeners many fine deutzias and mock oranges. His nursery in France was the birthplace of these hybrids.

However, many other hybridizers in other European countries and in North America also have hybridized the common lilac so the hybrids should not continue to be called "French."

There are hundreds of these cultivars. The best collection of them in the United States probably is that in Highland Park, Rochester, New York, and a visit there at lilac time will provide a real thrill if you love lilacs. The Arnold Arboretum, Jamaica Plain, Massachusetts, also has a fine collection of lilacs, and there are others on the continent.

Syringa vulgaris, tree form

Some nurseries grow this lilac with a single main stem like a tree.

TAMARIX
(Tamarix, Tamarisk)

Tall, sometimes leggy shrubs with graceful, feathery foliage and large, fluffy clusters of tiny florets, usually borne at the tips of the branches, tamarix plants are grown mostly for their light, airy appearance, so different from that of most shrubs. They usually grow well in dry soil and will tolerate seaside conditions and even salt water spray.

The tall-growing species need to be pruned occasionally so that they do not grow too tall. The lower parts of the branches become bare of foliage if the plants are not pruned and so are unsightly.

Tamarix africana

This shrub is listed in many northern catalogs but, since it is a native of the Mediterranean region and hardy only in the south, it is obvious that this name is incorrectly used. Usually the shrub sold under this name is *Tamarix tetrandra.*

Tamarix amurensis
(see T. pentandra)

Tamarix pentandra

Tamarix gallica
(French tamarix)
Zone 4; 7'–25'
This may grow as a shrub or as a small tree. It has slender, arching, wide-spread, brown branches with dull green or bluish-green leaves and white to rose-pink flowers in compact clusters in July and August. This shrub has escaped from cultivation and may be found growing wild in the south and as far north as Indiana and Massachusetts.

Tamarix hispida
(Kashgar tamarix)
Zone 4, even the northern part if planted in a sheltered spot; 4'
Slender, upright branches, bluish-green foliage and pink flowers in large clusters at the ends of the branches all make this shrub desirable. The fact that it blooms in August and September makes it more so.

Tamarix hispida aestivalis
(see *T. pentandra*)

Tamarix odessana
(Odessa tamarix, Caspian tamarix)
Zone 4; 6'–7'
Upright in form, with slender branches, this has tiny leaves and little, pink, fluffy flowers in large, loose clusters in mid-July. This species flowers on wood of the same season's growth, so should be pruned in early spring, when necessary.

Tamarix parviflora
(Small-flowered tamarix)
Zone 5 to part of Zone 4; 15'
Blooming in late May, this species makes it possible to have the airy, pink flowers of tamarix in spring as well as summer. As both botanical and common names suggest, the flowers are tiny. The branches are slender, arching and dark purple.

Prune this tamarix, if and when pruning is necessary, directly after it finishes blooming as it flowers on wood grown the previous year and pruning it in spring would eliminate the flower buds for that year.

Tamarix pentandra
(Five stamen tamarix)
Zone 2, possibly part of Zone 1; 15'
Purple branchlets, tiny, pale green leaves that give the usual feathery effect, and small pink flowers in mid-July are the characteristics of this shrub. As you see, from its hardiness zone, this is the hardiest tamarix. It does have a tendency to legginess and therefore needs hard pruning occasionally.

Tamarix pentandra 'Pink Cascade'
Zone 5; 6'
Blue-green, feathery foliage and pink, feathery flower clusters borne well above the foliage and from July to September make this shrub a good choice for long-season bloom. Best results are said to be obtained if the shrub is pruned severely each spring.

Tamarix pentandra 'Rubra' (syn *Tamarix* 'Summer Glow')
Zone 5; 6'
Tiny blue-green leaves and tiny florets ⅛" in diameter, in spikes 9" long and 5" wide, colored deep purplish-pink will ornament your garden if you decide to grow this shrub. Flowers appear from the beginning of July for a month or more.

Tamarix 'Summer Glow'
(see *T. pentandra* 'Rubra')

TEUCRIUM

Teucrium chamaedrys
(Germander, Chamaedrys germander)
Zone 6 to southern part of Zone 5; 8"–10"
A neat little gray-leaved, almost evergreen shrublet, this has rose or purplish-rose flowers in thin spikes during most of the summer. It can be clipped to form a very low hedge for use as an edging for herb or rose beds. It also may be allowed to grow unclipped in a rock garden or at the front of a perennial border.

Tamarix parviflora

Vaccinium corymbosum

VACCINIUM

(Blueberry, Huckleberry)

This genus includes the wild huckleberries and the cultivated blueberries. It is listed here because the low bush blueberry is a good ground cover in dry soil and the high bush blueberry is an excellent ornamental, even if most people think of it only as a fruit-bearing plant.

Vaccinium corymbosum
(Highbush blueberry, Swamp blueberry, Whortleberry)
Zone 4 to part of Zone 3; usually about 6', but may grow taller in favorable situations.
Found growing wild in swamps and low areas, but sometimes in drier places, from Nova Scotia to southern Quebec and Maine, westward to Wisconsin and Minnesota, southward to Florida and Louisiana, this plant is the forerunner of our cultivated blueberries. The first cultivars were selected from wild plants for their extra-large fruits.

Highbush blueberries are used in gardens both for foliage and fruits, though their flowers are as pretty as those of many another ornamental and prettier than some. These shrubs may

be used for unusual and beautiful unclipped hedges. The autumn color of the foliage, which is yellow, orange and red, is so vivid that they even are occasionally used in house plantings.

Growth habit is upright, foliage (any time but autumn) is glossy green, and the flowers are white and waxy, borne in dense clusters in late May. The berries, as you know, are blue to blueblack and arrive at edible stage from the end of June to early September, partly because not all the fruits in a cluster ripen at one time and partly because different cultivars bear fruits at different times.

The *Vaccinium corymbosum* cultivars are the blueberries that are grown commercially and may be grown by any home gardener who possesses acid soil or is willing to acidify it (as explained in Chapter 4).

VIBURNUM

This is a large genus with many members useful to the gardener. Almost all viburnums are easy to grow, tolerant of almost any soil, and many will flower and fruit in semi-shade. Some are evergreen; most of these hardy only in the

south. Others are semi-evergreen in the north, evergreen in the south. And more are deciduous in any climate.

Some are grown primarily for their handsome foliage, which, in many, turns beautiful colors in autumn. Others are primarily interesting for their flowers or fruits and finally, some are grown for their branching habit.

A wide range of foliage form, flower form and fruit colors are available to the gardener in this single genus.

Not only that, but flowering times vary greatly and so do the months during which the fruit ripens. There is usually some viburnum in bloom in my garden from late April until mid-July.

All viburnums have florets arranged in groups, but the forms of these groupings vary, though all are borne at the tips of stems. Some clusters are flat, others almost half-round, still others almost completely ball-shaped. There also may be two different types of flowers: small, fertile blooms and large, sterile flowers, both borne in the same flower cluster in some viburnums.

When fruits mature they may be red, blue, black, or even yellow, and many of the species have fruits that change from one color to another during the ripening process. When fruits of several colors are on the plant at one time they present an interesting effect.

It must be remembered that fruits may not be produced every year on every plant, for fruits are "set" only when weather conditions encourage insects to fly and pollinate the flowers. It is best to plant viburnums in groups, to insure pollination as often as possible.

The usual use for viburnums in the garden is in a shrub border, but some are best suited to woodland planting and others are sufficiently handsome for use as specimen plants. Because there are tree-like viburnums (described in the next chapter), medium-sized and small viburnums, the specific uses will be indicated in the descriptions below.

Only viburnums listed in several to many of the catalogs are described here. You will find others available from specialists in this genus.

Viburnum acerifolium
(Mapleleaf viburnum, Dock-manie, Arrow-wood)
Zone 4; 6′

Found in dry woods from southwest Quebec to Minnesota, south to New England, Georgia, and Tennessee, this viburnum is best used in a wild garden or in the woods; there it will grow beautifully in deep shade where few other woody plants would grow at all. It will not, however, flower frequently under these conditions. It needs a little sun in order to bloom. The leaves are so prettily shaped that if flowers are not a prime consideration, they make this a satisfactory shrub for any shaded location. Leaves turn pinkish to purplish in autumn. Flowers are creamy-white and appear in late May to June, sometimes continuing to open occasionally until late July. The sparse fruits on upright stems are first crimson, later turning purplish-black.

Viburnum americanum
(see V. trilobum)

Viburnum bitchiuense
(Bitchiu viburnum, Yeddo viburnum)
Zone 5 to part of Zone 4; 10′

Flowering in early May, at the same time as the Koreanspice viburnum (*V. carlesii*), with white to pinkish blooms, the Bitchiu viburnum often has been confused with the Koreanspice.

Both are useful, but the Bitchiu has a more open form because its branches are smaller and thinner. The foliage and flower clusters also are smaller and the cluster form is less compact. Blooms of both species are equally fragrant and it would be hard to choose between the two if one could have only a single species in the garden. If this were the case, the fact that the Bitchiu viburnum is slightly hardier might be the deciding factor. Foliage color of the Bitchiu viburnum is bluish-green, turning dull red in autumn.

Viburnum × burkwoodii

Viburnum × bodnantense (V. fragrans × V. grandiflorum)
Zone 6 to southern part of Zone 5; 10′

This hybrid is hardier than *V. grandiflorum*, but still not sufficiently hardy to be used in the far north. In flower, leaf, and growth habit, it is intermediate between its parents. It has dark, rose-colored buds, but the loose flower clusters, opening in April, are only faintly pink. Fruits are black, ripening in early August. Although this hybrid was produced in the 1930s, it still is not widely listed by North American nurseries.

Viburnum × burkwoodii (V. carlesii × V. utile)
Zone 5 to part of Zone 4; 6′–8′

This shrub has glossy, dark green foliage that is evergreen in the south and in mild winters may be semi-evergreen in the north, changes to orange or bright red in autumn. Fragrant, pinkish white flowers in early to mid-May (much like those of the Koreanspice) and black fruits maturing in early August characterize this hybrid. Some nurseries describe it as "an improved *carlesii*," but I still prefer the Koreanspice viburnum to any of its hybrids and I own most of them.

Viburnum × burkwoodii 'Chenault' (V. carlesii × V. utile) (syn V. chenaultii)
Zone 5; 6′

This viburnum tends to be semi-evergreen in the south, but is deciduous in the north. It has finer-textured leaves and a more compact growth habit than *V. burkwoodii*, but not as compact as the Koreanspice viburnum (*V. carlesii*). It has pink florets, ⅜″ in diameter, in 2″ to 2¼″ clusters, is fragrant, but not as much so as either the Koreanspice or Judd viburnums. It blooms after the Judd viburnum.

Viburnum × carlcephalum (parentage uncertain)
(Fragrant snowball)
Zone 6 to southern part of Zone 5; 6′

This is a widely spreading, openly branched shrub with larger, coarser, and more shiny foliage than the Koreanspice and ball-shaped, 4″ to 5″ diameter flower clusters. These flowers are pinkish to white and clove-scented, open as those of the Koreanspice are fading in early to mid-May, with the flowers of *V. burkwoodii*. The foliage colors brilliant red in autumn.

Because of the growth habit and the large flowers, this shrub needs to be used as a specimen in a very special place where these characteristics will help the landscape plan. The plant does not blend well in a shrub border and, except in bloom, is not particularly helped by an evergreen background.

The fragrant snowball is hard to transplant and reestablish. It may take several tries before you can coax one to grow, but once it has reestablished its roots it will cause you no further trouble.

Viburnum carlesii
(Koreanspice viburnum, Fragrant viburnum)
Zone 5 to part of Zone 4; 5'

It is necessary only to pass within 30' of this viburnum or one of its hybrids when it is in bloom to notice the fragrance of the flowers. These, in the case of this viburnum, are produced on a compact, spherically shaped plant that has dull green leaves, grayish on the undersides and turning reddish purple in fall. The florets are pale pink, fading to white, $^9/_{16}''$ in diameter, and arranged in 3½" to 4" diameter clusters, rounded at the tops. They open in early May.

The fruits, in the infrequent times when they appear, are black and seldom seen because they are hidden under the foliage and the birds find and eat them as soon as they ripen. At that time in summer the birds can find few other fruits to eat.

Unfortunately, nurserymen too often graft or bud this lovely viburnum on vigorously growing understocks like *V. lantana*, the wayfaring tree. They do this to save time in getting a plant of saleable size, which is fine for them but not for the gardener who buys the plant. The understock too frequently sends out its own branches and if not cut back immediately when they are seen, these soon will outgrow the more desirable Koreanspice portion, either reducing it to a subsidiary plant or killing it altogether by shading it unduly. You will find further discussion of this subject in Chapter 11. You also will find that the common use of an understock makes the Koreanspice viburnum subject to a graft blight and so it often is considered a short-lived plant.

Occasionally a nursery grows—and lists—this viburnum on its own roots. In this case, of course, there will be no difficulty with constant pruning of an understock or with graft blight.

This shrub is ideal for use in an intimate setting such as a planting around an outdoor living area or near a house door. There you can enjoy its fragrance each year without any effort.

As with other shrubs like forsythias, some nurseries offer the Koreanspice viburnum grown to a single stem, as a standard or tree form.

Viburnum carlesii 'Compactum'

A dwarf form with an extremely compact growth habit. Its blooms also are fragrant, but the foliage is darker green than that of the species. This form should be even more useful in the small garden than its parent. It is not a hybrid but a seedling discovered by happy chance.

Viburnum cassinoides
(Withe rod, Swamp viburnum, Swamp black-haw, False Paraguay tea, Wild raisin, Appalachian tea, Teaberry)
Zone 4; 4'–6', sometimes taller

While the flowers of this viburnum do not compare with those of many others for beauty, they still are attractive. The tiny, creamy-white, fertile florets are arranged in clusters 3"–4" in diameter and slightly rounded at the tops. Blooms usually appear the second week in June. They are set off by the glossy, yellow-green leaves and are followed by berries that put on a real color show. They first are green, then yellowish-white, then pink, bright blue, dark blue and finally almost black. At some times all of these berry colors are present in one cluster at one time. The only difficulty is that birds love these berries and eat them as soon as each one ripens—in August and September.

In a garden this shrub is upright and compact, though in the woods, where the plants often lack sufficient light, they grow tall and straggly. This plant is found in thickets and near the edges of woods, as well as in swamps, from Newfoundland to Ontario, south to Nova Scotia, New England, Long Island, Delaware and Maryland, to upland Alabama, westward to Tennessee, Ohio, Indiana and Wisconsin.

The common name "withe rod" comes from the former use of its branches for switches by old-time schoolmasters.

Viburnum carlesii

Viburnum dilatatum

Viburnum chenaultii (see *V.* × *burkwoodii* 'Chenault')

Viburnum dentatum (syn *V. pubescens*)
(Arrow wood, Southern arrow wood)
Zone 3; 15'

In moist areas this viburnum may be found forming thickets, which it rarely does in dry, sandy soil. It is native from Rhode Island southward along the coast to New Jersey and Florida, westward to Pennsylvania, West Virginia, Tennessee and Texas.

It flowers in early to mid-June, bearing creamy-white, flat flower clusters to 2″ in diameter, followed by abundant, dark blue berries ripening in September. The leaves, sharply toothed at the edges, are glossy, dark green, and turn to rust-red in autumn.

The plant grows rapidly and vigorously, usually with many upright stems from the ground. It should be used in a large shrub border or in a wild garden but certainly never where space is limited. It grows in any soil in full sun or fairly heavy shade.

Viburnum dilatatum
(Linden viburnum, Japanese cranberry bush)
Zone 6 to southern part of Zone 5; 8'

The bright scarlet berries in clusters that may be 5″ across, coloring in September, combined with the purplish-red autumn color of its leaves, make this a handsome plant for any but the smallest garden. During the remainder of the season, the leaves are green and hairy on both sides, vary greatly in size and shape, and resemble those of the linden tree in general form. Flowers are cream-white, mildly fragrant, borne in 1″ diameter clusters in late May or early June. At that time a plant is covered with them. Growth habit is upright, rounded and compact.

One advantage in growing this viburnum is that the fruit stays on it for several weeks or more. More fruit is formed when several plants known to be grown from seeds are planted fairly close together.

There also is a yellow-fruited form, *V. dilatatum* 'Xanthocarpum', and a cultivar named 'Moraine', selected for its larger and more abundant fruits.

Viburnum fragrans
(Fragrant viburnum)
Zone 6 to southern part of Zone 5; 9'

Blooming before the forsythias in early April, this is the first viburnum to flower. Buds are deep pink to red, the flowers bluish-pink turning white and, of course, they are fragrant. They may be forced to bloom indoors even earlier since the flower buds were formed the previous autumn. In fact, forcing blooms is a good idea, for outdoors the flowers may last only two or three days. Except for their earliness and fragrance, the flowers are not outstanding. In severe winters in the north flower buds are killed, so that a plant should be set in a protected place.

The shrub grows upright, sometimes spreading by means of suckers. Leaves are 2″ to 3″ long, with a bronzy undertone to their green. They become even more bronze in color in summer and turn reddish-maroon in autumn. While the fruits are red, turning black, and mature in early summer, they are not effective in the garden for two reasons: there are not many of them and they are almost hidden by the leaves. They also are beloved of birds, so they soon disappear.

Viburnum dilatatum

Viburnum × juddii (V. carlesii × V. bitchiuense)
Zone 6 to southern part of Zone 5; 6′
More spreading in form and more bushy than *V. carlesii*, this has flowers and leaves that might be described as midway between those of its parents. The flower buds are pink, but flowers are white. They bloom in early May, with the Koreanspice viburnum, before the Chenault viburnum. They are almost as fragrant as those of the Koreanspice viburnum.

As usual with these hybrids, the black fruits, if formed, go unnoticed under the leaves or disappear down the gullets of birds. Nurserymen advertise this plant as "an improved *carlesii*" and many people consider it superior to that species. I cannot agree with them. I feel that each shrub has its points and neither one is superior to the other.

Viburnum lantana
(Wayfaring tree)
Zone 4; 10′ or more
Tall and upright, dense and rounded in outline, the wayfaring tree has round, gray-green leaves turning red in autumn and abundant clusters of creamy-white sterile flowers in late May to early June. The oval, 1¼″ long fruits are first green, then greenish yellow underneath and vivid red on top, then red, later turning black. Often all color stages appear on the shrub at the same time. The bright color of the fruits lasts only about a week, however, before they turn black. During winter they wrinkle like dried raisins and birds gradually eat them all.

The usefulness of this large, almost tree-like shrub, lies in its ease of growth and its adaptability to almost any soil, including one that is dry. It also is hardy. It may be used at the back of a shrub border or at the edge of the woods. Where there is plenty of room, it also might be used as a specimen plant.

Viburnum opulus

Viburnum × lantanaphyllum (V. lantana × V. rhytidophyllum)
Zone 6 to southern part of Zone 5; 8′
Larger and better looking leaves than the leatherleaf viburnum, *V. rhytidophyllum*, and red berries turning blackish are the characteristics of this hybrid.

Viburnum lentago
(see Chapter 13)

Viburnum molle
(Possum-haw, Silky viburnum, Kentucky viburnum)
Zone 6; 12′
Found on bluffs and in woods from Indiana to Missouri, south to Kentucky and Arkansas, this viburnum has light gray branches and shiny, dark green leaves that are paler green and hairy on the undersides. The older bark flakes off the branches, thus giving the shrub winter interest. The flowers, appearing in late May, are cream-white to white, the clusters attached to an exceptionally long stem. Fruits are blue-black and ripen in late August to early September.

Viburnum opulus
(European cranberry bush, Highbush cranberry, May rose, Ople-tree, Pincushion tree)
Zone 4 to southern part of Zone 3; 12′
Strong, dense growth; three-lobed leaves, turning orange to red in autumn; flowers in late May that are creamy-white and in flat clusters composed of fertile flowers in the center and sterile flowers around the outside; and vivid red berries that hang on the plant all winter, becoming translucent with age, are all reasons for growing this plant.

Another reason is that this plant is tolerant of dry situations and of heat. It may be massed for colorful effect when it is in bloom or in fruit, or used in a shrub border. One or two plants set along the edge of water are lovely in winter while their berries still hang and are reflected in the water. There is no sense in trying to use these fruits for jelly as they are much too bitter.

Viburnum opulus 'Compactum'
A dwarf form with many more berries than the larger-growing species.

Viburnum opulus 'Nanum'
Rarely, if ever, flowers or fruits. It is used solely for its dense, 2'-high growth, well covered with foliage. It may be used for a low hedge and, even if planted in a quite formal area, rarely needs pruning. The most interesting use for it that I have seen is at the Cooley Rose Garden in Lansing, Michigan, where it has been clipped to form a low balustrade on either side of a short flight of broad steps leading from one level of the garden to another.

Viburnum opulus 'Roseum' (syn V. o. sterile)
(European snowball, Common snowball, Guelder rose, Elder rose)
Zone 4 to southern part of Zone 3; 12'
The hardiest of the snowballs, those viburnums with fully-rounded clusters of all sterile flowers, this can be a gorgeous sight when in flower, but usually is marred by having its leaves contorted

Viburnum opulus sterile

by aphid infestations. Sometimes the stems also become oddly twisted. The new systemic insecticides will completely control this trouble if you wish to use them.

The blooms, which may be 3" in diameter, open in mid-May, are at first the same color as lime sherbet, gradually turning white as they enlarge in size. In some plants these white blooms gradually become tinged with pink to rose as they age.

Since the blooms are composed solely of sterile flowers, no fruits follow them. The foliage looks much the same as that of the species but does not turn red in autumn.

Viburnum opulus sterile
(see *V. o.* 'Roseum')

Viburnum opulus, tree form
Some nurseries grow this viburnum as a standard or tree, trained with a single stem.

Viburnum opulus 'Xanthocarpum'
The yellow-fruited form of *V. opulus.* Its ¼" fruits are borne in clusters to 4" in diameter and are brilliant yellow in color.

Viburnum plicatum (syn V. tomentosum sterile, V. t. plicatum)
(Japanese snowball)
Zone 6 to southern part of Zone 5; 9', and as wide as it is high
With wide-spreading horizontal branches arranged in tiers, this is a handsome shrub. The flower clusters are arranged along the top sides of these branches. They are composed entirely of large, sterile white flowers and are at their best in late May, about a week later than *V. plicatum tomentosum.* Of course there are no fruits to follow later since the blooms are sterile.

The leaves of this plant are oval and quite long, dull green, smooth on top and slightly hairy underneath. They turn red to bronzy-purple in autumn.

Viburnum plicatum 'Grandiflorum' (syn V. tomentosum 'Grandiflorum')
Has slightly larger flowers than the species.

Viburnum plicatum 'Mariesii' (syn V. tomentosum mariesii)
(Maries doublefile viburnum)
This is a selection with larger sterile flowers, to 1" in diameter, borne in larger clusters than those of the species. It is so beautiful in bloom that it has to be seen to be believed.

Viburnum opulus 'Roseum'

Viburnum plicatum 'Rotundifolium'
(Roundleaf doublefile viburnum)
Zone 5; 8'

This has broader leaves than the variety and blooms several weeks earlier. The foliage turns red in autumn; the flowers are of the fully rounded snowball type.

Viburnum plicatum tomentosum
(syn V. tomentosum)
(Doublefile viburnum)
Zone 5; 8'–10'

The common name of this plant refers to the placing of the flower clusters in a double file along the top sides of the branches, which may extend to 10' to 12' wide or even more on a fully-grown plant. The horizontal branching habit plus the length of the branches give this shrub a pyramidal form.

The leaves are dull yellowish-green with a few hairs scattered on the undersides. They are from 3" to 6" long. In autumn they change color to a dull, purplish-red. The flowers appear in mid-to-late May and the large clusters are composed of sterile flowers around the outsides with a group of small, fertile flowers in the center. Sterile flowers are white; fertile flowers cream-white.

In July the upright clusters of small, oval fruits ripen, first becoming red, then turning blue-black. They may be on the shrub for two full weeks before the birds devour them.

Viburnum prunifolium
(see Chapter 13)

Viburnum plicatum tomentosum

Viburnum rhytidophyllum (Leatherleaf Viburnum)

Viburnum pubescens
(see V. dentatum)

Viburnum × rhytidophylloides (V. rhytidophyllum × V. lantana)
Zone 6 to southern part of Zone 5; 8' to 10' in the south, lower in the north

Hardier than its evergreen parent, *V. rhytidophyllum*, this plant looks much like it but has broader leaves, not quite so wrinkled, and staying on the plant longer in late autumn. In late May small clusters of creamy-white fertile flowers open, to be followed by small clusters of fruits that first are red and later change to black.

The difference in appearance between this plant and the leatherleaf viburnum is not marked, so it might just as well be substituted for the less hardy viburnum.

Viburnum rhytidophyllum
(Leatherleaf viburnum)
Zone 6; 10'

This shrub has heavy branches growing upright and may be round-topped to pyramidal in form. Its semi-evergreen (in Zone 6) to evergreen (south of that zone) foliage is very dark green, leathery in texture, curling like the leaves of rhododendron in cold weather.

The plant should be set where it is sheltered from the wind, and it will grow well only in good soil. The flower buds form in autumn, remain on the plant all winter, to open in mid-May into large, yellow-white or cream-white flower clusters. Scarlet fruits, which turn black as they age, appear in September. This plant is used as a specimen and is particularly effective against a building. It does not blend well with other shrubs but looks better with needled evergreens.

Viburnum sargentii

Viburnum setigerum

early June and all are fertile. The berries are oval, ⅜″ long, ¼″ wide, and strong reddish-orange in color. With the first frost (provided the birds have left them on that long) they turn translucent and then brown. There is an orange-fruited form that is much handsomer when in berry than the species.

The common name refers to the use of the leaves for making a tea drunk by monks in the parts of China where this shrub grows wild.

Viburnum sieboldii
(see Chapter 13)

Viburnum theiferum
(see *V. setigerum*)

Viburnum tomentosum
(see *V. plicatum tomentosum*)

Viburnum tomentosum grandiflorum
(see *V. plicatum* 'Grandiflorum')

Viburnum tomentosum mariesii
(see *V. plicatum* 'Mariesii')

Viburnum tomentosum plicatum
(see *V. plicatum*)

Viburnum tomentosum sterile
(see *V. plicatum*)

Viburnum sargentii
(Sargent cranberry bush, Sargent viburnum, Manchurian cranberry bush)
Zone 5 to part of Zone 4; 12′
Resembling the European cranberry bush in form, flower and fruit, but slightly larger and more vigorous, this shrub may be substituted for the European cranberry bush and vice versa. The Sargent cranberry bush has darker branchlets that are more corky and a little more color in the foliage. The cream-white flowers are arranged in flat clusters with the small, fertile blooms in the center, ringed with the large, sterile flowers. Fruits are round or oval, red,

highly acid to taste, and stay on the shrub for months. There never are as many fruits on this viburnum as on *V. opulus*.

***Viburnum setigerum* (syn *V. theiferum*)**
(Tea viburnum)
Zone 6 to southern part of Zone 5; 10′, sometimes a little more
Narrowly upright in form, sometimes leggy, this shrub has arching branches, large, shiny, dark green leaves (to 4″ long) that turn yellow-orange and red in autumn. The flower buds are faintly pinkish-yellow. The fragrant flowers are borne in flat, 1½″ diameter clusters in

Viburnum trilobum (Highbush Cranberry)

An important breeding program involving Viburnums has been conducted at The National Arboretum under the supervision of Dr. Donald Egolf. Following is a list of the most important cultivars from this research.

Cultivar Name	Flower Color/Heritage	Fall Color	Height
'Allegheny' (1966)	Yellow-white-flowered hybrid involving *Viburnum* × *rhytidophylloides*	Red berries	11½'
'Catskill' (1966)	Creamy-white-flowered dwarf seedling selection of *Viburnum dilatatum*	Dark red berries	7'
'Cayuga' (1966)	White waxy-flowered hybrid involving several species		7'
'Chesapeake' (1981)	Pink-budded hybrid involving *Viburnum utile* and *Viburnum* 'Cayuga'	Black berries	3'
'Erie' (1971)	Creamy-white selection of *Viburnum dilatatum*	Coral-pink berries	4'
'Eskimo' (1981)	Pale cream-flowered hybrid involving *Viburnum* 'Cayuga' and *Viburnum utile*	Dull red berries	3'
'Huron' (1987)	Creamy-white hybrid involving *Viburnum lobophyllum* and *Viburnum japonicum*	Dark red berries	9' in 17 yrs.
'Mohawk' (1966)	White with red-blotch hybrid involving *Viburnum burkwoodii* and *Viburnum carlesii*	No fruit	6½'
'Iroquois' (1966)	Creamy-white-flowered hybrid involving *Viburnum dilatatum*	Cardinal-red berries	10'
'Shasta' (1979)	Pure white-flowered hybrid involving *Viburnum plicatum*	Black berries	Twice as wide as high
'Shoshoni' (1987)	Creamy-white-flowered selection involving *Viburnum plicatum tomentosum* 'Shasta'	Scarlet-red berries	4' x 8' in 17 yrs.

Viburnum trilobum (syn *V. americanum*)
(American cranberry bush, Cranberry bush, Highbush cranberry, High cranberry, Highbush, Pimbina, Cherry wood, Dow-rowan-tree, Water elder, Marsh elder, Gadrise, Gaiter tree, Gattan tree, Grouse berry, Love roses)
Zone 2; 12'
If you want to make delicious home-grown cranberry jelly, this is the shrub to choose. Its form, foliage, flowering and fruiting habits are quite similar to those of both the European cranberry bush and the Sargent cranberry bush,

but, being a native shrub, it is hardier than either of them.

It grows wild in cool woods and on slopes, as well as shores of bodies of water from Newfoundland to British Columbia and south to Nova Scotia, New England and Pennsylvania; is found in Ohio, Michigan, northern Indiana and Illinois and northeast Iowa, the Black Hills of South Dakota, Wyoming and Washington.

Though similar to the European form, this cranberry bush grows more widely spread and is generally more openly branched than its European counterpart. The foliage is smooth on

the undersides while the leaves of *V. opulus* are sometimes quite hairy. The fruits, if you do not cook them, stay bright and cheery all winter.

Flowers, too, are similar—flat clusters of both sterile and fertile flowers, the one around the outside of the other. The large (5/16" long), oval berries are first brilliant yellow on one side, vivid red on the other, and then gradually turn to red. If not picked and used for jelly, they will stay on the plant all winter, making a plant a real asset in the garden. The berries are particularly effective when seen against snow or the dark color of water in winter.

Vitex agnus-castus 'Latifolia'

**Viburnum wrightii
(Wright viburnum)
Zone 6 to southern part of Zone
5; 7'–8'**
This shrub is narrowly upright in form with oval to rounded leaves that turn crimson in autumn. The berries are showy, bright scarlet. They are produced in more quantity and are larger than those of *V. dilatatum* so that this species is preferable for garden purposes. The berries also begin to color early in August and still are on the plant several months later. Flowers are creamy-white, in clusters and all are fertile.

If you wish to buy this viburnum, remember that most nurserymen grow it from seeds and therefore offer for sale a variable group of plants. Actually it should be grown only from cuttings taken from a plant known to fruit well. Because it is confused with *V. dilatatum* by nurserymen, and also because of the variation in plants from seeds, I would advise you to see the plant you buy in fruit before you purchase it. Since the shrub can be moved satisfactorily in autumn as well as in spring, you could mark your plant and transplant it later in the season.

VITEX

(Chaste tree)

**Vitex agnus-castus 'Latifolia' (syn
V. macrophylla)
(Chaste tree, Hemp tree, Monks'
pepper tree)
Zone 6 to southern part of Zone
5; 3'**
Grown for its beautiful, cut-leaved foliage and its light violet flowers, which start to bloom in mid-August and continue through September, vitex is worth a place in your garden.

Vitex is a southern shrub. In the north it dies back to the ground in even a fairly mild winter. This makes no difference as far as the bloom is concerned for the shrub bears flowers on wood of the current season. In spring the dead branches should be cut to the ground and new ones will grow from the roots, forming a whole new shrub the flowers of which will be welcome in late summer.

Because of this lack of hardiness, the shrub never grows much higher than 3' in Zone 5b. In the south, of course, it is much taller, to 15'

The leaves are gray and aromatic. They contrast beautifully with the soft light violet flowers.

Except for the necessary drastic pruning in spring, this shrub is easy to grow and presents no problems. It is upright in growth, with almost vertical branches.

**Vitex macrophylla
(see *V. agnus-castus* 'Latifolia')**

Vitex agnus-castus

Weigela 'Eva Rathka'

WEIGELA

Please note the spelling of the name of this genus. It is not W-e-i-g-e-l-*i*-a, but W-e-i-g-e-l-a; not wy-gee′-le-uh, but wy-gee′-luh. It is so frequently misspelled in nursery catalogs and on nursery tags that, in the interests of accuracy, your attention is called to this here.

Weigelas (formerly classified as Diervillas) are a group of shrubs grown for their beautiful, trumpet-shaped flowers and, in several cases, for bronze or variegated leaves. They are easy to transplant and grow, mature rapidly, and bloom with the late lilacs, the early deutzias and mock oranges, and the last of the spring-flowering spireas. In addition to this blooming period, they are likely to bear occasional flowers during summer.

Weigela 'Abel Carriere'
Grows 5′ high, has deep pink flowers.

Weigela amabilis
(see *W. florida*)

Weigela 'Boskoop Glory'
Grown for its large, salmon-pink blooms.

Weigela 'Bristol Ruby'
Patented by Bristol Nursery, Bristol, Connecticut. It grows 2½′ high, has strong purplish-red flowers, 1¼″ in diameter with ½″ long tubes. There is a burst of bloom in June and occasional flowers during summer.

Weigela 'Bristol Ruby'

Weigela 'Bristol Snowflake'
(sometimes listed as 'Snowflake')
A white-flowered counterpart of 'Bristol Ruby'.

Weigela candida
(see *W. florida* 'Alba')

Weigela 'Eva Rathke'
This variety has strong purplish-red flowers, slightly lighter inside. Plants grow to 5′.

Weigela floribunda
(Crimson weigela)
Zone 5 to part of Zone 4; 6′–7′
Dark crimson flowers and hairy branches distinguish this weigela. It is best known for its popular cultivars, some of which are described above.

Weigela florida (syn *W. amabilis, W. rosea*)
(Rose weigela)
Zone 5 to part of Zone 4; 6′–9′
Growth habit is upright and spreading, sometimes with branches slightly arched. The leaves are long and pointed, dark green, smooth on top but hairy at the veins underneath. Flowers are ¾″ in diameter at the opening of the tube, which is ¾″ long and flared like a trumpet. New flowers are white, tinged deep purplish-pink on the outsides. Older flowers are moderate purplish-pink. Thus the effect is of two-toned blooms. The blossoms open in early to mid-June.

Weigela florida 'Alba' (syn *W. candida*)
(White weigela)
This is the white-flowered form of the species. It does not always grow into as large a plant as does the species.

Weigela florida 'Purpurea' (syn *W. purpurea, W. foliis purpureus, W.* 'Java Red')
A bronze-leaved form. Some nurseries call this foliage purple, but it is not at all like the color of the purple-leaved plums or similar plants.

Weigela florida

Weigela florida 'Variegata'
(Variegated weigela)
Zone 5; 4'
This shrub has leaves edged and variegated brilliant yellow green. Despite the coloring, it blends well with other shrubs, which many variegated shrubs do not.

New flowers are white, tinged on the outer sides of the petals and in the throats with light purplish pink. Older blooms are 1" in diameter and are strong, purplish-pink in color.

Weigela florida 'Venusta'
Zone 4
This is the hardiest of the weigelas. It has rose-pink flowers in May, several weeks before those of most weigelas. It has smaller leaves than those of the rose weigela and the flowers are borne in dense clusters. It is considered the most graceful of all weigelas.

Weigela foliis purpureus
(see *W. florida* 'Purpurea')

Weigela 'Henderson'
A strong-growing plant with deep rose blooms.

Weigela 'Java Red'
(see *W. florida* 'Purpurea')

Weigela 'Newport Red'
(see *W.* 'Vanicek')

Weigela purpurea
(see *W. florida* 'Purpurea')

Weigela rosea
(see *W. florida*)

Weigela 'Vanicek'
(also listed as *vanicecki*, syn *W.* 'Newport Red')
Zone 5; 6'–8'
A satisfactory weigela where a large plant is desirable. Flowers are 1¼" in diameter, strong purplish-red in two different tones with a yellow line down the tube to guide bees to the nectary.

Weigela variegata
(see *W. florida* 'Variegata')

XANTHORHIZA

Xanthorhiza apiifolia
(see *Xanthorhiza simplicissima*)

Xanthorhiza simplicissima
(syn *Xanthorhiza apiifolia*)
(Yellowroot, Shrub yellowroot)
Zone 5; 2'
This shrub is excellent for underneath trees, covering moist shady or sunny banks, or for edging a shrub border. It also makes a good ground cover as it is not only low-growing but its plants are uniform in height. It spreads rapidly by underground stolons. The leaves resemble those of celery and are yellow-green. Flowers are purplish and borne in clusters but are infinitesimal so that most people are certain that this shrub has none. Fruits also are inconspicuous. Both bark and roots are yellow and bitter to the taste. A dye is made from the roots.

Yellowroot is found in damp woods and along streams from New York to West Virginia and south to Florida and Alabama.

Weigela florida

13
SMALL TREES TO PLANT WITH SHRUBS

Small-size trees go with shrubs just as butter goes with bread. They lend a difference in flavor, a difference in texture, and a difference in form to what might otherwise be a monotonous picture.

They may be combined with shrubs or used as an accent for shrubs in many ways, for instance:

(a) in the back of a shrub border to lend height and also, perhaps, to screen an unsightly object that is sufficiently narrow so one or two trees will do the job;

(b) as the back row for a windbreak, when the other row or rows are of shrubs;

(c) near the front of a shrub border, at the end furthest from the house, to mark "finis" to the border;

(d) as a transition between an evergreen windbreak and a shrub border where there is plenty of room and the planting is 25 or 30 feet wide;

(e) as the center of a grouping of low shrubs, possibly to mark the outer corners of a property;

(f) in a house planting, to add needed height at the house corners, to balance a shrub planting on one side of the entranceway, or to add height and silhouette to a long line planting of shrubs along one house wall;

(g) to shade a terrace that is hedged or bounded by shrubs;

(h) to add their fall color and winter silhouettes as a strong contrast to a shrub planting and to break the skyline;

(i) as specimens, with shrubs framing the picture.

As you can tell, from reading the foregoing list, most of the situations described apply to small trees used with shrubs in a cultivated area. However, some also apply to small trees used with shrubs in a wild area. Therefore, in choosing the small trees to be included in this chapter, I have selected some suitable for the wild garden as well as many to use with shrubs in the cared-for garden area.

The hardiness zone references, height figures and color descriptions are from the same sources as already are given in the previous chapter, so are not repeated here.

Please remember that many small trees may be cut to the ground when young and permitted to produce many stems from the ground. This would classify them as shrubs according to the very broad definition given earlier. The reverse also is true. Many plants that usually are called shrubs because they grow with many stems from the ground can be called trees, by that same broad definition, if only one of their many stems is permitted to grow.

The line of demarcation between tree and shrub is fine— and often, particularly in the matter of large shrub or small tree, is a matter of personal opinion and therefore not worth quibbling about.

Now, let's consider the small trees available for use with shrubs. Alphabetically, according to botanical name, we have:

Crataegus oxyacantha

ACER
(Maple)

Of the many maples that might be considered small trees, only two species are included in this book, because they often are planted with shrubs. They might be considered shrubs too, since they often are grown with many stems from the ground. In fact, nurseries may offer both tree and shrub forms.

Maples, as you undoubtedly know, are considered satisfactory trees to grow. Their leaves are attractive, with their several lobes; their flowers are not particularly conspicuous, but are followed by winged seeds, called samaras, which may be colorful. Many maples have leaves that turn color in autumn and are at the height of their glory at that time.

Acer ginnala
(Amur maple)
Zone 3 to part of Zone 2; 20′

A very hardy maple, this has a densely branching, rounded form. The leaves, shiny, dark green, are small, about 3″ long; have three lobes, the middle one much longer than the others.

The yellowish-white flowers, appearing in May, are not conspicuous but are fragrant, so that you smell them when near a tree in bloom and thus look for them. The numerous clusters, to 4″ long and 1″ wide, of two-winged samaras are handsome in late August to September as they turn bright red. They often are so numerous that a tree may exhaust itself by producing too many seeds each year. Amur maple foliage turns brilliant scarlet in autumn, and if you know where there is a hedge of this tree, or even a specimen, be sure to visit it to enjoy the exquisite coloring.

Amur maple may be used as a hedge, either clipped or unclipped, as a windbreak or as a specimen tree. With shrubs, it is best used in the background of a border. It thrives in almost any situation with little care.

Acer palmatum
(Greenleaf Japanese maple)
Zone 5; 20′–25′

The heights given here rarely are reached in the northern states, but in the south and in Japan they are not unusual. This tree grows in rounded form and often a plant looks like a mound of foliage. Leaves are about 4″ wide with from five to nine lobes. In the varieties and cultivars of A. palmatum leaves may be deeply divided or cut, but not in palmatum itself. The flowers, which are purple, appear in mid-May to early June. The fruits are the usual two-winged samaras, but it is unusual to see them on a tree, since most trees never

fruit. Varieties and cultivars of Acer palmatum commonly found in the catalogs include the following.

Acer palmatum 'Atropurpureum'
(Bloodleaf Japanese maple)
Zone 5

If you like red-foliaged plants, this is one of the best. They remain the same color all season. Leaves are about 2¼″ long, 2¾″ wide.

The bloodleaf Japanese maple is best used as a specimen in a green lawn area or as an accent in a planting of lower growing shrubs with green leaves. It should never, never be planted near a red brick house.

Acer ginnala

Acer palmatum (Greenleaf Japanese Maple)

Acer palmatum 'Dissectum'
(Threadleaf Japanese maple)
Zone 5

This maple has green leaves, each divided so deeply that a segment is almost threadlike—hence the common name. This characteristic is lost when a plant is used in a border, but becomes an asset when the maple is used as the dominating plant with a few lower growing, glossy-leaved shrubs.

Acer palmatum 'Dissectum Atropurpureum'
(see *A. p.* 'Ornatum')

Acer palmatum 'Ornatum'
(Spiderleaf Japanese maple)

From spring through the early summer months the leaves of this cultivar are red. Later they turn bronze with undertones of green. Leaves are delicately and very deeply cut so that the effect is spiderlike. The branches tend to droop in weeping form, which gives the tree a graceful effect.

AMELANCHIER

(Shadbush, Shadblow, Juneberry, Service berry, Bilberry, Showy Mespilus, Canadian Medlar)

Amelanchiers are at their best when situated at the edges of wooded areas, by the sides of streams or ponds where their white flowers reflect in water.

Amelanchier laevis

Acer palmatum 'Dissectum'

They blend well with all other native shrubs. Though they seldom are used in cultivated areas, they look very much at home in such situations, in groupings with a few shrubs or as specimens at the end of shrub borders.

Blossom time is late April or very early May and blooms may be fleeting. If the weather turns warm flowers may last only two or three days, while in cool weather they may last a week or longer. The berries that follow the flowers usually stay for only a short time, but for a different reason: birds love them. The smooth gray bark and bright autumn foliage colors make amelanchiers attractive anywhere.

Amelanchier × grandiflora (A. arborea × A. laevis)
(Apple shadbush or Apple serviceberry)
Zone 5; usually about 10′ but may grow to 25′

Pale gray bark, dense foliage and narrow, upright growth characterize this tree. The newly opened leaves are purplish, the flower buds pinkish, but the flowers, though they may open faintly pink in color, soon fade to white. Flowers of this shadbush are larger than those of the others and are usually in bloom in early May. Edible fruits in early summer turn first red, then gradually black. Leaves turn yellow or orange in autumn.

Amelanchier laevis
(Allegany or Alleghany serviceberry, shadbush or shadblow)
Zone 5; usually 15′ or 20′ but may grow to 35′

Upright growth with spreading branches and clusters of white flowers in late April are this tree's assets. The young leaves are pink, and the bracts that set off the flowers are red. In late June or early July the fruits color—bluish-purple to blackish-purple. Leaves turn yellow to red in autumn.

CERCIS

(Redbud, Judas tree)

Small trees or large shrubs, the redbuds are dainty, delicate-looking plants with open form and very dark bark. They are native in the woods to Zone 5. They bloom in mid-May—at the same time as the flowering dogwoods, *Cornus florida*, and may be planted with them for a colorful effect. Do not, however, plant the pink-flowering dogwood with redbud as the flower colors clash. Seed pods of redbuds are shaped like those of edible peas, though narrower. They are at first pink, then turn tannish, then brown as they dry. Leaves are heart-shaped, turn from green to yellow in the fall.

In cold climates redbuds should be transplanted only in spring and purchased only with roots balled and burlapped.

Cercis canadensis
(Eastern redbud, American redbud, Junebud, Salad tree)
Zone 4; 30′
The flowers are shaped like those of edible peas, appear to grow directly from the branches (though actually they are on little spurs that grew when the branch had leaves in the same places where the flowers now appear) and usually are produced on older wood. They are ⅞″ long, the same in width at the widest part, and strong reddish-purple.

Cercis canadensis

Cercis chinensis

Cercis canadensis alba
(White redbud, Whitebud)
Identical with *C. canadensis* except for white flowers and a closer habit of growth. This variety is said to be not quite as hardy as *C. canadensis*. I have found just the opposite to be true as some of the plants of *canadensis* that I own die to the ground in severe winters but the white-flowered form never has done this.

Cercis canadensis 'Forest Pansy'
A strikingly beautiful purple-foliaged form, the new foliage even more intense than the old. In spring, before the tree is in full leaf it produces masses of purple-red pea-like flowers.

Cercis chinensis
(Chinese redbud)
Zone 5; usually about 20′ tall
The Chinese redbud is not as hardy as the eastern redbud—note the difference in northernmost hardiness zones as listed. It is tip-tender, that is the tips of the branches tend to be injured if the winter is severe, on the Michigan State University campus in East Lansing, which is in Zone 5b (that is the more southerly division of Zone 5). I live in the same part of the same zone and have had no difficulty wintering several small plants.

However, just to be on the safe side, it may be better to grow this redbud as a shrub in the north, with several stems, so that if one or two kill to the ground in winter the others will be left to grow. Flower color is strong reddish-purple. Blooms appear in mid-May.

CHIONANTHUS

(Fringe tree, Old man's beard, Grancy graybeard, Grandfather graybeard, Graybeard tree)

Fringe trees are handsome small trees with quite large leaves that turn yellow in autumn. They are grown, however, for their fringe-like white flowers that appear about the beginning of June. Similar in appearance are the male and female flowers, though the male flowers are slightly larger. These blooms are borne on separate trees, according to sex. Female plants bear dark blue berries on long, thin drooping stems after the flowers are gone.

Fringe trees may be used in wide shrub borders, as specimens, or planted against large, high buildings. It should be remembered, however, that the leaves appear late in spring, unfolding just before the flowers, so that the early spring effect is of bare branches. Gardeners not acquainted with these trees should be warned against thinking they are dead because leaves have not yet appeared though those on most other trees and shrubs are partly grown.

Chionanthus retusus
(Chinese fringe tree)
Zone 5; 20', but usually less
Leaves and flower clusters are shorter than in the native fringe tree discussed below, the petals of the individual florets ¾" long, the clusters 3" long. Leaves are more oval in form. The flowers appear a few days later than those of *virginicus* and the tree gives a more delicate effect in the landscape. It seems not to be quite as hardy as *virginicus*.

Chionanthus retusus

Chionanthus virginicus
(White fringe tree, Native fringe tree, Flowering ash, Poison ash, Shavings, Snowflower-tree, White-ash, plus the common names given for fringe trees in general)
Zone 5; 20'–25', though often less
Native from New Jersey to Florida, this tree has large leaves turning yellow in fall, very fragrant white, fringe-like flowers with petals of each floret 1" long and a cluster of florets 4" long.

CLETHRA
(White alder)

Clethra barbinervis
(Japanese clethra)
Zone 6 to Zone 5b; 30'
A spreading, irregularly formed tree that often has several trunks, this also has brown, shredding bark. The flowers are white and fragrant, appearing in late July, thus making it the first clethra to flower. They are produced in clusters that are held on the tree in an unusual way—horizontally.

CORNUS
(Dogwood)

The dogwoods are among the very best trees for use on home grounds. A glance at the list that follows will show that there are many worthwhile dogwoods besides the well-known flowering dogwood.

Dogwoods grow small enough to use on a city lot, yet are equally effective on a large acreage. Branching habit is horizontal in most tree dogwoods, thus they have interesting silhouettes in win-

Chionanthus virginicus

ter. Foliage is dark green in most of them. Flowers are yellow, inconspicuous in the kinds that have ornamental bracts, which may be white, pink or reddish. Colorful fruits usually follow the flowers and autumn foliage color is outstanding in most tree dogwoods.

In cold climates tree forms of dogwood should be moved in spring only and purchased with roots balled and burlapped.

Cornus alternifolia
(Pagoda dogwood, Umbrella tree, Alternate-leaved dogwood, Greenosier, Pigeonberry)
Zone 5; 20'
This tree grows naturally along the edges of woods and is prettiest when used with suitable shrubs in such a situation. The branches, greenish in color, are arranged in horizontal tiers and in irregular whorls, which gives the tree the shape of a pagoda. The winter pattern of these branches is particularly lovely. Leaves turn purplish in autumn. Flowers are greenish in clusters about 2" in diameter opening in late May and are followed by blue fruits borne on red stems. Damp soil and semi-shade are the chief requirements of this plant.

SHRUBS AND TREES TO KNOW AND GROW 217

Cornus florida

Cornus florida
(Flowering dogwood, Arrow wood, Boxwood, False boxwood, Nature's mistake)
Zone 5; 15′–25′

This dogwood is one of the most popular of flowering trees because of its beauty and its adaptability. It is at home in any situation, from the edge of a woodland (which is where it grows wild from Massachusetts to Florida and westward) to a place of honor on the lawn or to part of the house planting on a 40′ wide city lot.

The general effect of this dogwood is low and wide, because, under good growing conditions, a tree may spread to about 18′. If you compare this figure with the ultimate height figures given above you'll have a mental picture of the shape, so will realize that room should be allowed for this spread. Branches are arranged in tiers and grow horizontally.

Foliage is dark green, turning scarlet in autumn. What usually are called flowers are in reality white bracts coloring in mid-May around the inconspicuous yellow flowers in the center of the bracts. Bracts are notched, with the notched area usually pinkish or brownish (a result of cold injury during winter when the bract served as a bud scale). Bright red berries, borne in tight clusters, follow the flowers. Even brighter than the autumn color of the leaves, they contrast brilliantly with the foliage.

In winter the horizontal branches make a beautiful pattern against the sky (or a wall), while the flower buds, like little conical buttons, are prominent at the tips of the twigs. Birds frequently eat these buds so that there is little or no bloom the following spring.

Cornus florida 'Cherokee Chief'
Although this cultivar is described in several catalogs as having ruby red bracts, they are really a deep purplish-pink, slightly larger than those on most plants of *C. florida rubra*. This is a very pretty pink dogwood with reddish coloring in the new foliage. Although this cultivar and its white counterpart, listed below, are said to bloom when young, the word "young" is evidently subject to interpretation for my plant took 5 years from the time it was planted (2′ to 3′ high) to produce its first bloom and then presented me with a fine crop.

Cornus florida 'Cherokee Princess'
Like 'Cherokee Chief' this cultivar has larger bracts than the species but they are white.

Cornus florida 'Cloud 9'
Definitely shrubby in form, without a leader (main shoot or trunk such as a tree has) this plant probably should be described in the previous chapter, but is listed here because it is a cultivar of *C. florida*. The bracts are white, much more rounded in form and borne more horizontally than those of *florida*. This plant is said to flower at an early age. I have seen only fair sized specimen stock so cannot vouch for the validity of this claim.

Cornus florida multibracteata (see C. f. 'Pluribracteata')

Cornus florida 'Pendula' (Weeping dogwood)
A different form of *florida*, this has branches that bend downward or weep. It is best used as a specimen for an accent in a garden, with only low, ground-hugging shrubs around it. It looks very good drooping over a statue or a bird bath. I have seen it used in both situations. Do not depend on this dogwood for annual bloom. It is a shy bloomer at best.

Cornus florida plena (see C. f. 'Pluribracteata')

Cornus florida 'Pluribracteata' (syn C. f. multibracteata, C. f. plena) (Double-flowering dogwood)
The bracts in this dogwood number from six to eight arranged in two rows, whereas *florida* has but four bracts in a single row. This tends to make the double form more showy than the single.

Cornus florida 'Prosser Red'
This cultivar is identical with *rubra* but has flowers deeper in color and more nearly true red.

Cornus florida 'Pluribracteata'

Cornus florida 'Rainbow' (Variegated dogwood)

Wavy yellow and green leaves are ornamental all summer, turn bronze-red in autumn for a stunning fall display.

Cornus florida rubra (Red-flowering dogwood)

The bracts of this dogwood are not really red, but rose-colored. Otherwise the tree is identical with *florida* and exceptionally effective when planted with it.

Cornus florida rubra

Cornus florida 'Salicifolia' (Willow-leaved dogwood)

The foliage of this cultivar is narrow, like that of a willow (*Salix*), hence the name 'Salicifolia'. Furthermore the whole tree is smaller than *florida*, with shorter branches, more twigs and a more compact habit of growth. It does not grow as fast as *florida* either. The bracts are white; the fall foliage color is brilliant red.

Cornus florida 'Welchii'

A variegated form of *florida*, this has leaves that combine creamy white, green, and pink. The tree makes a handsome focal point in a garden because of the foliage colors. Flowers are sparse at best and the plant should not be grown for them. Foliage color becomes deeper in the fall. This plant is best set in light shade because the coloring may fade or the leaves burn when it is planted in a hot, sunny place.

Cornus florida 'Welchii'

Cornus florida xanthocarpa

This is the yellow-berried form of *Cornus florida*, like the species in every other way except berry color.

CRATAEGUS
(Hawthorn, Haw, Thorn apple)

A group of small trees most of which are native over a large part of America, down the east coast from Quebec to North Carolina, westward to Michigan. Their form is dense, they are twiggy; branching habit is horizontal and shape picturesque. Because of their shiny green leaves, close clusters of white (or pink or rose) flowers followed by red, scarlet, or crimson fruits, many hawthorns are excellent for garden use. Their thorns, which in some cases are an inch long, make them valuable for use as impenetrable hedges. They are useful in a border with shrubs, as tall plants in a house planting, or as specimens.

Crataegus 'Autumn Glory' Zone 5; 15'–18'

This tree is described as having a shapely head and deep green foliage, large clusters of white blooms in spring and immense clusters of brilliant red, giant berries in early autumn that remain on the tree well into winter.

Crataegus carrierei (see C. × lavallei)

Crataegus coccinea (see C. intricata)

Crataegus cordata (see C. phaenopyrum)

Crataegus crus-galli (Cockspur thorn, Pinthorn, Newcastle thorn) Zone 5; 40'

A low, broad native tree (20'–30' spread) with flat top and horizontal branches, this flowers in late May. The glossy green foliage turns orange to scarlet in autumn, thus making this one of the comparatively few hawthorns with good fall color. Fruits, first green, then bright red, color in late October and stay on for most of the winter. They are hard, taste tart, and are inedible.

Because of its dense branching habit, this tree makes a good clipped hedge that will be impenetrable because of the long thorns.

Crataegus intricata (syn C. coccinea) (Red haw, Scarlet thorn) Zone 6; 12'–20' with the same spread

This is a shrubby, rounded tree with a short trunk, upcurving branches, and yellow-green leaves in spring. These turn bright green in summer, tan in autumn and buff in winter. Flowers are white, appear in May and are followed in October by deep crimson, sweet edible fruits.

Crataegus × lavallei (C. crus-galli × C. pubescens) (syn C. carrierei) (Lavalle hawthorn) Zone 5; 20'

A spreading habit, clusters of white flowers in late May, leaves that remain on the tree longer than those of most hawthorns and turn bronze red in fall, and orange-red or brick red fruits in October distinguish this hawthorn from others. Fruits stay on all winter until February.

Crataegus mollis
(Downy hawthorn)
Zone 5; 30′
Native from southern Ontario to Minnesota and South Dakota, southward to Alabama, Arkansas, and Oklahoma, this hawthorn has spreading branches that form a broad-topped crown. Leaves are dark yellow-green; flowers opening in early to mid-May are white with red disks; and fruit, which is larger than that of most hawthorns (an inch in diameter) and pear-shaped, is scarlet with thick yellow flesh, sweet to taste, ripe in August to September.

Crataegus monogyna
(English hawthorn, Single-seed hawthorn, Haw bush, Hagthorn, Hag bush or tree, May bush, May bread, May bread and cheese tree or bush, Aglet tree, Fairy thorn, Glastonbury thorn, Hipperty Haw tree, Holy Innocents, Heg Peg bush, Moon flower, Peggall bush, Pixie pear, Quick thorn, Scrab, Scrab-bush, Shiggy)
Zone 5; 30′
This hawthorn is a shrub or tree with ascending branches and a rounded head. Its twiggy habit of growth and numerous thorns are the reasons it is so widely used for hedging purposes in England. Single white flowers in late May, red fruit in fall, are further characteristics. Fruits have only one seed, from which comes the botanical name "monogyna," which actually means "one woman," referring to the single carpel. The foliage of this hawthorn does not turn color in fall.

C. monogyna often is confused with C. oxyacantha, described below, but it is easy to tell them apart either in bloom or in fruit. When in bloom, *monogyna* has only one style in the center of the flower while *oxyacantha* has two; and when the trees are in fruit, *monogyna* has only one seed while *oxyacantha* has two.

Crataegus monogyna 'Stricta'
Zone 5; 30′
A columnar form of hawthorn, upright growing and extremely dense in habit, therefore useful in certain places in the garden. Unfortunately this cultivar seems to be quite subject to fireblight, a plant disease.

Crataegus × mordenensis 'Toba'
(C. succulenta × C. oxyacantha 'Paul's Scarlet')
Zone 3; 20′
This hybrid was introduced by the Dominion Experiment Station, Morden, Manitoba. It is hardier than C. oxyacantha 'Paul's Scarlet', the parent it resembles. Foliage is glossy; flowers are double, bright pink or deep rose, and fragrant. Fruits are half an inch in diameter and bright red.

Crataegus nitida
(Glossy hawthorn)
Zone 5 to part of Zone 4; 30′
Rounded in form, densely branched, with glossy dark green leaves that are lighter on the undersides, white flowers in late May, and dull red ⅜″ wide fruits coloring in October, this is a handsome hawthorn. Its leaves turn orange and scarlet in autumn and the fruits, while not bright in color, still are attractive against the snow for they remain on the tree throughout the winter and until early March (sometimes late March) of the following year.

This hawthorn is native from Ohio to Missouri and Arkansas.

Crataegus oxyacantha

Crataegus viridis

Crataegus oxyacantha
(English hawthorn, May, Quick, Quick-set-thorn)
Zone 5; 15′
A densely headed tree, rounded in form, with spreading branches that often touch the ground and leaves that do not turn color in autumn. White flowers are followed by small scarlet fruits in September to October. This species is planted all over England and is called "May tree" or simply "May" because it flowers late in that month. In the United States the varieties or cultivars of this species are more popular because many of them have double white flowers or pink or red blooms.

Crataegus oxyacantha 'Paul's Scarlet'
(Paul's scarlet hawthorn)
One of the most popular hawthorns because of its double florets, each ¼″ in diameter, borne in 1½″ clusters and colored a strong purplish red. In late May a tree in bloom is a lovely sight. When this hawthorn is used as a street tree, as it sometimes is in Europe, the entire street becomes colorful when the trees are in bloom.

Crataegus oxyacantha 'Rosea Plena'
Pale rose flowers, double in form.

Crataegus phaenopyrum (syn C. cordata of the catalogs)
(Washington thorn)
Zone 5; 30'
Native from Virginia southward to Alabama and west to Missouri, this hawthorn blooms later than the others and certainly is one of the best. It has at least one interesting feature during each season of the year: in winter the dense, upright silhouette; in mid-June the white flowers borne in 4″ diameter clusters, each floret ⅝″ in diameter with green center; in summer the shining, densely packed green leaves; and in autumn both the orange-scarlet leaves and the small, bright scarlet fruits with which the tree usually is heavily laden in September and October.

Crataegus viridis (syn C. 'Winter King')
Zone 5; 20'
An introduction of Simpson Orchard Co. of Vincennes, Indiana, this was described in the catalog of the company as follows: "A hawthorn with rather small, glossy leaves, silvery younger bark, only moderately thorny, white blossoms opening a few days later than Washington hawthorn, followed by

Crataegus viridis

masses of ⅜″ orange-red fruits that normally persist throughout the winter. It is characterized by relatively disease-resistant foliage, freedom from blight, attractive silvery bark, and masses of orange-red fruits that do not soften or discolor from cold. This selection fruits well at an early age, and has not been difficult to transplant."

Crataegus 'Winter King'
(see *C. viridis*)

DAVIDIA

Davidia involucrata
(Dove tree)
Zone 6; usually about 20' high in that zone, though taller further south
The handsome large, bright green leaves overlap one another and make this tree beautiful even without a flower on it. This is fortunate for, in many cases, gardeners have been disappointed in the lack of bloom or sparseness of bloom.

While certain specimens are known to bloom every year, more do not flower until quite old and then have only a few flowers at irregular intervals.

When this pyramidal-shaped tree does bloom it is beautiful beyond words. In mid-May the flower bracts appear. There are two of these, one 6″ to 7″ long and the other less than half that length, both white. It is these, waving in the breeze, that give the tree its common name. Between the two bracts is the true flower, a ball-shaped, creamy-yellow, inch-wide mass of stamens. If any fruit forms it is pear shaped, green with purple bloom like a plum.

ELAEAGNUS

Small trees and large shrubs with interesting, sometimes handsome, foliage and fruits. Flowers are inconspicuous and this genus definitely is grown for either foliage or fruits or both and not for flowers.

Davidia involucrata

Eleagnus angustifolia

Elaeagnus angustifolia
(Russian olive, Oleaster)
Zone 3; 20′
The grayish-green foliage makes this little tree outstanding in any landscape. Flowers are tiny ($^3/_{16}$″ in diameter), brilliant yellow, fragrant, so that you smell them from some distance away when, in early June, they perfume the air. Edible fruit, widely sold in Middle Eastern markets, also is yellowish, but covered with scales that appear silvery. This tree is very hardy, easily grown, adaptable to many soils and situations. One of my favorite foliage combinations is Russian olive planted with any of the purple-leaved plums.

EUONYMUS

(Spindle tree, Dagwood, Dogwood)

There are vine, shrub, and tree forms of euonymus. The taller shrubs may be grown trained to only one stem and called trees. The tree forms may be cut back to force several stems into growth and thus may be grown as shrubs. Several of the larger tree-like species are listed here with the small trees, for, whether grown in tree or shrub form, they are large enough to be used as or

in place of small trees. These plants are grown for foliage and fruit, not for flowers, because, in most species, these are inconspicuous.

Euonymus atropurpureus
(Wahoo, Burning bush, Bitter ash, Indian arrow)
Zone 5 to part of Zone 4; 25′
The flowers are purple and appear in June, fruits are crimson and are showy in October when the leaves also are brilliant so that they appear to be burning. This plant is native from northeastern America southward to Florida, westward to Montana, and usually is found growing along the banks of streams.

Franklinia alatamaha

Euonymus europaeus
(European burning bush, Spindle tree, Arrow-bean, Bitch-wood, Louse berry, Butchers-prick-tree, Cardinal's cap, Death alder, Dog timber, Dogbane, Dog tooth berry, European dogwood, Flower-ivy, Foul rush, Gaiter tree, Gattan tree, Hot cross buns, Ivy flower, Peg wood, Pincushion shrub, Pop corns, Prick timber, Prick wood, Skewer wood, Skiver)
Zone 4; 20′
The green, four-sided branches make this plant interesting even in winter. The flowers in mid-June are yellow-green and unpleasant to smell. Autumn foliage color is almost purple while the fruits, coloring pink on the outside in September and October, open to show the bright orange berries.

Euonymus europaeus 'Aldenha-mensis'
(Aldenham spindle tree)
Zone 4; 8′ or more
Even more colorful than *E. europaeus*, the dark green foliage turns reddish in autumn; the fruits are brilliant pink outside, opening to show bright orange berries. Fruits are borne on long stems and hang downward.

FRANKLINIA

Franklinia alatamaha (syn Gordonia alatamaha)
(Franklinia)
Zone 5; to about 6′ in that zone, but to 30′ further south
In Zone 5 this tree lives, dying to the ground in severe winters but growing again from the roots the following spring. It does not flower because it never seems to make sufficient growth in a year to bloom. It flowers in Zone 6, though not as profusely as in Zone 7. It is desirable for its rarity, for the fact that its white flowers with conspicuous yellow stamens appear in September to October, and for the bright red and orange autumn coloring of its large leaves. Plant in full sun for the best autumn foliage color.

GORDONIA

Gordonia alatamaha
(see *Franklinia alatamaba*)

HALESIA

(Silverbell, Snowdrop tree, Bell-olive tree, Wild olive tree, Possum-wood, Tiss-wood)

Silverbells are native trees from West Virginia to Florida and westward to Texas. The common name refers to the flowers, which are white, drooping, and bell-shaped, opening in mid-May on trees with an irregular habit of growth. This genus has no serious pests, a point in its favor. Silverbells should be planted close to the house or outdoor living room so their bells may be enjoyed. Blooms are not bulky enough to be effective at a distance. Seed pods are interesting, though not beautiful, much of the winter as they turn gradually from tan to brown. Foliage turns yellow in fall.

Halesia carolina (syn *H. tetraptera*)
(Carolina silverbell)
Zone 5; 30', but usually about 20'
Flower buds are pinkish, bells are ¾" long, ¾" in diameter at the widest point, white with prominent deep yellow stamens. The fruit is a pod with from two to four wings. The leaves turn light yellow in autumn.

Halesia monticola

Halesia monticola
(Mountain silverbell)
Zone 6 to part of Zone 5; said to grow to 90' but usually to about 30'
This species has longer flowers, to an inch long, and fruits the same shape as *H. carolina*, but slightly larger. The tree is larger in every way than *H. carolina*, but has the same general form and the leaves also turn yellow in autumn.

Halesia tetraptera
(see *H. carolina*)

ILEX

(Holly)

Hollies grow in both tree and shrub forms and the genus includes both evergreen and deciduous species. Some hollies are hardy in the north, and these are the ones included in this book. The inconspicuous white flowers of the two sexes are borne on different plants so that a male plant should be set in the same hole as a female plant (and kept pruned to minimum size) or a male plant should be set out for every four to eight females. This male plant should be within about 40' of the female plants to insure pollination. In the north it is best to move hollies only in the spring and the evergreen sorts always should have earth balls around the roots. Evergreen hollies are beautiful in the background of either deciduous or other broad-leaved evergreen shrubs or as specimens.

Halesia carolina

Ilex opaca
(American holly)
Zone 5; 40', but only to about 15'
in Zone 5

From Massachusetts southward and
west to southern Ohio and Illinois, Missouri and Oklahoma, this is the native
holly. It is evergreen and is the holly
you think of when you think of
Christmas.

American holly has light gray bark, a
dense, horizontal branching habit, and
large trees are pyramidal in form. The
leaves have sharp, sawtoothed edges and
the female plants bear tiny white
flowers in early June followed by bright
red berries in October, which will remain in good condition until the following April. There are many cultivars of
this holly, some better than others for a
given locality. If you wish to buy American hollies you should go to a nursery
specializing in them and see them in
berry the autumn before buying them.

American holly needs well-drained,
fertile soil and, in the north, a place
protected from wind and the hottest
winter sun so that the leaves are not
winter-burned. Good drainage is essential to hardiness of evergreen hollies in
the north.

The New Jersey Experiment Station
has been active in American holly
breeding, and currently recommend
'Jersey Knight'—a male for pollination
—and 'Jersey Princess'—a female for
berry displays. Plant one male to every
six females for best berry set.

Ilex opaca (American Holly)

Koelreuteria paniculata

Ilex opaca xanthocarpa
Has yellow berries instead of red ones.
It is particularly pretty when used with
any of the red-fruited hollies as the
berry colors contrast beautifully.

KOELREUTERIA

Koelreuteria paniculata
(Goldenrain tree, Varnish tree,
Pride of India, China tree)
Zone 5; 20'–30'

This is one of the few flowering trees
with yellow flowers. They are small,
bright yellow with an orange-red blotch
at the base of each, and are borne in
early summer (mid-July) in large, upright clusters. The fruits that follow are
bladder-like pods, yellowish or tannish
in color. The tree has spreading
branches and is flat-topped. It is not
considered long-lived, but is worth
planting anyhow. From observation of
many full-grown trees in assorted
northern states where hardiness is a factor, I think that the supposed lack of
longevity is one of those myths started
in the year one and copied by unin-
formed writers ever since.

LABURNUM
(Golden-chain)

Laburnums belong to the pea family
and have yellow flowers shaped like
those of edible peas borne in long clusters, much like those of wisteria vines.
These blooms open in late May or early
June and last about two weeks. Growth
habit is upright and narrow; leaves are
gray-green and graceful. In both England and Scotland I have seen long arbors made of laburnums pruned to
shape—an idea that might be used in
gardens here. Laburnums do not change
foliage color in autumn. All parts of laburnums are poisonous to eat.

Laburnum alpinum
(Scotch laburnum)
Zone 4; 30'

This is hardier than the more commonly listed *L. anagyroides*. It also is
taller, more upright in form, has larger,
darker leaves and longer flower clusters
that appear a little later. Fruits are pods,
like pea pods but larger. Flowers, fruits
and seeds are poisonous. Gardeners living in Zone 4 should buy this species
and this one only.

Laburnum × watereri

Laburnum alpinum 'Pendulum' (Weeping golden-chain)

A grafted, pendulous form of *L. alpinum*, this is useful where a weeping laburnum is desired—usually as a specimen tree.

Laburnum anagyroides (syn *L. vulgare*) (Golden-chain, Common laburnum, Bean tree) Zone 5; 20'

All the comparative remarks made above about the Scotch laburnum apply in reverse to this species. Only if you cannot obtain either of the other laburnum species described here should you grow this one.

Laburnumossii (see *L. × watereri* 'Vossii')

Laburnum vulgare (see *L. anagyroides*)

Laburnum × watereri (*L. alpinum × L. anagyroides*) (Waterer laburnum) Zone 5; 30'

This hybrid has larger flowers (¾" long, ½" diameter, in clusters 8" long) of a deeper color and has a denser habit of growth than *anagyroides*. It is a better plant in many ways. This probably is the reason it is more widely listed in the catalogs. Seed pods are borne in clusters 4½" long, are each 2" long and ⅜" wide. They are colored strong greenish yellow at first, turning gradually to tan.

Laburnum × watereri 'Vossii' (syn *L. vossii*) (Voss laburnum)

Usually listed as an improved form of *L. watereri*, this has longer flower clusters, to 18"-20" in length. It is otherwise similar to the species, except for denser growth.

MACLURA

Maclura pomifera (Osage-orange, Bois d'arc, Bowwood, Hedge tree) Zone 4; 60', but usually seen as a pruned hedge to about 20'

This tree has a vigorous, dense growth and many twigs, plus heavy thorns. All of these characteristics make it admirable for hedging purposes or as a hedge background for lower-growing shrubs. Leaves are glossy and change to yellow in autumn. Fruits, at their best in September, look like big, dull green oranges with very rough surfaces. They have an unusual and delightful aroma. They are used for ornament and also are excellent

Laburnum × watereri 'Vossii'

Maclura pomifera

moth repellents. Since male and female flowers are borne in June on separate plants, it is imperative that plants of both sexes be planted in order to insure fruits.

MAGNOLIA

Magnolias are grown primarily for their flowers in the northern states, while in the south many species are grown as well for their evergreen foliage. Blooms are large, may be white, various shades of pink and pinkish-lavender, or reddish to red-purple. Flowers are followed by oddly shaped fruits that, when they split open to show the bright red seeds inside them, are conspicuous for a week or two. Magnolias have no autumn foliage color, but the velvety buds that become apparent during winter are interesting to watch then, when so many other shrubs show no signs of having made preparations to bloom another year.

Magnolias have fleshy roots, easily broken and bruised. For this reason buy only balled and burlapped plants and move them in spring, preferably when in bloom, for two reasons: so you can tell the flower color and because they move more readily at that time. When roots are dormant and plants are moved, the roots often decay and the decay may spread to the rest of the plant. So, pay no attention to the neighbors who accuse you of being cruel for moving a plant in bloom.

Magnolia alexandrina
(see *M. × soulangiana* 'Alexandrina')

Magnolia 'Girls' hybrids
A new series of Asian magnolias, all with girls' names, has been developed at the National Arboretum. They have bold, beautiful colors, ranging from creamy yellow ('Ann') through deep pink ('Susan') to rosy purple ('Betty'). All produce masses of flowers ahead of the leaves and have the appearance of billowing large shrubs, rather than small trees.

Magnolia glauca
(see *M. virginiana*)

Magnolia kobus
Zone 6; 30′
Although this plant is a tree, it is more often seen growing with several stems from the ground. Dark, glossy, green leaves are lighter on the undersides. White, 5″ diameter blooms have a faint purple line on the outsides of the petals, near the base of the flowers, and are fragrant. They appear in late April to early May, early in the magnolia parade. The fruits are the usual odd-shaped pods, which split to show the red seeds inside in early autumn.

Magnolia kobus borealis

Magnolia × soulangiana
(Saucer Magnolia)

There is a hardier variety of this plant, *Magnolia kobus borealis*, which can be grown in Zone 5.

Both of these plants take years to flower, sometimes as many as twenty. For this reason, a hybrid magnolia, *M. × loebneri* 'Merrill' is described below.

Magnolia lennei
(see *M. × soulangiana* 'Lennei')

Magnolia 'Leonard Messel'
A hybrid between *Magnolia kobus* and *Magnolia stellata* 'Rosea', raised in Colonel Leonard Messel's Sussex (England) garden. A magnificent large shrub or small tree in full flower, displaying lovely rosy pink blooms.

Magnolia × loebneri **'Merrill' (*M. stellata* × *M. kobus*) (syn *M. stellata* 'Dr. Merrill' of the catalogs) Zone 5 to southern part of Zone 4; 20′**
This hybrid fills a very definite need. It is listed here because it blooms early yet grows rapidly and blooms when young, offering a substitute for *M. kobus* and its variety, listed above.

'Merrill' has blooms slightly larger than those of the star magnolia and, like *M. kobus*, is fragrant, only not as much so as its one parent.

Magnolia rubra
(see *M. × soulangiana* 'Rubra')

Magnolia rustica rubra
(see *M. × soulangiana* 'Rubra')

Magnolia × soulangiana (*M. denudata × M. liliflora*)
(Saucer magnolia)
Zone 5; 25′
Fragrant, 3¾″ wide flowers open in early May before the leaves unfold. These are cup-shaped or saucer-shaped, as you prefer, and are usually white suffused with pinkish or purplish. Depending on the weather at the time of bloom, flowers may last only four or five days or they may be in good condition for two weeks.

Following the blooms, slender pods grow to be rather like short cucumbers in shape. These gradually turn brown and then split to reveal bright red seeds inside. When the pods have split open and there are many of them on a tree, the effect is of a second, short season of beauty in early fall.

Growth habit may be that of either a tree or a shrub depending on early training. When grown with several trunks, a plant may be as wide as it is high. Leaves are quite large—to 8″ long.

Magnolia × soulangiana **'Alba'** (syn *M. s. amabilis*)
This variety has especially large, fragrant white flowers.

Magnolia × soulangiana **'Alba Superba'** (syn *M. s.* 'Superba')
Another cultivar with larger flowers than the parent.

Magnolia × soulangiana 'Alba'

Magnolia × soulangiana 'Lennei'

Magnolia × soulangiana 'Alexandrina'

Earlier to bloom than the saucer magnolia, this cultivar has 6″ diameter blooms, white inside, flushed with rosy purple on the outside.

Magnolia × soulangiana 'Lennei'

This cultivar has the deepest colored flowers of any of the saucer magnolias —they are white inside but deep, deep rosy purple outside and are borne in late May, almost at the end of the magnolia season of bloom.

Magnolia × soulangiana 'Rubra' (syn M. rubra and M. rustica rubra)

Flowers of this variety look much like those of 'Lennei', but are lighter in color. They may be 6″ in diameter and appear earlier than those of 'Lennei'.

Magnolia × soulangiana 'Superba' (see M. s. 'Alba Superba')

Magnolia stellata (Star magnolia) Zone 5; 20′

When grown in a sheltered place, this will be one of the first magnolias to flower. It blooms when just a few feet high. It is a tree with a dense, rounded growth habit but often is grown with several stems like a shrub. Buds are pale purplish-pink. The flowers are white, double, star-shaped and fragrant, the outsides of the petals tinged with the same color as the buds. Blossoms grow to 5″ in diameter when fully open. They appear before the leaves, about the middle to end of April.

Leaves are small compared with those of other magnolias and rather narrow. Following the flowers come the twisted, 2″ long fruits, rather like small cucumbers. When ripe, these split open disclosing bright red seeds.

Leaves of this magnolia change color in fall, becoming yellow or bronze.

Magnolia stellata 'Rosea' (Pink star magnolia)

Buds are pink and flowers are flushed pale pink on the outsides of the petals. They fade to white, however, as they age.

Magnolia stellata 'Rubra'

Flowers of this variety are a deep, purplish pink and this deeper color makes the plant more effective in the landscape than the paler 'Rosea'.

Magnolia stellata 'Waterlily'

Larger flowers and faster growth are the distinguishing characteristics of this cultivar.

Magnolia stellata 'Waterlily'

Magnolia virginiana

Magnolia virginiana (syn *M. glauca*)
(Sweetbay, Swampbay, Indian bark, Swamp laurel, White bay)
Southern part of Zone 5; 60′ in the south, but only about 25′ and shrublike in the north

In late May this magnolia has fragrant, white flowers to about 3″ in diameter and these continue to appear sometimes until August.

Evergreen in the south, this magnolia is deciduous in the north. Leaves are glossy on top and have a grayish fleece beneath. As one of the common names implies, this tree grows and thrives in the wild in swampy locations and in moist soil. However, it does not absolutely need such conditions.

It will grow in drier soil, but if you plant it in such a situation, it is a good idea to leave a large, cup-shaped depression around the plant when setting it out. Thus you can easily give it extra water in this cup.

MALUS

Malus includes apples and crabapples. For the purposes of this book, we consider only the crabapples grown for their flowers. There are dozens of varieties and cultivars of flowering crabapples, one lovelier in bloom than the other. I considered a shrub in the previous chapter. The rest are trees of varying heights and, since it has taken whole books to describe them, it is obviously impossible to describe them adequately in this chapter, especially since this is a book primarily about shrubs.

Just because I have not described too many of them, do not neglect flowering crabapples when you are planning groupings of small trees with shrubs. It is best to see flowering crabapples in bloom before purchasing any with flower colors other than white, because some of the colors do not combine well with the flowers of many shrubs.

Malus 'Dolgo'
Not only rewards the gardener with a blizzard of apple blossom-pink flowers that fade to white in early spring, it produces an avalanche of dark red fruits in autumn.

Malus 'Dorothea'
Displays pink flowers in spring that do not fade to white, and presents a bonus of beautiful golden yellow fruits in autumn.

Malus 'Hopa'
Has the distinction of dark red blossoms fading to pink, followed by bright

Malus 'Red Jade'

red fruit by autumn. The tree almost breaks under its quantity of fruit.

Malus 'Red Jade'
An introduction of the Brooklyn Botanic Garden, a fabulous small weeping tree with an ornamental effect first enhanced by deep pink flowers in spring, followed by ruby red fruits covering the slender, arching branches from tip to toe.

Malus 'Royalty'
Has handsome purple leaves with crimson flowers, followed by dark red fruits.

Malus 'Snowdrift'
Ah, was there *ever* a small tree so blindingly white in peak flower? Well grown specimens have a perfectly rounded shape, making one of the best lawn highlights. Fruit is orange-red.

Malus 'Snowdrift'

OXYDENDRUM

Oxydendrum arboreum
(Sourwood, Sorrel tree, Elk tree)
Zone 5; may grow 75' high, but usually is only 20'–25' high in the north

This plant forms a narrow pyramid, has lustrous, leathery leaves turning brilliant scarlet-red in fall. This bright color is its outstanding characteristic. Flowers are not pure white, but whitish, and appear from the middle of July through October. They are small, shaped like miniature urns, and are borne in slightly drooping clusters.

Oxydendrum grows naturally in regions with acid soil. Therefore, unless your soil is acid, it is good to replace it when planting this tree.

Oxydendrum arboreum

PRUNUS

This genus includes peaches, plums, cherries, almonds, and apricots. In addition to those species grown primarily for their fruits, there are many others grown primarily for their flowers. These are the ones listed below. In height these species vary from medium-size trees to small trees down to shrubs, which are described in Chapter 12. Many of the *Prunus* species are spectacular when in bloom.

Prunus cerasifera 'Atropurpurea'

Prunus × blireiana (P. cerasifera 'Atropurpurea' × P. mume)
(Blireiana plum)
Zone 6 to part of Zone 5; 25'

This rounded, densely branched tree blooms in early May. Flowers are light pink, double, and an inch in diameter, against red-purple leaves. Small, edible fruits that are the same color as the leaves and therefore not conspicuous are borne later in the season. This hybrid stays in flower longer than many of the other flowering plums.

Prunus cerasifera
(Cherry plum)
Zone 4 to part of Zone 3; 20'

A small tree, this sometimes grows as a shrub with several stems from the ground. It is dense and twiggy, sometimes has thorns. The leaves are light green, flowers are white or pale pink, appearing in late April, fruits are yellow or red, about an inch in diameter and delicious to eat. This species is not nearly as well known or as often used in gardens as its purple-leaved forms described below.

Prunus cerasifera 'Atropurpurea'
(syn P. pissardii, P. cerasifera pissardii)
(Pissard plum)
Zone 4 to part of Zone 3; 15' to 25'

Little pink flowers in late April, ¾" in diameter, are followed usually by a few tiny edible plums that are the same color as and often hidden by the leaves. This is one of the satisfactory, colorful plants for use where such foliage color is needed. I am particularly fond of this plum, or one of the others with similar leaf color, planted with Russian olive, which has gray leaves.

Prunus cerasifera blireiana
(see P. × blireiana)

Prunus cerasifera 'Newport'

Slightly lighter leaf color than the Pissard plum and slightly greater hardiness are characteristics of this tree. It grows 10'–12' high and has white to flesh pink flowers. It is a hybrid, developed at the State Fruit Breeding Farm, Zumbra Heights, Minnesota, and is hardy there.

Prunus cerasifera 'Nigra'
This has very dark purple leaves, which have earned it the common name of Black Myrobalan plum. The flowers are pale pink, single, and about ½″ in diameter.

Prunus cerasifera pissardii
(see P. c. 'Atropurpurea')

Prunus cerasifera 'Thundercloud'
(Ruby tree)
Growing a little taller and a little broader than 'Newport', this cultivar reaches 12′–15′ in height. It has white to pink, single flowers and few fruits.

Prunus 'Hally Jolivette'
Zone 5; ultimate height probably about 12′, but the tallest specimen I have seen was 8′
This densely branched, rounded little tree has pink buds, double white flowers 1¼″ across over a long period of time, sometimes from mid-April to mid-May. This, of course, is a decided asset, as is also the fact that it starts to flower when very young.

Prunus persica
(Ornamental Peach)
Zone 6; 20′–25′
Almost everyone knows the common peach with its pink single flowers in late April and its yellow or red fruits.

Prunus 'Holly Jolivette'

Prunus serrulata 'Sekiyama'

The cultivars listed in the catalogs as flowering or ornamental peaches have been bred and are grown for flowers rather than fruits. They may have white, varying shades of pink, carmine, or bright red flowers, which may be single or double in form, depending on the precise name of the cultivar. These are beautiful when in bloom and many a new gardener (and an experienced one as well) has exclaimed over them. However, they are not the most desirable of flowering trees for they are subject to all of the diseases that make the common peach the subject of frequent and regular spraying by orchardists. The flowering peaches also are not strong growers.

If you are willing to spray as necessary to control pests, and to prune the trees well, right after the flowers drop, to force as much new growth as possible, then the flowering peaches will delight you with their blooms. They grow as small trees or large shrubs and are best placed in the back of the border as they do not look good for some time after pruning is finished.

Prunus pissardii or pissardii nigra
(see P. cerasifera 'Atropurpurea')

Prunus serrulata
(Oriental cherry)
Zone 6; 30′
A wide-spreading tree that usually grows with the main trunk divided into several trunks just a few feet above ground level, this has handsome red bark and single white flowers appearing in early May. Its cultivars are hardy in Zone 6 and the southernmost part of Zone 5, but there only in protected places. There are many cultivars, one of the most popular of which is called 'Kwanzan' in the catalogs but is properly named 'Sekiyama'. This is one of the varieties used around the Tidal Basin in Washington, D.C. It grows to 18′ in height and is upright in form. Young leaves are copper-red. Flowers are deep pink and double, 2½″ in diameter.

Prunus serrulata 'Amanogawa'
Zone 6; 20′
The important character of this cherry, as far as the garden is concerned, is its tall, narrow growth, called "fastigiate." It has semi-double, light pink flowers. It is best placed in a spot where ice and snow will not collect on it in winter and gradually spoil its shape.

**Prunus serrulata 'Shirotae'
(also written 'Sirotae')
(Mt. Fuji cherry)
Zone 6; 30'**
This lovely cherry is grown for its double white flowers, which are fragrant. It is considered the finest of the cherries with either semi-double or double blooms.

**Prunus subhirtella
(Higan cherry, Rosebud cherry,
Equinox cherry)
Zone 6 to part of Zone 5; 25'–30'**
This is one of the earliest of the Oriental-type cherries to bloom, since the flowers appear in late April. They are light pink and single, about 1½" in diameter, and are borne before the leaves appear. They are so profuse that they practically hide the branches of the tree.

**Prunus subhirtella 'Autumnalis'
(Autumn Higan cherry)**
If this cherry were a rose or a raspberry it probably would be advertised as "ever-blooming" for it not only has flowers in spring, but occasionally blooms during summer and usually, but not always, has a few blossoms in autumn. These are semi-double, pale pink to white, ¾" in diameter.

**Prunus subhirtella 'Pendula'
(Japanese weeping cherry, Weeping Higan cherry)**
Long, slender leaves that stay green far into the fall, and the low, broad form with pendulous branches make this a picturesque tree during the entire year. However, it is no tree for a small yard as it will eventually grow 25' wide as well as 25' high. The form usually seen has single, mauve-pink flowers that appear before the leaves. When in bloom it looks like a flowering fountain. There is also a double-flowered form, usually listed in the catalogs as *Prunus subhirtella* 'Roseaplena' but properly named 'Plena Rosea'.

Prunus subhirtella 'Autumnalis' (Autumn Higan cherry)

Prunus subhirtella 'Pendula'

PYRUS

Pyrus americana
(see *Sorbus americana*)

Pyrus calleryana 'Fauriei'
(Dwarf callery pear)
Zones 4 to 8; 25'
Beautiful, white-flowering, pollution-resistant, disease-resistant small tree. A scaled-down version of the famous Bradford pear. Never needs pruning. Beautiful fall color from leaves turning orange, scarlet and crimson-purple.

Pyrus decora
(see *Sorbus decora*)

ROBINIA

Robinia hispida 'Monument'
(Upright rose-acacia)
Zone 4 to part of Zone 3; 10'–12'
The same foliage, flowers, and "moss"-covered seed pods as *Robinia hispida*, a shrub, are characteristic of this tree form. It is adapted to any type of soil, is pretty in the shrub border or used as a specimen and is covered with pendant clusters of flowers colored deep purplish-pink. These appear in late May to early June and are shaped like the blooms of edible or sweet peas. They are followed by pea-shaped pods that are hairy or mossy outside.

SALIX

(Willow)

Salix caprea
(Goat willow, because goats are said to be fond of the catkins, Sally, Sally withy tree, Great sallow, Palmer, Palm willow, Palm tree, Sallow, Black sally, Geese and goslings, Geese and gullies, Goose chicks, Gosling)
Zone 5; 25'
The handsomest of the pussy willows because the male plants have the largest catkins, this tree must be given plenty

Salix caprea

of room as it is vigorous in growth. The finest willows for forcing in water indoors are the result of cutting this tree to the ground every few years or of pruning it drastically every year.

Like all willows, it will grow in swampy as well as dry areas.

SORBUS

The genus *Sorbus* includes three small trees that may be used with shrubs.

Sorbus americana (syn *Pyrus americana*)
(American mountain ash, Dogberry, Quickbeem)
Zone 3; 30'
Native from Labrador to Manitoba and southward to the Great Lakes area and the mountains of North Carolina, this little tree has a rounded head, compound leaves that turn orange and red in autumn, white flowers in late May, and clusters of orange-red fruits in October. It grows naturally in partly-shaded situations where the soil is moist. Since it is weak-wooded, it should be set where winds will not break the branches.

Sorbus aucuparia
(European mountain ash)
Zones 4 to 7; 20'–30'
Though susceptible to the ravages of fireblight disease, a virus infection that turns berries black and causes early defoliation, this deciduous tree is good for late summer scarlet-red berry displays. The small white flowers, borne in flat clusters in spring, are also ornamental. Many cultivars are available, including a yellow-berried form. Good lawn highlight. Rarely needs pruning. Naturally forms a tidy, upright, oval outline and strong single trunk.

Sorbus decora (syn *Pyrus decora*)
(Showy mountain ash)
Zone 2; 30'
This native of southeastern Canada and the northeastern United States used to be considered a variety of *S. americana* and is much like it but with larger and more showy fruits. Small white flowers appear in late May and clusters of half-inch fruits turn bright red in early fall. Foliage, like that of *S. americana*, turns to brilliant hues in autumn.

STEWARTIA
(Stuartia, Malachodendron)

Stewartia pseudo-camellia
(Japanese stewartia)
Zone 5; 30'
This species is not quite as hardy as *S. ovata*. Its white flowers are slightly smaller, to 2½" in diameter, look like single camellias, but are more cup-like in form. Unlike camellias, they are slightly fragrant. Because they appear in early July, when few other trees are blooming, they make this tree particularly desirable.

The tree itself is pyramidal in shape, with bright green leaves appearing early in spring and turning a dull purplish in autumn. Additional seasonal interest is provided by the red, flaking bark on older plant parts.

Stewartia sinensis
(Chinese stewartia)
Zones 5 to 8; 15'–20'
A handsome large shrub or small tree with camellia-like glossy green oval leaves and waxy cup-shaped 2" fragrant white flowers with prominent yellow stamens.

Stewartia sinensis

Styrax japonica

STYRAX
(Storax, Snowbell)

Styrax japonica
(Japanese snowbell)
Zone 5; 10'–30'
Sometimes this grows as a tree or sometimes as a wide-spread shrub with a flat top. Room must be allowed for the width, which may be twice the height when the plant is mature.

In early June the white, ¾"-diameter bells, which are the flowers, appear, hanging conspicuously from the undersides of the branches, underneath the dark green leaves that are on the upper sides of the same branches.

This species prefers a moist but well-drained soil in partial shade in a protected place. It is prettiest when planted so that one can look upward into the flowers.

Styrax obassia
(Fragrant snowbell)
Zone 6 to part of Zone 5; 10'–30'
Ascending branches rather than the horizontal ones of *S. japonica*, and early June-blooming fragrant, white flowers that grow erect or almost erect in clusters make this species different from the preceding one. The flowers often are hidden by the extra-large leaves. This species is said to be less hardy than *S. japonica* but I have not found it so.

SYRINGA
(Lilac)

Syringa amurensis japonica (syn S. japonica of the catalogs)
(Amur lilac, Japanese tree lilac)
Zone 5; 25'–30'
While this lilac usually is seen growing with one trunk as a small tree, it also may be grown with several stems as a large shrub. It is particularly useful in the garden because it blooms from mid-June to early July, after all the other lilacs have finished flowering.

It has creamy-white flowers in large heads or groups of clusters, to 8" or 9" in diameter, a single cluster being 6" long and 3½" across. The individual florets are only ⅛" in diameter and smell like those of privet rather than those of other lilacs.

VIBURNUM

Some of the species of this large genus grow into very large shrubs or small trees. They are therefore included in this chapter rather than in the previous chapter with the shrubs.

Viburnum lentago
(Black-haw, Nannyberry, Sheepberry, Black thorn, Nanny plum, Sheep paw, Sheep haw, Sweet berry)
Zone 2; sometimes to 30' but usually nearer to 20'
Blooming white in late May and early June, growing usually in moist woods or along the banks of streams, this is a native viburnum that is vigorous in growth. Left to itself it is a shrub, with branches first growing erect, then arching over to touch the ground, where they sometimes take root. However, it can be trained to a single stem (tree form) if so desired.

The flowers are borne in flat clusters and are followed by edible, blue-black fruits in August. Foliage is shining green, turning to purplish red in autumn. The fruits are ¼″ in diameter, in drooping clusters to 2½″ or 3″ in diameter. They will be eaten by the birds in winter if not sooner.

Viburnum prunifolium

Viburnum prunifolium
(Northern blackhaw)
Zone 4 to part of Zone 3; 15'
This grows naturally in the same types of places as *V. lentago* but adapts better than it to drier soils. It has perfect white flowers in flat clusters, 3½″ to 4″ in diameter in late May, followed by edible blue-black berries on red stalks in September to October. The leaves are dark green, turning wine red in fall. It too is normally a shrub but also may be trained to a single trunk to grow in tree form.

Viburnum sieboldii
(Siebold viburnum)
Zone 5; usually about 20', but sometimes to 30'
If it were not for the unpleasant odor of the leaves of this viburnum, given off sometimes in the fall, it could be recommended for use near a house. As it is, it should be used only at a distance and, because of its size, usually as a specimen to begin or end a border.

It has an interesting branching habit, rich green leaves to 5″ and 6″ long, turning red in autumn. Creamy white flowers borne in large, flat clusters to 5½″ in diameter in late May to early June are followed in summer by fruit clusters of the same diameter. The fruits turn progressively from brilliant yellow to dark red to blue-black, starting in late July and becoming their final color in September. The little stalks on which the individual fruits are borne are red. A cluster in the process of changing color may consist of fruits of all three colors at once and is both beautiful and interesting to see.

XANTHOCERAS

Xanthoceras sorbifolia
(Chinese flowering chestnut, Shinyleaf, Yellowhorn)
Zone 6 to part of Zone 5; 25'
This little tree is not easy to transplant, but it is worthwhile trying to grow. It likes an open loamy soil and full sun. The form is upright.

The white clusters of feathery flowers are borne in somewhat the same manner as those of wisteria vines. They appear in late April to early May just as the leaves are unfolding. The petals have blotches at their bases, first yellow, later red. The flowers are followed in August to September by green burs that look like those of horse chestnuts, but with shiny, black seeds inside instead of nuts. The leaves, which are shiny and dark green, do not change color in autumn, though they remain on the tree until late in fall.

Xanthoceras sorbifolia

14
SOME FLOWERING VINES THAT MAKE GOOD SHRUBS

Clematis 'Henryii'

The following woody vines can be pruned to create attractive shrub-like forms. This is usually done by staking the main trunk of the vine and removing all side branches emanating from the trunk. Side branches and foliage growth are allowed to billow out above the trunk. By pruning this top growth back to the trunk each year when the plant goes dormant, a small tree form, or 'standard', is created.

With vines that don't form a main trunk, but produce a dense tangle of vining stems, such as *Clematis* × *jackmanii* and *Lonicera* × *heckrottii* (the Goldflame honeysuckle), a shrubby form can be created by heavy pruning to keep the plant squat and rounded.

Polygonum aubertii (Silverlace Vine)

Campsis radicans

ria vine, producing clusters of orange-red trumpet-shaped blossoms attractive to hummingbirds. Plants have aerial roots at each branch division, allowing them to cling to any type of support with a rough surface texture, such as brick or wood. Two cultivars are widely available—'Praecox' with orange-red flowers and 'Flava' with yellow flowers. A hybrid, *Campsis × tagliabuana* 'Mme Galen', developed in France, is large-flowered and superior to the other two for flowering effect. Beware of trumpetcreeper collected from the wild and offered by some nurserymen.

Celastrus scandens
(American bittersweet)
Zones 3 to 8; 20' and more

Though this native North American woody plant is considered a nuisance in parts of New England due to its ability to seed freely and choke farmland, it is an attractive vine that produces masses of orange-red berries in autumn. The oval pointed leaves drop shortly before the fruits ripen. The flowers are small, green, inconspicuous. Plants are not fussy about soil if drainage is good, and prosper in either sun or light shade. Both male and female plants are needed for pollination. The less hardy Oriental bittersweet (*C. orbiculatus*), growing from Zones 5 to 8, is self-fertile and very similar in appearance.

Celastris scandens

Actinidia arguta
(Hardy kiwi vine)
Zones 4 to 8; 30' and more

Heart-shaped hairy green leaves almost hide the creamy white clematis-like one" flowers borne in clusters in late spring, early summer, followed by cherry-sized oval green fruits that are edible and ripen in late summer. Usually requires a male and a female to set fruit. Plants grow in a wide range of humus-rich soils in sun or partial shade. Propagated from seeds, cuttings, or layering. Good to cover walls, arbors, and chain-link fences. Similar in appearance to the New Zealand kiwi (*A. chinensis*), which is not reliably hardy above Zone 7. Another related species (*A. kolomikta*) is hardy to Zone 4, produces inconspicuous white flowers but variegated pink and green leaves. Generally needs heavy pruning to keep it within bounds.

Akebia quinata
(Fiveleaf akebia)
Zones 4 to 8; 30' or more

Small nodding, purple flowers appear in spring, almost hidden by the dense foliage cover. Leaves are composed of five leaflets splayed out like a fan on thin vines that allow the plant to climb high without adding excessive weight, in the same manner as a wisteria or a climbing hydrangea does. Good to train up posts and trellises. Prefers well-drained humus-rich soil in sun or partial shade. Propagation by division, cuttings or seeds. Can be pruned close to the ground or left to climb.

Campsis radicans
(Trumpetcreeper, Hummingbird vine)
Zones 5 to 9; 30'–40'

A fast-growing deciduous climber with compound leaves that resemble a wiste-

Clematis hybrid

Clematis hybrids
(Clematis)
Zones 4 to 8; 8'–10'
A vast number of cultivars, with different flowering times, allows gardeners to have clematis in bloom from early summer to fall frost. Color range includes red, white, blue, pink, purple, lavender, plus some sensational bicolors. Both single- and double-flowered forms are available. Plants climb by twining so need a trellis or netting for support. Best flowering occurs in a humus-rich soil with the roots in shade and the top-growth exposed to sun. Pruning varies according to variety; some aggressive growers like *Clematis* × *jackmanii* (a large-flowered purple cultivar) may require hard pruning each season to keep them within bounds; others, like 'Nelly Moser' (a pale-pink, deep-pink bicolor), may need just tip-pruning and general clean-up of tangled stems to maintain shape. Other cultivars to consider include 'Mrs. Cholmondeley' (pronounced Mrs. Chumley), with huge blue flowers up to 9" across; 'Henryii', a stunning white; and 'Ville de Lyon', bearing beautiful round-petalled carmine-red flowers in tremendous profusion. 'Duchess of Edinburgh' is a stunning double-flowered white, and 'Vivyen Pennell' an unusual double-flowered blue.

Hydrangea anomola petiolaris
(Climbing hydrangea)
Zones 4 to 7; 60' or more
Invaluable deciduous vine for covering large expanses of brick or stone. Aerial roots attach to any rough surface. The lustrous, ivy-like green leaves accentuate the beautiful white flower clusters that appear throughout summer. Plants grow slowly at first, may take several years before they show any appreciable progress. Well-grown specimens drape their leaves in layers. Prefers full sun or light shade and a fertile, humus-rich, well-drained soil. Can be trained as a tree form shrub.

Lonicera × *beckrottii*
(Goldflame honeysuckle)
Zones 5 to 8; 10'–20'
Almost always in bloom from early summer to fall frost. The twining deciduous vines like trellis for support, but can be tied up to climb posts, walls and fences. Thrives even in poor soil. Prefers full sun or light shade. By severe pruning it can be kept low, spreading and shrub-like. See other *Loniceras* in shrub section.

Polygonum aubertii
(Fleeceflower, Silverlace vine)
Zones 4 to 7; 60' or more
This rampant deciduous vine is so vigorous and capable of growing to such incredible heights it can cover a barn. The light green, delicate foliage covers thin, wiry stems that climb by twining. Likes a framework of netting or trellis for support, but also surmounts poles and snakes its way along cables and wires. Flowers the first year from cuttings. The flowers are individually quite small, pure white or sometimes tinged with a faint pink blush, but borne in a cloud-like mass. Popular for covering arbors and pergolas. Can be kept shrub-like by hard pruning.

Wisteria floribunda
(Japanese wisteria)
Zones 6 to 9; 30' and more
Heavily fragrant blue flowers form long grape-like clusters, twining their way even to the tops of tall pines. Popular for training along walls, along balustrades and over archways. Requires frequent pruning to keep it from getting out of hand. Side shoots are best pruned back to 3 or 4 shoots in summer. Prefers fertile, humus-rich moist soil in full sun. A related species, *Wisteria sinensis* (Chinese wisteria) is hardly distinguishable from Japanese wisteria except for its violet-blue color. 'Black Dragon' is an especially good cultivar of Chinese wisteria, displaying dark-purple double flowers.

CONCLUSION

Flowering shrubs, small flowering trees, flowering vines, and even flowering woody ground covers, are highly desirable long-lived plants for today's home landscapes. They stand out, don't need constant pampering, carry color high into the sky, and help establish the design of a garden more successfully than any other plants.

What could be more uplifting than a wisteria vine smothered in fragrant blue blossoms? Or a slope planted with masses of multi-colored azaleas? Or a saucer magnolia flaunting huge pink blossoms on leafless branches in early spring? Not even the most colorful border of annuals, a rainbow bed of perennials or a shimmering bulb display can steal the show from these super-flowering shrub varieties that require such little care.

When wealthy British and French plant collectors of the nineteenth and early twentieth centuries began amassing huge private plant collections (even sending plant explorers into the vast uncharted mountain ranges of India, Burma and western China), it was flowering shrubs and small flowering trees they sought so diligently. Baron Lionel de Rothschild, at his Exbury Estate in England, J. C. Williams, at Caerhays Castle, England, and Sir Edmund Loder, at Leonardslee Estate, in England, made stupendous gardens from rhododendrons, camellias, magnolias, azaleas and dove trees, collected by men like Frank Kingdon Ward and George Forrest while criss-crossing Asia.

North America, too, has been a treasury of spectacular flowering shrubs and small trees. The servicetree (*Amelanchier canadensis*), the dogwood (*Cornus florida*), the oakleaf hydrangea (*Hydrangea quercifolia*), evergreen azaleas (especially *Rhododendron canescens*) and trumpetcreepers (*Campsis radicans*) are examples of native North American plants highly prized even in European gardens. Some of the most important collecting in North America was done by Philadelphian John Bartram in the eighteenth century.

North America seems to be well on its way to becoming a great gardening continent; Americans and Canadians have the land and now the inspiration to plant beautiful gardens. Flowering shrubs—particularly hardy varieties—are being planted on a scale never seen before, with special attention paid to new varieties and unusual kinds. The age of the flowering shrub has arrived. In their enthusiasm, Isabel and Myron Zucker were a little ahead of the surge in popularity when *Flowering Shrubs* was first printed. With the new "greening of America" it is a work whose time has come.

Derek Fell

Part Five

Appendices

I · FLOWERING SHRUBS
FOR EVERY PURPOSE

II · BLOOM TIME CHART

III · WAYS OF PROPAGATING
SHRUBS AND SMALL
TREES

IV · HARDINESS ZONE MAP

V · WHERE TO BUY SHRUBS:
A SOURCE GUIDE

I.
FLOWERING SHRUBS FOR EVERY PURPOSE

SHRUBS THAT EVENTUALLY GROW TALLER THAN 10 FEET

*Asterisk denotes a vine needing support

*Actinidia arguta
*Akebia quinata
 Amelanchier alnifolia
 Amorpha fruticosa
 Aralia spinosa
 Buddleia alternifolia
 Buxus sempervirens
*Campsis radicans
*Celastrus scandens
*Clematis hybrids
 Cornus sanguinea
 Corylus avellana
 Cotinus coggygria
 Cotinus coggygria 'Purpureus'
 Cotoneaster acutifolia
 Euonymus yedoensis
 Fontanesia fortunei
 Hamamelis japonica
 Hamamelis mollis
 Hamamelis virginiana
*Hydrangea anomola
 Hydrangea paniculata
 Hydrangea paniculata 'Grandiflora'
 Ilex opaca
 Ilex pedunculosa
 Ilex verticillata
 Kolkwitzia amabilis
 Ligustrum amurense
 Ligustrum ovalifolium
 Ligustrum vulgare
*Lonicera x becklerottii
 Lonicera korolkowii
 Lonicera maackii
*Polygonum anbertii
 Prunus triloba
 Pyracantha coccinea
 Pyracantha coccinea 'Lalandei'
 Rhododendron arborescens
 Rhododendron maximum
 Rhododendron schlippenbachii
 Rhus typhina
 Rosa multiflora
 Rosa setigera
 Salix discolor
 Sambucus canadensis
 Sambucus racemosa
 Syringa chinensis
 Syringa chinensis 'Saugeana'
 Syringa josikaea
 Syringa reflexa
 Syringa vulgaris
 Tamarix gallica

Tamarix parviflora
Tamarix pentandra
Viburnum americanum
Viburnum cassinoides
Viburnum dentatum
Viburnum lantana
Viburnum molle
Viburnum opulus
Viburnum opulus 'Roseum'
Viburnum prunifolium
Viburnum sargentii
Viburnum setigerum
Viburnum sieboldii
Viburnum trilobum
*Wisteria floribunda
plus all the small trees described in Chapter 13

SHRUBS THAT RANGE IN HEIGHT FROM 6 TO 10 FEET AT MATURITY

Aesculus parviflora
Berberis mentorensis
Berberis thunbergii
Buddleia davidii and cultivars
Buxus sempervirens
Buxus sempervirens 'Suffruticosa'
Clethra alnifolia
Cornus alba
Cornus amomum
Cornus 'Argenteo-marginata'
Cornus racemosa
Cornus 'Sibirica'
Cornus stolonifera
Cornus stolonifera baileyi
Corylus americana
Cotoneaster divaricata
Cotoneaster foveolata
Cotoneaster multiflora
Cotoneaster multiflora calocarpa
Cotoneaster racemiflora soongorica
Deutzia scabra
Deutzia scabra plena
Deutzia scabra 'Pride of Rochester'
Enkianthus campanulatus
Euonymus alata
Euonymus kiautschovica
Euonymus sachalinensis
Exochorda giraldii wilsonii
Exochorda racemosa
Forsythia 'Beatrix Farrand'
Forsythia intermedia
Forsythia intermedia 'Spectabilis'
Forsythia ovata
Forsythia suspensa
Forsythia suspensa fortunei

Forsythia viridissima
Fothergilla major
Hamemelis vernalis
Hibiscus syriacus
Hydrangea arborescens
Hydrangea quercifolia
Ilex glabra
Ilex serrata
Ligustrum ibolium
Ligustrum obtusifolium
Lonicera bella 'Candida'
Lonicera fragrantissima
Lonicera maackii podocarpa
Lonicera morrowii
Lonicera tatarica and varieties
Magnolia liliflora 'Nigra'
Malus sargentii
Myrica pensylvanica
Philadelphus coronarius
Philadelphus grandiflorus
Prunus besseyi
Prunus cistena
Prunus tomentosa
Rhododendron arborescens
Rhododendron calendulaceum
Rhododendron catawbiense
Rhododendron grandavense
Rhododendron kaempferi
Rhododendron mucronatum
Rhododendron obtusum arnoldianum
Rhododendron vaseyi
Rhododendron viscosum
Rhus glabra
Ribes odoratum
Rosa alba
Rosa eglanteria
Rosa foetida
Rosa foetida 'Persian Yellow'
Rosa glauca
Rosa harisonii
Rosa moyesii
Rosa rugosa
Rosa virginiana
Rubus odoratus
Salix gracilistyla
Salix purpurea
Spiraea billiardii
Spiraea macrothyrsa
Spiraea prunifolia
Spiraea trichocarpa
Spiraea vanhouttei
Syringa laciniata
Syringa microphylla
Syringa persica
Syringa persica 'Alba'
Syringa prestoniae

Syringa pubescens
Syringa swegiflexa
Syringa villosa
Tamarix odessana
Vaccinium corymbosum
Virburnum acerifolium
Virburnum bitchiuense
Virburnum bodnantense
Virburnum burkwoodii
Virburnum burkwoodii 'Chenault'
Virburnum carlcephalum
Virburnum dilatatum
Virburnum fragrans
Virburnum judii
Virburnum plicatum
Virburnum plicatum tomentosum
Virburnum rhytidophylloides
Virburnum rhytidophyllum
Virburnum wrightii
Weigela floribunda
Weigela florida
Weigela 'Vanicek'

SHRUBS THAT GROW 3 TO 6 FEET IN HEIGHT WHEN AT MATURITY

Abelia grandiflora
Aronia arbutifolia
Aronia arbutifolia 'Brilliantissima'
Berberis julianae
Berberis koreana
Berberis thunbergii 'Atropurpurea'
Berberis thunbergii 'Erecta'
Berberis verruculosa
Buddleia farquhari
Buxus microphylla
Buxus microphylla koreana
Callicarpa dichotoma
Callicarpa japonica
Calycanthus floridus
Caryopteris incana
Chaenomeles japonica
Clethra alnifolia
Clethra alnifolia 'Rosea'
Cornus stolonifera coloradensis
Cornus stolonifera 'Flaviramea'
Cotoneaster apiculata
Cotoneaster bullata floribunda
Cotoneaster dielsiana
Cotoneaster divaricata
Cotoneaster integerrima
Cytisus praecox
Cytisus scoparius
Daphne 'Somerset'
Deutzia gracilis
Deutzia lemoinei
Deutzia rosea
Deutzia rosea 'Pink Pompon'
Euonymus alata 'Compacta'
Euonymus americana
Euonymus fortunei 'Vegeta'
Euonymus nana turkestanica
Exochorda macrantha 'The Bride'
Forsythia suspensa sieboldii
Fothergilla monticola
Hypericum frondosum

Hypericum prolificum
Kalmia latifolia
Kerria japonica
Kerria japonica 'Pleniflora'
Leucothoë fontanesiana
Ligustrum obtusifolium regelianum
Lonicera korolkowii 'Zabelii'
Lonicera xylosteoides 'Clavey's Dwarf'
Mahonia aquifolium
Paeonia suffruticosa
Philadelphus coronarius 'Aureus'
Philadelphus lemoinei
Philadelphus virginalis
Pieris floribunda
Potentilla fruticosa
Potentilla parvifolia
Prunus besseyi
Prunus glandulosa and varieties
Prunus laurocerasus 'Schipkaensis'
Prunus maritima
Prunus tenella
Rhododendron carolianum
Rhododendron carolianum album
Rhododendron kosterianum
Rhododendron molle
Rhododendron mucronulatum
Rhododendron nudiflorum
Rhododendron obtusum 'Amoenum'
Rhododendron roseum
Rhododendron yedoense
Rhodotypos scandens
Rhus copallina
Rhus trilobata
Ribes alpinum
Ribes aureum
Ribes diacanthum
Rosa blanda
Rosa hugonis
Rosa pimpinellifolia
Salix purpurea 'Gracilis'
Spiraea arguta
Spiraea bumalda 'Froebelii'
Spiraea gemmata
Spiraea japonica 'Atrosanguinea'
Spiraea multiflora
Spiraea thunbergii
Spiraea tomentosa
Spiraea trilobata
Symphoricarpos albus laevigatus
Symphoricarpos orbiculatus
Syringa velutina
Tamarix hispida
Viburnum carlesii
Vitex agnus-castus 'Latifolia'
Weigela florida 'Alba'
Weigela florida 'Variegata'

SHRUBS THAT REACH 3 FEET OR LESS AT MATURITY

Amelanchier stolonifera
Aronia melanocarpa
Berberis candidula
Berberis julianae 'Nana'
Berberis thunbergii 'Atropurpurea Nana'
Berberis thunbergii minor

Buxus microphylla 'Compacta'
Buxus sempervirens 'Grand Rapids'
Buxus sempervirens 'Inglis'
Buxus sempervirens 'Suffruticosa'
Buxus sempervirens 'Vardar Valley'
Buxus sempervirens 'Welleri'
Calluna vulgaris
Caragana pygmaea
Caryopteris clandonensis
Ceanothus americanus
Chaenomeles japonica alpina
Cornus stolonifera 'Kelsey'
Corylopsis pauciflora
Cotoneaster adpressa
Cotoneaster adpressa praecox
Cotoneaster dammeri
Cotoneaster horizontalis
Cotoneaster horizontalis perpusilla
Cotoneaster microphylla
Cytisus battandieri
Daphne cneorum
Daphne mezereum
Deutzia kalmiaeflora
Deutzia lemoinei 'Compacta'
Erica carnea
Erica vagans
Euonymus alata 'Gracilis'
Forsythia intermedia 'Arnold Dwarf'
Forsythia viridissima 'Bronxensis'
Genista tinctoria
Hydrangea arborescens grandiflora
Hydrangea macrophylla and cultivars
Hypericum calycinum
Hypericum kalmianum
Hypericum moserianum
Ilex crenata 'Compacta'
Ilex crenata 'Convexa'
Ilex crenata 'Helleri'
Ilex crenata 'Hetzi'
Ilex crenata 'Microphylla'
Ilex crenata 'Repandens'
Ilex crenata 'Stokes'
Ilex glabra 'Compacta'
Kerria japonica 'Picta'
Lavandula officinalis
Leucothoë fontanesiana
Leucothoë fontanesiana 'Girard's Rainbow'
Ligustrum vicaryi
Mahonia bealii
Mahonia repens
Pieris japonica 'Compacta'
Pieris japonica 'Variegata'
Potentilla davurica
Potentilla davurica 'Veitchii'
Potentilla parvifolia 'Farreri'
Rhododendron canadense
Rhododendron yedoense poukhanense
Rosa nitida
Rosa wichuraiana
Spiraea albiflora
Spiraea arguta compacta
Spiraea bumalda 'Anthony Waterer'
Spiraea bumalda 'Crispa'
Symphoricarpos chenaultii
Symphoricarpos chenaultii 'Hancock'
Viburnum carlesii 'Compactum'
Viburnum opulus 'Nanum'
Xanthorhiza simplicissima

BRANCHES GROW UPRIGHT, THEN ARCH OR DROOP

Buddleia alternifolia
Cornus florida 'Pendula'
Cotoneaster dielsiana
Cotoneaster divaricata
Cotoneaster multiflora
Cotoneaster multiflora calocarpa
Cotoneaster racemiflora soongorica
Euonymus alata 'Gracilis'
Forsythia suspensa
Forsythia suspensa fortunei
Forsythia suspensa sieboldii
Forsythia viridissima
Leucothoë fontanesiana
Pieris japonica
Rosa multiflora
Rosa setigera
Spiraea arguta
Spiraea thunbergii
Spiraea trilobata
Spiraea vanhouttei
Symphoricarpos albus laevigatus
Syringa microphylla
Weigela florida

BRANCH HORIZONTALLY

Cotoneaster horizontalis
Crataegus (many)
Euonymus alata
Euonymus alata 'Compacta'
Ligustrum obtusifolium regelianum
Prunus laurocerasus 'Schipkaensis'
Viburnum plicatum 'Mariesii'
Viburnum plicatum tomentosum
Viburnum prunifolium

VARIEGATED OR COLORED LEAVES

•Yellow
Corylus avellana 'Aurea'
Ligustrum vicaryi
Philadelphus coronarius 'Aureus'
Sambucus canadensis 'Aurea'
Sambucus racemosa 'Plumosa aurea'
Xanthorhiza simplicissima

•Purplish-red
Acer palmatum 'Atropurpureum'
Berberis thunbergii 'Atropurpurea'
Berberis thunbergii 'Atropurpurea Nana'
Corylus avellana 'Fusco-rubra'
Corylus maxima 'Purpurea'
Cotinus coggygria 'Purpureus'
Erica carnea 'Vivellii'
Prunus cistena
Rosa glauca

•Gray or Gray-green
Amorpha fruticosa
Buddleia alternifolia
Caryopteris clandonensis
Cotoneaster racemiflora soongorica
Cytisus battandieri

Daphne cneorum
Elaeagnus angustifolia
Lavandula officinalis
Lonicera bella 'Candida'
Myrica pensylvanica
Viburnum lantana
Vitex (several species)

•Blue-green
Lonicera korolkowii
Lonicera korolkowii 'Zabelii'
Mahonia bealii
Mahonia repens
Tamarix gallica
Tamarix hispida
Viburnum bitchiuense

•Red turning Green or Greenish
Acer palmatum 'Ornatum'

•Variegated Green and White
Cornus alba 'Argenteo-marginata'
Kerria japonica 'Picta'
Pieris japonica 'Variegata'

•Variegated Green and Yellow
Cornus alba 'Spaethii'
Weigela florida 'Variegata'

•Variegated Green, White and Pink
Cornus alba 'Gouchaultii'
Cornus florida 'Welchii'
Leucothoë fontanesiana 'Girard's Rainbow'

COLORED BARK, TWIGS OR STEMS IN WINTER

•Gray
Buddleia alternifolia
Clethra alnifolia
Cornus racemosa
Ilex verticillata
Lonicera morrowii
Lonicera tatarica
Viburnum opulus
Viburnum sargentii
Viburnum trilobum

•Yellow
Cornus stolonifera 'Flaviramea'

•Green
Cytisus scoparius
Forsythia viridissima
Kerria japonica

•Purple
Cornus alba 'Kesselringii'

•Red
Acer palmatum
Cornus alba
Cornus alba 'Sibirica'
Cornus amomum
Cornus florida
Cornus sanguinea
Cornus stolonifera
Cornus stolonifera baileyi
Cornus stolonifera coloradensis
Cornus stolonifera 'Kelsey'
Rosa nitida
Rosa virginiana

BEAUTIFUL AUTUMN FOLIAGE

•Purple or Purplish
Berberis verruculosa
Cornus amomum
Cornus racemosa
Cotoneaster apiculata
Cotoneaster horizontalis
Forsythia intermedia
Forsythia viridissima
Hydrangea quercifolia
Ligustrum obtusifolium
Ligustrum obtusifolium regelianum
Mahonia aquifolium
Mahonia repens
Prunus maritima
Rhododendron roseum
Rhododendron yedoense
Symphoricarpus chenaultii
Viburnum acerifolium
Viburnum carlesii
Viburnum dilatatum
Viburnum lentago
Viburnum molle
Viburnum plicatum

•Bronze
Abelia grandiflora
Buxus microphylla koreana
Euonymus nana turkestanica
Leucothoë fontanesiana

•Red and Yellow
Berberis mentorensis
Cotinus coggygria
Franklinia alatamaha
Rosa rugosa
Rosa virginiana
Viburnum setigerum

GROW IN SHADY PLACES
(not necessarily deep shade)

Full (or complete) shade—that found under low-branching trees or under evergreens. Practically no shrubs will grow in this type of shade.

Dense (or deep) shade—that found in fairly dense woods where spring wildflowers bloom but there is little but foliage covering the ground during summer.

Semi- (or half) shade—that found in shade of buildings, trees, or large shrubs that cast a shadow for about half the day, allowing full exposure to sun the rest of the day. Because of half-time sun and half-time shade, it is difficult to find shrubs to grow in this type of shade.

Light shade—that found under high-branched trees that allow filtered sunlight to reach plants. The perfect type of shade for shade-loving shrubs and trees.

Abelia grandiflora
Actinidia arguta
Akebia quinata
Amelanchier species
Aronia arbutifolia and other species
Berberis julianae
Berberis thunbergii
Berberis verruculosa
Buxus (most species)
Calycanthus floridus
Ceanothus americanus
Cercis canadensis
Cercis chinensis
Chionanthus virginicus
Clematis hybrids
Clethra alnifolia
Clethra alnifolia 'Rosea'
Cornus alba
Cornus amomum
Cornus mas
Cornus racemosa
Cornus stolonifera
Corylus americana and other species
Daphne mezereum
Enkianthus campanulatus
Euonymus americana
Euonymus kiautschovica
Fothergilla (all species)
Hamamelis virginiana
*Hydrangea quercifolia
Hypericum calycinum
Hypericum frondosum
Hypericum prolificum
Ilex glabra
Ilex verticillata
Kalmia latifolia
Leucothoë fontanesiana
*Ligustrum obtusifolium regelianum
Ligustrum vulgare
Lonicera (many species)
Mahonia aquifolium
Mahonia bealii
Mahonia repens
Philadelphus coronarius
Pieris floribunda
Pieris japonica
Rhamnus cathartica
Rhododendron
Rhododendron calendulaceum
Rhododendron catawbiense

•Pink, Red, Scarlet or Crimson
Acer ginnala
Acer palmatum
Aralia spinosa
Aronia arbutifolia
Aronia arbutifolia 'Brilliantissima'
Aronia melanocarpa
Berberis koreana
Berberis mentorensis
Berberis thunbergii
Berberis thunbergii 'Erecta'
Berberis thunbergii minor
Chaenomeles speciosa
Cornus alba
Cornus alba 'Sibirica'
Cornus amomum
Cornus florida

Cornus kousa
Cornus mas
Cornus sanguinea
Cornus stolonifera
Cotinus coggygria
Cotoneaster adpressa
Cotoneaster dielsiana
Cotoneaster divaricata
Cotoneaster foveolata
Cotoneaster horizontalis
Crataegus crus-galli
Crataegus lavallei
Crataegus oxyacantha
Crataegus oxyacantha 'Paul's Scarlet'
Crataegus phaenopyrum
Enkianthus campanulatus
Euonymus alata
Euonymus alata 'Compacta'
Euonymus atropurpurea
Euonymus europaea
Euonymus yedoensis
Oxydendrum arboreum
Rhododendron arborescens
Rhododendron mucronulatum
Rhododendron schlippenbachii
Rhododendron vaseyi
Rhus aromatica
Rhus copallina
Rhus glabra
Rhus typhina
Ribes alpinum
Ribes aureum
Ribes odoratum
Rosa nitida
Rosa setigera
Rubus odoratus
Spiraea prunifolia
Syringa microphylla
Vaccinium corymbosum
Viburnum bitchiuense
Viburnum burkwoodii
Viburnum carlcephalum
Viburnum cassinoides
Viburnum dentatum
Viburnum fragrans
Viburnum lantana
Viburnum opulus
Viburnum plicatum tomentosum
Viburnum prunifolium
Viburnum trilobum
Viburnum wrightii

•Yellow and/or Orange
Aesculus parviflora
Amelanchiers (various)
Callicarpa japonica (and others)
Cercis canadensis
Cercis chinensis
Chionanthus retusus
Chionanthus virginicus
Clethra alnifolia
Clethra alnifolia 'Rosea'
Fothergilla (all species)
Halesia carolina
Hamamelis mollis
Hamemelis vernalis
Hamemelis virginiana
Hypericum calycinum and other species

Kerria japonica
Koelreuteria paniculata
Rhododendron calendulaceum
Sambucus canadensis
Spiraea thunbergii
Rhododendron gandavense
Rhododendron kaempferi
Rhododendron maximum
Rhododendron nudiflorum
Rhodotypos scandens
Ribes alpinum
Ribes odoratum
Rubus odoratus
Staphylea trifolia
Styrax species
Symphoricarpos albus laevigatus
Symphoricarpos orbiculatus
Vaccinium species
Viburnum acerifolium
Viburnum cassinoides
Viburnum dentatum
Viburnum lantana
Viburnum lentago
Viburnum plicatum tomentosum
Viburnum prunifolium
Viburnum sieboldii
Weigela (most)
Xanthorhiza simplicissima
*will grow in deep shade—if you cannot grow these, no shrub will grow

THRIVE IN MOIST SITUATION

Amelanchier species
Aronia arbutifolia
Calycanthus floridus
Clethra alnifolia
Clethra alnifolia 'Rosea'
Comptonia peregrina
Cornus alba
Cornus amomum
Cornus sanguinea
Cornus stolonifera
Cornus stolonifera baileyi
Hamamelis, many species
Ilex glabra
Ilex verticillata
Kalmia latifolia
Leucothoë fontanesiana
Rhododendron arborescens
Rhododendron canadense
Rhododendron nudiflorum
Rhododendron vaseyi
Rhododendron viscosum
Salix caprea
Salix discolor and other willows
Sambucus canadensis
Spiraea tomentosa
Staphylea trifolia
Vaccinium corymbosum
Viburnum acerifolium
Viburnum cassinoides
Viburnum dentatum
Viburnum lentago
Viburnum opulus
Viburnum sieboldii
Viburnum trilobum

THRIVE IN DRY SITUATION AND/OR SANDY SOIL

Acer ginnala
Amelanchier stolonifera
Amorpha fruticosa
Aralia spinosa
Berberis mentorensis
Berberis thunbergii
Buddleia alternifolia
Caragana aborescens
Ceanothus americanus
Chaenomeles speciosa
Cornus racemosa
Coronilla eremurus
Cotinus coggygria
Cytisus species
Deutzia scabra
Elaeagnus angustifolia
Genista species
Kolkwitzia amabilis
Lavandula species
Ligustrum obtusifolium regelianum and other
  privets
Lonicera morrowii
Myrica pensylvanica
Philadelphus coronarius
Potentilla fruticosa
Prunus besseyi
Prunus maritima
Rhodotypos scandens
Rhus aromatica
Rhus copallina
Rhus glabra
Rhus trilobata
Rhus typhina
Ribes alpinum
Ribes odoratum
Robinia hispida
Rosa multiflora
Rosa nitida
Rosa pimpinellifolia
Rosa rugosa
Rosa setigera
Rosa virginiana
Symphoricarpos species
Tamarix gallica
Tamarix parviflora
Viburnum lantana
Viburnum lentago
Vitex agnus-castus 'Latifolia'

THRIVE UNDER SEASHORE CONDITIONS

Aronia arbutifolia
Calluna vulgaris
Clethra alnifolia
Clethra alnifolia 'Rosea'
Comptonia peregrina
Cornus stolonifera
Cornus stolonifera baileyi
Cotoneaster acutifolia
Cotoneaster adpressa
Cotoneaster apiculata
Cotoneaster dielsiana
Cotoneaster divaricata
Cotoneaster foveolata
Cotoneaster multiflora
Cytisus scoparius
Elaeagnus angustifolia
Hibiscus syriacus
Hydrangea (all species)
Ilex glabra
Lavandula (all species)
Ligustrum amurense
Ligustrum ovalifolium
Lonicera morrowii
Lonicera tatarica
Myrica pensylvanica
Potentilla fruticosa
Prunus maritima
Ribes (many species)
Rosa blanda
Rosa eglanteria
Rosa multiflora
Rosa pimpinellifolia
Rosa rugosa
Rosa virginiana
Sambucus canadensis
Spiraea (many species)
Syringa vulgaris
Tamarix (all species)
Vaccinium corymbosum
Viburnum cassinoides
Viburnum dentatum

THRIVE UNDER CITY CONDITIONS

Acer ginnala
Aesculus parviflora
Amelanchier laevis
Amorpha fruticosa
Aralia spinosa
Aronia arbutifolia
Berberis thunbergii
Buxus microphylla koreana
Campsis radicans
Cercis canadensis
Chaenomeles japonica
Chionanthus virginicus
Cornus alba 'Sibirica'
Cornus amomum
Cornus mas
Cornus officinalis
Cornus racemosa
Cornus sanguinea
Cornus stolonifera 'Flaviramea'
Cotinus coggygria
Cotoneaster acutifolia
Crataegus crus-galli
Crataegus intricata
Crataegus mollis
Crataegus oxyacantha
Crataegus phaenopyrum
Deutzia scabra
Elaeagnus angustifolia
Euonymus alata
Euonymus alata 'Compacta'
Euonymus europaea
Forsythia intermedia 'Spectabilis'
Forsythia ovata
Forsythia suspensa
Forsythia suspensa fortunei

Hamamelis (several species)
Hibiscus syriacus
Hydrangea arborescens
Hydrangea paniculata
Hypericum frondosum
Ilex crenata
Kalmia latifolia
Kerria japonica
Leucothoë fontanesiana
Ligustrum amurense
Ligustrum obtusifolium regelianum
Ligustrum vulgare
Lonicera becklerottii
Lonicera fragrantissima
Lonicera tatarica
Magnolia soulangiana
Magnolia stellata
Mahonia aquifolium
Malus sargentii
Myrica pensylvanica
Philadelphus coronarius
Philadelphus virginalis
Pieris japonica
Potentilla fruticosa
Prunus subhirtella
Prunus tomentosa
Pyracantha coccinea 'Lalandei'
Rhododendron calendulaceum
Rhododendron carolinianum
Rhododendron catawbiense
Rhododendron mucronulatum
Rhododendron obtusum 'Amoenum'
Rhodotypos scandens
Rhus aromatica
Rhus glabra
Rhus typhina
Ribes alpinum
Ribes odoratum
Rosa multiflora
Rosa rugosa
Rosa wichuraiana
Sambucus canadensis
Spiraea bumalda 'Anthony Waterer'
Spiraea vanhouttei
Symphoricarpos chenaultii
Syringa amurensis japonica
Syringa villosa
Syringa vulgaris
Tamarix parviflora
Viburnum burkwoodii
Viburnum carlesii
Viburnum dentatum
Viburnum lantana
Viburnum lentago
Viburnum opulus
Viburnum plicatum
Viburnum plicatum tomentosum
Viburnum prunifolium
Viburnum trilobum
Vitex agnus-castus 'Latifolia'
Weigela florida

FOR HEDGES

*Abelia grandiflora
*Acer ginnala
*Berberis (several, see text)
Calycanthus floridus

*Chaenomeles japonica
*Chaenomeles speciosa
*Cornus mas
*Cornus racemosa
 Cornus stolonifera 'Kelsey'
 Corylus avellana
*Cotoneaster acutifolia
*Cotoneaster apiculata
*Crataegus (many, see text)
*Deutzia gracilis
*Deutzia lemoinei
*Deutzia rosea
*Elaeagnus angustifolia
*Euonymus alata
*Euonymus alata 'Compacta'
*Euonymus europaea
*Euonymus fortunei 'Vegeta'
*Euonymus kiautschovicus
*Fontanesia fortunei
*Forsythia intermedia
 Hamamelis mollis
 Hamamelis virginiana
*Hibiscus syriacus
 Hydrangea arborescens grandiflora
 Hydrangea paniculata
*Ilex (several, see text)
 Kolkwitzia amabilis
*Lavandula officinalis
*Ligustrum (many, see text)
*Lonicera (many, see text)
*Malus sargentii
*Myrica pensylvanica
 Philadelphus (several, see text)
*Rhodotypos scandens
*Ribes alpinum
*Ribes diacanthum
*Ribes odoratum
 Rosa blanda
 Rosa harisonii
*Rosa hugonis
*Rosa rugosa
 Rosa virginiana
 Salix purpurea 'Gracilis'
*Spiraea arguta
*Spiraea arguta compacta
 Spiraea bumalda 'Anthony Waterer'
 Spiraea bumalda 'Froebelii'
*Spiraea prunifolium
 Spiraea thunbergii
 Spiraea vanhouttei
*Symphoricarpos (several, see text)
*Syringa chinensis
*Syringa prestoniae
 Syringa pubescens
*Syringa villosa
*Syringa vulgaris
 Tamarix pentandra
 Vaccinium corymbosum
 Viburnum cassinoides
 Viburnum dilatatum
 Viburnum lantana
 Viburnum opulus
 Viburnum opulus 'Nanum'
 Viburnum plicatum tomentosum
 Viburnum prunifolium
 Viburnum sieboldii

*will tolerate clipping

FOR THORNY HEDGE

Berberis species
Chaenomeles species
Crataegus species
Rosa species (see text)
Malus sargentii
Rubus, all species

FRUITS ONLY WITH MALE AND FEMALE PLANTS

Actinidia arguta
Celastrus scandens
Cotinus
Ilex
Myrica
Rhus
Ribes

MOVE IN SPRING

Buddleia
Calycanthus
Cornus florida, its varieties and cultivars
Crataegus
Hibiscus syriacus and its cultivars
Kalmia latifolia
Magnolia
Rhododendron (including azalea)
Rhus
Tamarix

MUST HAVE ACID SOIL

Amelanchier
Calluna
Clethra
Cytisus
Enkianthus
Erica
Fothergilla
Ilex
Kalmia
Leucothoë
Magnolia virginiana
Myrica pensylvanica
Rhododendron (including most azaleas)
Vaccinium
Xanthorhiza simplicissima

EASY MAINTENANCE

Aronia arbutifolia
Berberis thunbergii
Campsis radicans
Celastrus scandens
*Clethra alnifolia
*Clethra alnifolia 'Rosea'
 Corylus americana
 Deutzia gracilis
 Deutzia rosea
 Elaeagnus angustifolia
 Forsythia intermedia
 Forsythia suspensa fortunei
 Hamamelis (all species)

Hypericum frondosum
Hypericum prolificum
*Ilex glabra
*Ilex verticillata
*Kalmia latifolia
 Ligustrum vulgare
 Lonicera (all species)
*Myrica pensylvanica
 Polygonum aubertii
 Potentilla fruticosa
*Rhododendron calendulaceum
*Rhododendron canadense
*Rhododendron carolinianum
*Rhododendron kaempferi
*Rhododendron maximum
*Rhododendron nudiflorum
*Rhododendron vaseyi
 Rhododendron viscosum
 Rhus (all species)
 Ribes (all species)
 Robinia hispida
 Rosa blanda
 Rosa glauca
 Rosa nitida
 Rosa virginiana
 Viburnum acerifolium
 Viburnum cassinoides
 Viburnum dentatum
 Viburnum lantana
 Viburnum lentago
*assuming soil is acid or is made acid

USE TO HOLD BANKS

Amelanchier stolonifera
Ceanothus americanus
Clethra alnifolia
Clethra alnifolia 'Rosea'
Cornus alba
Cornus amomum
Cornus stolonifera
Cotoneaster horizontalis
Cytisus scoparius
Forsythia intermedia 'Arnold Dwarf'
Forsythia suspensa
Forsythia suspensa sieboldii
Hypericum calycinum
Rhus aromatica
Rhus copallina
Robinia hispida
Rosa multiflora
Rosa rugosa
Rosa setigera
Rosa virginiana
Rosa wichuraiana
Rubus odoratus
Symphoricarpos (several, see text)
Xanthorhiza simplicissima

FOR GROUND COVERS

Aronia melanocarpa
Calluna vulgaris
Cotoneaster adpressa
Cotoneaster adpressa praecox
Cotoneaster horizontalis
Cotoneaster microphylla

Forsythia intermedia 'Arnold Dwarf'
Hypericum calycinum
Rhus aromatica
Xanthorhiza simplicissma

FOR ESPALIERING OR TRAINING AGAINST FENCE OR WALL

Actinidia arguta
Akebia quinata
Campsis radicans
Celastrus scandens
Chaenomeles japonica
Cotoneaster horizontalis
Cotoneaster horizontalis perpusilla
Forsythia suspensa
Forsythia suspensa sieboldii
Hydrangea anomola
Polygonum aubertii
Pyracantha coccinea 'Lalandei'
Wisteria floribunda

FRUITS RELISHED BY BIRDS

Amelanchier
Aralia spinosa
Aronia
Berberis
Chionanthus

Cornus
Cotoneaster
Crataegus
Elaeagnus
Euonymus fortunei 'Vegeta'
Ilex
Ligustrum
Lonicera
Malus
Myrica
Prunus
Pyracantha
Rhus
Ribes
Rosa
Rubus
Sambucus
Sorbus
Vaccinium
Viburnum

Viburnum molle
Viburnum prunifolium
Wisteria floribunda

FEW OR NO PESTS

Amorpha fruticosa
Buxus sempervirens
Calluna vulgaris
Clethra alnifolia

Clethra alnifolia 'Rosea'
Coronilla eremurus
Corylus avellana
Elaeagnus angustifolia
Enkianthus campanulatus
Forsythia (all species)
Fothergilla (all species)
Hamamelis (all species)
Hypericum (all species)
Ilex crenata
Ilex glabra
Ilex verticillata
Kalmia latifolia
Kerria japonica
Koelreuteria paniculata
Ligustrum vulgare
Lonicera fragrantissima
Lonicera korolkowii
Lonicera maackii
Lonicera morrowii
Lonicera tatarica
Magnolia stellata
Philadelphus (all species)
Pieris (all species)
Rhododendron (many)
Rhodotypos scandens
Rhus (all species)
Spiraea (all species)
Tamarix (all species)
Viburnum (all species except V. opulus 'Roseum')
Xanthorhiza simplicissima

II.
BLOOM TIME CHART

KEY

☐ Flowering Period   ☐ Fruiting Period

Fruit and Flower Color Abbreviations

Examples: B/BK = Blue with Black   C, RD & S = Cream, Red & Scarlet
P-PK = Purplish Pink   RD to BK = Red changing to Black

A = Apricot
B = Blue
BD RD = Blood Red
BK = Black
BN = Brown
C = Cream
CN = Crimson
DP PK = Deep Pink

DP R = Deep Rose
DP RD = Deep Red
G = Green
GLD = Gold
GRY = Gray
L = Lavender
LC = Lilac
M = Magenta

O = Orange
P = Purple
P/OE = Purple with Orange Eye
Pale PK = Pale Pink
PK = Pink
R = Rose
RD = Red
S = Scarlet

SN = Salmon
T = Tan
V = Violet
VS = Various
W = White
Y = Yellow

BLOOM TIME CHART SHRUBS	JANUARY	FEBRUARY	MARCH	APRIL	MAY	JUNE	JULY	AUGUST	SEPTEMBER	OCTOBER	NOVEMBER	DECEMBER	FLOWER COLOR	FRUIT COLOR
ABELIA														
A. 'Edward Goucher'							▓	▓	▓				PK	
A. × grandiflora							▓	▓	▓				PK	
A. × grandiflora 'Prostrata'							▓	▓	▓				PK	
AESCULUS														
A. parviflora								▓					W	T
A. pavia					▓								R	
ALTHEA (see HIBISCUS)														
AMELANCHIER														
A. alnifolia					▓								W	B-BK
A. stolonifera					▓								W	BK
AMORPHA														
A. fruticosa							▓						V, P	
ARALIA														
A. spinosa								▓	▓				W	BK
ARONIA														
A. arbutifolia	▓	▓			▓				▓	▓	▓		W	RD
A. melanocarpa					▓				▓	▓			W	P, B
AZALEA (RHODODENDRON)														
R. arborescens						▓							W	
R. calendulaceum					▓								Y, S, C	
R. canadense					▓								R, P	
Exbury hybrids						▓							Y, S, C	
Gable hybrids						▓							VS	
R. × gandavense						▓							VS	
Girard hybrids						▓							VS	
Glenn Dale hybrids						▓							VS	
R. kaempferi						▓							SN, O, RD	
Kaempferi hybrids						▓							VS	
Knap Hill hybrids						▓							VS	
R. × kosterianum						▓							VS	
Linwood hybrids					▓								VS	
R. molle				▓									Y	
R. mucronulatum				▓									L	
North Tisbury hybrids							▓						VS	
R. nudiflorum					▓								PK or W	
R. obtusum 'Amoenum'					▓								M	
R. obtusum × arnoldianum				▓									P, PK	
Robin Hill hybrids				▓									VS	
R. roseum				▓									W, R, DP PK	
R. schlippenbachii					▓								P-PK or W	
Southern Indian hybrids				▓									VS	
R. vaseyi					▓								W or P-PK	
R. viscosum							▓						W	

BLOOM TIME CHART
SHRUBS

	JAN	FEB	MAR	APR	MAY	JUN	JUL	AUG	SEP	OCT	NOV	DEC	FLOWER COLOR	FRUIT COLOR
R. yedoense					X								R, P	
R. yedoense poukhanense					X	X							RD-P	
BERBERIS														
B. julianae					X				X				Y	
B. koreana					X					X			Y	RD
B. thunbergii	X				X					X			Y	S, RD
B. thunbergii 'Atropurpurea'	X				X					X			Y	S, RD
B. thunbergii 'Atropurpurea Nana'	X				X					X			Y	S, RD
B. thunbergii 'Rose Glow'	X				X					X			Y	S, RD
B. thunbergii 'Sheridan Red'	X				X					X			Y	S, RD
B. verruculosa					X					X			Y	S, RD
BUDDLEIA														
B. alternifolia						X							L	
B. davidii							X	X	X				P/OE	
B. davidii magnifica								X	X				P/OE	
B. × farqubari							X						L	
BUXUS														
B. microphylla													Flowers are inconspicuous	
B. microphylla 'Compacta'														
B. microphylla koreana														
B. sempervirens														
B. sempervirens 'Newport Blue'														
B. sempervirens 'Suffruticosa'														
B. sempervirens 'Vardar Valley'														
CALLICARPA														
C. dichotoma							X		X				P	L to P
C. japonica							X		X				P	P
CALLUNA														
C. vulgaris							X						R, P	
CALYCANTHUS														
C. floridus					X	X							RD, BN	
CARAGANA														
C. arborescens					X								Y	
C. pygmaea					X								Y	
CARYOPTERIS														
C. clandonensis									X				B	
C. incana								X	X				B, V	
CEANOTHUS														
C. americanus							X	X					W	RD
CHAENOMELES														
C. japonica				X					X				RD, O	G to Y
C. japonica alpina				X					X				RD, O	G to Y
C. 'Maulei'				X					X				VS	G to Y
C. speciosa				X					X				S	G to Y

BLOOM TIME CHART
SHRUBS

	JANUARY	FEBRUARY	MARCH	APRIL	MAY	JUNE	JULY	AUGUST	SEPTEMBER	OCTOBER	NOVEMBER	DECEMBER	FLOWER COLOR	FRUIT COLOR
CLEMATIS														
C. paniculata								▓	▓				W	
CLETHRA														
C. alnifolia								▓	▓				W	
C. alnifolia ‘Rosea’													PK	
COMPTONIA														
C. peregrina													G	
CORNUS														
C. alba						▓							C, W	B, W
C. alba ‘Argenteo-marginata’						▓							C, W	B, W
C. alba ‘Gouchaultii’						▓							C, W	B, W
C. alba ‘Kesselringii’						▓							C, W	B, W
C. alba ‘Siberica’						▓							C, W	B, W
C. alba ‘Spaethii’						▓							C, W	B, W
C. amomum						▓							W	BK
C. baileyi						▓		▓					W	W
C. kousa						▓							W, Y	R
C. kousa chinensis						▓							W	R
C. mas				▓				▓					Y	RD
C. officinalis				▓				▓					Y	S
C. racemosa							▓			▓			W	W
C. sanguinea						▓							W	P, BK
C. sericea						▓							W	W
C. sericea ‘Flaviramea’						▓							W	W
CORYLOPSIS														
C. glabrescens				▓									Y	
C. spicata				▓									Y	
CORYLUS														
C. americana			▓	▓				▓					BN	BN
C. avellana			▓	▓				▓					BN	BN
C. avellana ‘Aurea’			▓	▓				▓					BN	BN
C. avellana ‘Contorta’			▓	▓									BN	
C. maxima ‘Purpurea’			▓	▓				▓					BN	RD-BN
COTINUS														
C. coggygria						▓	▓						PK to GRY	GRY
C. coggygria ‘Purpureus’						▓	▓						PK to P	GRY
COTONEASTER														
C. acutifolia						▓			▓	▓			PK, W	BK
C. adpressus						▓		▓					PK	RD
C. adpressus praecos						▓		▓					PK	RD
C. apiculatus						▓		▓					PK	RD
C. dammeri						▓							W	RD
C. horizontalis							▓		▓				PK	RD
C. horizontalis perpusilla							▓		▓				PK	RD

BLOOM TIME CHART
SHRUBS

SHRUBS	JANUARY	FEBRUARY	MARCH	APRIL	MAY	JUNE	JULY	AUGUST	SEPTEMBER	OCTOBER	NOVEMBER	DECEMBER	FLOWER COLOR	FRUIT COLOR
C. microphylla	▓					▓			▓	▓			W	S
C. multiflora					▓				▓	▓	▓	▓	W	RD
C. multiflora calocarpa					▓				▓	▓	▓	▓	W	RD
CYTISUS														
C. × praecox					▓	▓							Y	
C. × praecox 'Albus'					▓	▓							W	
C. × praecox 'Hollandia'					▓	▓							Y & RD	
C. purgans					▓	▓							Y	
C. scoparius					▓	▓							Y	
C. scoparius 'Andreanus'					▓	▓							Y & RD	
DAPHNE														
D. × burkwoodii 'Somerset'						▓							PK	
D. cneorum						▓							PK	
D. mezereum				▓									PK to P	RD
D. mezereum 'Alba'				▓	▓								W	Y
DEUTZIA														
D. gracilis					▓	▓							W	
D. × lemoinei						▓							W	
D. × lemoinei 'Compacta'						▓							W	
D. × rosea						▓							W	
D. × rosea 'Pink Pompom'						▓							L, PK	
D. scabra						▓	▓						W	
D. scabra 'Plena'						▓	▓						W	
ENKIANTHUS														
E. campanulatus					▓	▓							Y to O	
ERICA														
E. carnea				▓									R	
E. × darleynsis	▓	▓	▓								▓		L, PK	
E. vagans									▓	▓			P, PK	
E. vagans 'Alba'									▓	▓			W	
EUONYMUS														
E. alata										▓				RD
E. alata 'Compacta'										▓				RD
E. americana										▓				RD
E. fortunei*														
E. fortunei 'Carrierei'*														
E. fortunei 'Emerald' (or 'Corliss')*														
E. fortunei, erect form*														
E. fortunei radicans, erect form*														
E. fortunei 'Sarcoxie'*														
E. fortunei 'Vegetus'*														
E. kiautschovicus*														
E. nanus turkestanicus*														
E. sachalinensis*														

*Purchased for fall color: Flowers and fruits are not primary unless indicated

BLOOM TIME CHART SHRUBS	JANUARY	FEBRUARY	MARCH	APRIL	MAY	JUNE	JULY	AUGUST	SEPTEMBER	OCTOBER	NOVEMBER	DECEMBER	FLOWER COLOR	FRUIT COLOR
*E. yedoensis**														
EXOCHORDA														
E. giraldii wilsonii					▓								W	
E. × macrantha					▓								W	
E. racemosa					▓								W	
FONTANESIA														
F. fortunei						▓							W	
FORSYTHIA														
F. 'Beatrix Farrand'				▓									Y	
F. × intermedia				▓									Y	
F. × intermedia 'Arnold Dwarf'				▓									Y	
F. × intermedia 'Arnold Giant'				▓									Y	
F. × intermedia 'Lynwood'				▓									Y	
F. × intermedia 'Spectabilis'				▓									Y	
F. × intermedia 'Spring Glory'				▓									Y	
F. 'Karl Sax'				▓									Y	
F. ovata			▓										Y	
F. suspensa				▓									Y	
F. suspensa fortunei				▓									Y	
F. suspensa sieboldii				▓									Y	
Forsythia, tree forms				▓									Y	
F. viridissima				▓									Y	
F. viridissima 'Bronxensis'				▓									Y	
FOTHERGILLA														
F. major					▓								W	
F. monticola					▓								W	
GENISTA														
G. tinctoria						▓							Y	
HAMMELIS														
H. × intermedia													VS	
H. japonica			▓										Y	
H. japonica flavopurpurescens			▓										RD	
H. mollis			▓										Y	
H. mollis 'Brevipetala'			▓										O, Y	
H. vernalis		▓											Y	
H. virginiana									▓	▓	▓		Y	
HIBISCUS														
H. syriacus								▓					VS	
HYDRANGEA														
H. arborescens						▓	▓						W	
H. arborescens 'Annabelle'						▓	▓						W	
H. arborescens grandiflora							▓	▓					W	
H. macrophylla hortensis								▓	▓				B or PK	
H. paniculata								▓	▓	▓			W to PK	

*Purchased for fall color: Flowers and fruits are not primary unless indicated

BLOOM TIME CHART
SHRUBS

	JANUARY	FEBRUARY	MARCH	APRIL	MAY	JUNE	JULY	AUGUST	SEPTEMBER	OCTOBER	NOVEMBER	DECEMBER	FLOWER COLOR	FRUIT COLOR
H. paniculata 'Grandiflora'								▓	▓	▓			W to PK	
H. quercifolia							▓						W	
HYPERICUM														
H. calycinum							▓	▓	▓				Y	
H. frondosum							▓	▓					Y	
H. patulum henryi							▓	▓					Y	
H. patulum 'Hidcote'								▓	▓				Y	
H. prolificum								▓	▓				Y	
H. 'Sun Gold'								▓	▓				Y	
ILEX (*Berries on female plant only*)														
I. cornuta 'China Boy' *and* 'China Girl'	▓									▓	▓			RD
I. crenata														BK
I. crenata compacta										▓	▓			BK
I. crenata 'Convexa'										▓	▓			BK
I. crenata 'Green Island'								▓						BK
I. crenata helleri														BK
I. crenata 'Hetzi'														BK
I. crenata 'Latifolia'														BK
I. crenata 'Microphylla'										▓				BK
I. crenata 'Repandens'														BK
I. crenata 'Stokes'														BK
I. glabra									▓	▓				BK
I. glabra 'Compacta'									▓	▓				BK
I. × meserveae									▓	▓	▓			RD
I. serrata										▓				RD
I. verticillata								▓						RD
KALMIA													Flowers are inconspicuous	
K. latifolia						▓							PK	
KERRIA														
K. japonica					▓								Y	
K. japonica 'Picta'					▓								Y	
K. japonica 'Pleniflora'					▓								Y	
KOLKWITZIA														
K. amabilis						▓							PK	
LAVANDULA														
L. officinalis						▓	▓						L	
LEUCOTHOË														
L. axillaris					▓								C	
L. fontanesiana						▓							W	
L. fontanesiana 'Girard's Rainbow'						▓							W	
LIGUSTRUM														
L. amurense						▓							W	BK
L. × ibolium						▓							W	BK
L. obtusifolium						▓	▓							B, BK

BLOOM TIME CHART — SHRUBS

SHRUBS	JAN	FEB	MAR	APR	MAY	JUN	JUL	AUG	SEP	OCT	NOV	DEC	FLOWER COLOR	FRUIT COLOR
L. ovalifolium						■							C, W	BK
L. vicaryi						■							W	BK
L. vulgare						■	■						W	BK
L. vulgare 'Lodense'						■							W	BK
LONICERA														
L. bella 'Candida'						■							W	RD
L. fragrantissima				■									C, W	RD
L. japonica						■							Y, W	BK
L. korolkowii						■							R	RD, O
L. korolkowii 'Zabelii'						■							RD	RD, O
L. maackii						■			■				W	RD, O
L. maackii podocarpa						■							C	RD, O
L. morrowii						■							C-W	BD RD
L. sempervirens					■	■							S/Y	RD
L. tatarica					■	■							W or PK	RD, O
L. tatarica alba					■	■							W	RD, O
L. tatarica 'Arnold Red'					■	■							RD	RD
L. tatarica grandiflora					■	■							W	RD, O
L. tatarica rosea						■							PK/R	RD, O
L. tatarica 'Sibirica'					■	■							W/PK	RD, O
L. xylosteroides 'Clavey's Dwarf'						■							G	RD
MAGNOLIA														
M. soulangiana				■									W	G to T & RD
M. stellata					■			■					W	
MAHONIA														
M. aquifolium				■	■		■						Y	B, BK
M. beale				■	■								Y	B, BK
M. repens					■								Y	B, BK
MALUS														
M. sargentii					■				■				W	RD
MYRICA														
M. cerifera	■	■							■	■	■	■		GRY
M. pensylvanica	■	■							■	■	■	■		GRY
NANDINA														
N. domestica	■						■			■	■	■	W	RD
OSMANTHUS									■	■			G-W	B, BK
O. heterophyllus									■	■			G-W	B, BK
PAEONIA														
P. suffruticosa						■							VS	
P. suffruticosa 'Joseph Rock'						■							C, W	
PHILADELPHUS														
P. 'Atlas'													W	
P. aureus													W	
P. 'Belle Etoile'						■							W	

BLOOM TIME CHART SHRUBS	JANUARY	FEBRUARY	MARCH	APRIL	MAY	JUNE	JULY	AUGUST	SEPTEMBER	OCTOBER	NOVEMBER	DECEMBER	FLOWER COLOR	FRUIT COLOR
P. coronarius						▓							W	
P. coronarius 'Aureus'						▓							W	
P. 'Enchantment'						▓							W	
P. 'Glacier'						▓							W	
P. grandiflorus						▓							W	
P. 'Innocence'						▓							W	
P. inodorus grandiflorus						▓							W	
P. × lemoinei						▓							W	
P. × virginalis						▓							W	
P. × virginalis 'Minnesota Snowflake'						▓							W	
PIERIS				▓										
P. floribunda				▓									W	
P. japonica				▓									W	
P. japonica 'Compacta'				▓									W	
P. japonica 'Red Mill'				▓									W	
P. japonica 'Variegata'				▓										
P. taiwanensis				▓									W	
PONCIRUS														
P. trifoliata				▓	▓				▓				W	Y
POTENTILLA														
P. arbuscula						▓	▓	▓					Y	
P. davurica						▓	▓	▓	▓				W	
P. × friedrichsenii						▓	▓	▓	▓				Y	
P. fruticosa						▓	▓	▓	▓				Y	
P. fruticosa 'Moonlight'						▓	▓	▓	▓				Y	
P. 'Lemon Drop'						▓	▓	▓	▓				Y	
P. 'Mount Everest'						▓	▓	▓	▓				W	
P. parvifolia						▓	▓	▓	▓				Y	
P. parvifolia 'Gold Drop'						▓	▓	▓	▓				Y	
P. parvifolia 'Klondike'						▓	▓	▓					Y	
P. parvifolia 'Red Ace'						▓	▓	▓	▓				Y or W	
P. parvifolia 'Tangerine'						▓	▓	▓	▓				O to Y	
PRUNUS														
P. besseyi					▓				▓				W	P-BK
P. × cistena					▓				▓				W or PK	BK-P
P. glandulosa				▓		▓							W or PK	RD
P. glandulosa 'Albiplena'				▓		▓							W	RD
P. glandulosa 'Sinensis'					▓								P-RD	RD
P. laurocerasus					▓								W	RD to BK
P. laurocerasus 'Zabeliana'					▓		▓						W	RD to BK
P. maritima					▓				▓				W	P or CN
P. tenella				▓	▓								R	RD
P. tomentosa				▓			▓						W	RD
P. triloba				▓									PK	

BLOOM TIME CHART SHRUBS	JANUARY	FEBRUARY	MARCH	APRIL	MAY	JUNE	JULY	AUGUST	SEPTEMBER	OCTOBER	NOVEMBER	DECEMBER	FLOWER COLOR	FRUIT COLOR
PYRACANTHA														
P. coccinea cultivars						█			█				W	O, RD, VS
P. coccinea 'Lalandei'	█	█	█			█			█	█	█		W	O, RD
RHODODENDRON														
R. 'Album Elegans'						█							L-W to W	
R. 'America'						█							RD	
R. 'Caractus'						█							P, R	
R. carolinianum					█	█							R, P	
R. carolinianum album						█							W	
R. catawbiense						█							RD, P	
R. 'Catawbiense Album'						█							W	
R. 'English Roseum'						█							R	
R. × laetervirens						█							PK to P	
R. 'Lee's Dark Purple'						█							P	
R. maximum						█	█						R	
P.J.M. hybrid					█	█							VS	
R. 'Purpureum Eleganus'						█							BK, L	
R. 'Roseum Elegans'						█							R	
R. 'Roseum Superbum'						█							P, R	
R. 'Scintillation'					█								PK	
Shammarello hybrids						█							PK, RD & W	
R. 'Windbeam'						█							A to PK	
R. yakushimanum						█							W	
RHODOTYPOS														
R. scandens	█				█	█			█	█	█	█	W	BK
RHUS														
R. aromatica				█									Y	RD
R. coppalina								█	█				G/Y	RD
R. glabra							█			█			Y	RD
R. trilobata														RD
R. typhina						█							Y	RD
R. typhina 'Laciniata'						█				█			Y	RD
RIBES														
R. alpinum					█								G-Y	RD-P
R. aureum					█								Y	P to BK
R. diacanthum					█								Y	P to BK
R. odoratum					█								Y	P to BK
ROBINIA														
R. hispida						█	█						P, PK	RD
ROSA														
R. blanda						█							R, PK	
R. centifolia 'Muscosa'						█							VS	
R. eglanteria						█				█			R, P	O to S
R. foetida 'Bicolor'						█				█			Y & RD	RD

BLOOM TIME CHART
SHRUBS

	JANUARY	FEBRUARY	MARCH	APRIL	MAY	JUNE	JULY	AUGUST	SEPTEMBER	OCTOBER	NOVEMBER	DECEMBER	FLOWER COLOR	FRUIT COLOR
R. foetida 'Persian Yellow'						█							Y	
R. glauca						█				█			PK	RD-O
R. harisonii						█				█			Y	BK
R. hugonis						█							Y	
R. moschata													VS	
R. moyesii									█	█			RD	O, RD
R. multiflora	█										█		W	RD
R. nitida							█						R	RD
R. palustris						█	█						PK	RD
R. pimpinellifolia						█				█			W	BK to BN
R. pimpinellifolia altaica							█						C, W	RD, BN
R. rugosa							█	█	█				P, PK	O, RD
R. rugosa 'Alba'						█	█	█					W	O, RD
R. setigera							█			█			PK	RD
R. spinosissima							█	█					PK	
R. virginiana							█						PK	RD
R. wichuraiana								█	█				W	RD
RUBUS														
R. odoratus							█		█				R, PK	RD
SALIX														
S. discolor			█										G-Y	
S. gracilistyla			█										G-Y	
S. purpurea			█										G-Y	
S. purpurea 'Gracilis'			█										G-Y	
S. repens			█										G-Y	
SAMBUCAS														
S. canadensis							█						W	B, BK
S. canadensis 'Aurea'							█						W	B, BK
S. nigra 'Aurea'					█	█			█				W	BK
S. nigra 'Laciniata'						█							W	BK
S. racemosa					█			█					W	S
S. racemosa 'Plumosa Aurea'					█			█					W	S
SPIREA														
S. albiflora							█						W	
S. × arguta					█								W	
S. × billiardi													P, PK	
S. × bumalda													P, PK	
S. × bumalda 'Anthony Waterer'													P, PK	
S. japonica alpina						█							PK	
S. japonica 'Atrosanguinea'						█	█						P, PK	
S. lemoinei alpestris						█							PK	
S. media sericea													W	
S. multiflora													W	
S. nipponica tosaensis						█							W	

BLOOM TIME CHART
SHRUBS

	JAN	FEB	MAR	APR	MAY	JUN	JUL	AUG	SEP	OCT	NOV	DEC	FLOWER COLOR	FRUIT COLOR
S. × pikoviensis						▓							W	
S. prunifolia						▓							W	
S. × sansouciana					▓								P, PK	
S. thunbergii				▓									W	
S. tomentosa							▓	▓					R to R-P	
S. trichocarpa					▓								W	
S. trilobata					▓								W	
S. × vanhouttei					▓								W	
STAPHYLEA														
S. trifolia					▓					▓			W/Pale G	G to T
SYMPHOROCARPOS														
S. albus						▓	▓						PK & W	W
S. albus laevigatus						▓	▓						PK & W	W
S. × chenaultii								▓	▓	▓			W or P	RD & W
S. orbiculatus								▓					W or P	RD
S. 'White Hedge'								▓	▓				W or P	W
SYRINGA														
S. chinensis						▓							L, P	
S. chinensis 'Alba'						▓							W	
S. chinensis 'Saugeana'						▓							R, P	
S. josikaea						▓							L, P	
S. laciniata					▓								L	
S. microphylla					▓								L	
S. microphylla 'Superba'					▓								PK	
S. × persica					▓								L	
S. × persica 'Alba'					▓								W	
S. × prestoniae						▓							VS	
S. pubescens					▓	▓							LC or PK	
S. vulgaris						▓							L, P	
S. vulgaris 'Alba'						▓							W	
S. vulgaris, hybrids						▓							VS	
S. vulgaris, tree form						▓							VS	
TAMARIX														
T. africana								▓					PK	
T. gallica								▓					R-PK	
T. hispida									▓				PK	
T. odessana													PK	
T. parviflora						▓							PK	
T. pentandra								▓					PK	
T. pentandra 'Pink Cascade'								▓	▓				PK	
T. pentandra 'Rubra'								▓					PK	
TEUCRIUM														
T. chamaedrys								▓					PK	

BLOOM TIME CHART
SHRUBS

	JAN	FEB	MAR	APR	MAY	JUN	JUL	AUG	SEP	OCT	NOV	DEC	FLOWER COLOR	FRUIT COLOR
VACCINIUM														
V. corymbosum						X			X	X			W	B
VIBURNUM														
V. acerifolium						X			X				W	C to BK
V. bitchiuense					X								PK	BK
V. × bodnantense				X									PK	BK
V. × burkwoodii					X								PK to W	BK
V. × burkwoodii 'Chenault'					X								PK to W	BK
V. × carlcephalum					X								PK to W	
V. carlesii					X								PK to W	BK
V. carlesii 'Compactum'					X								PK to W	BK
V. cassinoides							X						W	P, B, BK
V. dentatum						X			X				C to W	B
V. dilatum						X							C to W	S
V. fragrans			X										PK to RD	RD to BK
V. × juddii					X								PK to W	BK
V. lantana						X							C, W	RD to BK
V. × lantanaphyllum						X							C, W	RD to BK
V. molle						X							C, W	B, BK
V. opulus	X	X				X				X	X		C, W	RD
V. opulus 'Compactum'	X	X				X				X	X		C, W	RD
V. opulus 'Nanum'						X							C, W	RD
V. opulus 'Roseum'						X							G, W	RD
V. opulus, tree form						X							C, W	RD
V. opulus 'Xanthocarpum'						X							C, W	Y
V. plicatum							X						W	RD to BK
V. plicatum 'Grandiflorum'						X							W	RD to BK
V. plicatum 'Mariesii'						X							W	RD to BK
V. plicatum 'Rotundifolium'						X							W	RD to BK
V. plicatum tomentosum					X		X						W	RD to BK
V. × rhytidophylloides						X							C, W	RD to BK
V. rhytidophyllum						X				X			C, W	RD to BK
V. sargentii						X					X		C, W	RD
V. setigerum						X			X				C, W	R
V. trilobum	X	X				X							C, W	RD
V. wrightii						X							C, W	S
VITEX														
V. agnus-castus 'Linifolia'								X	X				L	
WEIGELA													W, P, R-O	
W. 'Abel Carriere'						X							DP PK	
W. 'Boskoop Glory'						X							SN, PK	
W. 'Bristol Ruby'						X							P/RD	
W. 'Bristol Snowflake'						X							W	
W. 'Eva Rathke'						X							P/RD	

BLOOM TIME CHART
SHRUBS

	JANUARY	FEBRUARY	MARCH	APRIL	MAY	JUNE	JULY	AUGUST	SEPTEMBER	OCTOBER	NOVEMBER	DECEMBER	FLOWER COLOR	FRUIT COLOR
W. floribunda						█							CN	
W. florida						█							W/P	
W. florida 'Alba'						█							W	
W. florida 'Purpurea'						█							W	
W. florida 'Variegata'						█							W/P	
W. florida 'Venusta'					█								R-P	
W. 'Henderson'						█							DP R	
W. 'Vanicek'						█							P/RD	
XANTHORHIZA														
X. simplicissima													BN-P	
SMALL TREES														
ACER														
A. ginnala					█	█	█						Y	RD
A. palmatum						█							P	RD
A. palmatum 'Atropurpureum'						█							P	RD
A. palmatum 'Dissectum'						█							Y	
A. palmatum 'Ornatum'						█							Y	
AMELANCHIER														
A. × *grandiflora*				█			█						W	RD to BK
A. laevis				█			█						W	B, BK
CERCIS														
C. canadensis						█							RD, P	
C. canadensis alba													W	
C. canadensis 'Forest Pansy'						█							RD, P	
C. chinensis													RD, P	
CHIONANTHUS														
C. retusus					█				█				W	B, BK
C. virginicus					█				█				W	BK
CLETHRA														
C. barbinervis								█					W	
CORNUS														
C. alternifolia						█		█					W	B-BK
C. florida						█				█	█		W	RD
C. florida 'Cherokee Chief'										█			R	RD
C. florida 'Cherokee Princess'										█			R	RD
C. florida 'Cloud 9'													W	RD
C. florida 'Pendula'						█							W	RD
C. florida 'Pluribracteata'													W	RD
C. florida 'Prosser Red'													RD	RD
C. florida 'Rainbow'													W	RD
C. florida rubra						█				█			PK to R	RD

BLOOM TIME CHART
SMALL TREES

	JANUARY	FEBRUARY	MARCH	APRIL	MAY	JUNE	JULY	AUGUST	SEPTEMBER	OCTOBER	NOVEMBER	DECEMBER	FLOWER COLOR	FRUIT COLOR
C. florida 'Salcifolia'					■				■	■			W	RD
C. florida 'Welchii'									■	■				RD
C. florida xanthocarpa					■				■	■			W	Y
CRATAEGUS														
C. 'Autumn Glory'						■			■	■			W	RD or S
C. crus-galli						■			■	■			W	RD or S
C. intricata						■			■	■			W	RD or S
C. × *lavallei*	■					■			■	■			W	RD
C. mollis					■				■				W	S
C. monogyna						■			■	■			W	RD or S
C. monogyna 'Stricta'						■			■	■			W	RD or S
C. × *mordenensis* 'Toba'						■			■	■			PK	RD
C. nitida						■			■	■			W	RD or S
C. oxyacantha					■	■			■	■			W	RD or S
C. oxyacantha 'Paul's Scarlet'					■	■			■	■			S	RD or S
C. oxyacantha 'Rosea Plena'					■	■			■	■			R	RD or S
C. phaenopyrum						■			■	■			W	RD
C. viridis						■			■	■			W	RD or S
DAVIDIA														
D. involucrata					■								W	
ELAEAGNUS														
E. angustifolia						■			■				Y	Y
EUONYMUS														
E. atropurpurea						■							P	
E. europaea						■			■	■			Y-G	PK/O
E. europaea 'Aldenhamensis'						■			■	■			Y, G	PK/O
FRANKLINIA														
F. alatamaha									■				W	
HALESIA														
H. carolina				■									W	
H. monticola					■								W	
ILEX														
I. opaca						■			■	■			W	RD
I. opaca xanthocarpa						■							W	Y
KOELREUTERIA														
K. paniculata							■		■				Y	Y or T
LABURNUM														
L. alpinum						■							Y	
L. alpinum 'Pendulum'						■							Y	
L. anagyroides					■								Y	
L. watereri						■							Y	
L. watereri 'Vossii'						■							Y	
MACLURA														
M. pomifera									■					G

BLOOM TIME CHART
SMALL TREES

	JANUARY	FEBRUARY	MARCH	APRIL	MAY	JUNE	JULY	AUGUST	SEPTEMBER	OCTOBER	NOVEMBER	DECEMBER	FLOWER COLOR	FRUIT COLOR
MAGNOLIA														
M. 'Girls' hybrids													VS	
M. kobus				■				■					W	G to T & RD
M. 'Leonard Messel'				■									PK	BN
M. × *loebneri* 'Merrill'				■									W	BN
M. × *soulangiana*				■					■				W/PK	BN/RD seeds
M. × *soulangiana* 'Alba'				■									W	BN
M. × *soulangiana* 'Alba Superba'				■									W	BN
M. × *soulangiana* 'Alexandrina'				■									W/PK	BN
M. × *soulangiana* 'Lennei'					■	■							R-P	G to T & RD
M. × *soulangiana* 'Rubra'					■	■							R-P	G to T & RD
M. stellata				■									W	G to T & RD
M. stellata 'Rosea'				■									PK	G to T & RD
M. stellata 'Rubra'				■									P, PK	G to T & RD
M. stellata 'Waterlily'				■									PK	G to T & RD
M. virginiana						■	■	■	■				W	G to T & RD
MALUS														
M. 'Dolgo'					■	■			■	■			PK	RD
M. 'Dorothea'					■	■			■	■			PK	Y
M. 'Hopa'					■				■	■			RD	RD
M. 'Red Jade'					■	■			■	■			DP PK	RD
M. 'Royalty'					■				■	■			CN	RD
M. 'Snowdrift'					■	■			■	■			W	O, RD
OXYDENDRON														
O. arboreum								■	■				W	
PRUNUS														
P. × *blireiana*				■					■				PK	PK to P
P. cerasifera										■			PK/W	Y to RD
P. cerasifera 'Atropurpurea'										■			PK/W	Y to RD
P. cerasifera 'Newport'										■			PK/W	Y to RD
P. cerasifera 'Nigra'										■			PK/W	Y to RD
P. cerasifera 'Thundercloud'						■			■				PK/W	Y to RD
P. 'Hally Jolivette'					■								W	
P. serrulata					■		■						W or PK	BK
P. serrulata 'Amanogawa'					■								W or PK	BK
P. serrulata 'Shirotae'					■								W or PK	BK
P. subhirtella				■			■						PK	BK
P. subhirtella 'Autumnalis'				■			■						PK	BK
P. subhirtella 'Pendula'				■			■						PK	BK
PTELEA														
P. trifoliata						■							G	
PYRUS														
P. calleryana 'Faurei'													W	

BLOOM TIME CHART
SMALL TREES

	JANUARY	FEBRUARY	MARCH	APRIL	MAY	JUNE	JULY	AUGUST	SEPTEMBER	OCTOBER	NOVEMBER	DECEMBER	FLOWER COLOR	FRUIT COLOR
ROBINIA														
R. hispida 'Monument'					▓								P/PK	
SALIX														
S. caprea				▓									GRY, G	
SORBUS														
S. americana						▓							W	O, RD
S. aucuparia						▓							W	O, RD
S. decora						▓							W	O, RD
STEWARTIA														
S. pseudo-camellia							▓						W	
S. sinensis							▓						W	
STYRAX														
S. japonica						▓							W	
S. obassia						▓							W	
SYRINGA														
S. amurensis japonica					▓								W	
VIBURNUM														
V. lentago						▓		▓					W	B, BK
V. prunifolium									▓	▓			W	B, BK
V. sieboldii						▓		▓					W	Y to B, BK
XANTHOCERAS														
X. sorbifolia						▓			▓				W	G to BN
FLOWERING VINES														
Actinidia arguta							▓		▓				W	G
Akebia quinata				▓									P	
Campsis radicans							▓						O-RD	
Celastrus scandens									▓	▓			G	O & RD
Clematis, hybrids						▓	▓						VS	
Hydrangea anomola subspecies petiolaris						▓							W	
Lonicera ✕ *heckrottii*							▓	▓	▓	▓			GLD	
Polygonum aubertii						▓							W	
Wisteria floribunda					▓								B	

III.
WAYS OF PROPAGATING SHRUBS AND SMALL TREES

Note that many shrubs may be propagated in several ways. (D) indicates a difficult method for that shrub.

DIVISION

Some shrubs naturally sucker, as noted below. Suckers may be removed to make new plants.

Amorpha
Aralia (suckers)
Aronia (suckers)
Berberis, some species
Buxus
Calycanthus (suckers)
Cornus, some species (suckers)
Corylus, some species (suckers)
Erica, species
Euonymus (some)
Hypericum calycinum
Kerria
Kolkwitzia
Mahonia aquifolium
Philadelphus
Prunus glandulosa (and cultivars)
Ribes odoratum
Robinia (suckers)
Rubus (suckers)
Spiraea japonica & other dwarf varieties
Symphoricarpos (suckers)

LAYERING

(L) means it takes a long time for roots to form. Month or season indicates best time to layer.

Aesculus parviflora
Amelanchier
Amorpha
Aronia
Azaleas (May-June)
Berberis some species (Apr.)
Chaenomeles (own root plants only) (June or July)
Cornus (spring)
Corylus (fall)
Cotoneaster (spring)
Crataegus
Cytisus (spring)
Daphne cneorum
Daphne genkwa
Elaegnus angustifolia

Elaeagnus umbellatum
Enkianthus
Erica
Euonymus (early summer)
Exochorda
Fothergilla
Halesia (spring)
Hamamelis (L)
Ilex (fall) (L)
Kalmia
Magnolia (early spring)
Philadelphus (fall)
Pieris (fall)
Potentilla
Pyracantha
Rhododendron
Rhus
Ribes
Rosa
Staphylea
Stephanandra
Stewartia
Styrax
Symplocos
Syringa (early spring)
Vaccinium (fall)
Viburnum opulus & other varieties (June)
Tip layer—*Rubus species*
Mound layer—*Calycanthus*
              Cotoneaster
              Hydrangea arborescens,
                    paniculata,
                    quercifolia

CUTTINGS

(H) means with heel
(L) means it takes a long time for roots to form

Acer palmatum
Aesculus parviflora
Amelanchier
Amorpha
Aronia
Azalea (evergreen)
Buxus
Callicarpa
Calluna vulgaris
Calycanthus
Caryopteris
Ceanothus
Cephalanthus
Clethra

Comptonia
Comus florida
Corylopsis (H)
Cytisus (H)
Deutzia
Enkianthus
Euonymus
Exochorda
Fontanesia
Forsythia
Hibiscus
Hydrangea species, *H. macrophylla*
Hypericum (H)
Kalmia
Kerria
Lavandula (H)
Ligustrum
Lonicera
Magnolia species
Pieris
Potentilla
Prunus maritima
Prunus tomentosa
Prunus triloba
Rhodotypos
Salix
Sambucus
Spiraea
Staphylea
Stewartia
Styrax
Symphoricarpos
Syringa (H)
Tamarix
Vitex

•**Semi-hardwood cuttings**
Abelia (H)
Azalea (evergreen and deciduous)
Berberis (H)
Buddleia alternifolia
Buddleia davidii
Buxus (H)
Caryopteris
Ceanothus
Chaenomeles
Clethra
Cornus
Cotoneaster (H)
Cytisus (H)
Daphne burkwoodii 'Somerset'
Daphne cneorum
Daphne mezereum
Deutzia
Erica carnea

APPENDICES *265*

Euonymus
Exochorda
Forsythia
Hibiscus (H)
Hydrangea
Hypericum (H)
Ilex (D)
Kolkwitzia
Lavandula (H)
Lonicera
Magnolia (H, L)
Mahonia beale
Philadelphus
Pieris
Potentilla
Pyracantha
Rhododendron
Rhus
Ribes
Rosa
Spiraea
Syringa
Viburnum × burkwoodii
Viburnum carlesii
Viburnum fragrans and others
Weigela

•Hardwood cuttings

Amorpha
Berberis
Buddleia alternifolia
Buddleia davidii
Buxus
Caryopteris
Ceanothus (H)
Chaenomeles
Corus alba & varieties
Cornus some species but not florida
Cotoneaster (evergreen) (H)
Cytisus
Deutzia (H)
Diervilla
Eleagnus angustifolia
Erica
Forsythia
Hibiscus
Hydrangea
Hypericum
Ilex (L)
Kerria (H)
Kolkwitzia
Laburnum watereri 'Vossii'
Ligustrum vulgare & others
Lonicera
Philadelphus
Potentilla
Pyracantha
Rhododendron
Rhus
Ribes

Rosa
Salix
Sambucus
Spiraea
Symphoricarpos albus
Symphoricarpos orbiculatus
Syringa persica
Tamarix
Weigela

SEED

 (I) means plant immediately when ripe
(ES) means sow in early spring
 (S) means stratify
 (L) means long to germinate, possibly
     two years.

Acer species (I or S)
Aesculus (I)
Amelanchier (S, L)
Amorpha
Aronia
Azalea
Berberis thunbergii & others (S, ES)
Buddeia alternifolia
Buxus (L)
Callicarpa
Calycanthus
Caragana
Caryopteris
Ceanothus americanus
Cercis species
Chaenomeles (ES)
Chionanthus
Clethra
Comptonia
Cornus (ES)
Cornus florida (S, L and other species ES)
Corylopsis
Cotinus coggygria
Cotoneaster (S, L)
Crataegus (L, S for 18 months)
Cytisus (ES)
Daphne mezereum (I or S)
Deutzia (ES)
Eleagnus (S, L)
Enkianthus (ES)
Erica (ES)
Euonymus (ES)
Exochorda (ES)
Fothergilla
Hamamelis (ES, L)
Hibiscus (ES)
Hypericum (ES)
Ilex (L, S for 18 months)
Kalmia (ES)
Laburnum anagyroides (ES)

Leucothoë
Ligustrum (I or S)
Lonicera (I or S)
Magnolia (S)
Mahonia (S, L)
Malus species (S)
Myrica
Paeonia suffruticosa
Philadelphus
Photinia
Pieris
Potentilla (ES)
Prunus species
Pyracantha
Rhododendron (ES)
Rhodotypos
Rhus
Ribes
Robinia (ES)
Rosa (I)
Sambucus (ES)
Sorbus
Spiraea (ES)
Staphylea
Styrax
Symphoricarpos
Syringa species (ES)
Viburnum (S, L)
Vitex
Weigela (ES)

GRAFT

All cultivars in species listed below are
grafted or budded.

Cornus florida rubra on C, F
Crataegus (April)
Cytisus (May)
Ligustrum (variegated on common)
Hamamelis
Hibiscus
Laburnum
Malus
Prunus
Rhododendron (& azalea)
Syringa on S. vulgaris (NOT on Ligustrum)

BUD

Crataegus
Ilex
Malus
Prunus
Rosa
Sorbus
Syringa

IV.
HARDINESS ZONE MAP

Some shrubs and trees can withstand only a certain mean low temperature. This map, based on information gathered by the Agricultural Research Service of the United States and the Department of Agriculture of Canada, divides North America into ten regions and indicates their median winter temperatures. It is extremely important that you consult the hardiness zone map before buying seeds and plants. Of course there are many micro climates in parts of the country; so it is wise to find out from local gardeners what zone you are really in. If you live in a coastal area, it is also a good idea to determine which plants can withstand salt or sea-spray conditions.

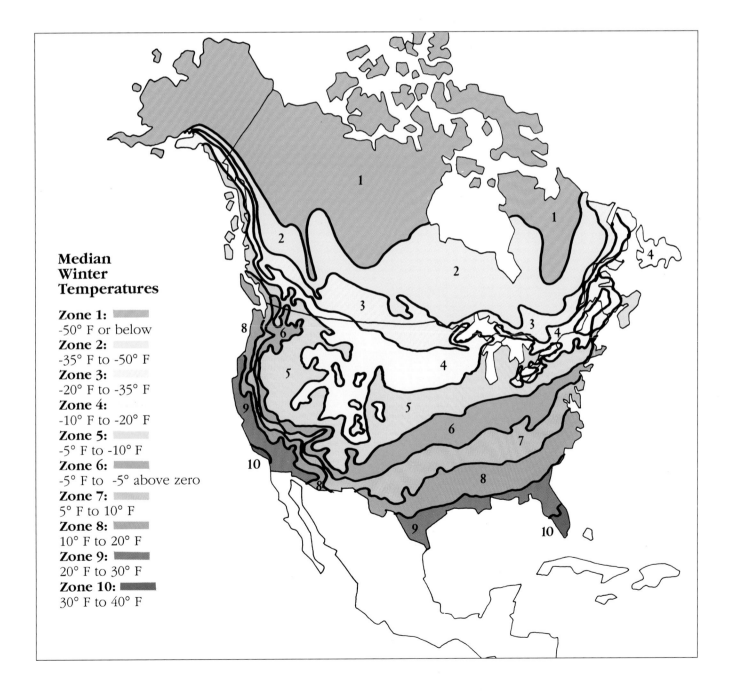

**Median
Winter
Temperatures**

Zone 1:
-50° F or below
Zone 2:
-35° F to -50° F
Zone 3:
-20° F to -35° F
Zone 4:
-10° F to -20° F
Zone 5:
-5° F to -10° F
Zone 6:
-5° F to -5° above zero
Zone 7:
5° F to 10° F
Zone 8:
10° F to 20° F
Zone 9:
20° F to 30° F
Zone 10:
30° F to 40° F

V.
WHERE TO BUY SHRUBS:
A SOURCE GUIDE

There are several ways to purchase flowering shrubs. The most convenient source is a local nursery or garden center. Some nurseries offer a big selection of varieties; others may specialize in a particular group of flowering shrubs. For example, there are many nurseries specializing in azaleas, rhododendrons, roses and camellias, usually offering a choice of sizes, from newly rooted cuttings sold bare-root to one- or two-year-old plants shipped in pots and containers.

Local nurseries that don't specialize will usually offer plants either containerized or balled-and-burlapped. Popular plant groups such as magnolias, crabapples and flowering cherries may be offered in several popular varieties, but anything unusual or new is not likely to be available. For the widest selection of flowering shrubs mail-order catalogs are generally the best place to turn. Following is a list of mail-order companies with good selections. They are divided into general nursery stock companies that carry a wide selection of flowering shrubs and specialist suppliers. Some of these publish simple catalogs—nothing more than mimeographed sheets stapled together—while other companies offer extravagant books with gorgeous photographs in full color. Some of the catalogs are free; for others there is a charge that is usually deductible from the first order.

Mail-order companies usually ship bare-root plants that have been grown in the field, dug up and the roots cleaned of soil. They are then wrapped in moist sphagnum moss, moist shredded newspaper or moist peat moss, and held tight with clear plastic film. In rare cases plants may be shipped in a container with soil.

Bare-root plants received through the mail need to be planted as soon as possible after receipt, weather permitting. If you cannot plant them into permanent positions right away, place them in temporary nursery beds, covering the roots with moist soil. Containerized plants that cannot be planted right away can be placed in a shady area and some kind of organic material heaped around the pot to keep it cool and prevent dehydration. Wood chips, shredded leaves and peat moss are ideal.

GENERAL NURSERY STOCK

Bear Creek Nursery
P.O. Box 411
Bear Creek Road
Northport, WA 99157-0411
Specializes in cold-hardy and drought-resistant shrubs for the home gardener. Catalog free.

Beaver Creek Nursery
7526 Pelleaux Road
Knoxville, TN 37938
Specializes in collector's trees and shrubs. Catalog $1.00.

Brittingham Plant Farms
P.O. Box 2538
Salisbury, MD 21801
Specializes in fruit-producing shrubs (blackberries, blueberries, etc.). Catalog free.

W. Atlee Burpee Co.
300 Park Avenue
Warminster, PA 18974
Offers a wide variety of plant material in a color catalog. Catalog free.

Carroll Gardens
P.O. Box 310
444 East Main Street
Westminster, MD 21157
Huge selection of plant material. Catalog $2.00.

Chiltern Seeds
Bortree Stile
Ulverston, Cumbria, England LA12 7PB
Extensive selection of plants from all over the world. Catalog $2.00.

Cold Stream Farm
2030 Free Soil Road
Free Soil, MI 49411-9752
Trees and shrubs useful for woodland planting in seedling size. Nice selection of native trees and shrubs. Catalog free.

Bill Dodd's Rare Plants
P.O. Drawer 377
Semmes, AL 36575
Nice selection of native azalea and rhododendron species and hybrids. Catalog free with 9½" self-addressed envelope.

Dutch Mountain Nursery
7984 N. 48th Street
Augusta, MI 49012
Offers number of flowering trees and shrubs specializing in plants to attract birds. Catalog twenty-five cents.

Emlong Nurseries
2671 W. Marquette Woods Road
Stevensville, MI 49127
Offers roses and general nursery stock. Catalog free.

Farmer Seed & Nursery
P.O. Box 129
818 N.W. 4th Street
Faribault, MN 55021
Broad selection of northern grown hardy stock. Catalog free.

Henry Field Seed & Nursery Co.
407 Sycamore Street
Shenandoah, IA 51602
Large and varied selection. Catalog free.

Gardens of the Blue Ridge
P.O. Box 10
U.S. 221 North
Pineola, NC 28662
Good selection of native trees and shrubs. Catalog $2.00.

Girard Nurseries
P.O. Box 428
6801 North Ridge (US 20)
Geneva, OH 44041
Broad selection of flowering shrubs. Catalog free.

Griffeys' Nursery
1680 Highway 25-70
Marshall, NC 28753
Broad selection of southeastern native plants. Catalog free.

Gurney Seed & Nursery Co.
2nd & Capital
Yankton, SD 47078
Broad selection of plant material including flowering shrubs. Catalog free.

Hall Rhododendrons
1280 Quince Drive
Junction City, OR 97448
Broad selection of species and hybrid rhododendrons and azaleas. Catalog $1.00.

Hastings
P.O. Box 4274
Atlanta, GA 30302-4274
Specializes in plant material for Southern gardens. Catalog free.

Holbrook Farm & Nursery
Route 2, P.O. Box 223 B
Fletcher, NC 28732
Broad selection of flowering shrubs. Catalog $2.00.

Hortico, Inc.
723 Robson Road, R.R. 1
Waterdown, ON, Canada L0R 2H0
Broad selection of garden perennials, including flowering shrubs. Ask for a rose or perennial list.

Krider Nurseries
P.O. Box 29
Middlebury, IN 46540
Broad selection of ornamental shrubs and roses. Catalog free.

Lakeshore Tree Farms, Ltd.
R.R. 3
Saskatoon, SK, Canada S7K 3J6
Good selection of ornamental trees, shrubs and perennials. Catalog $1.00.

Lawyer Nursery, Inc.
950 Highway 200 West
Plains, MT 59859
Offers large selection of shrubs and seeds including sub-tropical. Catalog free.

Louisiana Nursery
Route 7, P.O. Box 43 (Highway 182)
Opelousas, LA 70570
Offers unusual trees and shrubs. Ask for a catalog (M) $3.50.

McConnell Nurseries, Inc.
R.R. 1
Port Burwell, ON, Canada N0J 1T0
Large selection of general nursery stock. Catalog free.

Earl May Seed & Nursery Co.
P.O. Box 500
208 N. Elm Street
Shenandoah, IA 51603
Seasonal color catalogues offer general nursery stock, seeds, garden supplies, etc. Catalog free.

Mellinger's Inc.
2310 W. South Range Road
North Lima, OH 44452
Extremely large range of plants, gardening supplies, seeds, etc. Catalog free.

J.E. Miller Nurseries Inc.
5060 West Lake Road
Canandaigua, NY 14424
Broad selection of fruit and berry-producing shrubs. Catalog free.

Morden Nurseries, Ltd.
P.O. Box 1270
Morden, MB, Canada R0G 1J0
Good selection of ornamental trees and shrubs. Catalog free.

Mt. Leo Nursery
P.O. Box 135
603 Beersheba Street
McMinnville, TN 37110
Nice selection of trees and shrubs. Catalog free.

Musser Forests, Inc.
P.O. Box 340
Indiana, PA 15710-0340
Many varieties of shrubs in transplant sizes. Catalog free.

Powell's Gardens
Route 3, P.O. Box 21
Highway 70
Princeton, NC 27569
Broad selection of flowering shrubs. Catalog $1.50.

F.W. Schumacher Co.
36 Spring Hill Road
Sandwich, MA 02563-1023
Broad selection of seeds. Catalog $1.00.

Southwestern Native Seeds
P.O. Box 50503
Tucson, AZ 85703
Offers seeds of southwestern native plants. Catalog $1.00.

Spring Hill Nurseries Co.
P.O. Box 1758
Peoria, IL 61656
Broad selection of plant material. Catalog free.

Stark Bros. Nurseries & Orchards Inc.
Highway 54 West
Louisiana, MO 63353-0010
Good selection of roses, fruit-producing shrubs and ornamental shrubs. Catalog free.

Tripple Brook Farms
37 Middle Road
Southampton, MA 01073
Specializes in northeastern native shrubs. Catalog free.

Waynesboro Nurseries
P.O. Box 987
Route 664
Waynesboro, VA 22980
Good selection of plant material including flowering shrubs. Catalog free.

Wayside Gardens
P.O. Box 1
Hodges, SC 29695-0001
Wide selection of ornamental trees, shrubs, perennials, and roses. Catalog $1.00.

White Flower Farm
Route 63
Litchfield, CT 06759-0050
Broad selection of shrubs and perennials. Catalog $5.00.

SPECIALIST PLANT SUPPLIERS

Azaleas

The Bovees Nursery
1737 S. W. Coronado
Portland, OR 97219
Catalog $2.00.

Bull Valley Rhododendron Nursery
214 Bull Valley Road
Aspers, PA 17304
Catalog free with 9½" self-addressed envelope.

Carlson's Gardens
P.O. Box 305
South Salem, NY 10590
Catalog $2.00.

Cummins Gardens
22 Robertsville Road
Marlboro, NJ 07746
Catalog $1.00.

Bill Dodd's Rare Plants
P.O. Drawer 377
Semmes, AL 36575
Catalog free with 9½" self-addressed envelope.

Flora Lan Nursery
Route 1, P.O. Box 357
Forest Grove, OR 97116
Catalog free.

Girard Nurseries
P.O. Box 428
6801 North Ridge (US 20)
Geneva, OH 44041
Catalog free.

Greer Gardens
1280 Goodpasture Island Road
Eugene, OR 97401-1794
Large selection of rhododendrons and azaleas. Catalog $2.00.

Hall Rhododendrons
1280 Quince Drive
Junction City, OR 97448
Broad selection of species and hybrid rhododendrons and azaleas. Catalog free with 9½" self-addressed envelope.

Hass Nursery
24105 Ervin Road
Philomath, OR 97370
Specializing in rhododendrons, azaleas, and Pieris japonica. Catalog $2.00.

Holly Hills, Inc.
1216 Hillsdale Road
Evansville, IN 47711
Specializes in their own hardy H. R. Schroeder evergreen azaleas bred for midwestern winters. Catalog free with 9½" self-addressed envelope with 2 first class stamps.

Mowbray Gardens
3318 Mowbray Lane
Cincinnati, OH 45226
Specializes in hardy species and hybrid rhododendrons for cold climates. Catalog free.

Roslyn Nursery
P.O. Box 69
211 Burrs Lane
Dix Hills, NY 11746
Large selection of ornamental shrubs. Catalog $2.00.

Salter Tree Farm
Route 2, P.O. Box 1332
Madison, FL 32340
Good selection of southern shrubs. Catalog free with 9½" self-addressed envelope.

Stubbs Shrubs
23225 S.W. Bosky Dell Lane
West Linn, OR 97068
Specializing in newer, hybrid, evergreen azaleas. Catalog $2.00.

The Sweetbriar
P.O. Box 25
13825 132nd N. E. (Kirkland)
Woodinville, WA 98072
Collector's list of hybrid and species rhododendrons. Catalog $2.00.

Thomasville Nurseries
P.O. Box 7
1842 Smith Avenue
Thomasville, GA 31799-0007
Catalog free.

Trans Pacific Nursery
Parkertown Road
Lavonia, GA 30553
Offers Dexter rhododendrons, rare native deciduous azaleas, hybrid azaleas, kalmia, leucothoë and pieris. Catalog free.

Trillium Lane Nursery
18855 Trillium Lane
Ft. Bragg, CA 95437
Specializes in rhododendrons. No catalog, but you can send a want list.

Westgate Garden Nursery
751 Westgate Drive
Eureka, CA 95501
Large selection of species and hybrid rhododrons and azaleas and unusual ornamental shrubs and trees as companion plants. Catalog $1.00.

Whitney Gardens
P.O. Box F
31600 Highway 101
Brinnon, WA 98320
Large selection of hybrid and species rhododrons, azaleas and kalmias. Catalog $2.00.

Woodlanders, Inc.
1128 Colleton Avenue
Aiken, SC 29801
Offers southeastern native shrubs. Catalog $1.00.

Hollies

Appalachian Gardens
P.O. Box 82
Waynesboro, PA 17268
Catalog free.

Bill Dodd's Rare Plants
P.O. Drawer 377
Semmes, AL 36575
Catalog free with a 9½" self-addressed envelope.

Foxborough Nursery
3611 Miller Road
Street, MD 21154
Specializing in dwarf and unusual. Catalog $1.00.

Girard Nurseries
P.O. Box 428
6801 North Ridge (US 20)
Geneva, OH 44041
Catalog free.

Holly Hills, Inc.
1216 Hillsdale Road
Evansville, IN 47711
Catalog free with a 9½" self-addressed envelope with 2 first class stamps.

Magnolia Nursery
Route 1, P.O. Box 87
Chunchula, AL 36521
Good selection of southeastern native plants. Catalog free.

Roslyn Nursery
P.O. Box 69
211 Burrs Lane
Dix Hills, NY 11746
Catalog $2.00.

Terrapin Springs Farm
P.O. Box 7454
Tifton, GA 31793
Specializes in rare and native plants for the southeast. Catalog $1.00.

Washington Evergreen Nursery
P.O. Box 388
Brooks Branch Road
Leicester, NC 28748
Catalog $2.00.

Wavecrest Nursery & Landscaping Company
2509 Lakeshore Drive
Fennville, MI 49408
Catalog free.

Waynesboro Nurseries
P.O. Box 987
Route 664
Waynesboro, VA 22980
Catalog free.

Kalmias

Beaver Creek Nursery
7526 Pelleaux Road
Knoxville, TN 37938
Catalog $1.00.

Carlson's Gardens
P.O. Box 305
South Salem, NY 10590
Catalog $2.00.

Cummins Gardens
22 Robertsville Road
Marlboro, NJ 07746
Catalog $1.00.

Foxborough Nursery
3611 Miller Road
Street, MD 21154
Catalog $1.00.

Kelly Nurseries of Dansville, Inc.
19 Maple Street
Dansville, NY 14437
Catalog free.

E. B. Nauman, Nurseryman
688 St. Davids Lane
Schenectady, NY 12309
Specializes in broadleaf evergreens hardy in the northeast and midwest. Catalog free.

Roslyn Nursery
P.O. Box 69
211 Burrs Lane
Dix Hills, NY 11746
Catalog $2.00.

Trans Pacific Nursery
Parkertown Road
Lavonia, GA 30553
Catalog free.

Vineland Nurseries
P.O. Box 98
Martin Road
Vineland Station, ON, Canada L0R 2E0
Catalog $1.00.

Westgate Garden Nursery
751 Westgate Drive
Eureka, CA 95501
Catalog $1.00.

Whitney Gardens
P.O. Box F
31600 Highway 101
Brinnon, WA 98320
Catalog $2.00.

Lilacs

Heard Gardens, Ltd.
5355 Merle Hay Road
Johnston, IA 50131
Catalog $2.00.

Hortica Gardens
P.O. Box 308
Placerville, CA 95667
Good selection of dwarf lilacs. Also sells seeds. Catalog fifty cents.

Hortico, Inc.
723 Robson Road, R.R. 1
Waterdown, ON, Canada L0R 2H0
Catalog free.

Morden Nurseries, Ltd.
P.O. Box 1270
Morden, MB, Canada R0G 1J0
Catalog free.

Smith Nursery Co.
P.O. Box 515
Charles City, IA 50616
Catalog free.

Magnolias

Beaver Creek Nursery
7526 Pelleaux Road
Knoxville, TN 37938
Specializes in mostly southern natives. log $1.00.

Flora Lan Nursery
Route 1, P.O. Box 357
Forest Grove, OR 97116
Catalog free.

Gossler Farms Nursery
1200 Weaver Road
Springfield, OR 97478-9663
Specializes in magnolias. Catalog $1.00.

Greer Gardens
1280 Goodpasture Island Road
Eugene, OR 97401-1794
Catalog $2.00.

Louisiana Nursery
Route 7, P.O. Box 43 (Highway 182)
Opelousas, LA 70570
Offers 350 cultivars of magnolias. Ask for catalog (M) $3.50.

Magnolia Nursery
Route 1, P.O. Box 87
Chunchula, AL 36521
Good selection of southeastern native plants. Catalog free.

Wavecrest Nursery & Landscaping Company
2509 Lakeshore Drive
Fennville, MI 49408
Catalog free.

Yucca Do Nursery
P.O. Box 655
FM 359 & Brumlow Road (Hempstead)
Waller, TX 77484
Catalog free with 9½" self-addressed envelope.

Maples (Japanese)

Del's Japanese Maples
4691 River Road
Eugene, OR 97404
More than 200 varieties for collectors and bonsai. Catalog free.

Flora Lan Nursery
Route 1, P.O. Box 357
Forest Grove, OR 97116
Catalog free.

Foxborough Nursery
3611 Miller Road
Street, MD 21154
Broad selection of plants for bonsai. Catalog $1.00.

Greer Gardens
1280 Goodpasture Island Road
Eugene, OR 97401-1794
Large variety of palmatum cultivars. Catalog $2.00.

Harstine Island Nursery
E. 3021 Harstine Island North Road
Shelton, WA 98584
No catalog but send want list with 9½" self-addressed envelope for reply.

Hortica Gardens
P.O. Box 308
Placerville, CA 95667
Both seeds and plants available. Catalog fifty cents.

Hughes Nursery
1305 Wynooche West
Montesano, WA 98563
Collector's list of Japanese maples. Catalog $1.50.

Michael & Janet Kristick
155 Mockingbird Road
Wellsville, PA 17365
Hundreds of cultivars available. Catalog free.

Lamtree Farm
Route 1, P.O. Box 162
Warrensville, NC 28693
Catalog free.

Loucks Nursery
P.O. Box 102
14200 Campground Road
Cloverdale, OR 97112
Specializes in Japanese maples for bonsai and container growing. Catalog $1.00.

Maplewood Seed Company
6219 SW Dawn Street
Lake Oswego, OR 97035
Offers both seeds and plants. Catalog free with 9½" self-addressed envelope.

Matsu-Momiji Nursery
P.O. Box 11414
410 Borbeck Street
Philadelphia, PA 19111
Offers Japanese maples for bonsai. Catalog $1.25.

Miniature Plant Kingdom
4125 Harrison Grade Road
Sebastopol, CA 95472
Offers Japanese maples for bonsai. Catalog $2.50.

Sonoma Horticultural Nursery
3970 Azalea Avenue
Sebastopol, CA 95472
Catalog $1.50.

Stonehurst Rare Plants
1 Stonehurst Court
Pomona, NY 10970
Rare miniatures of dwarf conifers and Japanese maples. Catalog $1.00.

Trans Pacific Nursery
Parkertown Road
Lavonia, GA 30553
Catalog free.

Vineland Nurseries
P.O. Box 98
Martin Road
Vineland Station, ON, Canada L0R 2E0
Collector's list and wide selection of Japanese maples. Catalog $1.00.

Wavecrest Nursery & Landscaping Company
2509 Lakeshore Drive
Fennville, MI 49408
Catalog free.

Peonies, Tree

Busse Gardens
Route 2, P.O. Box 238
Cokato, MN 55321
Catalog $2.00.

Caprice Farm
15245 S. W. Pleasant Hill Road
Sherwood, OR 97140
Good selection, some very rare. Catalog $1.00.

Iris Country
118 S. Lincoln Street
Wayne, NE 68787
Specify Herbaceous and Tree Peony List. Catalog fifty cents.

Klehm Nursery
Route 5, P.O. Box 197
South Barrington, IL 60010
Catalog $2.00.

Reath's Nursery
P.O. Box 521
100 Central Boulevard
Vulcan, MI 49892
Offers only peonies. Catalog $1.00.

Pieris

Flora Lan Nursery
Route 1, P.O. Box 357
Forest Grove, OR 97116
Catalog free.

Foxborough Nursery
3611 Miller Road
Street, MD 21154
Catalog $1.00.

Hass Nursery
24105 Ervin Road
Philomath, OR 97370
A collector's list of plants, all well described. Catalog $2.00.

Roslyn Nursery
P.O. Box 69
211 Burrs Lane
Dix Hills, NY 11746
Large selection of choice plants. Catalog $2.00.

Vineland Nurseries
P.O. Box 98
Martin Road
Vineland Station, ON, Canada L0R 2E0
Wide selection of shrubs including pieris. Catalog $1.00.

Washington Evergreen Nursery
P.O. Box 388
Brooks Branch Road
Leicester, NC 28748
A collector's catalog of dwarf shrubs including pieris. Catalog $2.00.

Rhododendrons

The Bovees Nursery
1737 S.W. Coronado
Portland, OR 97219
Collector's catalog of species and hybrid rhododendrons. Catalog $2.00.

Briarwood Gardens
14 Gully Lane, RFD #1
East Sandwich, MA 02537
Specializes in Dexter hybrid rhododendrons. Catalog $1.00.

Bull Valley Rhododendron Nursery
214 Bull Valley Road
Aspers, PA 17304
Specializes in Dexter, Wister-Swarthmore and Gable hybrid rhododendrons. Catalog free with 9½" self-addressed envelope.

Cardinal Nursery
Route 1, Box 316
State Road, NC 28676
Selection of over 200 rhododendron hybrids. Catalog free.

Carlson's Gardens
P.O. Box 305
South Salem, NY 10590
Broad selection of azaleas and rhododendrons. Catalog $2.00.

Chambers Nursery
26874 Ferguson Road
Junction City, OR 97448
Broad selection of azaleas and rhododendrons. Catalog free.

Cummins Garden
22 Robertsville Road
Marlboro, NJ 07746
Specializes in rhododendron for the rock garden and bonsai. Catalog $1.00.

Eastern Plant Specialties
P.O. Box 40
Colonia, NJ 07067
Broad selection of hardy azaleas and rhododendrons. Catalog $2.00.

Ericaceae
P.O. Box 293
6 Kelsey Hill Road
Deep River, CT 06417
Offers only the rhododendron hybrids of David Leach. Catalog free.

Flora Lan Nursery
Route 1, P.O. Box 357
Forest Grove, OR 97116
Extensive list of rhododendron and azalea hybrids. Catalog free.

Louis Gerardi Nursery
R. R. 1, P.O. Box 428
Geneva, OH 44041
Catalog free.

The Greenery
14450 N. E. 16th Place
Bellevue, WA 98007
Broad selection of species rhododendrons and azaleas as well as hybrids. Catalog $2.00.

Greer Gardens
1280 Goodpasture Island Road
Eugene, OR 97401-1794
Large selection of plants, specializing in rhododendrons and azaleas. Catalog $2.00.

Hall Rhododendrons
1280 Quince Drive
Junction City, OR 97448
Broad selection of hybrid and species rhododendrons and azaleas. Catalog $1.00.

Harstine Island Nursery
E. 3021 Harstine Island North Road
Shelton, WA 98584
Wide variety of rhododendrons. No catalog, but will supply from want lists.

Holly Hills, Inc.
1216 Hillsdale Road
Evansville, IN 47711
Offer hybrid rhododendrons along with hollies, azaleas, dwarf conifers. Catalog free with 9½" self-addressed envelope.

Horsley Rhododendron Nursery
7441 Tracyton Boulevard N.W.
Bremerton, WA 98310
Ship only two rhododendrons: 'One Thousand Butterflies' & 'Arthur Harsley,' but will ship others along with them if you order one of "shippers." Catalog free.

Justice Gardens
107 Hight Drive
Watkinsville, GA 30677
Wide selection of hybrid azaleas and some rhododendrons. Catalog free with 9½" self-addressed envelope.

Mowbray Gardens
3318 Mowbray Lane
Cincinnati, OH 45226
Very hardy species and hybrid rhododendrons for cold climates. Catalog free.

E.B. Nauman, Nurseryman
688 St. Davids Lane
Schenectady, NY 12309
Specializes in broadleaf evergreens hardy in the northeast and midwest. Catalog free.

North Coast Rhododendron Nursery
P.O. Box 308
Bodega, CA 94922
Specializes in plants for mild climates, hot climates, and greenhouses in cold climates. Catalog $1.00.

Roslyn Nursery
P.O. Box 69
211 Burrs Lane
Dix Hills, NY 11746
Collector's list of hybrid and species rhododendrons. Catalog $2.00.

Sonoma Horticultural Nursery
3970 Azalea Avenue
Sebastopol, CA 95472
Broad selection of rhododendrons and acid-loving plants. Catalog $1.50.

The Sweetbriar
P.O. Box 25
13825 132nd N. E. (Kirkland)
Woodinville, WA 98072
Collector's list of hybrid and species rhododendrons. Catalog $2.00.

Trans Pacific Nursery
Parkertown Road
Lavonia, GA 30553
Collector's list of Dexter rhododendrons. Catalog free.

Trillium Lane Nursery
18855 Trillium Lane
Ft. Bragg, CA 95437
Offers 1,000 rhododendron cultivars and varieties (species, dwarf and standard hybrids). No catalog, but you can send want list.

Vineland Nurseries
P.O. Box 98
Martin Road
Vineland Station, ON, Canada L0R 2E0
Wide selection of plant material including rhododendrons. Catalog $1.00.

Westgate Garden Nursery
751 Westgate Drive
Eureka, CA 95501
Large selection of species and hybrid rhododendrons. Catalog $1.00.

Whitney Gardens
P.O. Box F
31600 Highway 101
Brinnon, WA 98320
Large selection of hybrid and species rhododendrons. Catalog $2.00.

Woodland Nurseries
2151 Camilla Road
Mississauga, ON, Canada L5A, 2K1
Offers plants for severe winter climates, including rhododendrons. Catalog $1.00.

Roses (Modern)

Armstrong Roses
P.O. Box 1020
Somis, CA 93066
Catalog free.

BDK Nursery
P.O. Box 628
2091 Hass Road
Apopka, FL 32712
Catalog free.

Emlong Nurseries
2671 W. Marquette Woods Road
Stevensville, MI 49127
Catalog free.

Gurney Seed & Nursery Co.
2nd & Capital
Yankton, SD 57078
Catalog free.

Hastings
P.O. Box 4274
Atlanta, GA 30302-4274
Catalog free.

Hortico, Inc.
723 Robson Road, R.R. 1
Waterdown, ON Canada L0R 2H0
Catalog free.

Jackson & Perkins Co.
P.O. Box 1028
Medford, OR 97501
Catalog free.

Krider Nurseries
P.O. Box 29
Middlebury, IN 46540
Catalog free.

McConnell Nurseries, Inc.
R.R. 1
Port Burwell, ON, Canada N0J 1T0
Catalog free.

Milaeger's Gardens
4838 Douglas Avenue
Racine, WI 53402-2498
Catalog $1.00.

Rose Acres
6641 Crystal Boulevard
Diamons Springs, CA 95619
Catalog free with 9½" self-addressed envelope.

Roses by Fred Edmunds
6235 S. W. Kahle Road
Wilsonville, OR 97070
Catalog free.

Savage Farms Nursery
P.O. Box 125
Highway 56 South
McMinnville, TN 37110
Catalog free.

Spring Hill Nurseries Co.
P.O. Box 1758
Peoria, IL 61656
Catalog free.

Stark Brothers Nurseries & Orchards Inc.
Highway 54 West
Louisiana, MO 63353-0010
Catalog free.

Thomasville Nurseries
P.O. Box 7
1842 Smith Avenue
Thomasville, GA 31799-0007
Catalog free.

Wayside Gardens
P.O. Box 1
Hodges, SC 29695-0001
Catalog $1.00.

Roses (Miniature)

Armstrong Roses
P.O. Box 1020
Somis, CA 93066
Catalog free.

Justice Miniature Roses
5947 S. W. Kahle Road
Wilsonville, OR 97070
Catalog free.

MB Farm Miniature Roses
Jamison Hill Road
Clinton Corners, NY 12514
Catalog free.

McDaniel's Miniature Roses
7523 Zemco Street
Lemon Grove, CA 92045
Catalog free.

Mini-Roses
P.O. Box 4255, Station A
Dallas, TX 75208
Catalog free.

Miniature Plant Kingdom
4125 Harrison Grade Road
Sebastopol, CA 95472
Catalog $2.50.

Nor'East Miniature Roses
58 Hammond Street
Rowley, MA 01969
Catalog free.

Rosehill Farm
Gregg Neck Road
Galena, MD 21635
Catalog free.

The Roses Garden & Mini Rose Nursery
P.O. Box 560
SC Highway 560 (Austin Street)
Cross Hill, SC 29332-0560
Catalog free.

Tiny Petals Nursery
489 Minot Avenue
Chula Vista, CA 92010
Catalog free.

Roses (Old Garden & Species)

Antique Rose Emporium
Route 5, P.O. Box 143
Breham, TX 77833
Catalog $2.00.

Greenmantle Nursery
3010 Ettersburg Road
Garberville, CA 95440
Catalog $3.00.

Heritage Rosarium
211 Haviland Mill Road
Brookville, MD 20833
Catalog $1.00.

Heritage Rose Gardens
16831 Mitchell Creek Drive
Fort Bragg, CA 95437
Catalog $1.00.

High Country Rosarium
1717 Downing Street
Denver, CO 80218
Catalog $1.00.

Historical Roses
1657 West Jackson Street
Painesville, OH 44077
Catalog free with 9½" self-addressed envelope.

Lowe's Own-root Roses
6 Sheffield Road
Nashua, NH 03062
Catalog $2.00.

Pickering Nurseries Inc.
670 Kingston Road (Highway 2)
Pickering, ON, Canada L1V 1A6
Catalog $2.00.

Roses of Yesterday & Today
802 Brown's Valley Road
Watsonville, CA 95076-0398
Catalog $2.00.

Shrubs, Dwarf

Alpenflora Gardens
17985 40th Avenue
Surrey, BC, Canada V3S 4N8
Broad selection of rock garden and alpine plants. Catalog $2.00.

Eastern Plant Specialties
P.O. Box 40
Colonia, NJ 07067
Large selection of unusual dwarf shrubs. Catalog $2.00.

Gossler Farms Nursery
1200 Weaver Road
Springfield, OR 97478-9663
Selection of dwarf shrubs among other unusual trees and shrubs. Catalog $1.00.

Holbrook Farm & Nursery
Route 2, P.O. Box 223B
Fletcher, NC 28732
Offers dwarf shrubs among a broad selection of plant material. Catalog $2.00.

Hortica Gardens
P.O. Box 308
Placeville, CA 95667
Good selection of dwarf shrubs. Catalog fifty cents.

Vineland Nurseries
P.O. Box 98
Martin Road
Vineland Station, ON, Canada L0R 2E0
Wide selection of dwarf plant material. Catalog $1.00.

Washington Evergreen Nursery
P.O. Box 388
Brooks Branch Road
Leicester, NC 28748
Collector's catalog of dwarf conifers and other dwarf shrubs. Catalog $2.00.

Wildwood Gardens
14488 Rock Creek
Chardon, OH 44024
Collector's list of dwarf conifers and other dwarf shrubs. Catalog fifty cents.

Yucca Do Nursery
P.O. Box 655
FM 359 & Brumlow Road (Hempstead)
Waller, TX 77484
Selection of unusual trees, shrubs and perennials. Catalog free with 9½" self-addressed envelope.

Vines

Clifford's Perennial & Vine
Route 2, Box 320
East Troy, WI 53120
Nice selection of flowering vines. Catalog $1.00.

Conley's Garden Center
Boothbay Harbor, ME 04538
Offers good selection of native vines among other plant material. Catalog $1.50.

The Fragrant Path
P.O. Box 328
Fort Calhoun, NE 68023
Offers seeds of fragrant, rare and old-fashioned plants, including vines. Catalog $1.00.

Griffey's Nursery
1680 Highway 25-70
Marshall, NC 28753
Broad selection of southeastern native plants including vines. Catalog free.

J. L. Hudson, Seedsman
P.O. Box 1058
Redwood City, CA 94064
Specializes in rare seeds from all over the world. Catalog $1.00.

Kartuz Greenhouses
1408 Sunset Drive
Vista, CA 92083
Offers many flowering plants for home, greenhouse, and warm areas. Catalog $2.00.

Little Valley Farm
R.R. 1, P.O. Box 287
Richland Center, WI 53581
Specializes in native plants of the midwest. Catalog twenty-five cents.

Logee's Greenhouses
55 North Street
Damielson, CT 06239
Extensive list of greenhouse and exotic plants suitable for outdoors in warm climates. Catalog $3.00.

Richard Owen Nursery
2209 E. Oakland Street
Bloomington, IL 61701
Offers variety of nursery stock including vines. Catalog free.

The Plant Kingdom
P.O. Box 7273
Lincoln Acres, CA 92047
Broad selection of tropical and greenhouse plants including vines. Catalog $1.00.

Smith Nursery Co.
P.O. Box 515
Charles City, IA 50616
Catalog free.

Stallings Exotic Nursery
910 Encinitas Boulevard
Encinitas, CA 92024
Offers about 1000 tropical and sub-tropical plants. Catalog $2.00.

Woodlanders, Inc.
1128 Colleton Avenue
Aiken, SC 29801
Collector's list of southeastern native plant material. Catalog $1.00.

INDEX

A

Acidity
   fertilizing and, 40–41
   plant hardiness and, 58
   soil levels, 34
Air, plant hardiness and dampness of, 58
Air layering, 85
Aphids, 62

B

Bagworms, 62
Balled and burlapped roots, planting technique
      for, 33
Banks, planting on, 27
Bare root planting, 31–32
Barriers, shrubs as, 26–27
Beetles, 62
Blights, 65–66
Bloom, pruning to increase, 43
Borders, planning, 24–25
Borers, 62–63
Botanical names
   changing of, 19–20
   common names and, 19
   explanation of, 16–17
   information contained in, 18–19
   logic for use of, 14–16
Bridge grafting, 92
Budding, propagation by, 93–94
Bugs, 63

C

Cankers, 66
Caterpillars, 63
Changes in shrubs
   from chemical injury, 55
   minor variations, 56
   reversion, 53–55
   soil reaction and, 56
   sporting and, 55
Chemicals, injury from, 55
Collected plants, nursery-grown vs., 79
Color, pruning for, 43
Cuttings
   aftercare, 88
   half-ripened, 87
   hardwood, 88–89
   rooting mediums, 87
   rooting under mist, 88
   semi-hardwood, 87
   softwood, 86
   types, 86

D

Delineation of space, shrub use for, 23–24
Density, pruning to increase, 43
Digging, for planting, 31
Diseases
   blights, 65–66
   cankers, 66
   galls, 66
   leaf spots, 66–67
   mildew, 68
   rots, 68
   rusts, 68–69
   wilts, 69
Division, propagation by, 83
Dormancy, of seeds, 97–98
Drainage, 58
Drought, 38

F

Fall planting, 36
Fertilizing, 39–40
   for acid-soil plants, 40–41
   chemical injury from, 55
   special fertilizers, 41
First aid, 69
Flowers, pruning dead, 44

G

Galls, 66
Gardens
   problem-solving in, 22–27
   shrub use in, 27
Grafting
   bridge, 92
   splice, 90–91
Ground cover, shrubs as, 27

H

Half-ripened cuttings, 87
Handling, prior to planting, 30
Hardiness, 57–58
Hardwood cuttings, 88–89
Hedges, rejuvenation of, 50
House planting, 22–23

I

Insecticides. *See* Pesticides
Insects and parasites, 62–65

L

Latin names. *See* Botanical names
Layering
   air, 85
   mound, 84
   serpentine, 84
   simple, 83–84
Leaf miners, 64
Leaf spots, 66–67

M

Maintenance
   drought, 38
   fertilizing, 39–41
   mulching, 38–39
   pruning, 41–44
   watering new plants, 37
   winter protection, 45
   See also Rejuvenation; Troubleshooting
Maturity, rejuvenation of shrubs past, 49
Measurement, of garden footage, 74
Microclimates, 57
Mildew, 68
Mites, 64
Mound layering, 84
Mulching, 38–39

PLANT INDEX

A

Aaron's beard. *See Hypericum calycinum*
Abelia sp.
    A. chinensis, 106
    A. 'Edward Goucher', 106, 249
    A. grandiflora, 243, 245
    A. rupestris, 106
    A. schumannii, 106
    A. uniflora, 106
    A. × *grandiflora*, 106, 249
    A. × *grandiflora* 'Prostrata', 106, 249
Acacia. *See Robinia hispida*
Acer sp., 214
    A. ginnala, 214, 245, 261
    A. palmatum, 214, 245, 261
    A. palmatum 'Atropurpureum', 214, 261
    A. palmatum 'Dissectum', 215, 261
    A. palmatum 'Ornatum', 215, 261
Actinidia arguta, 236, 242, 245, 264
Aesculus sp., 106-7
    A. parviflora, 106, 242, 245, 249
    A. pavia, 107, 249
Aglet tree. *See Crataegus monogyna*
Akebia quinata, 236, 242, 245, 264
Alabama fothergilla. *See Fothergilla monticola*
Aldenham spindle tree. *See Euonymus europaeus* 'Aldenhamensis'
Alleghany serviceberry. *See Amelanchier laevis*
Almond. *See Prunus* sp.
Alpine currant. *See Ribes alpinum*
Alternate-leaved dogwood. *See Cornus alternifolia*
Althea. *See Hibiscus*
Amelanchier sp., 107, 215, 245
    A. alnifolia, 107, 242, 249
    A. laevis, 215, 261
    A. stolonifera, 107, 243, 249
    A. × *grandiflora*, 215, 261
American bittersweet. *See Celastrus scandens*
American bladdernut. *See Staphylea trifolia*
American burning bush. *See Euonymus americana*
American cranberry bush. *See Viburnum trilobum*
American elder. *See Sambucus canadensis*
American hazelnut. *See Corylus americana*
American holly. *See Ilex opaca*
American laurel. *See Kalmia* sp.
American mountain ash. *See Sorbus americana*
American pussy willow. *See Salix discolor*

American redbud. *See Cercis canadensis*
American spindle tree. *See Euonymus americana*
American witch hazel. *See Hamamelis virginiana*
Amoena azalea. *See Rhododendron obtusum*
Amorpha sp., 107-8
    A. fruiticosa, 107-8, 242, 249
Amur honeysuckle. *See Lonicera maackii*
Amur lilac. *See Syringa amurensis japonica*
Amur maple. *See Acer ginnala*
Amur privet. *See Ligustrum amurense*
Amur River privet. *See Ligustrum amurense*
Amygdalus nana. *See Prunus tenella*
Andromeda. *See Pieris* sp.
Angelica-tree. *See Aralia*
Appalachian tea. *See Viburnum cassinoides*
Apple. *See Malus* sp.
Apple serviceberry. *See Amelanchier* × *grandiflora*
Apple shadbush. *See Amelanchier* × *grandiflora*
Apricot. *See Prunus* sp.
Aralia spinosa, 108, 242, 245, 249
Arbutus. *See Abelia*
Aronia sp., 108
    A. arbutifolia, 108, 243, 245, 249
    A. arbutifolia 'Brilliantissima', 243, 245
    A. melanocarpa, 243, 245, 249
Arrow-bean. *See Euonymus europaeus*
Arrow wood. *See Cornus florida*; *Viburnum acerifolium*; *Viburnum dentatum*
Ash. *See Sorbus* sp.
Ash barberry. *See Mahonia repens*
Austrian copper brier. *See Rosa foetida* 'Bicolor'
Autumn clematis. *See Clematis paniculata*
Autumn Higan cherry. *See Prunus subhirtella* 'Autumnalis'
Azalea. *See Rhododendron* sp.

B

Bailey's dogwood. *See Cornus baileyi*
Bamboo. *See Nandina domestica*
Barberry. *See Berberis* sp.
Basket willow. *See Salix purpurea*
Bastard indigo. *See Amphora*
Bayberry. *See Myrica cerifera*; *Myrica pensylvanica*
Beach plum. *See Prunus martima*
Bean tree. *See Laburnum anagyroides*
Bearberry cotoneaster. *See Cotoneaster dammeri*
Beauty berry. *See Callicarpa* sp.
Beauty bush. *See Kolkwitzia amabilis*
Bell-flower tree. *See Enkianthus campanulatus*
Bell-olive tree. *See Halesia* sp.
Berberis sp., 116
    B. candidula, 243
    B. julianae, 116, 243, 245, 250
    B. julianae 'Nana', 243
    B. koreana, 116, 243, 245, 250
    B. mentorensis, 242, 245
    B. thunbergii, 117, 242, 245, 250
    B. thunbergii 'Atropurpurea', 117, 243, 250
    B. thunbergii 'Atropurpurea Nana', 117, 243, 250
    B. thunbergii 'Erecta', 243, 245
    B. thunbergii 'Minor', 243, 245
    B. thunbergii nana, 117
    B. thunbergii 'Rose Glow', 117, 250
    B. thunbergii 'Sheridan Red', 117, 250
    B. verruculosa, 117, 243, 245
Big-leaf ivy. *See Kalmia latifolia*
Big scentless mock orange. *See Philadelphus inodorus grandiflorus*
Bilberry. *See Amelanchier* sp.
Billiard's spirea. *See Spiraea* × *billiardii*
Bissum. *See Hydrangea arborescens*
Bitchiu viburnum. *See Viburnum bitchiuense*
Bitch-wood. *See Euonymus europaeus*
Bitter ash. *See Euonymus atropurpureus*
Bittersweet. *See Celastrus scandens*
Black alder. *See Ilex verticillata*
Black-haw. *See Viburnum lentago*
Black plum. *See Prunus martima*
Black sally. *See Salix caprea*
Black thorn. *See Viburnum lentago*
Bladdernut. *See Staphylea* sp.
Blireiana plum. *See Prunus* × *blireiana*
Bloodleaf Japanese maple. *See Acer palmatum* 'Atropurpureum'

C. maxima atropurpurea, 131
C. maxima aurea, 130
C. maxima 'Purpurea', 131, 251
Cotinus sp.
C. coggygria, 131, 242, 245, 251
C. coggygria 'Purpureus', 131, 242, 251
C. coggygria rubrifolius, 131
Cotoneaster sp., 132
C. acutifolia, 132, 242, 247, 251
C. adpressa, 132, 243, 245, 251
C. adpressa praecox, 132, 243, 251
C. apiculatus, 132, 243, 247, 251
C. bullata floribunda, 243
C. bumifusa, 133
C. dammeri, 133, 243, 251
C. dielsiana, 243, 245
C. divaricata, 242, 243, 245
C. foveolata, 242, 245
C. borizontalis, 133, 243, 245, 251
C. borizontalis perpusilla, 133, 243, 251
C. integerrima, 243
C. microphylla, 133, 243, 252
C. multiflora, 133, 242, 252
C. multiflora calocarpa, 134, 242, 252
C. praecox, 132
C. racemiflora soongorica, 242
Cow-plant. See Rhododendron maximum
Crabapple. See Malus sargentii
Cranberry bush. See Viburnum trilobum
Cranberry cotoneaster. See Cotoneaster
    apiculatus
Crataegus sp., 219, 247
C. 'Autumn Glory', 219, 262
C. cordata, 221
C. crus-galli, 219, 245, 262
C. intricata, 219, 262
C. lavallei, 245
C. mollis, 220, 262
C. monogyna, 220, 262
C. monogyna 'Stricta', 220, 262
C. nitida, 220, 262
C. oxyacantha, 220, 245, 262
C. oxyacantha 'Paul's Scarlet', 220, 245, 262
C. oxyacantha 'Rosea Plena', 221, 262
C. pbaenopyrum, 221, 245, 262
C. viridis, 221, 262
C. 'Winter King', 221
C. × lavallei, 219, 262
C. × mordenensis 'Toba', 220, 262
Creeping cotoneaster. See Cotoneaster adpressus
Creeping hollygrape. See Mahonia repens
Creeping mahonia. See Mahonia repens
Creeping service-berry. See Amelanchier
Creeping willow. See Salix repens
Crimson Pigmy. See Berberis thunbergii nana
Crimson weigela. See Weigela floribunda
Currant. See Ribes sp.
Cutleaf lilac. See Syringa laciniata
Cut-leaved European elder. See Sambucus nigra
    'Laciniata'
Cut-leaved staghorn sumac. See Rhus typhina
    'Laciniata'
Cydonia. See Chaenomeles sp.
Cydonia japonica, 125
Cytisus sp., 134
C. battandieri, 243
C. praecox, 243
C. purgans, 134, 252
C. scoparius, 134, 243, 252
C. scoparius 'Andreanus', 135, 252
C. × praecox, 134, 252
C. × praecox 'Albus', 134, 252
C. × praecox 'Hollandia', 134, 252

D

Dagwood. See Euonymus sp.
Dahurian cinquefoil. See Potentilla davurica
Daphne sp., 135
D. cneorum, 135, 243, 252
D. mezereum, 135, 243, 245, 252
D. mezereum 'Alba', 136, 252
D. 'Somerset', 243
D. × burkwoodii 'Somerset', 135, 252
Darley heath. See Erica × darleyensis
Davidia involucrata, 221, 262
Death alder. See Euonymus europaeus
Deutzia sp., 136
D. crenata, 137
D. gracilis, 136, 243, 247, 252
D. gracilis rosea, 136
D. gracilis rosea 'Pink Pompon', 137
D. kalmiaeflora, 243
D. lemoinei, 243, 247
D. lemoinei 'Compacta', 243
D. rosea, 243, 247
D. rosea 'Pink Pompom', 243
D. scabra, 137, 242, 252
D. scabra crenata, 137
D. scabra 'Plena', 137, 242, 252
D. scabra 'Pride of Rochester', 242
D. × lemoinei, 136, 252
D. × lemoinei 'Compacta', 136, 252
D. × rosea, 136, 252
D. × rosea 'Pink Pompom', 252
Devil's walking stick. See Aralia
Dockmanie. See Viburnum acerifolium
Dogbane. See Euonymus europaeus
Dogberry. See Sorbus americana
Dog hobble. See Leucothoë fontanesiana
Dog laurel. See Leucothoë fontanesiana
Dog timber. See Euonymus europaeus
Dog tooth berry. See Euonymus europaeus
Dogwood. See Cornus sp.; Euonymus sp.
Doublefile viburnum. See Viburnum plicatum
    'Mariesii'; Viburnum plicatum
    'Rotundifolium'; Viburnum plicatum
    tomentosum
Double-flowering almond. See Prunus
    glandulosa 'Albiplena'; Prunus glandulosa
    'Sinensis'
Double-flowering dogwood. See Cornus florida
    'Pluribracteata'
Dove tree. See Davidia involucrata
Downy hawthorn. See Crataegus mollis
Dow-rowan-tree. See Viburnum trilobum
Drooping leucothoë. See Leucothoë fontanesiana
Dwarf Arctic willow. See Salix purpurea
    'Gracilis'
Dwarf callery pear. See Pyrus calleryana
    'Faurei'
Dwarf flowering almond. See Prunus
    glandulosa
Dwarf Japanese quince. See Chaenomeles
    japonica alpina
Dwarf Korean lilac. See Syringa velutina
Dwarf purple osier. See Salix purpurea
    'Gracilis'
Dwarf Russian almond. See Prunus tenella
Dwarf Russian pea tree. See Caragana pygmaea
Dwarf sumac. See Rhus coppalina
Dyer's greenweed. See Genista tinctoria

E

Early forsythia. See Forsythia ovata
Eastern redbud. See Cercis canadensis
Eatin' rose. See Rosa rugosa
Edging box. See Buxus sempervirens
    'Suffruticosa'
Eglantine. See Rosa eglanteria
Elaeagnus sp., 221
E. angustifolia, 222, 247, 262
Elder. See Sambucus sp.
Elderberry. See Sambucus canadensis
Elder rose. See Viburnum opulus Roseum
Elk tree. See Oxydendrum arboreum
English hawthorn. See Crataegus monogyna;
    Crataegus oxyacantha
English lilac. See Syringa vulgaris
English privet. See Ligustrum vulgare
Enkianthus campanulatus, 137, 242, 245, 252
Equinox cherry. See Prunus subbirtella
Erica sp., 137
E. carnea, 137, 243, 252
E. vagans, 138, 243, 252
E. vagans 'Alba', 138, 252
E. × darleyensis, 138, 252
Euonymus sp., 138, 222
E. alata, 138, 242, 245, 247, 252
E. alata 'Compacta', 139, 243, 245, 247, 252
E. alata 'Gracilis', 243
E. americana, 139, 243, 245, 252
E. atropurpurea, 222, 245, 262
E. europaea, 222, 247, 262
E. europaea 'Aldenhamensis', 222, 262
E. fortunei, 139, 252
E. fortunei 'Carrierei', 140, 252
E. fortunei 'Corliss', 252
E. fortunei 'Emerald', 140, 252
E. fortunei radicans, 140, 252
E. fortunei radicans vegetus, 140
E. fortunei 'Sarcoxie', 140, 252
E. fortunei 'Vegeta', 243, 247
E. fortunei 'Vegetus', 140, 252
E. kiautschovicus, 140, 242, 245, 247, 252
E. nanus koopmannii, 141
E. nanus turkestanicus, 141, 243, 252
E. patens, 140
E. sachalinensis, 141, 242, 252
E. yedoensis, 141, 242, 245, 253
European burning bush. See Euonymus
    europaeus
European cranberry bush. See Viburnum opulus
European dogwood. See Euonymus europaeus
European elder. See Sambucus nigra Aurea;
    Sambucus nigra 'Laciniata'
European hazelnut. See Corylus avellana
European mountain ash. See Sorbus aucuparia
European privet. See Ligustrum vulgare
European red elder. See Sambucus racemosa
European snowball. See Viburnum opulus
    'Roseum'
Ever-blooming lilac. See Syringa microphylla
Exbury hybrids, 111
Exochorda sp., 141
E. giraldii wilsonii, 142, 242, 253
E. grandiflora, 142
E. macrantha 'The Bride', 243
E. racemosa, 142, 242, 253
E. × macrantha, 142, 253

F

Fairy thorn. *See Crataegus monogyna*
False boxwood. *See Cornus florida*
False indigo. *See Amphora*
False Paraguay tea. *See Viburnum cassinoides*
False syringa. *See Philadelphus coronarius*
Father Hugo rose. *See Rosa bugonis*
February daphne. *See Daphne mezereum*
Fernleaf euonymus. *See Euonymus nanus turkestanicus*
Fetter bush. *See Leucothoë fontanesiana; Pieris floribunda*
Filbert. *See Corylus* sp.
Firebush. *See Chaenomelis japonica*
Firethorn. *See Pyracantha* sp.
Fish wood. *See Euonymus americana*
Five finger blossom. *See Potentilla* sp.
Five finger grass. *See Potentilla* sp.
Fiveleaf akebia. *See Akebia quinata*
Five stamen tamarix. *See Tamarix pentandra*
Flame azalea. *See Rhododendron calendulaceum*
Fleeceflower. *See Polygonum aubertii*
Florists' hydrangea. *See Hydrangea macrophylla*
Flowering almond. *See Prunus glandulosa*
Flowering ash. *See Chionanthus virginicus*
Flowering cherry. *See Prunus glandulosa*
Flowering chestnut. *See Xanthoceras sorbifolia*
Flowering dogwood. *See Cornus florida*
Flowering quince. *See Chaenomeles* sp.
Flowering raspberry. *See Rubus odoratus*
Flower-ivy. *See Euonymus europaeus*
Fontanesia fortunei, 142, 242, 247, 253
Forsythia sp., 142–43
   F. 'Beatrix Farrand', 143, 242, 253
   F. intermedia, 242, 247
   F. intermedia 'Arnold Dwarf', 243
   F. intermedia 'Spectabilis', 242
   F. 'Karl Sax', 144, 253
   F. ovata, 144, 242, 253
   F. suspensa, 144, 242, 253
   F. suspensa fortunei, 144, 242, 253
   F. suspensa sieboldii, 145, 243, 253
   F. viridissima, 145, 242, 253
   F. viridissima 'Bronxensis', 145, 243, 253
   F. × *intermedia*, 143, 253
   F. × *intermedia* 'Arnold Dwarf', 143, 253
   F. × *intermedia* 'Arnold Giant', 143, 253
   F. × *intermedia* 'Lynwood', 143, 253
   F. × *intermedia* 'Spectabilis', 144, 253
   F. × *intermedia* 'Spring Glory', 144, 253
Fortune forsythia. *See Forsythia suspensa fortunei*
Fothergilla sp., 145, 245
   F. major, 145, 242, 253
   F. monticola, 145, 243, 253
Foul rush. *See Euonymus europaeus*
Fountain butterfly bush. *See Buddleia alternifolia*
Fragrant currant. *See Ribes odoratum*
Fragrant honeysuckle. *See Lonicera fragrantissima*
Fragrant mock orange. *See Philadelphus coronarius*
Fragrant snowball. *See Viburnum × carlcephalum*
Fragrant snowbell. *See Styrax obassia*
Fragrant sumac. *See Rhus aromatica*
Fragrant viburnum. *See Viburnum carlesii; Viburnum fragrans*

Fragrant winterhazel. *See Corylopsis glabrescens*
Franklinia alatamaha, 222, 262
French hydrangea. *See Hydrangea macrophylla*
French tamarix. *See Tamarix gallica*
Fringe tree. *See Chionanthus* sp.

G

Gable hybrids, 112
Gadrise. *See Viburnum trilobum*
Gaiter tree. *See Euonymus europaeus; Viburnum trilobum*
Gallberry. *See Ilex glabra*
Garland flower. *See Daphne cneorum*
Garland spirea. *See Spiraea × arguta*
Gattan tree. *See Euonymus europaeus; Viburnum trilobum*
Geese and goslings. *See Salix caprea*
Geese and gullies. *See Salix caprea*
Genista sp., 146
   G. tinctoria, 146, 243, 253
Germander. *See Teucrium chamaedrys*
Ghent hybrids. *See Rhododendron × gandavense*
Girard hybrids, 112
Glastonbury thorn. *See Crataegus monogyna*
Glaucous willow. *See Salix discolor*
Glenn Dale hybrids, 112
Globeflower. *See Kerria japonica* 'Pleniflora'
Glossy abelia. *See Abelia*
Glossy hawthorn. *See Crataegus nitida*
Goat willow. *See Salix caprea*
Golden bell. *See Forsythia* sp.
Golden-chain. *See Laburnum* sp.
Golden currant. *See Ribes aureum; Ribes odoratum*
Golden elder. *See Sambucus canadensis* 'Aurea'
Golden European elder. *See Sambucus nigra* 'Aurea'
Golden filbert. *See Corylus avellana* 'Aurea'
Golden mock orange. *See Philadelphus coronarius* 'Aureus'
Golden privet. *See Ligustrum × vicaryi*
Goldenrain tree. *See Koelreuteria paniculata*
Golden rose of China. *See Rosa bugonis*
Golden St. Johnswort. *See Hypericum fronosum*
Goldentwig dogwood. *See Cornus sericea* 'Flaviramea'
Golden Vicari privet. *See Ligustrum × vicaryi*
Goldflame honeysuckle. *See Lonicera × beckrottii*
Goose chicks. *See Salix caprea*
Gordonia alatamaha, 222
Gosling. *See Salix caprea*
Gotha honeysuckle. *See Lonicera bella* 'Candida'
Gouchault dogwood. *See Cornus alba* 'Gouchaultii'
Grancy graybeard. *See Chionanthus* sp.
Grandfather graybeard. *See Chionanthus* sp.
Graybeard tree. *See Chionanthus* sp.
Gray dogwood. *See Cornus racemosa*
Great sallow. *See Salix caprea*
Greenleaf Japanese maple. *See Acer palmatum*
Greenosier. *See Cornus alternifolia*
Greenstem golden bell. *See Forsythia viridissima*
Grouse berry. *See Viburnum trilobum*
Guelder rose. *See Viburnum opulus* 'Roseum'

H

Hag bush. *See Crataegus monogyna*
Hagthorn. *See Crataegus monogyna*
Hag tree. *See Crataegus monogyna*
Hairy lilac. *See Syringa pubescens*
Halesia sp., 223
   H. carolina, 223, 245, 262
   H. monticola, 223, 262
Hamamelis sp., 146
   H. japonica, 146, 242, 253
   H. japonica flavopurpurescens, 146, 253
   H. mollis, 147, 242, 245, 247, 253
   H. mollis 'Brevipetala', 147, 253
   H. vernalis, 147, 242, 245, 253
   H. virginiana, 147, 242, 245, 247, 253
   H. × *intermedia*, 146, 253
Hardhack. *See Spiraea tomentosa*
Hardhack spirea. *See Spiraea tomentosa*
Hardy butterfly bush. *See Buddleia alternifolia*
Hardy kiwi vine. *See Actinidia arguta*
Hardy orange. *See Poncirus trifoliata*
Harison's yellow rose. *See Rosa harisonii*
Harry Lauder's walking stick. *See Corylus avellana* 'Contorta'
Haw. *See Crataegus* sp.
Haw bush. *See Crataegus monogyna*
Hawthorn. *See Crataegus* sp.
Hazel. *See Corylus* sp.
Hearts-a-bustin'-with-love. *See Euonymus americana*
Heath. *See Erica* sp.
Heather. *See Calluna* sp.
Heavenly bamboo. *See Nandina domestica*
Hedge tree. *See Maclura pomifera*
Heg peg bush. *See Crataegus monogyna*
Hemp tree. *See Vitex agnus-castus* 'Latifolia'
Henry St. Johnswort. *See Hypericum patulum benryi*
Hercules' club. *See Aralia*
Hibiscus sp., 148
   H. syriacus, 148, 242, 247, 253
Higan cherry. *See Prunus subbirtella; Prunus subbirtella* 'Autumnalis'; *Prunus subbirtella* 'Pendula'
Highbush. *See Viburnum trilobum*
Highbush blueberry. *See Vaccinium corymbosum*
Highbush cranberry. *See Viburnum opulus; Viburnum trilobum*
High cranberry. *See Viburnum trilobum*
High geranium. *See Hydrangea arborescens*
Hills of Snow. *See Hydrangea arborescens grandiflora*
Hipperty Haw tree. *See Crataegus monogyna*
Holly. *See Ilex* sp.
Holly barberry. *See Mahonia aquifolium*
Hollygrape. *See Mahonia* sp.
Holly osmanthus. *See Osmanthus heterophyllus*
Holy innocents. *See Crataegus monogyna*
Honeysuckle. *See Lonicera* sp.; *Rhododendron nudiflorum*
Honeysuckle azalea. *See Rhododendron nudiflorum*
Hortensia. *See Hydrangea macrophylla*
Hot cross buns. *See Euonymus europaeus*
Huckleberry. *See Vaccinium* sp.
Hungarian lilac. *See Syringa josikaea*
Hydrangea sp., 148–49
   H. anomola, 242

S

W

X

Y

Z